CAMBRIDGE STUDIES
IN ENGLISH LEGAL HISTORY

Edited by

Harold Dexter Hazeltine, Litt.D., F.B.A.

Of the Inner Temple, Barrister-at-Law;
Downing Professor of the Laws of England in
the University of Cambridge

A HUNDRED YEARS OF
QUARTER SESSIONS

THE GOVERNMENT OF MIDDLESEX
FROM 1660 TO 1760

by

E. G. DOWDELL, M.A., D.Phil.

*Lecturer in Economics at St John's College
Oxford*

With an Introduction by

SIR WILLIAM HOLDSWORTH

K.C., D.C.L., Hon. LL.D.

*Vinerian Professor of English Law in the University of
Oxford; Fellow of All Souls College; Fellow of the
British Academy; Bencher of Lincoln's Inn*

CAMBRIDGE
AT THE UNIVERSITY PRESS
1932

CAMBRIDGE UNIVERSITY PRESS
Cambridge, New York, Melbourne, Madrid, Cape Town,
Singapore, São Paulo, Delhi, Mexico City

Cambridge University Press
The Edinburgh Building, Cambridge CB2 8RU, UK

Published in the United States of America by Cambridge University Press, New York

www.cambridge.org
Information on this title: www.cambridge.org/9781107638143

© Cambridge University Press 1932

This publication is in copyright. Subject to statutory exception
and to the provisions of relevant collective licensing agreements,
no reproduction of any part may take place without the written
permission of Cambridge University Press.

First published 1932
First paperback edition 2013

A catalogue record for this publication is available from the British Library

ISBN 978-1-107-63814-3 Paperback

Cambridge University Press has no responsibility for the persistence or
accuracy of URLs for external or third-party internet websites referred to in
this publication, and does not guarantee that any content on such websites is,
or will remain, accurate or appropriate.

CONTENTS

Author's Preface	vii
General Preface: The Justice of the Peace *by* H. D. Hazeltine	ix
Introduction by Sir William Holdsworth	xlv
Table of Statutes	lxxiv
I. Organisation of the County	1
General and Quarter Sessions	1
Relation to other organs of Local Government	4
Growth of Petty Sessions	6
County Officials	10
Relation to Central Government	14
II. Law and Order	16
The Constables	17
Watch and Ward	21
The Reformation of Manners	27
Liquor Control	33
Recusancy and Sunday Observance	37
III. The Poor Law	44
Employment of the Poor	44
Destitute Children	52
Relief and Maintenance	61
The Overseers	63
Rating and Expenditure	64
Settlement	66
Vagrancy	69
Inmates and Cottages	79
Briefs	82
Conclusion	86

CONTENTS

IV.	Highways and Bridges	89
	The Parish and Road Maintenance	92
	Statute Labour	97
	Road Finance	100
	The Surveyors	105
	Paving	107
	Cleansing	112
	Lighting	117
	Nuisances	119
	Bridges	124
	Turnpike Trusts	130
	Conclusion	133
V.	The Labour Code	137
	Apprentices	137
	Servants and Journeymen	146
VI.	The Regulation of Production and Distribution	158
	The Aleconner and the Clerk of the Market	160
	Forestalling, Engrossing and Regrating	165
	Badgers, Kidders and Drovers	170
	Apprenticeship	173
	The Assize of Bread	176
	Other Regulations	182
Conclusion		190
Appendix: Specimen Documents		193
Bibliography		202
Index		205

AUTHOR'S PREFACE

This volume is based upon research which I undertook as George Webb Medley Senior Scholar of Oxford University from 1926 to 1928. My original object in sifting the Middlesex Quarter Sessions Records was to discover how far and in what way the Tudor policy of elaborate control in economic affairs was carried on in the period after the Restoration. In the sequel it appeared that a very large proportion of the Justices' attention was occupied by economic and cognate matters, so that the scope of my enquiry needed to be broadened very little in order to cover all the more prominent branches of local government action. The following pages are therefore an attempt to give a fairly complete picture of the administrative work of Quarter Sessions, including judicial proceedings wherever they are directly complementary to administration. A very few routine matters have been neglected, but such omissions have generally been noted in passing.

Among the many obvious shortcomings of the book, perhaps that which calls most for explanation is the fact that I have made comparatively little use of outside sources. No doubt a careful search through other contemporary records would throw fresh light on many topics here discussed. However, having examined the Sessions Records thoroughly, I wished to make the fullest possible use of the material they afforded, which was extensive enough to demand all the space at my disposal. Indeed, it may well be complained that at times I have summarised too ruthlessly.

Lack of space has also prevented extensive quotation, the more so as the sources, which are described in the first part of the Bibliography, are prolix. For purposes of illustration, a few specimen documents are printed in full in the Appendix. The short extracts embodied in the text have been modernised.

My obligations are too numerous to be all acknowledged here. I am very much indebted to E. S. W. Hart, Esq., Clerk of the Peace and Clerk of the County Council of Middlesex, and to

AUTHOR'S PREFACE

Miss J. Cameron, Assistant in charge of the Records, for putting the Records at my disposal and affording me such enviable facilities during my work at the Middlesex Guildhall. My thanks are due to Professor Hazeltine for his helpful interest, to the Syndics of the Cambridge University Press for undertaking publication, and to the staff of the Press for the way in which they have carried out the work. Professor Holdsworth has advised me on several points and suggested improvements in my manuscript, in addition to writing the Introduction. Mr G. D. Bone of this College has helped me in various ways, especially with the proofs, while Mr W. C. Costin, also of this College, has given me some valuable material.

E. G. D.

ST JOHN'S COLLEGE, OXFORD
April 1932

THE JUSTICE OF THE PEACE

I

A QUICKENING of interest in the origin and development of the office of Justice of the Peace came at the very time when changes in the machinery of English local government, during the latter part of the nineteenth century, had already deprived the Justices of much of that administrative work which had been entrusted to them, in ever-increasing degree, both during and after the age of the Tudors. The Justices still preserve, however, their judicial functions; and, owing to the importance alike of their past and of their present position in the framework of local government, these ancient officers in the shires and boroughs richly deserve the study of all who concern themselves with English institutions. From investigations which the critical scholarship of our time has devoted to their past, the Justices have now in fact emerged upon the historical scene as one of the most continuous and vital of all the factors that have been operative in the constitutional, legal, and social evolution of England. It is this outstanding feature of history, slowly revealed by recent labour, which makes valuable any fresh contribution to our knowledge of the Justices, any study that portrays their activities within some definite region during a particular age.

The older literature dealing with the powers and duties of the Justices is abundant; and this has been much used in recent historical research. While William Lambarde's *Eirenarcha* (1581) has long been viewed as the classic work, it is now seen, thanks to Miss Putnam's learned and extensive studies, that this was but one of many early treatises on the office and practice of the Justices in the fifteenth and sixteenth centuries.[1] There was, for example, Marowe's *Reading on the Justices* which, written by a leading member of the Inner Temple at the end of the fifteenth century, both Fitzherbert and Lambarde regarded as of high authority and from which the latter derived considerable por-

[1] Putnam, *Early Treatises on the Practice of the Justices of the Peace in the fifteenth and sixteenth Centuries* (published in *Oxford Studies in Social and Legal History*, ed. Vinogradoff, vol. VII, 1924).

x   GENERAL PREFACE

tions of his own *Eirenarcha or of the Office of the Justices of Peace*. Sir Anthony Fitzherbert wrote the *Boke of Justices of the Peace*, now valuable for historical purposes; and of other early treatises special mention may be made of Dalton's *Justice* (1618) and of William Sheppard's *Sure Guide for His Majesty's Justices of the Peace* (1649) and *Justice of the Peace's Clerk's Cabinet* (1654), a collection of precedents. Richard Burn's *Justice of the Peace* (1755) was in one sense an epoch-making book, for Burn was the first of all English writers, as Professor Winfield has reminded us, to apply the idea of an abridgement to a part only of the law.[1] Coming to the literature of our own day it may be said with fairness that Maitland's *Justice and Police* (1885), in which the Justices could still be described as the governors of the county, marked the beginnings of the present tendency in scholarship to devote attention not only to the powers and duties of the Justices at a given time, but also to their history as shown by their own records and by the long series of statutes which deal with the Justices, age by age, as instruments of local government. Especially since the appearance of Mr Beard's *Office of the Justice of the Peace in England* (1904), already a classic work on the medieval development, the number of historical studies has rapidly increased. If special mention be made of the researches of Mr and Mrs Webb, Mr Crump, Mr Johnson, Miss Putnam, Miss Cam, Sir William Holdsworth,[2] Mr Jenkinson, and the late Professor Tout, it should not be forgotten that the writings of these scholars represent only part of a still larger historical literature. In addition many county records, including the records of Quarter Sessions, have been published in recent years; and it is more and more evident that future studies must be largely based on original materials of this character.[3]

To this growing literature on the history of Justices of the

[1] Winfield, *Chief Sources of English Legal History*, pp. 247, 329.
[2] See Holdsworth, *History of English Law*, 3rd ed., *passim*.
[3] For a list of some of the recent works dealing with the history of the Justices in particular counties or in England as a whole, see *Quarter Sessions Records with other Records of the Justices of the Peace for the County of Surrey*, edited by Mr Hilary Jenkinson, 1931, pp. 2-3; and for a list of some of the recent publications containing records, see *op. cit.*, pp. 34-5. Mr Jenkinson's Introduction (pp. 1-38) is of much historical value.

GENERAL PREFACE xi

Peace Mr Dowdell's present monograph, *A Hundred Years of Quarter Sessions: The Government of Middlesex from 1660 to 1760*, is a most welcome addition: it is a study, both scholarly in character and fruitful in results, based on a patient examination of the original materials. Prefixed to Mr Dowdell's essay the reader will find, moreover, a valuable Introduction by Professor Sir William Holdsworth. Written by a scholar who had already illumined in his *History of English Law* some of the leading features of the long history of Justices of the Peace, these introductory pages, which place the work of the Middlesex Justices in the larger environment of local government in England during the special period which Mr Dowdell has studied, not only form an integral part of the subject-matter of this volume, but constitute at the same time a continuation of the *History of English Law* in regard to this particular aspect of institutional growth. Combining the work of two scholars who have given much time to the historical investigation of English local government, the present book is a notable contribution to our knowledge of English social, economic, legal, and institutional history.

A long development of absorbing interest lies behind the special period which Sir William Holdsworth and Mr Dowdell have presented to us in such an attractive manner; and, as already observed, on that earlier history much light has been thrown by scholars of our own time. While it is generally agreed that the predecessor of the Justice of the Peace was the *Conservator Pacis*, or, in other words, the *Custos Pacis*, the origin and the early history of this office are still but imperfectly known. It may well be, as some scholars hold, that the origin of the *Conservator Pacis* is to be found in the well-known proclamation of Hubert Walter in 1195, under which knights were called upon to swear all men of fifteen years or over to the duty of assisting the sheriff in preserving the peace;[1] but clear historical evidence of the effect of this proclamation, issued in the unpeaceful reign of Richard I, is still lacking. Whatever may have been the influence of the great Archbishop's *edictum*

[1] For the text of the proclamation, see Hoveden (ed. Stubbs), vol. III, p. 299; Stubbs, *Select Charters*, 9th ed. (Davis), p. 257.

regium on the origin of the office, it is clear that in the reign of Henry III the *Custodes Pacis* were already performing useful functions, predominantly military, in the maintenance of the peace; and it is equally certain that, as time went on, their civil and judicial duties increased at the expense of their military activity.[1] After a considerable period of steady development Parliament in the reign of Edward III finally established the *Conservator Pacis*, the *Custos Pacis*, or, in other words, the Justice of the Peace, as a permanent institution; and, moreover, in this same age the jurisdiction of the Courts of Quarter Sessions was founded. Continuously filling a position of ever-increasing importance in the judicial and administrative life of the shires, during the reconstruction of local government in Tudor times the Justices of the Peace were made the rulers of the county. Placing their chief trust in the Justices the Tudor sovereigns continually imposed new duties upon them; and their double capacity as judges and administrators appears clearly from the Commission of the Peace as revised by Sir Christopher Wray in 1590, a form of the Commission which lasted unchanged until 1875. In rising to be the proud rulers of the county the Justices became at the same time its over-worked servants; or, to employ a simile already used by writers in describing them, the Justices became, in fact, judicial and administrative "beasts of burden".

Respecting the history of the Justices there are still many problems awaiting their solution. For one thing, the social standing of the Justices in all the ages of their development needs further study; it must not be too lightly thought, for example, that a well-known pirate who served as a Cornish Justice from 1451 onwards[2] was the only man of the later middle ages who in his own person represented both law and

---

[1] Conservators of the Peace were sometimes used by the King in the execution of his political policy. See Davies, *Baronial Opposition to Edward II*, p. 488.

[2] Kingsford, *Prejudice and Promise in XVth Century England*, p. 97. The social position of Justices may help to explain in part their willingness, or unwillingness, to enforce the law against drunkenness and immorality. See Gardiner, *History of the Commonwealth and Protectorate*, ed. 1903, vol. IV, pp. 29–40.

GENERAL PREFACE xiii

lawlessness. The place of the constable in the history of the Justices is, again, a topic that has never been fully examined. In many other directions there is still a field for the exploration of the historian; and, as an illustration of one of these directions, the charter of a trading company granted by Charles I, whereby the officers of the company were invested with the powers and functions of Justices of the Peace in certain English counties, may be cited in passing.[1]

The history of Justices of the Peace in England from the time of Richard I into the seventeenth century gives clarity to many of the details in Mr Dowdell's book; and, furthermore, it is of considerable importance to observe that there is still another aspect of the general history of the Justices which helps to place the work of the Quarter Sessions of Middlesex from 1660 to 1760 in a wide historical setting. This feature of the development is a part of the history of the Empire alike in medieval and modern times. Originating in the English middle ages at a time when in many respects the central and local courts were "an unwieldy judicial machine creakingly stretching out to the farthest corners of the kingdom",[2] the *Custodes Pacis*, gradually transformed into the Justices,[3] proved to be among the most effective of all the instruments of the King for the preservation of his peace in the shires;[4] and in course of time the office of *Custos Pacis*, or of Justice of the Peace, like other English institutions, such as the itinerant justices, the jury, and the forms of action begun by original writ, spread to many regions outside the Kingdom of England. This wide diffusion of the English system of local government by the Justices has as yet received but scant attention on the part of scholars; and in fact

---

[1] *Select Charters of Trading Companies*, A.D. 1530–1707 (Selden Society), ed. Carr, pp. 142–8.
[2] Stenton, *Lincolnshire Assize Rolls*, A.D. 1202–9, p. xix.
[3] See Putnam, "The Transformation of the Keepers of the Peace into the Justices of the Peace" (*Transactions of the Royal Historical Society*, Fourth Series, vol. XII, 1929, pp. 19–48).
[4] Fresh light has been thrown on the office of *Custos Pacis* by very recent research, as, for example, the point that at least in one period the appointment of the *Custodes* was made under the great seal, "chiefly by the chancellor and treasurer in conjunction with the knights of the counties". See Wilkinson, *Chancery under Edward III*, 1929, p. 28.

DQS

no investigator has sought to study this broader history of the Justices in its entirety. A scholarly historical examination of the extensive use of the office of Justice of the Peace beyond the borders of England is urgently needed; for such a study, if pursued from the point of view of social, political, and institutional development, would illumine many features of that vast historical process which we know as the expansion of England into an imperial and world power. In the meantime, until studies of this character shall have been undertaken and carried to fruition, we do well to remember that when we fasten our attention upon the work of the Justices in any particular English county or borough in any particular period of English history we are concerned with special and local features of the development of an institution that has a British imperial and not merely an English significance. The materials are abundant for a history of Justices of the Peace in regions outside the English shires and boroughs. A comparative study of the English Justices and of those in other lands, on historical lines, would have the effect of presenting upon a broad field the social, political, and legal causes that have led to the establishment, the growth, and the gradual decline of one of the most remarkable offices known to the constitutional and legal systems of the Empire. The extent of that enquiry may be judged by this dominant fact:—Formed slowly in the later middle ages in response to English needs, the office of Justice of the Peace has found acceptance not only among scattered peoples of English derivation and English civilisation, but also in communities that owe many of their leading characteristics to sources of a different and non-English character.

Not even a sketch of this development, so interesting in its details and so important as an aspect of world-history, can be attempted at the present time. A few indications of its scope may, however, attract the attention of historical students to a large and unexplored realm of enquiry.[1]

[1] In the paragraphs which follow no attempt will be made to deal with the technical distinctions between the *Custodes Pacis* and their successors, the Justices of the Peace; nor will special attention be paid to such matters as the scope of the Commission, the oath of the Justice, the Quorum, the *Custos*

II

Let it be noted, therefore, as the first of these indications, that one of the earliest manifestations of the historical process of extending the English Commission of the Peace was the adoption of the office of *Custos Pacis*, or Justice of the Peace, by the palatinates. The distinguishing characteristic of those great franchises of the middle age was, as Mr Lapsley has remarked, "the exercise of local sovereignty...a kind of limited royalty".[1] The palatinate was in fact the reproduction on a small scale of

Rotulorum, the Clerk of the Peace, and the Records of the Justices. The sole object will be to indicate briefly the wide diffusion of the offices of *Custos Pacis* and Justice of the Peace.

Although recent research has brought us much information on the origin and early history of the *Custodes Pacis*, or Keepers of the Peace, and their transformation into Justices of the Peace in the time of Edward III, there is still some obscurity surrounding the whole subject. One difficulty is occasioned by the fact that during the early history of the Keepers of the Peace various other agencies were employed in the effort to keep the King's peace and to punish crimes of violence. Developing in this complicated environment of communal, feudal, and royal courts and of various kinds of special commissioners, the Keepers of the Peace gradually acquired certain definite characteristics which marked them out from all the other authorities charged with the preservation of the peace and the punishment of crime; and in the middle of the fourteenth century the Keepers were transformed by practice into the Justices of the Peace, a practice which was sanctioned by the famous statute of 1361. In this development of the Justices in the fourteenth century the Commons, in Miss Putnam's view, appear to have played the leading rôle; and, contrary to older views, it is her conclusion that in the time of Edward III "the Crown preferred to rely on the feudal lords, the magnates, rather than on the local gentry, in its fight for suppressing disorder". "Eventually, of course", she remarks, the Justices "helped the central government overthrow feudalism; it was not only the county courts and sheriffs' tourn that were superseded by Quarter Sessions, but also the courts of private jurisdiction". See, further, Miss Putnam's valuable article, which has been mentioned in note 3, p. xiii, *supra*. But cf. Tout's views: *Bull. J. Rylands Library*, vol. viii, No. 1, pp. 22, 23.

The history of the transformation of the Keepers into the Justices of the Peace in England has already involved much elaborate and detailed research and there are still marked differences of opinion among scholars on vital points. It is obvious, therefore, that in a few brief paragraphs the present writer cannot deal with the similar problems connected with the early history of the Keepers and their transformation into Justices in regions outside the realm of England. In some of these regions the Keepers preceded the Justices, who gradually took their own place as judges commissioned to deal with crime by the normal processes of the law; and thus the course of development, as in Ireland, was similar to that in England. The details of this evolution must be left, however, for future research.

[1] Lapsley, *The County Palatine of Durham*, p. 11.

the kingdom itself: the ruler of the palatinate possessed within his dominion a power comparable only with that of the King in the realm as a whole. "The power and authority", said Coke, "of those that had counties palatine was king-like".[1] In their relations to the kingdom the palatinates were never, however, entities with full sovereignty. Even in the periods of their earlier history, when they were strongest, they were at best, if one may adopt a vague but expressive term, only *quasi*-independent states; and various historical factors, not least of all their geographical position on the fringe of the royal domain and their subjection to Parliament, tended to bring them more and more within the general scheme of English royal government. When they were still in their early vigour the palatinates began to copy the judicial system of the common law of England: and this fact, too, contributed to a gradual coalescence of their institutions with those of the realm and to the ultimate disappearance of the palatinates themselves as lordships that were almost royal.[2] It is this imitation of the judicial system of the kingdom, in the days when palatine power was at its height, which concerns us at the present moment.

Of the great medieval franchises the palatinate of Durham was, perhaps, the most powerful. In Durham the peace was the bishop's, not the King's; and in fact there, as in the other palatinates, the King's writ did not run. For our present purposes let us note merely that, in accordance with the general tendency to adopt the institutions of the common law of the realm, the *Custos Pacis*, appointed by the bishop, made his appearance in the palatinate, as a special instrument for the punishment and suppression of vagabondage and disturbance of the peace, during the early years of the fourteenth century. In 1385 "Justices of the Peace", under that title, were for the first time appointed by the bishop; and, as in the kingdom, it was not long before the county court was effectively superseded by the Justices of the Peace in Quarter Sessions.[3]

---

[1] *Fourth Institute*, 205.
[2] See Lapsley, *op. cit.*, pp. 1–11; Holdsworth, *op. cit.*, vol. I, pp. 108, 109.
[3] See Lapsley, *op. cit.*, pp. 32, 33, 178, 179, 197; Holdsworth, *op. cit.*, vol. I, pp. 109–14.

GENERAL PREFACE

While these early commissions of the peace, which served as the beginnings of a special peace magistracy in the palatinate, are of great historical interest, let it not be thought that in this respect Durham stands alone among the palatinates. In the fourth quarter of the fourteenth century the judicial system of the palatinate of Lancaster was framed, under powers conferred by royal charter, on lines that made it similar to the judicial system of the Durham palatinate; and in this framework of judicial organisation Justices of the Peace were given a place alongside the other Justices of Lancaster.[1]

In the palatinate of Chester there existed from an early time an organisation of Serjeants of the Peace, under the control of a Grand Serjeant who held his office by hereditary right. The Serjeants of the Peace were palatine officers to whom the preservation of law and order was entrusted; and they constituted the early police system in the county. Attended by assistants, known as bedells, the Serjeants perambulated the hundreds and there took cognisance of all offences against the peace. Originally there appear to have been twenty Serjeants, with many sub-serjeants, for the whole of the palatinate of Chester; but by the general charter of privileges granted by the third Randle, Earl of Chester, early in the thirteenth century, the number of Serjeants in time of peace was reduced to twelve, while in time of war the number was to be regulated in accordance with the advice of the barons and the judges. Mr Stewart-Brown, who has given in his *Wapentake of Wirral* a learned account of this perambulating body of Serjeants, the Earl's officials, informs us that "they had power to arrest offenders, and in early days might instantly behead them, if caught in the

---

[1] Holdsworth, *op. cit.*, vol. I, p. 114. Coke, *Fourth Institute*, 205; "Justices of assise, of gaol delivery, and of the peace are and ever since the erection of the county palatine of Lancaster have been made and assigned by commission under the seal of the county palatine of Lancaster". It is clear, however, that at least on one occasion in the latter part of the fourteenth century the Duke of Lancaster requested the Chancellor of England to assign certain persons to keep the peace in Lancaster, since "the present guardians of the peace are not as intendant on their work as they ought to be". See Wilkinson, *op. cit.*, p. 28. Early in the fourteenth century the Crown appointed *Conservatores Pacis* for the county of Durham during a vacancy of the see: Lapsley, *op. cit.* p. 178.

act, or if sufficient evidence was immediately forthcoming", but that "otherwise they had to present the robber or wrongdoer for judgment at the Hundred Court, or before the Earl's justice. Their duties also included making proclamations, the execution of attachments and distresses, and the service of summonses and writs". Apart from the Earl's Serjeants a similar system of Serjeants for the forests of Cheshire was in force; and, moreover, as Mr Stewart-Brown has stated, "each of the great barons of Cheshire had his own organisation of serjeants and bedells, who exercised, within the limit of their lord's district, much the same jurisdiction as the serjeants of the Earl".[1] Before the institution of *Conservatores Pacis* and Justices of the Peace this early system of Serjeants of the Peace performed, therefore, useful functions in all parts of the palatinate of Chester.

A further stage of development was reached with the frequent appointment of special commissioners *ad hoc*. Thus, in the Hundred of Wirral the system of presenting breaches of the peace to the Hundred Court did not always prove effective in the keeping of law and order; and, the King learning of serious disturbances of the peace, special commissions were issued from time to time whereby the appointed commissioners were empowered, as in 1386 and 1392, to arrest all malefactors and disturbers of the peace in the hundred. In this connection it is instructive to observe that, in view of the near approach of Owen Glendower who, it was reported, was already in the marches of the county, it again became necessary in the autumn of 1403 to appoint special conservators and guardians for the Hundred of Wirral. While these examples of special com-

---

[1] For an account of the system of Serjeants of the Peace in Cheshire, see Stewart-Brown, *The Wapentake of Wirral: A History of the Royal Franchise of the Hundred and Hundred Court of Wirral in Cheshire*, pp. 17-27, 38, 163, 176. Mr Lapsley has kindly called the present writer's attention to the existence of a class of persons in Lancashire—"witness-men"—with similar duties, under a tenurial obligation which may have had a pre-Conquest and possibly Scandinavian origin. Whether these officials stood in the line of development of the Justices of the Peace would be worth investigating. See *Lancashire Court Rolls*, ed. Farrer (Lancs. and Ches. Rec. Society), Introd., pp. viii-ix, xii, and Index, *s.v.* "witness-men". The future investigator of the Cheshire Serjeants and of the early legal and administrative system of that palatinate should consult the learned Introduction to Mr Stewart-Brown's *Calendar of County Court Rolls of Chester*, 1259-97 (Chetham Society publications, vol. 84), 1925.

GENERAL PREFACE

missions have been drawn exclusively from the history of the Hundred of Wirral, no doubt similar special commissions were issued for the other hundreds of Cheshire whenever they became necessary in the interests of the preservation of peace;[1] and, again, it may well be imagined that these Wirral commissions, which date from the reigns of Richard II and Henry IV, had their forerunners in still earlier appointments for Wirral or for one or more of the other hundreds. But, however this may have been, it seems clear that in these special commissions for the Hundred of Wirral we have to do with a specific illustration of those early "*ad hoc* institutions" which became in time parts of the ordinary machinery of the common law.[2]

The Wirral commissions which have been mentioned are not in fact the only instances of special temporary commissions of the peace granted by Richard II for Cheshire. From at least as early as 1387 the King made many appointments of such commissioners;[3] and he also appointed special commissioners to arrest malefactors.[4] It would seem that the King had reference to these commissions *ad hoc* when, in a writ of 1396, he directed the sheriff of Cheshire to cause proclamation to be made that *all commissions of the peace* "lately" granted by the King be returned into the Exchequer, before the next county, *to be cancelled*.[5] Three years later Conservators of the Peace for all the hundreds of Cheshire were appointed[6]. As Mr Stewart-Brown has explained, "in 1399 the disturbed state of Cheshire, consequent upon the conflict between Richard II and Henry of Lancaster, and the risings in Wales, made it necessary for Con-

[1] On the special commissions *ad hoc* for Wirral, see Stewart-Brown, *op. cit.*, pp. 40–1, 53.
[2] On the historical significance of *ad hoc* authorities, see the comments of Sir William Holdsworth, pp. lvi–lviii, *infra*.
[3] See *Calendar* in the 36th Report of the Deputy-Keeper of the Public Records, p. 95 *et seq*. The first appears to have been January 6th, 1387–8 (see *Calendar*, p. 95).
[4] E.g. in 1392, Sir Ralph de Vernon. See *Calendar*, cited above, p. 497.
[5] Cheshire Recognisance Roll 19/20 Richard 2, M. 11d (12). See *Calendar*, cited above, p. 98.
[6] The commissions are dated January 23rd, 1399–1400. See *Calendar*, cited above, p. 100.

Mr Stewart-Brown has kindly furnished the present writer with all the above items of information as to special commissions of the peace for Cheshire and the writ of 1396.

servators of the Peace to be appointed for all the hundreds. These Conservators were the predecessors of Justices of the Peace, and to their appointment may be partially ascribed...the decline in the jurisdiction of the Hundred Courts. The appointment of these Conservators was made, not by the King or by the people, but by the Prince of Wales, to whom the County Palatine had been granted a few years before by Richard II when he created it a principality".[1]

In the history of the preservation of the peace in Cheshire the early system of Serjeants of the Peace and the issue of commissions *ad hoc* are of much interest; but special significance attaches to the appointment in 1399 of Conservators of Peace, for they were the true predecessors of the Justices of the Peace in Cheshire.[2] In this connection, moreover, it is to be borne in mind that by Henry VII's charter of 1506, known as the "Great Charter", later confirmed by James I and Charles II, the city of Chester was constituted a county by itself; and this charter provided, among other things, that the mayor, the ex-mayors, and the recorder were to be jointly and severally "keepers of the peace", "as also Justices of the Peace".[3] The introduction of Justices of the Peace into the city of Chester by Henry VII is of interest as an early and special instance of the great reliance placed by the Tudors on these officers; and, owing to the close historical relations between the county palatine of Chester and the principality and marches of Wales, it is also of significance as the prelude to the process whereby Justices of the Peace, under that title, were introduced by Henry VIII into all the counties of Wales at the time of the incorporation of Wales and the marches in the Kingdom.[4]

---

[1] Stewart-Brown, *op. cit.*, p. 47.

[2] The present writer wishes to acknowledge his obligation to Mr Stewart-Brown for drawing his attention to the historical importance of the appointment of Conservators of the Peace in 1399.

[3] For the Latin text and an English translation of Henry VII's charter of 1506, see Morris, *Chester in the Plantagenet and Tudor Reigns*, pp. 524-40. The provisions as to the powers and jurisdiction of the Justices of the Peace will be found on pp. 530-1, 538-9.

[4] See pp. xxxii-xxxiv *infra*. It may be observed in passing that the distinctive privileges of Cheshire as a county palatine were much abridged in the reign of Henry VIII.

GENERAL PREFACE

Historical problems in regard to the introduction of the office of Justice of the Peace in the palatinates cannot be solved by taking into account only the officers who bore that title; for in still earlier times there were various officers, more particularly the Keepers or Conservators of the Peace, who were the forerunners of the Justices of the Peace. Thus, to take only one illustration, Coke's statement that in the county palatine of Chester the chamberlain, who was the judge in the court of exchequer, "time out of mind hath been a conservator of the peace by virtue of the same office [of chamberlain]",[1] needs investigation at the hands of the historian. Since the history of the office of Justice of the Peace involves the history of the institutions which that office gradually displaced, or modified, a study of the early communal, feudal, franchisal, and royal authorities that were charged with the duty of preserving the peace must of necessity form a part of the history of the Justices themselves. Not only the palatine and the *quasi*-palatine lordships, but also the lordships in the Welsh and Scottish marches should be subjected to searching examination from this point of view; and, to gain a complete historical picture, they ought all to be brought into the same scheme of study. In some of these entities, such as Durham, Lancaster, and Chester, the lord possessed *iura regalia* "as fully as the King hath in his palace";[2] and in others the rights of the lord were nearly as extensive.[3] By a comparative study of all these franchises of the medieval era, from the institutional view-point, the forerunners of the Justice of the Peace, such as the *Custodes Pacis* of Durham and Chester, could then be envisaged in a much broader historical perspective. Indeed, it is only by comparative studies of all the great lordships that clear ideas as to the origin and early

---

[1] *Fourth Institute*, 212. For a list of the Chamberlains of Chester during the first half of the fourteenth century, see Tout, *Place of Edward II in English History*, pp. 383–4; and on the history of the Chamberlain of Chester, see Tout, *Flintshire: Its History and its Records* (Flintshire Historical Society), 1911, pp. 27–9.

[2] Blackstone, *Commentaries on the Laws of England*, 2nd ed., vol. I, pp. 116–17.

[3] An idea of the fertility of the middle ages in producing great territorial franchises may be gained by reading Holdsworth, *op. cit.*, vol. I, p. 92. Cf. also Pollock and Maitland, *History of English Law*, 2nd ed., vol. I, p. 582.

history of Justices of the Peace in those regions can be obtained.[1]

III

As Maitland remarked: "Certainly to any one who has an eye for historical greatness it is a very marvellous institution, this Commission of the Peace, growing so steadily, elaborating itself into ever new forms"; "and then", as he continued, "it is so purely English, perhaps the most distinctively English part of all our governmental organisation".[2] Its historic greatness is due, however, not only to its origin and growth in the Kingdom as a special manifestation of the English genius in the matter of law and order; its importance in history has been partly occasioned by its extension to many parts of the world. In a broad sense its adoption and development in the palatinates are features of its English history; for these exalted jurisdictional franchises, because of the very fact that they were king-like, were closely related to the realm and they formed in fact parts of the realm. In the words of Coke, "the county palatines were parcell of the realm of England and divided in jurisdiction".[3] It is the adoption and adaptation of the office of Justice of the Peace in regions outside the realm of England which makes a far more dramatic appeal to the historical imagination of the present-day

---

[1] Coke, *Fourth Institute*, 205, states generally that the rulers of counties palatine could "make justices of eyre, justices of assize, of gaol delivery, and of the peace". The generalisations of lawyers are not necessarily, however, those of the historian; and Coke's lawyerly statement may easily mislead the historian of the Justices of the Peace. From the view-point of history, is it true to say that Justices of the Peace were introduced into all the counties palatine of the middle ages? They were introduced into Durham and Lancaster; but, to all seeming, they were not introduced into Chester (save in the case of the city of Chester under Henry VII) before the time of Henry VIII. In justice to Coke, however, it is only fair to quote from the *Fourth Institute*, 214: "Before the statute of 27 Hen. VIII the lord chancellor of England appointed no justices of peace, justices of quorum or gaol delivery within the county of Chester". Here Coke was writing as an historian; and here he seems to have been upon sure ground. So far as the county palatine of Chester is concerned, the truth seems to be this: *Conservatores Pacis*, the forerunners of the Justices, were appointed as early as 1399, but Justices of the Peace, under that title, were not introduced until the reign of Henry VIII. The whole problem needs, however, fuller investigation.
[2] *Collected Papers*, vol. I, p. 470.
[3] *Fourth Institute*, 223.

GENERAL PREFACE   xxiii

observer; and it is possible, although not clearly certain, that the first example of this world-wide spread of the English institution is to be found in the legal history of Ireland.[1]

The history of Irish laws and institutions, including the introduction of the Justice of the Peace, cannot be understood, however, unless we study it, not in isolation, but as part of a far broader and more extensive development. There is, in fact, a unity in the institutional and legal history of the British Isles which is too often overlooked. Each of the successive invasions, Anglo-Saxon, Scandinavian, and Norman, left its imprint on the laws, customs, and institutions of many regions that were, and have always remained, outside the realm of England; and of these external influences caused by invasion the Norman was the last and the most important. Not only in England, but also in Wales, Scotland, and Ireland, the coming of the Normans meant a vast change in legal and institutional development,[2] and in that Norman epoch of the history of the British Isles the foundations of the later polity of each of these regions were laid. Norman ideas of feudalism and of the strong rule of the King, as overlord and sovereign, were not of course the only factors making for the remoulding of these several societies in the British Isles: the influence of Roman ecclesiastical institutions was also an accompanying feature of the process that had far-reaching effects. But it was the Norman factor which determined, in the field of law and of government, the main lines of future development; and it is precisely this aspect of British history which the student of the spread of English laws and institutions must always bear in mind. The fact that the Normans had penetrated into Wales, Ireland, and Scotland, and there worked their characteristic changes in the framework of social, political and legal life, made it easier, as time progressed, for English laws and institutions, which had themselves been reshaped, expanded, and supplemented by the Normans, to gain admittance. The laying of emphasis on the Norman factor should not, however, lead us to

[1] On the question as to the introduction of the *Custos Pacis* into Scotland in 1197, see p. xxxv *infra*.
[2] See e.g. Rhys and Brynmor-Jones, *The Welsh People*, 1909, *passim*; Hume Brown, *History of Scotland*, vol. I, chaps. I, II; Orpen, *Ireland under the Normans*, vols. I and II, *passim*.

forget the Angevin forces that began to exert their influences on the legal and institutional history of the British Isles with the coming of Henry II; but, although Henry II and his immediate successors effected changes that were specifically Angevin as contrasted with Norman, in its broadest aspect the Angevin factor was essentially a continuation of the Norman. In England, to go no further afield, the work of Henry I in the direction of the centralisation of justice and the formation of the common law served as the basis of Henry II's epoch-making reforms. Without, however, pursuing these reflections further, let us not fail to observe that in the study of the spread of English laws and institutions into Ireland, Wales, and Scotland, the special and peculiar conditions prevailing in each one of these regions, and not least of all the varying effects of Norman feudal influence, must be borne in mind.

In Ireland the coming of the Normans meant a clash between native tribalism and foreign feudalism; and the introduction of English laws and institutions into this environment of conflicting ideas in large measure determined the whole course of Irish legal history during the later middle ages. By the close of the twelfth century the English system of law and government, a system coloured by Norman and Angevin ideas, had already entrenched itself in parts of Ireland; and the ground was prepared, therefore, for the enforcement of English law in Ireland by the ordinances of John and Henry III.[1] Although it may be said that the influence of England was partly institutional and partly legal, it is hardly possible to distinguish neatly between these two aspects of one and the same historical process; for the establishment of courts on the English model went hand in hand with the introduction of the English writ-system and the rules and principles of English law. Without, therefore, drawing the distinction too sharply, let us take note of the fact that it is the local government of medieval Ireland, as an aspect of its institutional development, which has special bearing on the history of the introduction of Justices of the Peace. The formation of counties, administrative units where justices in eyre

[1] See Maitland, "The Introduction of English Law into Ireland" (*Collected Papers*, vol. II, pp. 81–3).

GENERAL PREFACE

heard pleas and where sheriffs executed the processes of the law, was a gradual development; but by the end of the reign of Henry III some progress had been made in this direction.[1] In course of time came the *Custos Pacis*; and, although the introduction of this officer into Ireland is wrapt in some obscurity, it would seem to date from an early age. Speaking of the time of John and Henry III, Maitland has observed that "when a change was made in English law a corresponding change was made in Irish law";[2] and the same remark seems to be equally applicable to changes in institutions.[3] By the time of Henry III the *Custos Pacis*, whose office may have originated on the basis of Hubert Walter's proclamation of 1195, was already functioning in England; and, whatever may have been the precise date, it cannot be doubted that the *Custos Pacis* and the Justice of the Peace made their entry into the local government of Ireland long before the middle of the fifteenth century, when the Commission of the Peace was already regarded as based on ancient custom.[4]

The Justiciary Rolls furnish in fact clear evidence that *Custodes Pacis* were appointed, at least in some parts of Ireland, as early as 1305;[5] and no doubt these instances were based on a much earlier practice. By the year 1287 knights as *Custodes Pacis* were being commissioned in England with the specific purpose of administering the Statute of Winchester[6] for keeping the peace; and soon after the accession of Edward II this com-

[1] See Orpen, *op. cit.*, vol. II, pp. 270–7.
[2] *Collected Papers*, vol. II, p. 81.
[3] Irish administration "reproduced that of England with extreme fidelity". Tout, *Place of Edward II in English History*, p. 385.
[4] Through the kindness of Sir Lynden Macassey, K.C., and Mr Arthur Cox the present writer was enabled to consult the Honourable Mr Justice Murnaghan, learned in the early legal history of Ireland, on certain points; and to him the present writer is under obligation for the reminder that the historical problem in regard to the introduction of Justices of the Peace into Ireland is complicated by the fact that there is considerable difficulty in saying how far the statutes of the Edwards passed in England were regarded as having any force in Ireland. The Irish Act of 1449, mentioned later, referred to commissions issued to Justices of the Peace in Ireland "after the old custom".
[5] See *Calendar of the Justiciary Rolls of Proceedings in the Court of the Justiciar of Ireland*, A.D. 1305–7, pp. 116, 518.
[6] 13 Edward I (1285).

mission included all counties.¹ Now it is a striking fact that in this very same period Edward II, by a writ of the year 1308 directed to the Justiciar of Ireland, ordered that the Statute of Winchester be strictly kept throughout his whole land of Ireland: in every county of Ireland two knights were to be appointed who, together with the sheriff, were to enforce the Statute in order that peace might be preserved. The Statute was to be observed, moreover, in all cities, burghs, hundreds, market towns and other places, as well within liberties as without, throughout the whole land of Ireland; and bailiffs and constables in towns and hundreds, "appointed for the conservation of the peace in the counties", as well within liberties as without, were strictly enjoined to be diligent in the conservation of the King's peace.² Two years later, in 1310, for the better conservation of the King's peace in Ireland, it was ordained, on the initiative of the King, by an Irish legislative body at the so-called Parliament of Kilkenny, that "in every county [there] be established ten men of note or more" who, together with the sheriffs and coroners, were to enquire of all manner of malefactors and to punish and imprison them; and these men of note were to be appointed by the King.³ Again, in Irish legislation of the time of Edward III there were various provisions in regard to the election, commission, and duties of "wardens of the peace" (*gardeines del peax, gardeins du peas*) for the counties; and, while it is impossible in the present place to consider these provisions in detail, one may at least hazard the suggestion that they picture to us a stage in the process whereby the *Custodes Pacis*, the *gardeins du peas*, were transformed, in Ireland not less than in England, into the "Justices of the Peace".⁴ Leaving this pro-

[1] Putnam, "The Transformation of the Keepers of the Peace into the Justices of the Peace" (*Transactions of the Royal Historical Society*, Fourth Series, vol. XII, 1929, pp. 19–48, at p. 23); Jenkinson, *op. cit.*, p. 7.
[2] 1 Edward II (1308). See *Early Statutes of Ireland: John to Henry V*, ed. H. F. Berry (under the direction of the Master of the Rolls in Ireland), pp. 245–53.
[3] 3 Edward II (1310). See *Early Statutes of Ireland: John to Henry V*, pp. 259–68, at p. 267.
[4] 25 Edward III (1351), *Early Statutes of Ireland: John to Henry V*, p. 375, at pp. 379, 383, 385, 387; 31 Edward III (A.D. 1357), *ibid.* p. 408, at p. 411; 40 Edward III (A.D. 1366), the "Statutes of Kilkenny", *ibid.* p. 431, at p. 455.

blem, for the moment, to the historian of Irish law and institutions, it should be carefully observed, as a fact of more than a little significance, that in Irish legislation of the time of Henry IV (1410) the "Justices of the Peace" not only appear before us under that title, but that, to all seeming, the "Guardians" or "Keepers" of the peace are identified with the "Justices".[1] By the middle of the fifteenth century, after the Commission of the Peace had undergone four more decades of development, the same identification of the "Keeper" and the "Justice" is to be observed; and, moreover, by that time the office was viewed as founded on ancient custom. The proof of this is an Act passed by the Irish Parliament in the reign of Henry VI (1449) which provided that certain of the superior judges should be included in the Commission of the Peace and in the *Quorum* in enquiries as to treasons and certain other crimes in certain counties. Not only does this Act assume that Justices of the Peace had long been active in Ireland, but it expressly saved "the commissions made or to be made to justices or keepers of the peace after the old custom".[2]

In Ireland, as in England, therefore, the first stages in the history of the Justices of the Peace appear to have been marked by the introduction of officers whose duties were partly military and partly judicial; and it was only gradually that the early "custodians", "guardians", or "wardens" of the peace finally

[1] 11 Henry IV (1410), *Early Statutes of Ireland: John to Henry V*, p. 520, at pp. 521, 523, 526, 527.

[2] 27 Henry VI (1449): "IV. Also, it is ordained and established that no commission be henceforth made out of the Chancery of our lord the King of his land of Ireland to any person, to enquire, hear and determine, or to enquire, hear and certify of treasons, felonies, trespasses, contempts and all other excesses and offences, in the counties of Dublin, Kildare, Meath and Uriel, except the commissions made or to be made to the Justices or wardens of the peace, according to the ancient custom of the said land (*forsprisez lez comissions faitz ou affaire as Justicez ou gardeins de peas solonq launcient custume del dit terre*); and if any such commission be made to the contrary, that it be void in law and held for null, and that this statute continue until the next parliament".

For the text of the statute as given above, see *Statute Rolls of the Parliament of Ireland* (Henry VI), being vol. II of the Irish Record Office series of early Statutes, ed. H. F. Berry, p. 110, at p. 112. See also *Statutes at Large passed in the Parliaments held in Ireland*, vol. I, p. 14. For later Irish statutes on Justices of the Peace, see the latter collection, vol. VIII (an Index covering the years 1310 to 1798), *s.v.* Justices of Peace.

emerged clearly as the "Justices of the Peace" of later history. In Ireland this early development was influenced by the corresponding development in England; and, in general, the changes in England were soon reflected by similar changes in Ireland. But while the office in Ireland seems to have gone through processes of evolution similar to those which characterised the history of the office in England, no doubt in the Irish development there were certain features which represented a variation due to the difference of environment. This, however, is a matter for future research: what is now needed is a comparative study of the two processes, the original in England and the derivative in Ireland. But only after the materials for the history of the office in Ireland have been carefully studied and their contents made known will it be possible to determine, with any accuracy, the similarities and the differences between two processes of growth which had their common origin in the King's determination to preserve the peace alike within his realm and all his other lands and dominions.

IV

The Welsh aspects of the process of extending the office of Justice of the Peace will demand the attention of an historical scholar whose mind is alert and whose study is carried into the minutest details. Special caution is needed by reason of the intricacies incident to all features of the institutional and legal history of the Welsh regions and the adjacent English counties. Geographically contiguous, the English county palatine of Chester, the principality of Wales, and the franchises of the lords marchers were not united in a political and constitutional sense; and these regions formed in fact no single entity, but a group of entities that were in process of coalescing into one. They possessed many social and legal characteristics in common; and, moreover, in their relations one to another they were closely interwoven. Their relations were marked, however, by disunity rather than unity: disunity was inherent in the prevalence of tribalism and feudalism. Feudalism, common to them all, was far from being a consolidating force; and, since its main effect was disruptive, the only ultimate promise of peace and unity lay in the power of a strong King. Surveying them as a group, but comparing each one of them with the others, the historical observer sees clearly that, as in the history of other similar groups of political entities in various parts of the world, variety was a dominant note in the development of the Welsh regions during the later middle ages. Variety was a striking feature of the process of English influence. In general the introduction of English institutions into any one of them did not necessarily mean that they were also introduced into one or more, or all, of the others; and this was as true of the Justice of the Peace as it was of the jury, the itinerant justices, the original writs, and all the other parts of the English system which gradually found lodgement in the system of Wales. Our fundamental question emerges, therefore, into view. Was the office of Justice of the Peace introduced into any one of these regions before their unification, or consolidation, under the strong hand of the Tudors? Was it introduced, before Tudor times, into the principality of Wales, the palatinate of Pembroke, the lordship of Glamorgan, or any one or more of the many franchises of the lords marchers? Our studies have already shown us two things. *Conservatores Pacis* were introduced into the county palatine of Chester at the very end of the fourteenth century; and in the time of Henry VII the Justices of the Peace were incorporated by royal charter in the government of the city of Chester. But what of the extensive area dominated by the Welsh? Were *Custodes Pacis* introduced? Were they transformed into Justices of the Peace? These and other similar problems of an historical character are directly connected with our general subject; and they are problems of more than a little difficulty and complexity that still await their solution. The results of future research in regard to the course of development must not, and cannot, be anticipated in the present place; but a few suggestions, a few references to authority, may be made.

From the time of Edward I onwards the extension of English laws and institutions to Wales proceeded stage by stage;[1] and

[1] Rhys and Brynmor-Jones's *The Welsh People* is a useful introduction to Welsh institutional and legal history.

yet, to all seeming, Justices of the Peace were not introduced into the principality until the reign of Henry VIII. Before he came to the throne Edward I had endeavoured to establish in his Welsh lands an organisation similar to that of the shires in England;[1] but these efforts do not appear to have been very successful. After he became King, however, his conquest of the principality and its annexation to the Crown gave Edward the opportunity of reviving his earlier plans and of introducing the English shire system and the English laws into Wales on a far more extensive scale.[2] By the Statute of Wales (1284)[3] the King divided his "dominion" of Wales into shires, made provision for the appointment of sheriffs and coroners, introduced the system of writs, and otherwise declared his will in regard to courts, government, and law.[4] But, although *Conservatores Pacis* already formed a part of the English system of local justice in his time, Edward I does not appear to have introduced them into the shires of his principality either by the Statute of Wales or by other means.[5]

In the centuries which immediately followed Edward's conquest of the principality, Welsh institutions represented in general a combination of Celtic and English elements; and while there is no doubt that certain features of the English system of preserving the peace were introduced, such as the "serjeant of the peace",[6] there was apparently no influence of the office of Justice of the Peace upon the Welsh system before the time of Henry V; and even then that influence, as we shall see, did not mean the

---

[1] Thus, "at Carmarthen Edward instituted a county court, or *comitatus*, to which the neighbouring lords marchers were constrained to do suit and service". Morris, *Welsh Wars of Edward I*, p. 23.

[2] Tout, *Edward the First*, ed. 1913, pp. 107–19; Rhys and Brynmor-Jones, *op. cit.*, ed. 1909, p. 347.

[3] 12 Edward I. The text of this and many other statutes concerning Wales will be found in Bowen's *The Statutes of Wales*, 1908.

[4] See Bowen, *op. cit.*, pp. 2–27; Rhys and Brynmor-Jones, *op. cit.*, pp. 349–56.

[5] On *Conservatores Pacis* in England in the time of Edward I, see Beard, *Office of Justice of the Peace in England*, 1904, pp. 21–8.

[6] See Vinogradoff and Morgan, *Survey of the Honour of Denbigh 1334*, 1914, pp. lxxiv–lxxxvi, 48, 152, 209, 270, 314. Cf. the Serjeants of the Peace in the county palatine of Chester, pp. xvii–xviii *supra*. In future studies of the origins and early history of the offices of *Custos Pacis* and Justice of the Peace the "Serjeants of the Peace" should form the subject-matter of careful investigation.

introduction of the office as an integral part of the Welsh system itself. Edward I's legislation had applied only to the principality as it then existed and did not touch the march in which many lordships were held of the English King, on terms of vassalage, by the descendants of Norman lords or Welsh chieftains. In these extensive feudal regions private wars between lords, conflicts of jurisdiction between courts of lordship, and the general disorder and lawlessness that prevailed, were long a matter of deep concern to the Kings of England; and finally, in the second year of Henry V (1414), a statute was passed[1] which gave power to Justices of the Peace within English counties both to enquire into and to determine charges against Welshmen who had committed offences "with force and arms in the manner of war, sometimes by day and sometimes by night", in these bordering counties of England.[2] While this statute did not establish Justices of the Peace either in the principality or in the marches, it is of interest as being the first step taken by the King to place those of his Welsh subjects who had committed offences in English counties within the jurisdiction of Justices of the Peace in those counties. The jurisdiction thus established in the time of Henry V was not only continued, but further strengthened and extended by legislation of Henry VI and Henry VIII; and, beginning with the statute of Henry V, already mentioned, the jurisdiction was made as effective as possible by the institution of processes by which Welsh offenders in English counties could be followed into the principality and the marches and brought to justice.[3]

The absence of Justices of the Peace in the principality and marches of Wales had long been felt as one of the chief reasons why so many crimes had gone unpunished.[4] In the regions of the march difficulties had been caused by the conflicts of

[1] 2 Henry V, Statute 2, c. 5.
[2] The Act specially mentions the counties of Salop, Hereford, and Gloucester, and "other places bordering upon" Wales. See Bowen, *op. cit.*, pp. xlvii, 38.
[3] 20 Henry VI, c. 3 (1441–2); 23 Henry VI, c. 4 (1444–5); 27 Henry VI, c. 4 (1448–9); 26 Henry VIII, c. 5, 6, 12 (1534). The nature of these processes, which have parallels elsewhere, forms a neglected aspect of English legal history.
[4] The absence of the Justices is expressly mentioned in the statute 26 Henry VIII, c. 12.

jurisdiction and the easy flight from one lordship to another of persons accused of crime, while in the principality itself many criminals appear to have been at large untroubled by the fear of punishment. In the time of Edward IV the prevalence of disorder in the principality as well as the continuance of lawlessness in the marches[1] led to the establishment of a new court known as the President and Council of Wales and the Marches (1478); and in the reigns of Henry VII and Henry VIII this tribunal was given an extended jurisdiction and made permanent.[2] Under the presidency of Rowland Lee (1535–43), Bishop of Coventry and Lichfield, "the court became a terror to the evil-doers in the marches and a powerful weapon for keeping the peace and dispensing justice throughout the West"; and Lee's "tenure of office prepared the way for the practical application of the great statutes by which Henry VIII united Wales and the marches to England".[3] The legislation of Henry VIII (1535–43) completed the work begun by Edward I.[4] Not only were the lordships of the march converted into shire-land, but in all parts of Wales, which now included both the ancient principality and the lands that had formed the marches, English institutions and laws, following the model set by Edward I in the principality of his time, were either re-established on firmer foundations or introduced for the first time as a further stage in the assimilation of the constitutional and legal systems of England and Wales.[5]

Only one aspect of the constitution of Wales as thus established by Henry VIII, with the assistance of Thomas Cromwell, concerns us at the present moment. By Henry's legislation the whole of the Welsh region was divided into twelve shires, of

---

[1] Evans, *Wales and the Wars of the Roses*, p. 197: "Wales had almost become one vast lordship-marcher".

[2] On the history of the tribunal, see Skeel, *The Council in the Marches of Wales*.

[3] Rhys and Brynmor-Jones, *op. cit.*, pp. 362–6. See also Skeel, *op. cit.*, pp. 49–80; Fisher, *History of England* (1485–1547), 1910, p. 376. Lee not only sat at Ludlow for the hearing of causes, but, either alone or in company with Sir Thomas Englefield, the Justice of Chester, travelled throughout his jurisdiction, after the manner of the English justices in eyre of medieval times.

[4] For the text of Henry VIII's statutes, see Bowen, *op. cit.*, pp. 50–135.

[5] See Rhys and Brynmor-Jones, *op. cit.*, pp. 346–94.

which eight had existed "of long and ancient time";[1] and for the first time in the history of Wales all of these shires were now to be governed, like the counties of England, through Justices of the Peace who were subject to the orders of the King's Council and the laws of Parliament. As remarked by Professor Trevelyan, "thus supported by the strong arm of the central government, the Justices of the Peace were able to rule in the wild hill region where tribalism and feudalism had run riot for centuries. These magistrates, under the system inaugurated by Henry VIII, were not Englishmen imported to hold down the natives, but Welsh gentlemen who were the natural leaders of the people".[2] It is in truth one of the most striking features of Henry VIII's Welsh constitution that the King, following the general policy of the Tudors in England, placed his chief reliance on Justices of the Peace as instruments for the preservation of peace and the maintenance of good government in all the shires of Wales.

As a matter of historical sequence and accuracy it should be noticed that Justices of the Peace were first of all introduced by statute into the eight ancient shires (1535)[3] and that only on the division of the whole land into twelve shires was it provided, by a later statute, that there should be "Justices of Peace and Quorum, and also one *Custos Rotulorum*, in every of the said twelve shires" (1542–3).[4] The statutes of Henry VIII made in fact elaborate provision for the establishment and working of the courts of the Justices; and in general the mode of appointment, qualification, and jurisdiction of the Justices were patterned after the system at that time in force within England. The institution of Justices of the Peace in Wales fell within the period when the old form of the Commission of the Peace, before Sir Christopher Wray's revision (1590), was still in use in England; and to all seeming the Commission of the Peace for Wales followed this ancient form of the English Commission until 1590. Apparently the statute of 1535 was sufficient authority for the holding of Quarter Sessions, even though they were not

---

[1] See Bowen, *op. cit.*, pp. lx, lxvi; Holdsworth, *op. cit.*, vol. I, pp. 122–32.
[2] Trevelyan, *History of England*, 1929, p. 359.
[3] 27 Henry VIII, c. 5 (1535).
[4] 34 and 35 Henry VIII, c. 26 (1542–3).

expressly mentioned; but in the Act of 1542-3 it was definitely provided that Quarter Sessions should be held, "in like manner as is used in England". Henry VIII's legislation had limited the number of Justices of the Peace in each of the shires of Wales to eight.[1] But in the time of William and Mary this provision was repealed and the Crown was given power to nominate and appoint any such number of Justices of the Peace in any of the counties of Wales as should be deemed fitting and convenient, according to the "ways and methods" commonly employed for the appointment of such Justices in English counties.[2]

Before passing from Wales to Scotland the point should be stressed that there is urgent need for a scholarly historical study of the entirety of Welsh medieval regions from the institutional and legal point of view: and this is particularly true of that institution which forms the subject-matter of the present pages. The presence of special commissioners of the peace *ad hoc* and of "Conservators of the Peace" in medieval Cheshire, to which reference has already been made, is a suggestive fact. Although a cursory reading of modern historical books does not disclose the existence of the Conservators or Keepers of the Peace, the forerunners of the Justices, in the Welsh regions during the later middle ages, it may well be that these early officers of the peace, not less than special commissioners of the peace *ad hoc*, lie hidden away, awaiting their finder, in the original sources of Welsh history. The Keepers may be there, just as the Justices themselves may be there, concealed in part, it is possible, by language, by names and terms which mask their office and its function.

V

In the history of Justices of the Peace in Scotland there is a remote period still shrouded in mystery. In earlier medieval times Germanic folk, not less than Celtic, played a rôle in the beginnings and consolidation of Scotland: Angle, Saxon, and Norman left their distinct imprint on social and legal institutions.[3] While differing each from the other in many essential

[1] 34 and 35 Henry VIII, c. 11, § 55 (1542-3).
[2] 5 and 6 William & Mary, c. 4 (1693).
[3] See Hume Brown, *History of Scotland*, vol. I, pp. 1-87.

GENERAL PREFACE xxxv

particulars, the early legal and institutional systems of England and Scotland both possessed, nevertheless, certain features which made them similar to each other; and while some of these resemblances were due to common origins, others were caused by common influences from the same external sources. Scholars still dispute, however, as to the nature and extent of the mutual influences, each upon the other, of English and Scots law during the earlier centuries of their growth; and, in particular, historians are not in agreement upon the question as to whether or not in the twelfth century Henry II of England (1154–89) borrowed at least some of his reforms in law and police from the measures which David I of Scotland (1124–53), one of the greatest of the northern kings, had already adopted. Without entering upon this controversy, it seems clear that there was a marked imitation of English institutions by the Scots in the twelfth century, and that not until the wars of Edward I threw the Scots upon the alliance with the French was this tendency largely displaced by a preference for the principles of law and the modes of government that had established themselves in France.[1] On the particular matter which concerns us at the moment it is not without interest to recall that Hoveden is an authority for English influence; for he tells us that in the year 1197 William I, "the Lyon", King of the Scots, introduced into his dominions that oath for the preservation of the peace which two years earlier, in 1195, had been prescribed in England by the proclamation of Hubert Walter.[2] The question as to whether William's introduction of the oath resulted in the appointment of *Custodes Pacis* in Scotland seems never to have been investigated; but, however this problem of early history may be ultimately resolved, from a study of later conditions it is safe to conclude that when James VI came to the throne of Scotland in 1567 there were no Justices of the Peace in that kingdom.

The first appearance of Justices of the Peace in Scotland fell in fact within the reign of James VI (1567–1625), who in 1603 was to become, as James I, the first of the Stuart Kings of Eng-

---
[1] See Stubbs, *Historical Introductions to the Rolls Series*, p. 309.
[2] Hoveden (ed. Stubbs), vol. IV, p. 33. See Stubbs's comments, *op. cit.*, pp. civ–cv.

land. In Scottish history the half-century of James's ascendency was notable as a period in which the constitution was transformed and the administration of justice improved. The personality of the King was not the least of the causes of this change in Scottish institutions. As Rait has remarked: "James did not exaggerate when he said [in a speech at Whitehall, 31st March, 1607]: 'Here I sit and governe it [Scotland] with my pen, I write and it is done, and by a Clearke of the Councell I governe Scotland now, which others could not do by the sword'".[1] What James VI did for Scotland was similar to the work done for England and Wales by the Tudors, for France by Louis XI, and for Spain by Ferdinand and Isabella; and in truth the masterful achievement of James was like that of all the other strong rulers of the epoch of the Renaissance. In the consolidation of the institutions of Scotland, at the beginnings of our modern age, James VI was concerned with judicial reform as a leading part of his policy; and the introduction of Justices of the Peace, on the English model, formed one of its features. Partly as a result of the fact that the Justice-Ayres, which were circuit courts of justiciary, had ceased to be held with any regularity in the time of Mary (1561-7) and during the early years of James's reign (1567-1625), the lesser crimes committed throughout the country were left unpunished.[2] It was accordingly enacted by the Scottish Parliament in 1587[3] that in every shire Justice-Ayres should be held twice each year and that Justices of the Peace, who were to sit in both Petty and Quarter Sessions, should be commissioned in every shire. One purpose of the appointment of Justices of the Peace, as appears from the statute, was to commit "all persones delated as culpable in the first degree" to the cognizance of the Justice-Ayres; but, "upon all persones delated and suspected, as culpable of the

[1] Rait, *Scottish Parliament*, p. 101.
[2] The "special and highest crimes" could be dealt with by the Court of Session in Edinburgh. Hume Brown, *op. cit.*, vol. II, p. 217.
[3] James VI, 11th Parliament, 1587, c. 82, *Acts of the Parliament of Scotland*, vol. III, pp. 458-9. The text of the Act will also be found in Walker, *Justice of the Peace: A Manual for the Use of Justices of the Peace in Scotland*, 1931, pp. 98-101. The attention of the present writer was drawn to Mr Walker's book by Mr A. D. Gibb, who has also been kind enough to make more than one valuable suggestion as to the Scottish aspect of the history of the Justices.

GENERAL PREFACE

uther crimes and defaultes, in the second degree, the said justices and commissioners in the schires [should] proceede and do justice themselves, at their courtes and meetings to be kept four times every zeir". Although the Act of 1587 was primarily intended as a measure for the regulation of the holding of the Justice-Ayres, it is at the same time notable as being the first statutory provision for the appointment of Justices of the Peace in Scotland. After fixing the number of Justices to be appointed in each individual shire, the Act provided that the Justices should be landed gentlemen of good standing and repute who were actual dwellers within the shires to which they were appointed; and the statute further enacted both that the Justices were to sit in Quarter Sessions at the head burgh of the shire and that three should be a quorum.[1]

The Act of 1587 proved, however, to be inadequate; and, indeed, it may well be doubted whether, in the disturbed condition of the country at that time, it was productive of much effect in introducing Justices of the Peace. In fact it appears to have been found difficult to incorporate the office of Justice of the Peace in the Scottish system of criminal justice; and it is possible that the very multiplicity of Scottish statutes dealing with Justices of the Peace proves this to have been the case.[2] However this may have been, after the Union of the Crowns of England and Scotland in 1603 James was brought into immediate touch with the English machinery of justice; and apparently it was his observation of the working of the system of Justices of the Peace in England which led him to the conclusion that, so far as the Justices in Scotland were concerned, the Act of 1587 needed supplementation.[3] Accordingly, in 1609 the Scottish Parliament passed an Act authorizing the appointment of Justices of the Peace in every shire; and this was followed by active measures on the part of the Privy Council of Scotland. The Justices were given extensive powers; and to make their orders effective two constables in every parish were to be appointed. "Generally", it has been said by Masson, "the

---

[1] See Walker, *op. cit.*, pp. 97–101.
[2] Walker, *op. cit.*, p. 1.
[3] See Hume Brown, *op. cit.*, vol. II, p. 218.

justices in each shire were charged with all the duties of magistracy in that shire, except that they were to refer all matters capital, and the cases of all offenders of high rank, to the Council, and also that they were to avoid interference with the powers of provosts and bailies of burghs, and with other constituted jurisdictions."[1] The Act of 1609 was ratified by a later Parliament of James's reign; and this Scottish statute of 1617 contained important general instructions to the Justices. Further ratifications by the Scottish Parliament followed in the time of Charles I (1633), in the Usurpation (1655), at the Restoration (1661), and in the reign of James II (1685).[2] The Scottish Acts of 1617 and 1661, passed in the reigns of James VI and Charles II respectively, are to be regarded as in some measure the legislative basis of the activity of Justices of the Peace in Scotland at the present day.

That the introduction of Justices of the Peace had proved to be a gain to Scotland may be inferred from the Act of 1661,[3] in which Charles II declared that the appointing of such Justices and constables within all the shires of Scotland in the time of his predecessors had contributed to "the peace, quiet, and good government" of the country and to "the speedy and impartial execution of law and justice". While it may well be true that as a result of more peaceful social conditions and of the reorganisation of the shrievalty the Justices of the Peace lost something of power and position in the course of the seventeenth century,[4] a perusal of this important Act of Charles II's time (1661) leads one to the conclusion that at the time when the Act was passed the judicial and administrative work of the Justices, including that of their courts of Quarter Sessions, was still very extensive.

Although the Union of North and South Britain in 1707 meant the absorption of the Scottish Parliament and Privy Council in those of England, it left the judicial and legal in-

---

[1] See Hume Brown, *op. cit.*, vol. II, pp. 217–18; Peters, *Der schottische Rechtskörper in Vergangenheit und Gegenwart*, 1907, § 6; Walker, *op. cit.*, pp. 1–2. Masson quoted by Hume Brown, *loc. cit.*, p. 218.
[2] Walker, *op. cit.*, pp. 2, 97–8.
[3] Charles II, 1st Parliament, 1661, c. 38. For the text of the Act, see Walker, *op. cit.*, pp. 101–14.
[4] Peters, *op. cit.*, § 6.

GENERAL PREFACE

stitutions of the two countries intact as two separate systems. At the first Parliament of the United Kingdom (1707-8) the question of Justices of the Peace in Scotland came forward, however, for discussion; and the debate showed that the Scottish representatives were themselves divided.[1] It was contended by the official party that the powers which it was proposed to confer on the Justices would be destructive of the baronial feudal jurisdictions, which the Treaty had expressly preserved. The "Squadrone Volante", the independent and powerful "New Party" which, led by such men as the Marquis of Tweeddale and the Earls of Rothes and Roxburgh, had worked for the Union, maintained, on the other hand, that the Privy Council had exercised the very powers which it was now sought to entrust to the Justices, who had already occupied a place in the Scottish judicial system ever since the time of James VI. In respect of the Privy Council and of the Justices alike the Squadrone Volante ultimately had their way. The same Act not only abolished the Scottish Privy Council, but authorized the appointment of Justices of the Peace for Scotland with a jurisdiction practically identical with that of the contemporary Justices in England.[2] By the Act[3] authority was given to the Queen to appoint a "sufficient number of good and lawful men to be Justices of the Peace within their respective shires, stewartries, cities, boroughs, liberties, or precincts" in Scotland; and the Act further provided that over and above the "powers and authorities vested in Justices of the Peace by the laws of Scotland", such Justices should be "authorized to do, use, and exercise" whatever "doth pertain to the office and trust of a Justice of the Peace, by virtue of the laws and Acts of Parliament made in England", provided nevertheless that "in the Sessions of the Peace the methods of tryal and judgment shall be according to the laws and customs of Scotland".[4]

---

[1] On the temper of the situation, see Leadam, *History of England* (1702-60), pp. 93-108.
[2] Hume Brown, *op. cit.*, vol. III, pp. 105-6. See also Peters, *op. cit.*, § 6.
[3] 6 Anne, c. 6. The text is set out in Walker, *op. cit.*, pp. 114-16.
[4] On the later history of Justices of the Peace in Scotland, see Peters, *op.cit.*, § 18; Walker, *op. cit.*, *passim.*

VI

In modern times the history of the extension of the office of Justice of the Peace to remote regions of the world has been an integral part of British imperial history. The spread of the office to many parts of the British Empire has been in fact one of the leading features of that vast historical process by which English institutions and English laws have been given a world-wide significance. So far as the nature of that process is concerned there has been no break with medieval times: from the early period of English expansion under the Normans and Angevins to our own day conquest and colonisation have carried the English system into regions farther and farther away from the homeland. If the modern history of the process be studied in its entirety it will be found that this peculiarly English institution, the Commission of the Peace, has been worked into the institutional systems of many scattered regions; and of this process two or three illustrations may be given.

Sometimes under a new name, and often with an adaptation to local conditions, the office of Justice of the Peace found in the seventeenth century a fresh field for development within the King's American colonial possessions;[1] and in still later times, following the expansion of the Empire, it has entered into the legal and constitutional systems of both ancient and youthful communities. Thus, to take but one illustration out of many, in the earliest days of British settlement in Australia the governors, in the exercise of the powers conferred upon them by their commissions, appointed Justices of the Peace. Not only did these early Australian Justices of the Peace exercise a summary jurisdiction over the convict class, but in the preliminary stages of proceedings in the higher criminal courts they served to some extent as protectors of the accused. As a barrier against oppressive proceedings on the part of the Crown the Justices of the

[1] See Osgood, *The American Colonies in the Seventeenth Century*, 3 vols., 1904–7, *passim*; Reinsch, "The English Common Law in the early American Colonies" (*Essays in Anglo-American Legal History*, vol. I, 1907, pp. 367–415); Thompson, *The Development of the Anglo-American Judicial System*, Part I, 1932 (reprinted from *Cornell Law Quarterly*, vol. XVII, Nos. 1, 2, and 3), p. 23.

GENERAL PREFACE xli

Peace in those early times were, however, in a position of disadvantage; for, added to their general lack of professional and legal knowledge, they were dependent on the will of the Government. Apparently the first introduction of Justices of the Peace into New Zealand was due to the action of Governor Macquarie, of New South Wales, early in the nineteenth century. Although his commission as Governor did not in the year 1814 include the Maori islands, he actually appointed magistrates to reside in New Zealand with the chief object of checking the outrages of the white settlers.[1]

Without pausing even to sketch the later history of the Justices in Australasia, attention may be centred for a moment on India. In the period of the union of the Old and New Companies, when the Company bore the title of "The United Company of Merchants of England trading to the East Indies", a charter was granted in 1726 which established or reconstituted municipalities at Madras, Bombay, and Calcutta; and at the same time the charter either set up or remodelled mayor's courts and other tribunals at each of these places. In this judicial charter of 1726 it was provided, among other things, that the Governor or President and the five seniors of the Council should be Justices of the Peace and that they were to hold Quarter Sessions four times in every year, with jurisdiction over all offences except high treason. The well-known Regulating Act of 1773 marks another stage in the history of the Justices in India; for by its terms the Governor-General and Council and the Chief Justice and other judges of the Supreme Court were to act as Justices of the Peace and in that capacity to hold Quarter Sessions. Twenty years later the Charter Act of 1793 conferred power to appoint covenanted servants of the Company or other British subjects to be Justices of the Peace in Bengal; while by the Charter Act of 1813 it was provided that Justices of the Peace were to have jurisdiction not only in cases of assault or trespass committed by British subjects on natives of India, but also in cases involving small debts due to natives from British subjects. In 1832 an Act of Parliament both repealed the pro-

[1] Jenks, *A History of the Australasian Colonies*, pp. 153, 154, 169, 170; Stout, *New Zealand*, p. 109.

visions requiring jurors to be Christians and gave authority for the appointment of persons other than covenanted civilians to be Justices of the Peace in India.[1]

VII

Surveying for a moment the historical development outlined in such a fragmentary way in the preceding pages, the fact comes clearly into our cognisance that before the opening of the century illumined by Sir William Holdsworth and Mr Dowdell this ancient office of local government in England, the Justice of the Peace, had already been incorporated in the institutional systems of Ireland, Wales, and Scotland. There is, moreover, a further fact that comes vividly into light. Even before the beginning of Mr Dowdell's period in Middlesex the forces that were making British imperial history had begun to carry the office into remote quarters of the world, there to serve the same purposes for which it had been originally created in the days of the Angevins.

Those purposes had been, primarily, the conservation of the King's peace. The prevalence of lawlessness and disorder required that a new office be established in the local government of the realm; and in slowly developing that new instrument of judicial and administrative government our forefathers unwittingly created an institution which in all subsequent ages and in large parts of the world has proved to be, with all its defects, a benefit of inestimable value to many political societies differing one from another in their origin and in their culture. Of the several causes, partly political and partly social, which have led to the introduction of Justices of the Peace in these scattered domains, there is one that stands out in great prominence. It is, in truth, a notable fact that, as in early England, the existence of lawlessness and crime has nearly everywhere been one of the chief historical factors in the adoption and adaptation of the office of Justice of the Peace; and, moreover, it is equally striking that, as in England, once firmly established in the interests of peace and justice the office has been used for many

[1] Ilbert, *The Government of India*, 3rd ed. (1915), pp. 32, 48, 70, 79, 81, 165.

GENERAL PREFACE

of the other purposes of local government and has in this way been adapted to functions that are political, social, and economic in character.

At the present day the office of Justice of the Peace, not only in the British Isles but elsewhere, is in process of decay, its functions usurped by other institutional machineries; and it is not impossible, indeed it is probable, that in course of time this heritage from the middle ages, at least in the form in which it has filled so much of history, is destined to disappear from the life of society, taking its place among those institutions of the past which men study only in order to understand the course of historical development that has produced the local government of their day. Lord Coke could write: "The whole Christian world hath not the like office as justice of the peace if duly executed". To-day no observer, lawyer or other, would think of writing of the Justice of the Peace, as an instrument of present government, in these terms. What causes lie at the basis of this gradual decline?[1] The introduction of new methods and new offices of local government gives a partial, but not a complete, answer. Some of the causes of that slow decay lie far back in history. In Mr Dowdell's book the thoughtful reader may detect more than one of them; and others will be found in the events of later centuries. The growth of democratic ideas in Great Britain may partly account for the curtailment of the functions of an office the holder of which is appointed by the Lord Chancellor as a representative of the Crown; and generally democracies, as in the case of the United States of America, show a decided preference for elected officers and elected bodies.[2] The historical

---

[1] Since the decline seems to be general in all, or at least in nearly all, the countries where the office of Justice of the Peace was established, it seems unnecessary to do more than cite one or two illustrations. The Honourable Mr Justice Murnaghan has informed the present writer that although the Justice of the Peace remained in Ireland until 1922 and still remains in Northern Ireland, in the Irish Free State since 1922 a District Justice has the former jurisdiction of the Justice of the Peace, with an added statutory jurisdiction. Thompson, *op. cit.*, p. 23: "This great institution was transplanted to America, and the office of justice of the peace is still to be found in most of our states, although sadly diminished from its ancient dignity both in power and prestige".

[2] The present writer is indebted to Sir William Holdsworth for this suggestion.

causes which lie at the basis of the decline, whatever they may be, have been operative in various parts of the world; and those causes have not yet ceased to produce their effect. Indeed, in all the countries where the Justices have flourished, the forces of our own day, uncompromising and unyielding, ever diminish and never increase the power of these ancient rulers of the shire: the processes that make for extinction, though gradual, seem relentless in their trend. But, whatever the ultimate fate of the Justices of the Peace may be, they stand out in world-history as one of the most remarkable expressions of the English genius for government, a genius that is legal, but also more than legal, for in it there are elements of a justice that is social and political, a justice which makes the law and its instruments the servants of the community.

H. D. H.

INTRODUCTION

I

MAITLAND, in his brilliant paper on *The Shallows and Silences of Real Life*, said that some day "a history of the eighteenth century which does not place the justice of the peace in the very foreground of the picture, will be known for what it is—a caricature"; because, unless the Justice of the Peace is given this prominent position, we can never know "what the laws made in Parliament, what the liberties asserted in Parliament, really meant to the mass of the people".[1] In other words, in the eighteenth century, as in all other periods of English history, we must know something of the machinery of local government, and of the legal and political ideas of the men who worked that machinery, if we wish to attain a thorough knowledge of the public and much of the private law of the English state. In the middle ages the constitutional historian must begin his story by telling us of the many varied kinds of courts—communal, feudal, franchise, manorial—through which the work of government was done. It is only when their position and functions have been explained that he can go on to tell us of the series of encroachments made upon their jurisdictions by a strong central court, and, as the result of these encroachments, of the growth of a centralised system of government to which those local courts are gradually subordinated. In the Tudor period the constitutional historian must tell us of the rise of a new system of local government based on the Justices of the Peace and the parish, and of the manner in which it was pieced on to the medieval system, in such a way that the new organisation inherited much of the medieval spirit and many of the medieval forms. As in the middle ages, the Justices performed their functions under judicial forms, and, subject to the law, they had a large measure of autonomy; and, as in the middle ages, the whole system rested upon a basis of unpaid service, which was obligatory on

[1] *Collected Papers*, vol. I, pp. 468–9.

all classes of the community, from the dignified Lord-Lieutenant to the humble parish officers. In the Tudor and early Stuart period this complex system was kept in working order by the strict supervision of the Council, the Star Chamber, and the Provincial Councils; and it is quite clear that, without some knowledge of this system thus controlled, it is impossible to understand either the strong and the weak points of the balanced Tudor constitution, or the strength of the opposition to the Stuart kings. Similarly, in the eighteenth century, the local government was based upon the autonomous powers of the Justices of the Peace, upon the community of the parish, and upon the unpaid services of all classes. The Justices of the Peace were the centre of a system which contained elements which came from all periods in English history; and the manner in which they adapted that system to the new economic and social conditions which were emerging in the latter half of that century, enables us to understand the success with which the statesmen of the century built up, on a basis of legislation, custom, and convention, that balanced constitution of separated powers which won the admiration of foreigners as well as of Englishmen, and enables us also to understand the essential truth of Maitland's aphorism.

Maitland's words were written in 1888. When he wrote them the history of local government was something in the nature of a *terra incognita*. There were the practitioners' books on the Justices of the Peace and the Sheriff; and there were a few published series of county records. But there was no authoritative book on the history of local government as a whole. After the reign of Edward I Stubbs ceased to give that attention to local government which he had given in the earlier part of his history; and the later constitutional historians, such as Hallam and Erskine May, pay very little attention to it. In 1906 was published the first volume of the Webbs' *History of Local Government*. That history, which is remarkable for the success with which its authors combine the qualities of literary style and human interest with the qualities of erudition and accuracy, gave to the students of English public law the opportunity of acquiring that knowledge of the eighteenth-century system of local government,

INTRODUCTION

which is the necessary foundation for an accurate knowledge of eighteenth-century constitutional history. Those who have studied it must, I think, agree that it proves the truth of Maitland's view that a constitutional history of the eighteenth century which neglects the topic of local government is a caricature.

Some of the most important authorities for the history of local government are the records of the proceedings of the Justices at the Quarter Sessions. A number of these records are in print.[1] But they deal for the most part with rural areas. It is true that, in the eighteenth century, the distinction between rural and urban or suburban areas was less distinct than it became in later times. "*Summa rusticitas*", says Maitland,[2] "the pig was ubiquitous.... In Cambridge, even under Elizabeth, there was a strong smack of the farmyard"; and Mr Dowdell tells us that in the Middlesex records the keeping of pigs was the most frequently prosecuted of nuisances.[3] But, allowing for the truth of these facts, I think that the records of more especially rural areas ought to be supplemented by the records of an area which, at the beginning of the eighteenth century, was coming to be of a distinctively urban or suburban character. Mr Dowdell's account of the records of the county of Middlesex from 1660 to 1760 supplies this want by giving us an account of the records of such an area. Though in many respects the business done by the Middlesex Quarter Sessions does not differ materially from the business done at the Quarter Sessions of other counties, it is clear that these Sessions, by reason of their urban or suburban character, were faced with different problems. The manner in which they faced these problems, either with the help of the Legislature, or by methods which the Justices, by virtue of their autonomous powers, devised to deal with them, presents us with a valuable picture of the initial stages of a transitional period in the history of local government. After 1760 the progress of the industrial revolution, and the social and economic changes which came in its train, made the transition more rapid both in

---

[1] See, for instance, J. C. Atkinson, *North Riding Sessions Records*; *The Shropshire County Records*; J. C. Cox, *Three Centuries of Derbyshire Annals*.

[2] *Township and Borough*, pp. 68–9; cp. Webb, *Local Government, The Manor and the Borough*, p. 303.

[3] *Vide infra*, pp. 123–4.

Middlesex and in other parts of the country. But it is interesting to see how these problems were tackled in their initial stages, in a county where the process of urbanisation had begun several decades before the industrial revolution had begun to make its influence felt elsewhere.

It was this process of urbanisation which made it necessary to modify, to add to, and gradually to change the system of local government which the eighteenth century had inherited. Mr Dowdell's book gives us a picture of the first stages of this gradual revolution in what was then the most important urban and suburban area in England. It therefore gives us a picture of the beginnings of a series of changes which, in the later years of the eighteenth century, were destined to modify the system of local government in many parts of England; and, in the first quarter of the nineteenth century, to create a demand for still more radical changes. It was the need to make these changes which was the driving force behind that demand for Parliamentary reform, which was attained in 1832 by a statute which has had a more profound effect than any other single statute upon the development of the government of England both central and local.

In the ensuing sections of this Introduction I propose to sketch very shortly and summarily some of the leading features of the local government of the eighteenth century; to describe the relations between the local and central government; to say something of the light which these relations throw upon the extent to which the powers of government in the English state were separated; and to summarise the strong and weak points of the eighteenth-century system of local government.

II

The system of local government which the eighteenth century had inherited was remarkable for the diversity of the origin of its parts, for the autonomy of the Courts and officials by which it was conducted, and, consequently, for a curious combination of old ideas and old machinery with a power and a will to adapt those ideas and this machinery to new needs.

INTRODUCTION

The collapse of central control, which followed the Great Rebellion and the Revolution, left the Justices of the Peace very free to carry out their duties in their own way;[1] and their autonomy was increased by the fact that, in the course of the eighteenth century, they came to be in effect permanent officials.[2] This absence of central control made also for the preservation of many local diversities. Though the county and borough records show that there were many uniformities in the system of local government which the eighteenth century had inherited, the autonomous character of the units of local government, past history, and present conditions, left room for many of these diversities. Local customs might vary the part which the inhabitants of the parish took in its management.[3] The existence of a franchise, occasionally in the county and more often in a borough, might create differences in the style and jurisdiction of the Courts through which the government was administered.[4] The personality of some one member of a bench of Justices might improve the whole tone of the government of a county or a borough.[5] On the other hand, some of the urban and suburban districts of Middlesex suffered from the fact that it was impossible to get men of education and property to act as justices— hence we get the notorious "trading justices" who figure in many of the plays and novels of the period.[6] Local government had not yet been mechanised as it is now mechanised in this age of machines. Therefore it is the historical continuity of much of the machinery of local government, the autonomy of its units, and the necessity of adapting old machinery to new needs, which are the principal causes for the leading characteristics of the eighteenth-century system of local government. The

---

[1] Webb, *Local Government, The Parish and the County*, pp. 309-10; vide infra, p. 14.
[2] Holdsworth, *History of English Law*, vol. I, p. 291.
[3] Webb, *Local Government, The Parish and the County*, pp. 21-2.
[4] Webb, *Local Government, The Manor and the Borough*, pp. 337, 340-1.
[5] Webb, *Local Government, The Parish and the County*, pp. 354-6, 364-70.
[6] *Ibid.*, pp. 326-37; Burke said in 1780 of some of the Middlesex Justices that they were "the scum of the earth—carpenters, bricklayers, and shoemakers; some of whom were men of such infamous character that they were unworthy of any employ whatever, and others so ignorant that they could scarcely write their own names", *Parl. Hist.*, vol. XXI, p. 592, cited Webb, *The Parish and the County*, p. 325.

INTRODUCTION

leading characteristics of that system can be summarised as follows:

(1) It was remarkable for the survival of many medieval ideas and institutions—a characteristic which it shared with much of the judicial machinery of the common law courts,[1] and some parts of the executive machinery of the central government.[2] One illustration of this characteristic is to be found in the extensive use which was still made of the machinery of presentment. As in the thirteenth century, when the Justices in Eyre travelled round the country, the machinery of presentment and indictment was used, not only for purposes of criminal procedure, but also as an essential part of the machinery of local government.[3] Thus, before a rate could be made for the repair of a bridge, a presentment was required. Mr Dowdell tells us[4] that "the obstruction which the Court encountered over several years was based partly on the neglect of this procedure"; and a statute of 1739[5] required a presentment before money could be spent on the repair of bridges, gaols or houses of correction. A second illustration of the survival of medieval ideas is the wide and undifferentiated powers of the Justices. They were judges, administrators, and sometimes even legislators. The Quarter Sessions was very free to make its own rules of procedure. Thus, the Middlesex Quarter Sessions "sought to establish a regular system of licensing sessions half a century before Parliament took the step".[6] Under cover of putting down nuisances the Justices had large power to suppress courses of conduct of which they disapproved;[7] and in the orders issued or the procedure adopted by them in the exercise of their statutory powers we can see the beginnings of the law upon such matters as licensing,[8] vagrancy,[9] and rating.[10] A third illustration of the survival of medieval ideas is to be found in the extensive use made of unpaid

---

[1] For illustrations see Holdsworth, *op. cit.*, vol. I, pp. 246–60.
[2] The best series of illustrations will be found in Burke's speech on Economical Reform in 1780, *Works* (Bohn's ed.), vol. II, pp. 55–126.
[3] *Vide infra*, pp. 2–3.　　　[4] *Vide infra*, p. 126.
[5] 12 George II, c. 29, § 13.
[6] *Vide infra*, p. 34; for other anticipations of a statutory requirement *vide infra*, pp. 62, 92.
[7] *Vide infra*, pp. 119–24.　　　[8] *Vide infra*, p. 37.
[9] *Vide infra*, pp. 70, 71–2.　　[10] *Vide infra*, pp. 75–6.

INTRODUCTION   li

and compulsory service. Jurymen, overseers of the poor, surveyors of the highways, high and petty constables, must all serve gratuitously; and landowners and labourers must assist with their horses, their money, or their labour to maintain the roads.[1] In the case of *The King* v. *Welch*[2] Lord Mansfield held that it was illegal to pay a person to act as an assistant overseer; and he refused to allow the overseers to credit themselves with a sum paid for this purpose, although the payment had been sanctioned by the majority of those present at a vestry meeting.

(2) The eighteenth-century system of local government was remarkable for the manner in which it was developed to meet the new needs of the eighteenth century. That development was effected partly by the Legislature, and partly by Justices themselves. A few general statutes, and very many local statutes, added to the duties and powers of the Justices of the Peace and other officials and units of the local government. The manner in which these statutory duties and powers were performed was left very much to the discretion of the persons or bodies on whom they were conferred; and these persons or bodies, in the exercise of their discretion, devised machinery for their performance which was often new, often extra-legal, and sometimes even illegal.[3] The result was that much of the machinery of local government was, like much of the machinery of central government, based on conventions.

The stream of statutes, which gave to the Justices of the Peace their position of decisive importance in the government of the counties and boroughs, had begun to flow in the Tudor period;

---

[1] *Vide infra*, pp. 97–9.

[2] (1785) 4 Dougl. 236; Lord Mansfield said at p. 237, "it is very hard, especially upon the officers who have paid the money, but I cannot make it a legal act. It is a great burden, but the statute meant to throw it on the overseers, and that they should do it without fee or reward"; the hardship was remedied by 59 George III, c. 12, § 7, which allowed vestries to appoint paid assistant overseers—though overseers were still bound to serve gratuitously, *R.* v. *Glyde* (1813), 2 M. at S. 323 (*note*).

[3] The Webbs, speaking of the orders issued by Quarter Sessions, say that many were issued without either common law or statutory authority, and that "even the eighteenth-century law courts must have held their orders, if they had been challenged, to be extra-legal—that is, not legally enforceable on anyone who chose to disobey them—or else positively illegal—that is, in direct contravention of existing statutes", *Local Government, The Parish and the County*, p. 534.

lii   INTRODUCTION

and it has never ceased to flow. The vast variety of topics which were brought within their cognisance is apparent from a glance at the alphabetical headings, under which the eighteenth-century books on the Justices grouped their powers and duties. These books make it clear that the Justices were brought into contact with very many branches of the law, public and private. How multifarious their duties were is apparent from Mr Dowdell's chapters on Law and Order, the Poor Law, Highways and Bridges, the Labour Code, and the Regulation of Production and Distribution. This multiplicity of duties did not make for efficiency; and the lack of efficiency was most felt in urban districts like Middlesex. Largely for this reason, the Middlesex Justices failed to keep the peace in and around London,[1] failed to deal adequately with the problem of the pauper and the vagrant,[2] and neglected their duties in respect of the maintenance of the highways.[3] On the other hand, though this multiplicity of duties militated against efficiency in many of the spheres of local government, it had a compensatory advantage. It gave the Justices a practical acquaintance with many branches of law, public and private; it gave them a comprehensive view of the working of the law, statutory and otherwise, upon those whom it affected; and it thus enabled them both to make well considered proposals for legislation, and to criticise intelligently proposals made by others. All this has a considerable bearing upon the efficiency of the House of Commons in the eighteenth as in earlier centuries. The lessons learned by the many members of the House of Commons who were Justices of the Peace had no small share in fitting Parliament to fill the great position which the Revolution settlement had given to it.

The approach to many of the subjects over which the Legislature had given the Justices of the Peace jurisdiction was by way of the criminal law. Their connection with many branches of the law—with the law, for instance, as the regulation of commerce and industry, as to food prices, as to master and servant—was based to a large extent on the administration of this branch

[1] *Vide infra*, pp. 23–6; cp. Lecky, *History of England*, vol. VII, p. 339. See Walpole, *Memoirs of George III*, vol. III, 219–21, for a striking illustration of the inefficiency of the way in which the peace was kept in London.
[2] *Vide infra*, p. 86.   [3] *Vide infra*, p. 134.

INTRODUCTION

of the law. Similarly much of the law relating to local government was approached through it and grew up under its shadow. This method of approach came very naturally to a system which still worked, to a large extent, through the machinery of presentment and indictment. A curious and a late instance of this point of view occurs in a Parliamentary debate of 1777. Reflections had been cast by a member on the Justices for their negligence in allowing unlicensed theatrical performances. To these reflections another member replied that, "as a magistrate the honourable gentleman ought to have known that it was no part of the duty of a magistrate to act in the first instance, but officially on a complaint made or information given".[1]

But long before the beginning of the eighteenth century it had become clear that this narrow view of a magistrate's duty was becoming obsolete. Legislation on such matters as the poor law, vagrants, rating, prisons, liquor licensing, and highways, had cast upon the Justices and other officials of the local government much administrative work, which made it necessary that they should act "in the first instance" and take the initiative in putting the law into force. This legislation, therefore, introduced ideas as to the conduct of local government which were very different from the medieval ideas, and created the need for a machinery of government very different from the medieval machinery through which the Justices still did much of their work. It introduced a distinction between the enforcement of duties upon officials and others through the agency of the criminal law, and the performance of administrative functions. Mr Dowdell's book shows the growth of this distinction, partly through the agency of general statutes upon such subjects as the poor law, vagrancy, highways, liquor licensing, and commerce and industry; and partly through the agency of local Acts which gave special powers to particular districts. It was chiefly in urban and suburban districts that these local Acts were necessary; and, since it was largely through these local Acts that new ideas in local government began to emerge, it is necessary to say a few words about their place in the evolution of the system of local government.

[1] *Parl. Hist.*, vol. XIX, p. 204.

In the days when travel was difficult, slow, and dangerous, and the modes of conveying news were primitive, the different units of local government had an individuality which they have lost in an age of mechanical transport and transformed methods of communication. This individuality was increased by the autonomous character of units not subject to any effective control by the central government. Mr Spencer, in his able book on *Municipal Origins*,[1] has explained graphically and truly the legal results of this individuality of the units of local government. He says: "Peckham, or the parish of St. Andrews Holborn, or Marylebone wanted a watch. The old machinery of watch and ward was not only rusty and ruined, but even had it been capable of refurbishment it would have remained inadequate. These parishes did not wait until, a hundred, or ninety, or sixty years later, the national Government made up its mind that there should be a police system. Each parish applied to Parliament for power to raise a local force and obtained such power".

From a very early period localities of different kinds had applied to Parliament to give them special powers to meet their special needs. There are one or two local statutes of this kind in the middle ages. They are more numerous in the Tudor and Stuart periods; and, during the eighteenth century, they gradually come to outnumber the general statutes. It is clear from the character of the statutes passed in this century that the cause for this increase was the urbanisation of the country. Besides numerous turnpike Acts, there are Acts which give powers to pave, light, watch, cleanse the streets, to construct sewers, to regulate buildings, to control harbours, docks, and markets, and to administer the poor law. In fact, these Acts cover the whole field of local government.[2]

It was largely due to these Acts that the system of local government was able to shed some of its medieval characteristics, and to develop new organs and new methods of administration. But this result was also due in part to the fact that these autonomous units had retained one of their medieval characteristics—the

---

[1] *Vide* p. 314.
[2] F. H. Spencer, *Municipal Origins*, pp. 115–16.

power of adapting their procedure and their activities to new conditions.

Very many of the organs of government, both central and local, were very free, subject to the control of the law, to perform their functions in their own way. Therefore they could both make and vary rules as to the methods of performing their functions as and when they saw fit to do so. It followed that the machinery evolved by all these organs of government, central and local, created institutions of government; and that the working of this machinery created a body of constitutional law which defined the rights, duties and powers of these institutions. Just as in the sphere of private law the working of the forms of action created the principles of substantive law, so in the sphere of government and administration the machinery and the procedural rules of these autonomous organs of government have created much constitutional law.

From an early period we can see these processes at work in many departments of government. In the eighteenth century their working was especially fruitful. Central control was weak; and, at the same time, it was necessary to adapt and develop medieval machinery to the needs of a state which, in the latter part of the century, was being transformed through the working of new political, economic, and intellectual forces and ideas. In the sphere of local government the beginning of this process can be discerned in the sixteenth and early seventeenth centuries. We can discern a differentiation of the Sessions of the Justices and the beginning of an official staff.[1] During the seventeenth and eighteenth centuries there are many similar developments; and, as Mr Dowdell's book shows, the urban and suburban problems of Middlesex caused it to be a pioneer in these developments. We can see, in the first place, a more elaborate organisation of the machinery of government in the differentiation of the Sessions for different functions of government, in the differentiation of the judicial from the administrative sides of the Justices' work, and in the development of a committee system. We can see, in the second place, the rise of a more numerous paid staff. The urban and suburban counties and parishes were com-

[1] Holdsworth, *op. cit.*, vol. IV, pp. 145–51.

pelled to depart from the medieval system of compulsory and unpaid service. Many of them, acting not by virtue of any statute or common law rule, but by virtue of their autonomous powers, gradually acquired a staff of paid officials, in order to cope with the new work which was being placed upon them. But in the counties the process was very slow,[1] and in many places the Justices eked out the deficiences of their staffs by recourse to a contractor. This contract system pervades all parts of the local government of the eighteenth century, and marks the transition stage between the medieval system of unpaid and compulsory service and the modern system of paid officials.[2] We can see, in the third place, the rise of what the Webbs have rightly called "a provincial legislature".[3] The Justices issued many orders as to the administration of the poor law, as to hawkers and pedlars, as to fairs, as to vagrants, as to nuisances, as to rating, and as to licensing, which were legislative in character. One of the most famous of these legislative orders was the Speenhamland order of the Berkshire Justices, which was followed by many other benches of Justices, as to the principles upon which out-relief was to be given.[4]

In these ways—partly by the help of the Legislature, and partly by the efforts of the Justices—the system of local government was being adapted to new needs. But these devices were not sufficient. Because they were not sufficient recourse was had to another device which introduces us to a third characteristic feature of the eighteenth-century system of local government—the use made of the *ad hoc* authority.

(3) If we trace the course of English history back to a sufficiently early period, we come to a time when much of what has long been part of the regular machinery of law and government took the form of an *ad hoc* device, invented to meet a local, a personal, or a temporary need. In the twelfth century many parts of that centralised machinery of law and government, in which the common law originated, took the form of *ad hoc* devices. Commissions to the itinerant Justices were then devices of this character, since neither their form nor the occasions on

---

[1] See Webb, *Local Government, The Parish and the County*, pp. 512–24.
[2] *Ibid.*, p. 525.   [3] *Ibid.*, pp. 533–50.   [4] *Ibid.*, pp. 545–8.

INTRODUCTION lvii

which they were issued were regularised;[1] and even permission to have a case tried by a jury was sometimes in the nature of an *ad hoc* expedient, which was procurable by a payment to the King.[2]

Many of these early *ad hoc* institutions became parts of the ordinary machinery of the common law. But the power of the Crown to create such institutions to supplement the ordinary machinery of government was not lost. The creation of the Justices of labourers by royal ordinance in 1349 is one illustration.[3] Another is the issue of numerous commissions to enquire into the condition of particular roads, bridges, rivers or sewers.[4] These commissions created temporary *ad hoc* authorities, which developed into the body known as the Commissioners of Sewers—the oldest and most long-lived of all these *ad hoc* authorities.

The rise of the legislative power of Parliament during the fourteenth and fifteenth centuries caused Parliamentary consent to be given in some cases to the creation of these *ad hoc* bodies. It was beginning to be seen that more could be effected by a statute than by an exercise of the prerogative. There is, for instance, a series of statutes which give extensive powers to the Commissioners of Sewers;[5] and there are one or two other instances in which such bodies were created in the sixteenth and early seventeenth centuries.[6] After the Restoration there are several statutes which created *ad hoc* authorities to administer the poor law;[7] and very many such authorities were created for this purpose in the eighteenth century. In the early years of the eighteenth century there begin the series of Acts which created *ad hoc* bodies to make and administer turnpike roads. Later in the century the growth of urban districts led to the creation of

[1] Holdsworth, *op. cit.*, vol. I, pp. 49–51, 264.
[2] *Ibid.*, vol. I, p. 323; Pollock and Maitland, vol. II, pp. 615–16.
[3] Holdsworth, *op. cit.*, vol. I, p. 288.
[4] For illustration see *Public Works in Medieval Law* (S.S.), vol. II, pp. xxxv–xxxvi.
[5] 23 Henry VIII, c. 5; 3 and 4 Edward VI, c. 8; 13 Elizabeth, c. 9, § 1; 3 James I, c. 14; 7 Anne, c. 33.
[6] See, for instance, 1 Henry VIII, c. 9; 6 Henry VIII, c. 17; 2 and 3 Philip & Mary, c. 16; 18 Elizabeth, c. 17; 3 James I, c. 20.
[7] *Vide infra*, p. 46.

many bodies of Improvement Commissioners, in whose organisation and powers we can see the origins of much of the organisation and many of the powers of our modern municipalities. Mr Dowdell's book shows us that the creation of these *ad hoc* authorities was necessary to enable the overburdened Justices to cope with the problems of urbanisation. They found it quite impossible to deal adequately with such services as poor law administration, road making, paving, lighting, scavenging, and sanitation, in their rapidly growing urban areas; and so in the latter part of the eighteenth century very many of these bodies were created all over England, and more especially in the suburban parishes in and around London.[1]

(4) Just as the growth and multiplication of these *ad hoc* authorities testify to the emergence of modern problems, so the records of the Middlesex Quarter Sessions testify to the passing of the sixteenth-century ideas on such matters as the relation of employer and employed, and the organisation of commerce and industry. The two concluding chapters of Mr Dowdell's book are a careful and original study of the reason for the passing of the older economic ideas, and the beginnings of the substitution of a policy of laissez-faire for the paternal regulation which commended itself to the Elizabethan statesmen. In fact the commercial men had begun to demand greater freedom of action at the end of the seventeenth century,[2] and the government was inclined to favour this demand.[3] The feeling in favour of this greater freedom was growing all through the eighteenth century; and it was naturally reflected in the policy pursued by benches of magistrates sitting in commercial and industrial areas. Adam Smith's book was published in 1776; but it reflected a current of economic thought which had been increasing in strength all through the eighteenth century; and the acclamation with which it was greeted was due in no small degree to this fact.

In 1772 a statute was passed which repealed many of the laws

[1] Webb, *Local Government, Statutory Authorities*, pp. 242-3.
[2] Holdsworth, *op. cit.*, vol. VI, pp. 355-60.
[3] As early as 1684 the Privy Council disallowed a Jamaica Act against engrossing and forestalling, on the ground that it was "contrary to that freedom of Trade which we are willing to encourage amongst our subjects", *Acts of the Privy Council (Colonial Series)*, vol. II, p. 833.

INTRODUCTION

against engrossers, forestallers and regrators;[1] and it was recited in the preamble to the statute that "it hath been found by experience that the restraints laid by several statutes upon the dealing in corn, meal, flour, cattle, and sundry other sorts of victuals, by preventing a free trade in the said commodities, have a tendency to discourage the growth and to enhance the price of the same"; and that these statutes, "if put in execution, would bring a great distress upon the inhabitants of many parts of this kingdom, and in particular upon those of the cities of London and Westminster". That the Middlesex Justices had long been in sympathy with these ideas is shown by Mr Dowdell. They "had come to the conclusion that it was impracticable to enforce the old labour code";[2] and they allowed most of the laws which regulated production and distribution to fall into desuetude—"trade was left mainly to look after itself, subject to such scrutiny as consumers could exercise; and experience was to show that this freedom was fraught with pernicious consequences".[3]

That the Middlesex Justices showed themselves so responsive to new economic ideas was due partly to the character of the area over which they exercised jurisdiction, and partly to the nature of the relations between the local and central government. We shall now see that the nature of these relations kept the Justices both in Middlesex and in other parts of England in touch with the current political and economic ideas held by the executive government and by Parliament.

III

In a modern state the independent and autonomous development of the organs of government has its limits. All the organs

---

[1] 12 George III, c. 71; see a speech by Governor Pownall in 1772 which illustrates the prevalence of the new economic ideas, *Parl. Hist.*, vol. XVII, pp. 553–4; in 1776 Jackson, the counsel to the Board of Trade, objected to an Act passed by the Assembly of Montserrat to regulate the price of provisions on the ground "that the price of provisions can only be reduced by increasing the plenty of them...; that a price fixed above the natural rate will be useless, a price equal to the natural rate impossible because the natural rate will frequently vary, and one below the natural rate may operate to decrease the product, but can never augment it or lower the product", *Acts of the Privy Council (Colonial Series)*, vol. V, p. 437.
[2] *Vide infra*, p. 156.   [3] *Vide infra*, p. 189.

of government form part of the same constitution. They must work together; and, since they must work together, rules must be devised to settle their relations *inter se*. It was necessary, therefore, for eighteenth-century statesmen to devise rules to settle the relations between the local government and the executive, legislative, and judicial departments of the central government.

If we looked only at the letter of the law we might suppose that the executive had large powers over the organs of local government. The Lord-Lieutenants, the Sheriffs, and the Justices of the Peace held their offices at the pleasure of the Crown. They were subject in the exercise of their jurisdiction to the rulings of the Courts of Common Law and the Judges of Assize. Through the Judges of Assize or otherwise the Privy Council could issue instructions to them. Moreover counties and hundreds could be indicted and fined for breach of the duties laid on them by law. We might, therefore, suppose that the executive had many means of enforcing its wishes. But these appearances are fallacious. After the Revolution the executive government had very little coercive force. Thus, when the county of Derby failed to comply with the Militia Acts of 1757, 1765 and 1769, the executive was obliged to apply to the courts for a writ of mandamus; and, even then, nothing was done till a second writ was threatened.[1] Nevertheless there were certain kinds of conventional or extra-legal forms of control which established some very real links between the local and the central government. In the first place, the Lord-Lieutenant was always a great nobleman, a member of the House of Lords, and generally a Privy Councillor; and the fact that the Justices of the Peace were, as a rule, appointed on his nomination gave him a certain measure of control over them,[2] and sometimes induced them to seek his help.[3] It was partly for this reason that the victories of Whigs or Tories, during the

---

[1] Cox, *Three Centuries of Derbyshire Annals*, vol. I, pp. 184–9.
[2] *Vide infra*, p. 40, for a direction of the Privy Council in 1745 to the Duke of Newcastle, the Lord-Lieutenant of Middlesex, to warn the Justices to enforce the laws against Roman Catholics and non-jurors, with which the Justices readily complied.
[3] *Vide infra*, p, 25, for an appeal by the Middlesex Justices to the Duke of Newcastle on the subject of street robberies.

INTRODUCTION

reigns of William III, Anne, George I and George III, were accompanied by the dismissal of some of the Lord-Lieutenants. In the second place, the practice of appointing only county gentlemen to the office of Justice of the Peace made the governing class very homogeneous. As Francis Bacon had said in the seventeenth century, "the noblemen and the gentlemen were knit together".[1] Since many of the noblemen were Lord-Lieutenants or Privy Councillors, this was a very real link. In the third place, it is clear from these records that the Middlesex Justices were very ready to listen to the advice and admonitions of the Privy Council.[2]

In 1617 Francis Bacon had remarked upon the intimacy of the relations between the local government and Parliament, and upon the reason for that intimacy. "Those that have voices in Parliament to make laws", he said, "for the most part are those which in the country are appointed and administer the same laws."[3] This was even more true in the eighteenth century than in 1617. In the House of Commons the knights of the shire, and very many of the members for the smaller boroughs, were drawn from the same class of landed gentry as that from which the Justices of the Peace were drawn; and the House of Lords was composed of the richer members of the same class. The result was that Parliament was willing to increase the powers of the Justices by general Acts; and when, at their request, it passed local Acts, or Acts creating *ad hoc* bodies, it was equally willing to entrust the control of these bodies to the Justices. "Parliament", say the Webbs,[4] "seemed to imply, alike in the occasional general statutes, and the multitudinous local Acts, that it assumed the court of Quarter Sessions to stand, towards the other local authorities of the county, in much the same position as is to-day occupied by the Home Office, the Board of Education, and the Local Government Board"; and, "the House of Commons felt itself to be but the legislative clearing house of the several courts of Quarter Sessions".

[1] Spedding, *Letters and Life of Bacon*, vol. VI, p. 303.
[2] *Vide infra*, p. 28; for another instance see Webb, *Local Government, The Old Poor Law*, pp. 368–9.
[3] Spedding, *op. cit.*, vol. VI, p. 304.
[4] *Local Government, The Parish and the County*, p. 554.

The most effective control to which the units of local government were subject was the control exercised by the Courts of Common Law, and principally by the Court of King's Bench. It is necessary, therefore, to deal with this form of control at somewhat greater length.

The control exercised by the Courts of Law manifested itself in three main directions. First, there was the control exercised by means of proceedings initiated in the name of the Crown either by indictment, information, or the prerogative writs. Secondly, there was the control exercised in proceedings initiated at the suit of private persons either by setting in motion the machinery of indictment, information, or the prerogative writs, or by a civil action. Thirdly, there was the control exercised through the litigation arising from disputes between the different units of local government. The continuous exercise of these different forms of judicial control, and the growth in the elaboration of the law, which was its necessary concomitant, are the most striking of all proofs of the essential continuity of English public law. In the eighteenth, as in the thirteenth, century the Judges, by means of these various judicial processes, were defining spheres of jurisdiction, controlling the exercise of jurisdiction, and, as the result, producing uniformity in the rules of law.

In the exercise of this wide jurisdiction the Judges never attempted to override the discretion of the Justices when they had been entrusted with a discretion by the common law or by statute.[1] But they were always ready to act if there was any allegation of corruption, oppression or partiality.[2] It is impossible to overestimate the value of this intelligent and impartial control over the many persons and bodies entrusted with large and ill-defined powers. Squire Western was inclined to listen to the admonitions of his clerk, and to refrain from carrying into effect his resolution to commit his sister's maid to Bridewell for impertinent language to her mistress, because "he had already had two informations against him in the King's Bench, and had no curiosity to try a third".[3] It is clear that if the Courts had not

[1] R. v. *Young and Pitts*, (1758) 1 Burr. 556, at pp. 561–2.
[2] Ibid.
[3] *Tom Jones*, Bk VII, chap. ix.

INTRODUCTION

exercised their powers sternly and impartially the large powers of the Justices might in many cases have become a tyranny of the worst kind.[1]

The exercise of the jurisdiction not only protected the subject, it also developed the law. It was, in fact, creating new bodies of public law on such matters as the poor law, highways, licensing and rating. It was creating modern local government law. It was bringing the common law and statutory rules relating to local government into line with the principles of English law. It was so adjusting the relations between the separate parts of the eighteenth-century constitution that they were able, in spite of their independence and autonomy, to work harmoniously together.

It is true that the technicality of the procedure of the Courts, and the strictness of the rules of pleading, sometimes pressed hardly on the Justices and other officials. Mr Dowdell has given us an illustration of the manner in which an unscrupulous opposition could use legal technicalities to impede the course of county business.[2] But Parliament intervened, and made it impossible to resort to this expedient in this particular case. In fact Parliament was generally ready to intervene to stop an abusive use of legal technicalities. A series of one hundred and eight statutes, beginning with the Poor Relief Act of 1601 and extending to the Inland Revenue Act of 1890, contains clauses which give procedural advantages to Justices of the Peace and other public authorities. This long series of statutes was repealed by the Public Authorities Protection Act, 1893,[3] and a uniform set of rules was laid down in that Act for the protection of persons acting in the execution of statutory and other public duties.

Both the Courts and the Legislature thus attempted, not without success, to hold the balance between the conflicting interests of the executive government, of the local government, and of the subject. It was a difficult task because all these bodies

---

[1] Fielding tells us in *Tom Jones, loc. cit.*, that "many justices of peace suppose they have a large discretionary power, by virtue of which under the notion of searching for and taking away engines for the destruction of game, they often commit trespass, and sometimes felony, at their pleasure".
[2] *Vide infra*, p. 76.   [3] 56 and 57 Victoria, c. 61.

and persons had their separate and independent rights, powers, and duties. The Courts preserved the separation and autonomy of the units of local government, and yet secured a certain measure of control over them. They upheld the large powers of the Justices and other officials entrusted with the conduct of local government, and yet secured the liberty and rights of the subject. The result of their work was to adjust the rights and powers of very many separate bodies and separate interests—to adjust the rights and powers of the different units of the local government *inter se*, and the rights and powers of the units of the local government in their relation to the central government. The nature of the separation of the rights and powers of these separate bodies and separate interests will help us to understand the real nature of that separation of powers, as between different parts of the central government, to which the excellence of the eighteenth-century constitution was then generally attributed.

IV

Montesquieu put forward the theory that it was to the separation of the legislative, the executive, and the judicial functions of the central government that Englishmen owed their liberty.[1] But, though there was a separation between the functions of the institutions of central government on these lines, it was by no means the clear-cut separation which Montesquieu envisaged; and it is obvious that his theory is still less applicable to the functions of the organs of local government. Both Quarter and Petty Sessions, in town and county alike, exercised functions which were legislative, executive, and judicial; and some of the *ad hoc* authorities, such as the poor law incorporations, exercised a similar variety of functions. There is little, if any, separation of powers in the functions of the organs of local government. Yet there is a sense in which there was a separation of functions in the eighteenth-century system of local government; and it is necessary at this point to say a word about it, because it will help us to understand what is perhaps the most salient characteristic of the public law of the eighteenth century.

[1] *De L'Esprit des Lois,* Bk xi, chap. vi.

INTRODUCTION

All the organs of local government were independent autonomous bodies, not subject to any continuous supervision by the central government, but subject only to the legislative power of Parliament, and to control by the Courts, if they infringed the law which defined their powers and duties. It is true that Quarter Sessions exercised powers of supervision over the Petty Sessions, and that the actions of vestries were also controlled by the Justices and by Quarter and Petty Sessions. But these powers of control were limited and definite; and, subject to that control, these organs of local government could act freely and independently. It is true that their powers varied. The powers of vestries and the officers of the parish were very much smaller than the powers of Quarter Sessions. But, within the sphere of their powers, they could act as they pleased, provided that they did not break the law. Thus the system of local government was composed of a series of separate and autonomous organs. Because these organs were separate and autonomous, each, to some extent, acted as a check upon the others, and prevented the others from using their large and undifferentiated functions tyrannically. Because the Courts were always ready to interfere to prevent any encroachment by one of these organs on another, and because they were always ready to prevent any illegal action on the part of these organs, there was both an additional security against a tyrannical exercise of powers, and a security that these organs would not overstep the powers entrusted to them by the law. This was the true sense in which there was a separation of powers in the eighteenth-century system of local government. It was very much more in this sense, and very much less in the sense indicated by Montesquieu, that there was a separation of powers in the system of central government. England, as Professor Lévy-Ullmann has truly said, is not the classic country of the separation of powers.[1] In fact it is hardly possible to create the complete separation which Montesquieu envisaged; for, as the writers of *The Federalist* said,[2] " experience has instructed us, that no skill in the science of Government has yet been able to discriminate and define, with sufficient cer-

---
[1] *Le Système Juridique de l'Angleterre*, vol. I, p. 376.
[2] No. xxxvi.

tainty, the three great provinces, the Legislative, Executive, and Judiciary".

V

I must now try to sum up the strong and the weak points of this eighteenth-century system of local government.

Its strong points can be summarised as follows:

(1) It safeguarded the rights and liberties which the law gave to individuals and to the units of local government. Both individuals and the units of local government had abundant remedies, civil and criminal, if their rights and liberties were infringed; and thus a spirit of independence was fostered in individual citizens, and the autonomy of the units of local government was preserved. But it should be noted that what the law thus safeguarded was not liberty in general, but particular rights and liberties. This was then, and always has been, the attitude of the common law.[1] No doubt some rights and liberties, such as the right to personal freedom and the right to protection against attacks upon person or property, were common to all citizens; but other liberties, such as the right to vote for members of Parliament, the right to be appointed to the office of Justice of the Peace, the right to become a mayor or other official or member of a municipal corporation, could only be enjoyed by certain classes of persons. There were degrees and grades in the rights and liberties of individuals; and there were degrees and grades in the rights and liberties of the units of local government. Vestries, Petty Sessions, Quarter Sessions, municipal corporations, had different rights and liberties, which gave them various degrees of autonomy—degrees of autonomy which were often different in different places. The various units of local government had, it is true, a family likeness to one another; and the pressure of a common law made for a certain measure of uni-

---

[1] "If it be allowable to apply the formulas of logic to questions of law, the difference in this matter between the constitution of Belgium and the English constitution may be described by the statement that in Belgium individual rights are deductions drawn from the principles of the constitution, whilst in England the so-called principles of the constitution are inductions or generalisations based upon particular decisions pronounced by the Courts as to the rights of given individuals", Dicey, *Law of the Constitution* (7th ed.), p. 193.

INTRODUCTION lxvii

formity. But no eighteenth-century statesman ever supposed that the attainment of a standardised uniformity was a possible or a desirable ideal. It was seen that, just as between individuals it is impossible to produce an absolute equality, so as between the higher and lower units of local government, and as between those units in different environments, there must be variety in structure and function. Differences between individuals, and varieties in the units of local government, which were imposed by natural causes, were accepted as inevitable, and were therefore reflected in the different contents of the rights and liberties which the law gave to these individuals and to these units of local government. It was recognised, perhaps half unconsciously, that equality and liberty are not necessary concomitants; and that attempts to produce an absolute and necessarily fictitious equality and uniformity are fatal both to an ordered liberty and to national fraternity. The eighteenth-century system of local government helped to preserve those definite yet flexible class distinctions which had emerged in the sixteenth century,[1] because those class distinctions were reflected in its organisation, and because the different rights and liberties of each of these classes were recognised and protected by the law.

(2) The eighteenth-century system of local government, though it protected rights and liberties, stressed the duties of citizens rather than their rights. From all sorts and conditions of men—from the Lord-Lieutenant and the Justices of the Peace to the labourer bound to perform his "statute labour" on the roads—the law exacted gratuitous service. Different classes of citizens were called on from time to time to serve on juries of many different kinds, to serve as surveyors of highways, as constables, as churchwardens, as overseers of the poor, to take parish apprentices.[2] These different classes of citizens, who were thus compelled to serve the State in these different capacities, received a practical education in the duties of citizenship appropriate to their station. Bagehot, speaking of the higher classes of the eighteenth-century society, truly says that "in all the records of the eighteenth century the tonic of business is seen

[1] Holdsworth, *op. cit.*, vol. IV, pp. 402–7.
[2] *Vide infra*, pp. 18, 57–8, 63, 106.

to combat the relaxing effects of habitual luxury ".[1] Similarly, in the lower classes of that society, the duty imposed upon them to serve the State took those on whom the duty was placed out of the rut of their daily work, and gave them sometimes the rudiments of a political education, and always the reminder that there were public duties involved in citizenship which must be fulfilled. What De Tocqueville has said of the educative effects of the jury system[2] applies also to many of those compulsory and unpaid duties in the system of local government, which were exacted from the citizen in the eighteenth century.

(3) Because the system of local government depended upon bodies and officials which were autonomous within their own spheres, because these bodies and officials were educated by the performance of the duties imposed on them by the law, they were able to appreciate the consequences of a foolish policy or a neglect of duty. In these small autonomous and separate units the consequences of folly or neglect were immediately apparent; and it was comparatively easy to put the blame on the right shoulders. There was no paid staff of bureaucrats in the service of the local authorities to warn them against the consequences of a mistaken policy, and there was no department of the central government to advise or control. The local authorities were obliged to shoulder responsibility for their neglects and defaults. This helped to foster the qualities of initiative and readiness to learn from experience. As a locality suffered from folly and neglect of its rulers, so it profited by their ability and industry. Many public-spirited administrators in many different places devoted many years to the work of improving the standard of government in their districts.[3] Their example was not wasted upon administrators, who were the better able to judge a policy by its results, since they did not gain office by means of promises to pursue policies, adopted without consideration, because those policies were likely to captivate an ignorant electorate.

(4) The fact that there were great varieties in the constitu-

---

[1] *Literary Studies*, vol. I, p. 241.
[2] *Démocratie en Amérique*, vol. II, p. 190.
[3] *Vide supra*, p. xlix and note 5.

INTRODUCTION

tion of the various units of local government enabled the public opinion of the country to come to some fairly definite conclusions as to the methods of administration which were the most effective. On the one hand, the examples of administration by a turbulent open vestry,[1] and the conduct of the trading Justices in the City of London;[2] on the other hand the examples of a vestry like St George's, Hanover Square, which was controlled by noblemen and gentlemen,[3] and of the close corporation of Liverpool[4]—showed that the government was most successfully run when it was in the hands of the higher and most enlightened classes. This appeared to be an obvious truism in the eighteenth century; for it was not a century which was blinded by the universal prevalence of democratic theories. The result was that there was a general acquiescence in the rule of the landed gentry in the country, and in the rule of the more substantial traders in the towns. The most important part of the work of local government was thus entrusted to a ruling class responsible to itself. And, because it was in the hands of a class of this type, it was possible to modify the machinery of local government, and to adapt it to new needs, by means of extra-legal conventions.[5] A class which had progressed so far as this in the art of self-government had learned all that was necessary to fit it to manage and to adapt to changing needs the complex constitutional machinery of the English state. To the political abilities of this class, which were created and fostered by the eighteenth-century system of local government, are due the success of Parliamentary government in England. At the same time, though the control of the local government was in the hands of a ruling class, some share in the government was left to the other classes who were called upon to serve on juries and to fill the lower offices in that government. Just as the classes of society were graded, so were the degrees of political power and responsibility.

(5) The system of local government was a cheap government. Those who have been trained to manage small estates, or to live

---
[1] Webb, *Local Government, The Parish and the County*, pp. 91–2.
[2] *Vide supra*, p. xlix and note 6.
[3] Webb, *Local Government, The Parish and the County*, p. 245.
[4] Webb, *Local Government, The Manor and the Borough*, pp. 481–91.
[5] *Vide supra*, p. li.

upon moderate incomes, are the persons who understand the need for thrift and economy; and the class who managed the local government of the county fell, for the most part, into these categories. Moreover they were the class upon whom the burden of the rates mainly fell. Administrators who come either from a small rich class or from the class of the poor, will be extravagant because, for opposite reasons, neither class appreciates the value of money or the necessity for economy. The fact that the eighteenth-century system of local government was a cheap government meant that no impediment was placed upon that economic expansion which, at the end of the century, the growth of the overseas dominions of the Crown and scientific and mechanical inventions were producing.

The eighteenth-century system of local government had the defects of its qualities. Its weak points can be summarised as follows:

(1) There was too little central control over the units of local government—their autonomy was excessive. It was a mistake to leave the entire control of matters of such national interest as main roads, and the management of the poor and prisons, to the unfettered discretion of small, often very small, units. The Legislature, it is true, passed many general Acts in order to bring the law into conformity with modern needs; and something was effected by this legislation. But, as Mr Dowdell has shown, it did not effect very much because, in many cases, the agencies trusted to work this legislation were defective. It was of little use to direct over-burdened officials, working with inadequate machinery, to perform new duties; and, even if the machinery had been more adequate, it was futile to expect that they could perform them without any sort of supervision.

(2) Though the old machinery sufficed fairly well for backward rural areas, where life ran on in the accustomed ways, these Middlesex Records show that it was obviously quite insufficient for the needs of growing towns and suburban districts. The problems of government in such centres were increasing in complexity, and the old machinery was quite incapable of solving them. The Legislature adopted the only expedient which the autonomy of the units of local government left open to it—

INTRODUCTION

the expedient of creating *ad hoc* authorities. Though the powers conferred on these *ad hoc* authorities foreshadow later developments in local government, notably developments in municipal government, they were partial and purely local in their operation; and they immensely complicated an already complicated system. They left the existing machinery untouched; and so they often raised difficulties, for instance in the case of the turnpike trusts, as to the relation of the old machinery to the new statutory machinery.[1]

(3) Though the cheapness of the system of local government had its good side—a side which we who live in an age when all parties in the state compete in extravagance are the more disposed to admire—it also had its bad side. Essential services, such as the building and maintenance of roads, bridges, and prisons, were inadequately performed because not sufficient money was spent on them. Too great reliance was placed on unpaid and compulsory service. Too great reluctance was shown to pay adequately for competent service. And this policy often, in the long run, made for extravagance, corruption, and illicit exactions. It was impossible to compel the autonomous units of local government to raise the money needed to perform adequately the duties laid upon them by the law, or, in the case of urban and suburban districts, to undertake the new duties of police, of cleansing, of lighting, and of sanitation, which were urgently required. This was another reason why it was necessary to employ the device of the creation of an *ad hoc* authority. It was possible to create an *ad hoc* body with power to rate or to charge money for its services. It is clear that the device of laying a toll on the users of the roads was the only way in which the sums requisite for road making and repair could have been raised.

In the latter half of the eighteenth century it was becoming clear that what was needed was a comprehensive overhauling of the machinery of local government—an overhauling as comprehensive as that effected by the Tudor legislation.[2] Possibly something of the kind, in, at any rate, some of the departments

[1] *Vide infra*, pp. 131–2.
[2] Holdsworth, *op. cit.*, vol. IV, pp. 137–66.

of local government, might have been attempted by the younger Pitt, if the war with France and the passions engendered by the French Revolution had not intervened. But such a task would have been difficult. It would have been difficult to persuade the governing class as a whole that comprehensive measures of reform were necessary or expedient. Even if this difficulty had been overcome, the making of the necessary reforms would have been a delicate task, because all classes would have feared to disturb the existing equilibrium of powers and forces in the constitution. Parliament would have been reluctant to give departments of the central government larger powers of supervision or control, because that would have meant an increase in the power and influence of the Crown. The Crown and the peers and large landowners would have been opposed to changes in the machinery of government in the counties and the boroughs which might have had the effect of diminishing their electoral influence. The Justices of the Peace, whose representations were all powerful in the House of Commons,[1] would have opposed measures which diminished their autonomous powers to rule their counties; and the borough corporations would have opposed changes which aimed at thoroughgoing municipal reforms. Pitt might have made some reforms, but it is difficult to see how any really comprehensive measure of reform could have been got through the unreformed Parliament.

Mr Dowdell's book deals with a district in which the problems of dealing with an urban society, by means of the machinery which England had inherited from the sixteenth century, were becoming acute. The problems which the Middlesex Justices were called on to face were the same problems as those which, later in the century, as the result of the industrial revolution, faced the Justices in many other parts of England. The policy which the Legislature and the Justices adopted foreshadows the policy which was later adopted in other parts of England. Its inadequacy to deal thoroughly with the problem is clear; and the later years of the eighteenth and the first years of the nineteenth century were to show that far more drastic measures were necessary—measures which it was only possible to take when

[1] *Vide supra*, p. lxi.

INTRODUCTION lxxiii

the new classes and interests which the industrial revolution had created obtained an adequate representation in the House of Commons.

After 1832 the long task of reforming the system of local government was begun by the passing of the Poor Law Amendment Act of 1834[1], and the Municipal Corporations Act of 1835;[2] and it was continued by many statutes which culminated in the Acts of 1888[3] and 1894[4] which created the system of county, district and parish councils. These reforms amended the deficiencies of the eighteenth-century system of local government, and adapted it to modern needs—though not without sacrificing some of the strong and good points in the eighteenth-century system.

W. S. HOLDSWORTH

ALL SOULS COLLEGE
    OXFORD

[1] 4 and 5 William IV, c. 76.
[2] 5 and 6 William IV, c. 76.
[3] 51 and 52 Victoria, c. 41.
[4] 56 and 57 Victoria, c. 73.

TABLE OF STATUTES[1]

mentioned in the author's text

Assisa Panis et Cervicie; 176, 180, 183
13 Edward I, st. Wynton; 22, 23
22 Henry VIII, c. 5; 124, 126
23 Henry VIII, c. 4; 183, 186 n.
25 Henry VIII, c. 2; 169 n.
32 Henry VIII, c. 40; 18 n.
34 & 35 Henry VIII, c. 12; 108 n.
5 & 6 Edward VI, c. 14; 165 n., 170, 201
— c. 25; 33
2 & 3 Philip and Mary, c. 8; 89, 98, 105
5 Elizabeth, c. 4; 137, 146, 149, 149 n., 153, 174, 176
— c. 13; 94
18 Elizabeth, c. 3; 62
31 Elizabeth, c. 7; 80 n., 81 n., 82
43 & 44 Elizabeth, c. 2; 52, 55 n., 57, 59, 65, 66 n., 198
1 James I, c. 9; 183 n.
4 & 5 James I, c. 4; 35
16 Charles I, c. 19; 161 n.
12 Charles II, c. 25; 184
14 Charles II, c. 2; 108, 109, 112 n., 113, 114, 115, 118 n.
— c. 6; 101, 101 n., 121 n.
— c. 12; 18, 45–7, 67, 69, 75, 86
15 Charles II, c. 7; 168 n., 171 n.
18 & 19 Charles II, c. 8; 149 n.
22 Charles II, c. 8; 160 n., 188 n.
— c. 12; 95, 99, 102, 103, 121, 121 n.
22 & 23 Charles II, c. 18; 48, 50, 51 n.
— c. 19; 167 n., 170 n.
30 Charles II, c. 3; 66 n.
1 James II, c. 17; 67 n.
1 William and Mary, c. 15; 39, 39 n.
2 William and Mary, c. 8; 175
— Sess. 2, c. 8; 91, 110, 111 n., 115, 115 n., 118, 123

3 William and Mary, c. 11; 67 n.
— c. 12; 90, 91, 92, 96, 104, 105, 110 n., 120 n., 185 n.
7 & 8 William III, c. 29; 98, 121 n., 122
8 & 9 William III, c. 17; 12 n., 112 n.
— c. 25; 71 n., 167 n.
— c. 30; 58, 62
10 William III, c. 4; 168 n.
— c. 13; 167 n.
11 William III, c. 18; 75, 77
1 Anne, c. 9; 188 n.
— c. 12; 125 n., 126
4 & 5 Anne, c. 25; 85 n.
6 Anne, c. 56; 121 n., 122
— c. 58; 85 n.
7 Anne, c. 17; 85 n.
8 Anne, c. 2; 169 n.
— c. 19; 169 n., 177, 180, 181
9 Anne, c. 23; 121 n., 122
10 Anne, c. 7; 136 n.
— c. 33; 136 n.
12 Anne, c. 19; 132 n., 136 n.
1 George I, c. 11; 136 n.
— c. 26; 181, 181 n., 182 n.
— st. 2, c. 11; 121 n.
— st. 2, c. 52; 104, 117 n.
— st. 2, c. 57; 123 n.
— (private), c. 25; 131 n., 136 n.
3 George I (private), c. 4; 130 n., 136 n.
— (private), c. 14; 136 n.
4 George I, c. 7; 66 n.
5 George I, c. 12; 121 n.
— c. 25; 182 n.
— c. 26; 85 n.
7 George I, c. 13; 151, 152
— c. 26; 112 n.
8 George I, c. 26; 85 n.
10 George I, c. 17; 182 n.
12 George I, c. 35; 188 n.
13 George I, c. 31; 132 n.

---

[1] The references are to the Statutes of the Realm down to the close of that series in 1714, after which they are to the Statutes at Large.

TABLE OF STATUTES

2 George II, c. 11; 110, 111
— c. 15; 188 n.
— c. 28; 34
3 George II, c. 22; 189 n.
— c. 29; 180 n.
8 George II, c. 12; 132 n.
10 George II, c. 15; 27 n., 112 n.
— c. 25; 27 n., 85 n.
— c. 28; 32 n.
11 George II, c. 35; 27 n., 85 n., 119 n.
12 George II, c. 29; 1 n., 5, 5 n., 6, 12, 76, 126, 128
13 George II, c. 24; 78
14 George II, c. 42; 121 n.
15 George II, c. 32; 85 n.
16 George II, c. 18; 8, 73 n.
17 George II, c. 5; 73, 78 n., 88 n., 157 n.
19 George II, c. 35; 187 n.
20 George II, c. 19; 57, 143, 154

21 George II, c. 38; 85 n.
22 George II, c. 50; 27 n., 117 n., 119 n.
23 George II, c. 35; 27 n., 88 n., 117 n.
24 George II, c. 26; 27 n., 117 n., 119 n.
— c. 40; 37
— c. 43; 123 n.
25 George II, c. 23; 88 n., 117 n.
26 George II, c. 31; 34
— c. 97; 88 n., 117 n.
— c. 98; 88 n.
27 George II, c. 20; 121 n.
— c. 25; 27 n., 117 n., 119 n.
29 George II, c. 53; 27 n., 88 n., 117 n.
— c. 87; 27 n., 112 n., 117 n., 119 n.
31 George II, c. 29; 182 n.
32 George II, c. 18; 182 n.

CHAPTER I

ORGANISATION OF THE COUNTY

In view of the amount of work already done on the subject,[1] it is unnecessary to give here an elaborate account of local government generally. Some sketch of its organisation is, however, needed, in order to indicate the place and importance of the Justices in Sessions assembled and the methods by which they could carry their policies into execution. Refinements will be omitted, except when the Records appear to throw new light on some aspect or when they suggest that Middlesex machinery was exceptional.

The main authority for the county was the Assembly of Justices in General Sessions.[2] These Sessions were not all on an equal footing. General Sessions might be held in the intervals between Quarter Sessions and were regularly so held in Middlesex, thus making the exceptionally large total of eight Sessions each year.[3] Although in some respects the competence of General Sessions was more restricted than that of General Quarter Sessions, the differences are not of great moment for our purposes[4] and, unless the contrary is explicitly stated, reference to the sessional activities of the Justices may be interpreted as covering their work at either or both types of meeting. The

[1] E.g. Webb, *Parish and County*; Holdsworth, *History of English Law*, especially vol. IV, p. 137 *et seq.*

[2] The administrative county did not include the City of Westminster or the Tower Liberty, which had Sessions of their own. The Tower Liberty may be ignored normally, owing to the virtual completeness of the separation. The relations of Westminster with the county were complex and somewhat obscure, but it has seemed unnecessary to go into this matter in detail. Westminster may be left out of account, except in certain connections where such a separation appears too arbitrary a departure from facts.

[3] These Sessions were all held at Hicks Hall in St John Street, Clerkenwell, except that the April and October Sessions were opened at Westminster.

[4] After the Justices had exposed themselves to attack by doing at General Sessions certain things which were strictly only cognisable at General Quarter Sessions, 12 George II, c. 29 gave them equal authority at both types of Sessions. For a case in which an order made at General Sessions was confirmed at Quarter Sessions, in view of doubts as to its validity, *vide* S.B. Jan. 1689–90, p. 44.

General Sessions of the Peace was, first and foremost, a Court working with a jury and following judicial procedure, the Justices of the Peace being the judges.[1] It might therefore be thought that the Justices had no scope to follow their own opinions, that they were merely parts of a legal machine whose motive power was supplied by others, or ministerial agents in the enforcement of obligations determined not by policy but by law. This, however, would only be a part of the truth. The Grand Jury was empowered not merely to find bills of indictment upon evidence supplied by outside prosecutors, but also to take the initiative by presenting offenders on its own knowledge. Hence the importance of the charge delivered by the Chairman of Sessions, which reminded the jurors of their duty in this respect and directed their attention to some few of the innumerable matters within their purview. Thus the Chairman had great influence on the character of the presentments initiated by the Grand Jury and, one suspects, not a little affected their willingness to find bills at the instance of others. It is very unfortunate that charges were not regularly preserved among the Records of Sessions, for they would have afforded us a clear reflection of the principal Justices' views as to the relative importance of the various branches of the law which they were expected to administer—law which was so overwhelming in its comprehensiveness as to make eclecticism inevitable. Certain chairmen were, however, requested by their colleagues and the jurors to have their charges printed for the benefit of the general public[2] and, by comparing these with the model charge given by Lambard,[3] we can see how comparatively narrow were the live interests of the chairmen. Of the indictments which originated outside the Court, a large proportion were due to the action of officials—high and petty constables, surveyors of highways, churchwardens and overseers of the poor and aleconners. The Justices could clearly make their influence felt by issuing orders

[1] The titular head was the *Custos Rotulorum*, but he seems never to have attended Sessions during our period and need only be noticed when he constitutes the channel of communication between the central government and the Justices. For an illustration of this, *vide* p. 40.
[2] E.g. Sir William Smith, Whitlocke Bulstrode and Sir Daniel Dolins.
[3] Reprinted in Holdsworth, *op. cit.* vol. IV, p. 543 *et seq.*

ORGANISATION OF THE COUNTY 3

for these officers to prosecute certain types of offenders and by punishing them if they neglected to comply. Such action would, of course, include also types of case cognisable out of Sessions. The Court's method of dealing with many evils was, in fact, to issue directions of this kind, and it is sometimes possible to suggest either a positive or a negative correlation between the promulgation of such orders and the number of prosecutions, although the official description of prosecutors is not usually given with their names on the backs of the bills.[1] Again, we may look for a reflection of the Justices' views in the vigour with which prosecutions were followed up and the nature of the judgments passed. Dilatoriness is an obvious characteristic of the period, but it was always possible to speed up cases by punishing offenders or prosecutors who held up proceedings by failing to appear. Variation in the actual judgments is also of interest, for, within the statutory limits, there was usually room for the exercise of discretion as to penalties and, when we find the Court actually transgressing these limits, the interpretation of its views becomes much easier. So, too, when it grants license to commit an offence or to compound for it, we have good ground for concluding that no great social evil was thought to be involved.

Thus even while we regard the Sessions as a purely judicial body, charged with the enforcement of obligations which it had no share in defining, we are not debarred from trying to reconstruct a policy or policies inspiring its action. Successive statutes had given it very wide legal powers to be exercised without formal legal procedure. In this sphere, its views are clearly expressed in the orders issued and it is from these orders that we must seek our chief light on the principles and problems which directed its

[1] From the Sessions of April 1682 there survives a table of "Articles to be presented by the High and Petty Constables to the Grand Jury and to be enquired into by the said Grand Jury", Charge of Sir William Smith, p. 10. This list of articles, which was read by the Clerk of the Peace, seems to have been a substitute for the usual comprehensive charge, so that it is doubtful whether we can rightly use it as a clue to the functions of the somewhat mysterious juries of constables which appear at Sessions in the eighteenth century, *vide*, for instance, Sir D. Dolins, Charge, Oct. 1725, title-page and pp. 1 and 28; Whitlocke Bulstrode, Charge, Oct. 1718, p. 4. On the way in which the Justices were hampered by neglect to present offences, *vide* especially Sir D. Dolins, Charge, Oct. 1725, p. 24.

administration. Naturally, the two spheres are not separable. Administration implies enforcement and, at the period with which we are dealing, this meant judicial enforcement far more than it does now. The Court had no large staff of paid officials to carry out its wishes, who could be dismissed in case of non-compliance. Its agents were, for the most part, persons whom it had no share in choosing and who would have been only too pleased to be relieved of their responsibilities. Judicial proceedings were consequently needed, not merely to punish those actively responsible for the evils that were being combated, but also against officials who failed to carry out the remedial measures. The Court rolls are therefore an indispensable supplement to the administrative minutes. Even in the matter of form, there are cases in which the one method shades into the other—when presentments, either by officers or by Justices, themselves have the force of bills of indictment regularly found, or when the Court begins to act on its own initiative in matters where a jury presentment has been previously required.[1]

It is necessary here to sketch the relation between the Justices in Sessions and the other organs of local government, partly because a large proportion of their work was, strictly speaking, the supervision of the activities of these other organs, partly because, as already indicated, the Court depended on these organs for the execution of work which was more particularly its own. The most important of these units were the parishes which went to make up the county. The Court spent a large amount of its time in enforcing the obligations settled by Common and Statute Law upon these bodies. This might be achieved by proceeding against the parish collectively, or against the officers responsible for any particular service, or against the inhabitants who were to participate in its performance. This is especially true in the case of highway maintenance, where the corporate character of the parish was more marked than, for instance, in connection with poor relief, the main responsibility for which rested more definitely on its officers. These suits might, of course, be commenced, either at the instance of the Justices themselves, or by outsiders pursuing some aim of their own. In the former

[1] *Vide* pp. 94, 126.

ORGANISATION OF THE COUNTY

case, the Court would naturally proceed by way of an order to local Justices, constables or other officers to return offenders, and this was its method of dealing with a large proportion of the abuses brought to its notice. In addition to the bare enforcement of the parish's obligations, there was the further question of interpretation and method, and we constantly find the Court laying down detailed instructions as to how the officers and inhabitants were to proceed. It would do this, sometimes in face of disputes within the parish, sometimes on its own initiative or upon representation by some of its members or other influential personages. It is unfortunate that these orders do not always show at whose instance they were issued. Even where the Court was expected to act more on its own account, it still depended on the organisation of the parish, as it had the merest nucleus of an administrative staff of its own. In particular, it had no body of tax-gatherers to collect its revenue and had to rely upon the parishes for the final assessment and collection of the county rates.[1] It will be shown that the Court was severely handicapped by this dependence on semi-independent authorities for the funds which it needed. The bare right to indict for disobedience proved an insufficient means of exercising control, and Parliament felt obliged to strengthen the Justices' authority by the Act, 12 George II, c. 29. For the sake of logical completeness we must also include the individual householder or landholder in the category of administrative organs, since, apart from his duty to participate in the performance of parochial services, certain responsibilities rested upon him personally. What has already been said as to the Court's part in enforcing and defining parochial obligations is also applicable here, and need not be repeated. It is only necessary to notice, in connection with the duty of lighting the streets which was imposed upon householders, the interesting phenomenon of numbers of these individuals combining together to arrange for the performance of a service for which they were severally responsible. These loose

---

[1] Strictly speaking, the constables who collected the county rates were not parish officers, but they may practically be regarded as such and 12 George II, c. 29, transferred the payment of county rates to the churchwardens and overseers.

aggregations of persons had, of course, no legal status, and the Court found them difficult to deal with.[1]

Between the county and the parish stood the hundred. Of the Middlesex hundreds, that of Ossulston, including the metropolitan district, was divided into several separate divisions, so that, for administrative purposes, we are concerned with the entire hundreds of Edmonton, Gore, Elthorne, Spelthorn and Isleworth, and in place of the hundred of Ossulston, the divisions of Kensington, Holborn, Finsbury, and the Tower. The hundred court was decadent, but the official head of the hundred, the high constable, was an important link between the Court and the petty constables and headboroughs, and so with local administration generally. This link was the closer since, owing to the decay of the hundred courts, Quarter Sessions had come to appoint the high constables. It was of most importance in connection with the various branches of the maintenance of law and order[2] and the levying of county rates. For the latter, the high constable issued his precept to the petty constables to levy the money, which was paid to him after collection. Generally speaking, he was then expected to pay it over to a treasurer appointed specially for the purpose in question. The slackness of high constables in collecting the county rates and submitting their accounts caused the Court great embarrassment[3] and eventually the Act, 12 George II, c. 29, empowered it to commit to prison high constables and collectors who neglected to collect or to account for or to pay over such county money. In other cases, when the Court wished certain things to be done or left undone, its method was often to instruct high constables to issue their precepts to petty constables to return or apprehend offenders, and here, also, there was difficulty in securing ready compliance.

Parliament had entrusted not a little judicial, and a great deal of administrative, work to Justices out of Sessions, acting singly, or in pairs or threes. The Justices out of Sessions must therefore

---

[1] *Vide* p. 118.
[2] The high constables' position is therefore further discussed in the following chapter, *vide* p. 17.
[3] *Vide* p. 76.

ORGANISATION OF THE COUNTY

be included among local government authorities, and they were brought into constant relations with the general body of Justices in Sessions, since, in many cases, appeal against their actions and decisions lay to the General Sessions and also because the latter had to rely upon its individual members for the execution of a large proportion of its orders. Many of these orders simply take the form of instructions to the several Justices acting out of Sessions, usually in the neighbourhood of their residence. Corporate spirit and the common perception of what was needful would doubtless go far to ensure a more or less thorough compliance with such instructions, but it is obvious that the policy of the Court would be far less certain of prompt execution than if it had had a body of really subordinate officials, paid for their work and dismissible at pleasure. This would be especially so if there was a strong minority opposed to the common decision, a contingency which appears very probable when we remember that a considerable number of Justices seldom attended Sessions. We shall, in fact, see that the Court had difficulty with individual Justices who flouted its decisions. It also at times sought to prevent members of the Commission from turning their office into a source of profit[1], and more frequently dealt with the exactions of magistrates' clerks, usually by precise regulations as to their fees. In the last resort, flagrant misconduct might be met by a representation to the Lord Chancellor, through whom the Court did, at various times, secure the exclusion from the Commission of conspicuously unfit persons;[2] but this was an extreme measure and could hardly be used in case of mere slackness or even of moderate opposition to the Court's policy.

From the constitutional point of view, the main interest in connection with the extra-Sessional activities of the Justices lies in the attempt to give them greater regularity, an attempt in which the Court played some part. In law, any member of the Commission of the Peace for a county might for many purposes

[1] The old wage of 4s. per day for Justices attending Sessions continued to be allowed out of the sheriff's fines, though for a customary number, not for those who actually attended. The proceeds were devoted to providing dinners for the Bench.
[2] *Vide* pp. 41 n. and 195. For further cases, *vide* Webb, *op. cit.*, p. 559 n.

act in any part of that county and, although Parliament had often given Justices authority which was to be exercised in or near their own parishes, its injunctions were too vague to be interpreted as precluding recourse to more remote magistrates. It was therefore not difficult for one who wished to extend his sphere of action to interfere in the affairs of parishes about which he knew little or nothing. This tended to destroy the main advantage possessed by single or "double" Justices as against the general body in Sessions, namely, that they could acquire detailed knowledge and experience of a limited field which were essential for the satisfactory execution of a large part of the duties of their office. Again, there was danger that magistrates would come into conflict with one another, perhaps quite unintentionally, for anyone aggrieved by the action of the neighbouring Justices could usually expect to find favour somewhere in the county at large and, if several officers and inhabitants with conflicting interests adopted this eclectic policy, chaos would ensue.[1] Another difficulty was that parish officers were liable to be summoned before several Justices at different places at the same time. A partial solution was to confine Justices within the limits of their own parishes. Some parishes, however, would not have resident Justices at all times. Magistrates, too, would often as ratepayers have personal interests at stake, so that their right to act in their own parishes was at one time questioned,[2] though it was reaffirmed by the Act, 16 George II, c. 18. The hundred or division was clearly a more satisfactory unit and it formed a possible basis for the organisation of periodic meetings of all the Justices within a given area. Such unification was also desirable as providing a local organ that would command more confidence than single or "double" Justices. The Court, consequently, would feel less obliged to institute minute enquiries into cases of appeal. Further, it could place more responsibility on these meetings than on the isolated Justices and so could reduce somewhat its own multifarious business, while saving others the expense and trouble of journeys to Clerkenwell or Westminster. Thus many good purposes might be served by the

[1] For illustrations, *vide* S.B. April 1715, p. 107; April 1727, pp. 65–7.
[2] *Vide* p. 73.

ORGANISATION OF THE COUNTY

development of small sessions for areas much narrower than the county, but wider than the parish, which would combine the advantages of impartiality and local knowledge, of detachment and accessibility.

The perception of these advantages led to the gradual and spontaneous organisation of such meetings by the Middlesex Justices. The one which earliest attained something approaching the regularity of a sessions was that at New Brentford, where remoteness from Westminster and Clerkenwell made the need particularly acute and where—one suspects—a feeling that the General Sessions were immersed in the problems of the suburban district would make magistrates anxious to have some other organisation to co-ordinate their policy.[1] For the hundred of Gore, a meeting at Edgware had reached a fairly advanced state of development by the end of the reign of George I.[2] In the part of the county adjacent to London, which was more immediately under the eye of the General Sessions, local organisation of Justices was hardly necessary for the formulation of general policy, but rather for the co-ordination of administrative action and, as such, was fostered by the Court.[3] For the Tower Division and Holborn, there is early evidence of meetings which were probably fairly well organised,[4] and, for the parish of Marylebone, magistrates met continuously from 1730 until after the end of our period.[5] For the metropolitan division of Finsbury and for the more rural division of Kensington and hundred of Edmonton, there is no indication of permanent organisation, but the Court at times seems to assume that it

[1] The proceedings of the Brentford Justices from 1651 to 1714 are recorded in a volume entitled *The Brentford Journal*, a calendar of which is among the Guildhall Records. Meetings were held fairly regularly at one of the inns, usually the Red Lion, New Brentford, the number of gatherings ranging from eight to nearly thirty a year.

[2] O.C. vol. III, f. 47.

[3] A characteristic early order is that of Feb. 1665-6 for Justices to meet in their divisions to execute the orders of the Council Board for preventing the spread of the Plague, S.Reg. vol. IX, p. 294.

[4] For the Tower Division in 1666 and 1681, S.Reg. vol. IX, p. 320; S.B. May 1681, p. 40. For Holborn in 1690 and 1705, S.B. Jan. 1689-90, p. 46; April 1705, p. 60.

[5] Two volumes of their minutes are preserved at the Town Hall, Marylebone.

existed.[1] We must not, however, exaggerate the extent to which such meetings were regularised. The Court continued to refer very many local matters to certain Justices by name or to magistrates in a division without mentioning any particular meeting. It felt obliged to urge that the meetings should be held at the known and usual places and that there should not be more than one in a division,[2] but its views regarding frequency varied from once a month to once a week,[3] while, in the matter of area, it did not always make definite ruling as to whether the meetings should be for parishes or divisions.[4] It is, however, clear that Middlesex witnessed an early growth of the tendency which, at a later date, was to produce a regular local organisation of Justices throughout the country.[5]

Of the county officials, little need be said. Strange as it may now seem, they played little part in local government, as has, in fact, appeared from what has already been said of the administrative hierarchy. The sheriffs who, it will be remembered, were also sheriffs of the City of London, are not of great interest, though they (or under-sheriffs on their behalf) figured constantly as recipients of forfeitures due to the King and also had the important function of returning juries. On the one or two occasions in which they come before us more definitely, it is because they are engaged in conflict with the Justices.[6] The

[1] In 1679, in connection with a proposal for the employment of the poor, it directed churchwardens and overseers of all parishes within the Bills of Mortality to give various particulars to the Justices of each division at their monthly meetings, S.B. Oct. 1679, p. 80. In 1682 it directed "that petty sessions be frequently held by the Justices within their several divisions" and assigned to them important functions in the supervision of parish administration, so apparently anticipating that such bodies would cover the whole county, S.B. April 1682, p. 37. In 1740 it referred the question of engrossing corn for export to petty sessions, O.C. vol. IV, ff. 180–81.
[2] S.B. April 1705, p. 41; Feb. 1715–16, p. 36.
[3] S.B. July 1696, p. 65; O.C. vol. III, f. 266.
[4] O.C. vol. I, ff. 109–10.
[5] As regards local meetings provided for by Parliament, there is, as we should expect, no sign of action under the Statute of Artificers. For "Brewster Sessions" and gatherings for highway business, *vide* pp. 34, 90 respectively.
[6] During the political and religious conflict of the latter part of the reign of Charles II, the Court complained to the King that the sheriff returned persons on juries "who regard not the laws but will take upon them to find bills contrary to evidence", etc., also that the sheriff's bailiffs were infringing the liberties of lords with bailiffs who ought themselves to summon jurors. S.B.

ORGANISATION OF THE COUNTY

Coroners also need not detain us, though the duty of paying them for inquisitions *post mortem* was imposed upon the Sessions.

The holder of the combined offices of Lord-Lieutenant and *Custos Rotulorum* is hardly more important. The duties of the former office do not concern us, while those of the latter were performed by deputy. Only occasionally do we hear of the *Custos*, when he forwards, sometimes with a covering letter, a communication from the Privy Council or one of the Secretaries of State. For his main duties, he appointed a deputy known as the Clerk of the Peace, who actually kept the Records and acted as principal official of the Court. The Justices relied on him to carry out various administrative functions, such as printing orders and writing letters. He was usually treasurer for the more private funds of the magistrates—colt money, sockett money, honour money and county rents[1]—and sometimes also for more public purposes. There was plenty of room for friction between the Court and its independent secretary, but relations appear in fact to have been quite satisfactory.

The offices of Housekeeper of Hicks Hall and Cryer of the Court were usually held by the same person, who was at times employed for business to which the Clerk of the Peace at other times attended. He was appointed and dismissed by the Court and the income which he derived from fees made him amenable to control. The same is true of the keepers of the New Prison and House of Correction.[2] These offices were at first held during good behaviour, tenure at pleasure being substituted in 1720. Their work was supervised by the Court with no little care, but

July 1681, p. 43. At the following Michaelmas Sessions, Sir George Jeffreys, the Chairman, by order of Court, commanded the under-sheriff to remove certain persons from the jury panel and put others in. On his refusal and the refusal of the sheriffs to attend, the Court adjourned from day to day and ultimately no Grand Jury was sworn, S.B. Oct. 1681, p. 56. On the difficulty of suppressing conventicles in the time of the "ignoramus juries" and the difference made by the appointment of loyal sheriffs, *vide* S.B. Sept. 1684, p. 56.

[1] The disposal of these funds claimed a good deal of the Justices' attention, but has seemed of insufficient importance to demand discussion here.

[2] The Keeper of the New Prison was expected to derive such a substantial income that he at first paid a rent of £50, but his profits later fell off and he was allowed a salary of £30 a year.

was mainly of a routine character and has therefore not been described, except for one or two incidental references.[1]

For its financial business, the Court appointed treasurers who were, of course, honorary, though some of them sought to remunerate themselves by keeping too tight a hand on the county's money. For several of the funds, Middlesex was divided into two parts, the one comprising the hundreds of Ossulston, Edmonton and Gore, the other covering Elthorne, Spelthorn and Isleworth. This was so in connection with the funds for the Maimed Soldiers and Mariners, for the King's Bench, Marshalsea and Hospitals,[2] for vagrants after they had become a charge upon the county and for the House of Correction when money had to be raised for its maintenance. The bridge treasurer was usually named *ad hoc* in the order for the rate.[3] There was always some tendency for these financial spheres to overlap. When one fund was depleted and unable to meet urgent demands upon it while another was prosperous, the Court quite naturally instructed the treasurer for the latter to advance money to the former. It was also no doubt difficult to discover sufficient gentlemen upon whom to lay these numerous offices and we find them holding more than one at a time, often for quite long periods. Unification had obvious advantages and there was a decided tendency in that direction from the end of the reign of George I.[4] The financial position of the county was much simplified, as well as strengthened, by the Act, 12 George II, c. 29, which unified the rates for bridges, gaols and houses of correction, King's Bench, Marshalsea and Hospitals, and vagrants. They were in future to be included by the Justices

---

[1] The business of maintaining the fabric and equipment of Hicks Hall, the New Prison and House of Correction has also been ignored, though it occupied a great deal of the Court's time.

[2] The management of these two funds was a matter of routine and they were of no great importance. They have therefore been left with this bare mention.

[3] After the Act, 8 and 9 William III, c. 17, regarding the maintenance of the Haymarket, a treasurer and collector were appointed by a general meeting of Justices for Middlesex and Westminster, *vide* p. 112 n.

[4] Mr John Higgs was General Treasurer from 1731 until after the close of our period and clearly looked after practically all the county finances. He was granted a salary of £25 per annum, with 1s. in the pound for all above £500 received, not exceeding £40 altogether.

ORGANISATION OF THE COUNTY

in one general rate, to be paid by the churchwardens and overseers out of the poor rate for each parish. Henceforward the advantage of having a single treasurer was much greater, since he could submit a single account comprising all these heads, and book-keeping was greatly simplified.[1] It was no longer necessary to conduct a large number of separate audits and, no doubt, effective supervision became much simpler.

It is perhaps unnecessary to emphasise the importance of committees in the work of Sessions. The committee of local Justices appointed to consider particular cases as they arose will appear in the following pages as the indispensable means to inform the Court, and often also to take decisions on its behalf. So, too, for the formulation of county policy and the elaboration of measures for its execution, there was generally need of more detailed investigation than the Court as a whole could spare time for, and committees were the obvious means to these ends. The audit committee, at first *ad hoc*, later becoming more general and permanent, was also a necessity. Towards the close of our period, a committee meeting between Sessions, which might apparently be attended by any magistrates who pleased, seems to have considered most of the important business which was known to be coming on. These gatherings had the advantage of informality and secrecy, besides saving the time of Sessions, and it is likely that they virtually decided a considerable proportion of the questions with which they dealt. Considering the amount and variety of business which the Justices were expected to transact, it is clear that they might advantageously have made more use of the standing committee. This would have ensured that some magistrates were regularly giving attention to each of the important branches of administration, whereas, in the absence of some degree of specialisation, there was a danger that the energies of all would be absorbed in a comparatively small number of problems which appealed to them more immediately.[2] It would also have made for continuity and efficiency of action by enabling

[1] A comprehensive volume of orders for payment commencing in 1763 survives at the Guildhall.
[2] A good picture of the pre-occupations of an active urban magistrate is given in the *Memoirs of the Life and Times of Sir Thomas Deveil*, which show him to have had no time or thought to spare for economic questions.

each group of Justices to become really conversant with their work, which they certainly could not be expected to master in its entirety. Such an anticipation of the modern method of local government was, however, very difficult owing to the complex rôle which the Justices played in and out of Sessions. The Justice in his parish or division must needs be a man of many parts, and it would have been hard to induce him to make himself an expert in one branch of the business of the county, to him, probably, the most remote sphere of his activity. Hence the position of the Justices themselves has all the appearance of being a source of weakness in administration. Our preliminary survey, therefore, points in no uncertain manner to the conclusion that the county was not provided with a really serviceable governmental organisation, and this view will receive ample corroboration in the subsequent chapters.

In conclusion, it is necessary to say a few words as to the relation between the county and the central government. This had originally been very close. Successive Sovereigns and Parliaments had heaped powers upon the Justices, largely because they could be controlled and stimulated in a way which was hardly practicable when dealing with the clumsy communities forming the basis of the older administrative machinery. Under the Tudors, the Council and Assize Judges supervised the Justices of Peace very much as the latter did the parishes and parish officers; but with the Civil War and the passing of the Star Chamber the central government was crippled and, when we commence our survey after the Restoration, it had little opportunity for systematic intervention in local government. Occasionally we find a letter from the Privy Council or one of the Secretaries of State, enjoining the execution of certain laws, sometimes prescribing details as to the method to be followed. Once or twice a Lord Chief Justice attended the Court and issued instructions in person. Letters coming direct from the Sovereign are also not quite unknown.[1] Proclamations were extensively employed to recommend the general enforcement of particular laws, but these were weak instruments unless addressed to willing ears. The Justices were, of course, obliged

[1] For such intervention by central authorities, *vide* pp. 23, 40, 41, 109.

ORGANISATION OF THE COUNTY 15

to act within limits prescribed by law. Except in certain cases where it had been explicitly taken away, there was a right of appeal from their action to the higher courts, a right which was clearly much used. The Common Law courts could also intervene on their own account by means of prerogative writs.[1] Orders and convictions by Justices in and out of Sessions might thus be challenged and quashed, perhaps merely owing to minute technical irregularities. This exposed magistrates to the constant danger of being involved in expensive legal proceedings and to the humiliation of having their action reversed.[2] On the other hand, it seems that Justices who neglected to perform their duties were never compelled to pay the comparatively heavy penalties which Parliament had in many cases prescribed. There was thus danger in action, but little, if any, in inaction. The Justices worked, so to speak, under negative, but not under positive, supervision. Here was a very powerful incentive to a laissez-faire attitude, the more so since, in the absence of a vigorous co-ordinating authority, there was no hope of simultaneous action throughout the country and measures taken in a single county would for many purposes be futile, if not positively harmful. The condition of the central government therefore tended rather to aggravate than to remedy the deficiencies of local administrative machinery. This reflection lends further emphasis to the conclusion that Justices who sought to make their administration really thorough and vigorous were hampered by very serious difficulties inherent in their constitutional position, and this must be borne in mind when judgment is being passed upon the achievement of the magistrates of the time.

[1] Owing to the unsystematic character of the Law Reports at this period, it has unfortunately not been possible to follow the fortunes in King's Bench of cases removed by Certiorari.
[2] For the difficulty so caused in regard to levying county rates, *vide* pp. 76, 127.

CHAPTER II

LAW AND ORDER

It is perhaps somewhat surprising that, in a volume on the work of Justices of Peace, it should be possible to deal with the maintenance of law and order in a single special chapter. The explanation is of course to be found in the fact that, until comparatively recent times, the officers with whom we are concerned were very much more than conservators of the peace in the widest sense that we could give that term to-day. For centuries before the Restoration they had seemed to successive kings and parliaments the most reliable and convenient instruments for carrying out measures of almost every description and had consequently been loaded with powers which are quite astonishing in their variety. A glance at any contemporary manual on the duties of Justices of Peace gives a vivid impression of the breadth of their functions. Quarter Sessions had, in fact, become the most important organ of local government as well as the chief seat of local jurisdiction. The problem of classifying its activities is therefore no small one. The entire work of the Justices was to a great extent then thought of as an attempt to introduce good order and rule into the whole of the community's life, including, for instance, its industrial and commercial relations. Such an interpretation is clearly too broad to help us in classification, while the adoption of a purely modern standpoint would narrow our outlook unduly. It thus becomes necessary to compromise between ancient and modern usage and to regard the maintenance of law and order as covering, not only present-day police functions, but also what we may style the moral regimentation of the people. This latter aimed at maintaining certain approved standards in the more personal sides of conduct, partly with a view to morality for its own sake, but partly also with an eye on the closely connected overt acts which concern a police court more directly. Such a treatment tends to make this chapter lack unity, superficially at least, but it appears the best mode of dealing with a rather awkward section of our material

LAW AND ORDER

and it does help to bring out the underlying connection between the matters here discussed. The more definite police duties naturally fall first for discussion and, before proceeding, something must be said regarding the officers concerned.

High constables had, before the opening of our period, lost their former position of independence and were mainly occupied in carrying out the instructions of Justices in and out of Sessions. They were perhaps the most important of the magistrates' instruments in county administration, for their functions included such duties as the levying of county rates. Here, however, we are concerned with them as the superior peace officers and, since the bulk of their work undoubtedly came to them in that capacity, a brief discussion of their whole position will not be out of place. They were properly officers of hundreds, but it must be remembered that in Middlesex the important hundred of Ossulston was split up into divisions for this as for other purposes.[1] The position of these officers as subordinates of the Justices of Peace was reflected in the manner of their appointment. The details doubtless varied, but the commonest method of selection seems to have been for the magistrates of the hundred or division to suggest one or more names which the Sessions would then either confirm or use as a panel from which to make the final appointment.[2] Owing to the danger of interested negligence or partiality, the Court, at the time of its campaign against excessive drinking, found it necessary to recommend magistrates not to return dealers in brandy, beer, etc., for the office.[3] It also, at least on occasions, discharged high constables for misconduct,[4] but this obviously could not be pushed to any great length, owing to the difficulty of finding suitable substitutes. There was further the possibility of indicting recalcitrant officers, though this was far too clumsy a method to ensure the desirable smooth working of the official hierarchy.

[1] Some hundreds and divisions had more than one high constable, *vide* the list of those forming the constables' jury at the beginning of the second Charge of Sir Daniel Dolins, April 1726.
[2] S.B. Feb. 1674–5, p. 38*a*; O.C. vol. II, f. 2, Jan. 1721–2.
[3] O.C. vol. IV, f. 14.
[4] E.g. for taking money from unlicensed alesellers in Welsh Fair, O.C. vol. IV, f. 155; also, for discharging arrested persons without carrying them before a Justice, S.B. Feb. 1711–12, p. 45.

Even it, however, was resorted to in connection with protracted negligence in levying and paying over county rates.[1] The difficulties of the Court in this connection were doubtless exceptional, but it seems clear that the high constables, though theoretically servants of the Justices, had ample scope for acting, or neglecting to act, as their own inclinations dictated.

Petty constables and headboroughs were strictly speaking not parochial, but manorial, officials, their offices dating from before the time when the parish became an organ of secular government. With the decay of the manor, however, they came to be associated more and more with the parish, co-operating in much of its business, though they often covered an area smaller than the parish. At the same time, their appointment by court leet tended to break down, as that type of court fell more and more into abeyance, and the Act, 14 Charles II, c. 12, empowered Justices in Sessions to make appointments when courts leet were not held. The Middlesex Sessions had made such an appointment as early as 1610[2] and, in the period under review, it constantly made appointments, usually upon petition of existing officers that they had served a full year and that there was no prospect of the holding of a court leet which would release them.[3] Whatever the mode of selection, there was always great eagerness to escape these offices and, in consequence, there were constant applications to the Court for relief. This was granted on such pleas as that the nominee kept a grammar school by license of the Bishop of London,[4] that he was poor, old and had children dependent upon him,[5] that he was a physician[6] or a parish clerk.[7] Where the system of rotation was well established, the Justices were prepared to recognise it and to discharge any one chosen out of his turn.[8] One unwilling prospective candidate, being intimate with the Steward of the Duchy Liberty, procured the

---

[1] *Vide* pp. 76, 127.
[2] Cal. of Sessions Rolls, etc., vol. II, p. 52.
[3] E.g., S.B. Oct. 1679, p. 65; July 1709, p. 48.
[4] S.B. April 1669, p. 34.
[5] S.B. Oct. 1694, p. 38.
[6] S.B. Sept. 1674, p. 43, under the Act, 32 Henry VIII, c. 40.
[7] S.B. April 1725, pp. 60–61, under a patent of Charles I to the Company of Parish Clerks.
[8] S.B. Dec. 1690, p. 59.

LAW AND ORDER

postponement of the Easter Thursday meeting at which he expected to be chosen, but the Court came to the rescue of the then constable who had no desire to have his term prolonged.[1] One widely-used mode of escape for nominees was to compound with their fellows. If carried to any great length, this would have the effect of causing the offices to be generally in the hands of the poorer inhabitants, and the Court objected to the practice,[2] without, however, being able to stop it.[3]

How far the system of unpaid and compulsory offices was normally supplemented or replaced by extra-legal professionalism it is impossible to say, but something was undoubtedly done in this direction.[4] Indeed, the expedient of finding substitutes might be employed with something of this effect. We hear, for instance, that at Lower Wapping "Robert Sturgion of the said hamlet and parish hath served as headborough there for himself and others for the space of four years past and is now also hired again to serve for another year". The Justices discharged him, not because, as was alleged, he had been "very abusive, oppressive and contentious amongst the neighbourhood to the prejudice of many of his neighbours", but because they conceived it "to be unreasonable that any one person should be continued in that office for so many years together".[5] Such an attitude, though quite in keeping with the views of the time, must appear strange to modern eyes, since it precluded the expertness which could only be expected to follow long experience. However, a later order instructing high constables to desire leet stewards not to appoint alehouse keepers as hired constables[6] suggests that paid substitutes were rather a usual phenomenon in the urban divisions of Ossulston.

The Court found it necessary to lay down and, from time to time to repeat, one important disqualification from the office of constable or headborough, owing to the evils likely to arise from

---

[1] S.B. April 1680, p. 51.   [2] S.B. Feb. 1681–2, p. 30.
[3] S.B. April 1683, p. 54.
[4] Our records throw little light on the part played by beadles at this time, but there are sporadic references to such officers, e.g. S.B. Feb. 1694–5, p. 39; O.C. vol. 1, f. 28. One man was beadle of the hamlet of Church End and Hoxton in Shoreditch for at least twelve years in succession, S.B. July 1700, p. 38; Jan. 1708–9, p. 47.
[5] S.B. May 1662, p. 37.   [6] S.B. April 1712, p. 55.

the appointment of persons interested in the sale of liquor. In January 1683-4, the Grand Jury presented "that no peace officers may be permitted to keep alehouses during the time they are in such an office"[1] and, on another occasion, we learn that such persons were wont to take arrested people to their houses, keep them there till they had spent great sums in eating and drinking and lodging, and then release them without bringing them before a Justice.[2] The Court therefore forbade alehouse keepers to be headboroughs or beadles.[3] A kindred danger was that of bribery, whereby peace officers might remunerate themselves for their unsought and unpleasant duties. We hear, for instance, that constables countenanced the vice and debauchery prevalent at Whetstones Park in St Giles' in the Fields because they were treated, a recent dinner being mentioned.[4] This was more difficult to deal with,[5] as also were the far more extensive cases of negligence which had no more definite motive than lack of interest in the duties of the office. What would nowadays appear the obvious step of dismissal was, of course, not open to the Court, since most of these officers would have been only too pleased to gain their release. On one occasion, however, William Brind, a constable of St Giles' in the Fields, was dismissed for refusing to execute a Justice's warrant to seize fruit exposed for sale.[6] For the rest, the Court could and did issue orders to the peace officers to carry out their duties. When, for instance, it was informed "that many of His Majesty's good subjects have been oftentimes set upon, assaulted, beaten and wounded in the day-time in the public lanes, streets and highways of this county near the city of London as they have been quietly and peaceably passing and going about their necessary occasions, and that the said offenders, through the extreme negligence and default of the petty constables and headboroughs, have escaped without any pursuit made after them by the said petty constables and headboroughs", and that the officers absented themselves

---

[1] S.B. Jan. 1683-4, p. 29. [2] S.B. Feb. 1694-5, p. 39.
[3] *Ibid. Vide* also S.B. April 1712, p. 55.
[4] S.B. Oct. 1671, p. 35.
[5] On the corruption of officers, especially peace officers, *vide* Sir D. Dolins, Charge, Oct. 1725, p. 28.
[6] S.B. July 1691, p. 65.

LAW AND ORDER

very much "on purpose to shun and avoid the execution of warrants and preservation of the peace", it ordered them to be attendant and diligent, to have their staffs fixed at their doors and, if called away, to leave notice where they were.[1] In its judicial capacity, too, it could punish specific offences and we find it fining men who refuse to serve the office when duly nominated,[2] or who omit particular duties of the office, such as failing to levy a rate under a Justice's warrant[3] or to attend a high constable to Tyburn.[4] In 1684 when a vigorous attempt was being made to suppress conventicles, great difficulty was experienced by some Justices in inducing the parish officers—of whom the constables would be the most important—to present offenders, and heavy fines were inflicted.[5] In this case feeling was running high and it is unlikely that peace officers normally went so far as to oppose actively the policy of the Justices. Mere negligence, however, must have been very serious, and have greatly hampered the work of the Magistrates.

The high and petty constables, serving their offices for a brief term without direct remuneration, were, of course, only the core of the police system. Alone they could, even with the best will in the world, have done very little and, for the prevention of crime and apprehension of wrong-doers, they depended largely on the even more sporadic labours of ordinary citizens whose duty it was to watch by turns. It need hardly be said that the latter were no more anxious to participate than were the constables and headboroughs to assume the duty of organising their services. The loss of rest was in itself no small matter and the Justices, at one time at least, were prepared to exempt the poor, as they ordered that no person not paying poor rate should be called to serve, thinking it unreasonable that those who by their labour got their daily bread should, by a night watch, be disabled for the next day's work.[6] Apart from this, it requires no vivid

---

[1] S.B. Oct. 1671, p. 41. For a further order to affix staffs to door-posts, vide S.B. Sept. 1693, p. 49.
[2] E.g. in S.R. July 1751, where the fine is only 12d.
[3] S.R. Aug. 1728.
[4] S.R. Dec. 1752.
[5] S.B. Sept. 1684, p. 56. There were fines of £100 and £50.
[6] S.B. April 1682, p. 37. The order is unfortunately decayed, but this appears to be its intention.

imagination to realise that watching was far from being a pleasant occupation. There was obvious danger in interfering with wrong-doers who, in the existing state of the criminal law, would be tempted to commit assault and murder in order to escape the very heavy punishments attached to crimes which would now be viewed more leniently. In addition, long exposure to the vagaries of the elements was in itself no small matter. In 1690, men of St Sepulchre's, in petitioning to be allowed to erect a watch house "wherein to shelter them from the extremity of the weather when on their watch", stated that the want of a roof had already occasioned the death of several of the inhabitants. The Court permitted them to erect, near the whipping post at Cow Cross, a house with a flat roof not more than five feet high above the street surface,[1] and overrode the objection of certain people living near the proposed site, who thought that the scheme would be prejudicial to their trade.[2] Thus it was possible, at public expense, to ameliorate the lot of those on watch, but this was probably at the cost of a further reduction of their efficiency, moderate as that must have been in any case. Such measures could not, of course, make watching a popular pursuit and there was constant need to exercise compulsion upon the inhabitants if anything approaching an adequate force was to be secured. There was a large and persistent stream of prosecutions, with a good many fines, though these tend to be small.[3] As might be expected, the names of constables frequently appear on the backs of the bills of indictment.[4] By the Statute of Winchester, watching was only compulsory from Lady Day to Michaelmas and, though the constable had power to watch at other times and might be ordered by Justices to do so, there was some doubt as to whether the ordinary inhabitants could be compelled to play their part in the winter.[5] The Middlesex Justices at times tried to

---

[1] S.B. Jan. 1690–91, p. 61.
[2] *Ibid.* p. 67 and S.B. Feb. 1690–91, p. 25. Similar action was taken in other cases.
[3] Probably so large a penalty as 13*s*. 4*d*. was rare, but there is an instance in S.R. April 1734.
[4] E.g. a number in S.R. Oct. 1719, presented by Thomas Barnes, constable of St Giles', Cripplegate.
[5] Burn seems to suggest that they could, but is not very explicit, *Justice of the Peace*, p. 749.

LAW AND ORDER

enforce winter watching,[1] but later they were definitely of opinion that there was no obligation upon the inhabitants[2]—and, as will be seen shortly, partly attributed their inability to keep order to this want of provision at the very time of year when it was most needed. The more detailed regulation of the manner in which the peace officers managed their watches was naturally carried out by the local magistrates. Evidence of this is at times forthcoming when the Court adds its authority by confirming orders so made.[3] The Court itself issued injunctions from time to time. In 1690, for instance, in response to a complaint that watches were set too late and discharged too early in the morning, and that no ward was kept in the day time, it ordered that double watch should be kept at night from 9 p.m. to 5 a.m., as well as ward during the day.[4] The sequel, however, suggests that the growing problem of the metropolitan area could not be solved simply by such an extended use of old methods. In the following September, the high constable and several petty constables of the Tower Hamlets explained that the inhabitants of their district were generally very poor and unable to sustain the charge of a double watch. Relief was accordingly granted to them.[5]

That this amateur organisation failed to do its work efficiently is quite clear. This may be attributed partly to the remissness of those concerned, but certainly largely to the fact that, in an important section of the county, the needs which the Statute of Winchester had sought to meet were not the needs of the year 1700. The growth of a densely packed population in the suburban area had immensely complicated the task of the constables and their assistants and, however hard they worked, they could not

[1] S.B. Jan. 1702–3, p. 25; Sept. 1707, p. 41.
[2] O.C. vol. I, f. 90; vol. v, f. 47.
[3] *Vide*, for instance, an order confirming detailed regulations made by the Petty Sessions of the Tower Division, S.B. May 1681, p. 40. This may have been due to the King's wishes for, before removing to Oxford, he had summoned the Middlesex Justices to attend him in Council and, by himself and by the Lord President, ordered them to use their utmost endeavour to preserve the peace and, for that purpose, to keep Petty Sessions in their several divisions one day every week, S.B. Feb. 1680–81, p. 32. For another confirmation of an order by Petty Sessions, *vide* S.B. Jan. 1702–3, p. 25.
[4] S.B. June 1690, p. 51.
[5] S.B. Sept. 1690, p. 44.

be expected to provide a really adequate police service.[1] Towards the end of the reign of Queen Anne, the Justices addressed to the Queen a memorandum on riots and other street disorders, explaining that, in obedience to royal command, they had done what they could and had caused the watches to be doubled. Among other outrages, they mentioned one in which Lord Hinchinbrook, Sir Mark Cole, Thomas ffanshaw, Thomas Sydenham, Captain John Reading, Captain Robert Bard, Robert Squibb and Hugh Jones assaulted John Bouch, watchman, in Essex Street, St Clement Danes.[2] The inadequacy of medieval machinery to cope with the problems of a modern metropolis is, however, shown most clearly by the outbreak and long continuance of a severe epidemic of street robbery.[3] In 1720, thirty-four Justices signed a representation to the House of Commons, stating that several persons of quality and others had lately and in an unusual manner been attacked in their coaches and chairs and some had been robbed in the high streets within the Bills of Mortality, but those concerned had not been apprehended through want of a proper and regular watch. The constables were not making good the deficiencies of the Statute of Winchester in the matter of provision for the winter season by their system of appointing paid watchmen at their own discretion, though, in the process, they were making oppressive levies. The Justices considered that a real solution could only be found by fresh legislation[4] and, a few months later, fifty of their number signed a petition to the House of Lords in support of a

---

[1] It is not clear whether much was done in the way of using paid watchmen, but these were not unknown in the Stuart period, as is shown by a complaint that the constable of Spitalfields was not summoning the inhabitants to watch, but was hiring a standing watch and levying exorbitant charges for the purpose, S.B. April 1672, p. 44.
[2] S.B. Feb. 1711–12, pp. 44–6. For the activities of the "Mohocks", and the proclamation issued against them, *vide* Lee, *History of Police in England*, p. 145.
[3] There is evidence during the period that the old suit against the hundred in which a robbery was committed had not fallen into complete disuse. From time to time, the Court made provision for the defence of the inhabitants of Ossulston in such suits, e.g. in S.B. June 1690, p. 43; April 1694, p. 70. It also received petitions as to money that had been levied in this connection, S.B. April 1694, p. 72. This procedure was, however, clearly no longer effective.
[4] O.C. vol. I, f. 90.

bill then depending.[1] After another decade, the Court issued a long order on the subject, directing Justices to hold weekly petty sessions, to proceed against those not hanging out lights at night, to suppress night-houses, gaming-houses or other disorderly houses where felons were harboured or encouraged and also to deal with all kinds of vagabonds and sellers of distilled spirits.[2] In 1744, the Justices addressed a long and comprehensive—one might almost add pathetic—representation to the Duke of Newcastle, who was one of the Principal Secretaries of State, as well as *Custos Rotulorum* of the county. They expressed the hope that their vigorous action against street robbers and other disorderly persons who had of late infested the town had produced some good effect "by repressing their boldness and forcing them to shift their habitations and seek for shelter in more obscure and distant places, by the frequent searches we have caused to be made by day and night, wherein we most thankfully acknowledge His Majesty's great goodness and paternal care of his subjects in sending his guards to our assistance whenever required". They were obliged, however, to admit that outrages continued and, unless some more effectual provision was made, were likely to persist " and, from robbing of foot passengers in the streets, soon reach to the coaches and dwelling-houses of His Majesty's subjects, not to mention the damages which may accrue to the public from the confederacies of so many armed villains or what use our enemies may find means to make of them on any future occasion". They considered that rewards must be offered, "for it is not to be expected that the constables or others will hazard their lives and the ruin of their families in apprehending these desperate fellows without being secure of a reward in some degree proportionable to the hazard they run", especially as rescues and attempted rescues were so frequent. Apart from this suggestion of a partial system of payment for service in keeping the peace, they stressed the need for fresh general legislation to strengthen the watch system, particularly in the winter, and for a better

---

[1] O.C. vol. I, f. 98.
[2] O.C. vol. III, f. 266. The acuteness of the evil is emphasised by Henry Fielding's elaborate *Enquiry into the Causes of the Late Increase of Robbers*.

enforcement of street lighting, as well as the suppression of various social evils which were thought to predispose men to highway robbery, such as gaming-houses, night-houses, fairs, pleasure-gardens and excessive spirit drinking.[1]

All this was in spite of certain supplementary agencies that had been introduced already. Where, for instance, the Government was specially interested, it sometimes interfered to reinforce the ordinary machinery, generally by the offer of a reward to those who apprehended offenders. That it should do this in an attempt to repress highway robbery in and about London and Westminster is quite understandable,[2] though it is somewhat surprising to find proclamations issued in cases of robbery and murder committed upon private persons.[3] Where inhabitants were prosperous enough to be able and willing to pay an additional price for good order, they could take special steps on their own account and, in so doing, could rely on the friendly interest of the Justices. When, for instance, the Lord Chief Justice of Common Pleas, Sir Henry Pollexfen, and other distinguished residents in the Great Square in St Giles' in the Fields complained, just after the Revolution, that many robberies had recently been committed in their square owing to the negligence of constables and asked liberty to provide and maintain a watch at their own expense, the Court gave them leave and directed that their watch, though under the constables, was only to be removed in cases of emergency.[4] More radical measures of reform followed towards the end of the period, when most of the local improvement acts passed for districts within the suburban area contained provisions for better regulating the nightly watches and beadles. These had the effect of substituting a paid professional watch for the compulsory personal service of the inhabitants, though the old peace officers might be left still with

---

[1] O.C. vol. v, f. 46.
[2] *Vide* the Proclamation of Jan. 21, 1719–20 in Crawford's *Hand-List*.
[3] Illustrations of such proclamations dealing with specific offences in Middlesex during the reign of George I may be found in Crawford's *Hand-List* under the following dates: Dec. 8, 1718; July 14, 1721; Sept. 8, 1721; April 13, 1722; Jan. 28, 1722–3; Dec. 11, 1723; Feb. 7, 1725–6.
[4] S.B. Jan. 1690–91, p. 71. For a similar order at the same time regarding Little Lincoln's Inn Fields, Sheir Lane and Bell Yard, *vide ibid*. p. 72.

LAW AND ORDER

the duty of active supervision and of watching by turns.[1] At Christ Church the constables and headboroughs remained, but the vestry were empowered to appoint a proper number of watchmen and beadles, to set down in writing the manner and number of their rounds, their arms, hours of watching and wages, and to pay them out of the proceeds of a pound rate. Probably more often, as at Red Lion Square and Saffron Hill, an entirely new body of trustees was established. At all events Parliament was accepting as proved the contention that the old machinery was no longer adequate for the new needs created by the growth of London.[2]

In a chapter dealing with the maintenance of law and order in the reigns of the later Stuarts and early Hanoverians it is convenient, even necessary, to treat of various topics which would nowadays be regarded as belonging to the domain of personal morality rather than to that of the public courts of justice. Some of these matters, however, are still on the borderline and are taken notice of by our legislators, while some of them were then dealt with largely as being likely to lead to overt disorder. Persons who refused to conform to the Established Church were punished for political reasons quite as much as, if not more than, for their religious convictions as such, while those who took part in the campaign for the encouragement of piety and virtue certainly felt that the vices they combated were likely to lead to open disturbance of the peace.[3] Questions so closely allied to the subject of this chapter must therefore be discussed here.

The campaign for the encouragement of piety and virtue and

---

[1] Such acts were 10 George II, c. 15, for Red Lion Square; 10 George II, c. 25, for Saffron Hill, Hatton Garden and Ely Rents; 11 George II, c. 35, for Christ Church; 22 George II, c. 50, for Shoreditch; 23 George II, c. 35, for St Martin's in the Fields; 24 George II, c. 26, for Bethnal Green; 27 George II, c. 25, for St Luke's; 29 George II, c. 53, for Marylebone; 29 George II, c. 87, for Wapping, Shadwell, Ratcliffe, St Ann and Well Close.

[2] The Bow Street Police Office was within the Liberty of Westminster, but the patrols instituted by Sir John Fielding did useful work in the County at large, Lee, *op. cit.* p. 156.

[3] For instance, in 1744 the Court attributed the then rampant evil of street robbery largely to the effects of gaming-houses, night-houses, fairs, wells, gardens and excessive spirit drinking, O.C. vol. v, ff. 46–7. In addition, it must be remembered that an increase of poverty, with its consequent burdens to the rates, was threatened by such practices as gaming and, in some degree, by all amusements that diminished industry.

for preventing and punishing vice, profaneness and immorality was waged with considerable energy and persistence in the eighteenth century, and in its prosecution the Justices received an unwonted amount of stimulus from the central Government.[1] They were naturally concerned at many points by a movement with such wide objects; so much so that the proclamation issued under George I was ordered to be read in open Court and the Chairmen of Sessions were, in their charges, to enjoin the punishment of those who offended or neglected to prosecute offenders.[2] That this was a congenial task is made clear, not only by orders of the Court, but also by the stress laid on these matters by chairmen such as Whitlocke Bulstrode and Sir Daniel Dolins.[3] One Order in Council for the discovery and punishment of profaneness, immorality and debauchery is reproduced in the Orders of Court.[4] The King had received information about "certain scandalous clubs or societies of young persons who meet together and, in the most impious and blasphemous manner, insult the most sacred principles of our holy religion, affront Almighty God Himself and corrupt the minds and morals of one another", and, being resolved to punish these enormities, commanded the Chancellor to stir the Justices of Middlesex and Westminster to action. The Lord Chancellor summoned the Justices to attend him and gave them appropriate instructions. Their appeal for informers to come forward and give evidence was, however, unanswered, though they assured the Chancellor of their resolve to do all they could in the matter. The prevalent and increasing profaneness and debauchery proceeded chiefly, they thought, from masquerades and gaming-houses, play-houses and public-houses, and they lamented the fact that the number of alehouses, brandy and Geneva shops was

---

[1] For various proclamations explicitly directed to these objects, *vide* Crawford's *Hand-List*.
[2] Evidence that these instructions were carried out is supplied by the Charges of Sir D. Dolins, Oct. 1725, p. 29, April 1726, p. 36 and Oct. 1726, p. 42. Cf. a letter from Lord Chesterfield, one of the Principal Secretaries of State, reporting the concern of George II at the prevalent immoralities and robberies, and strictly charging the Justices to take remedial measures and to return an exact account of what was done and by whom, in order that the King might reward the energetic and punish the remiss, O.C. vol. v, f. 130.
[3] *Vide* their printed charges. [4] O.C. vol. I, f. 118.

increasing, though already in some of the largest parishes every tenth house at least retailed strong liquors of some kind. The results were growing poverty, vice, debauchery, felonies and other disorders; and yet they could not supply a remedy, owing to the difficulty of finding willing informers, to the defeat of searches by closing doors which the officers had no authority to break open, and to the elaborateness and expense of securing convictions.[1] The attitude here portrayed inspired a very considerable proportion of the Court's orders throughout the reigns of the first two Georges, and our picture of county administration will be incomplete without some account of the steps taken to deal with the various disorders complained of.

From about the year 1700, the Justices took not infrequent action against fairs and similar gatherings. These were frowned on as they usually comprised booths for acting, and facilities for gaming, and attracted concourses of people which were very liable to be disorderly. "The acting of such plays and drolls and the keeping of public gaming tables or gaming houses are contrary to the laws and statutes of this realm and do manifestly and directly tend to the encouragement of vice and immorality and to the debauching and ruining of servants, apprentices and others, as well as to the disturbance of the public peace by occasioning quarrels, riots, tumults and other disorders."[2] Later we read that, owing to the increase of these fairs, "numbers of innocent persons are debauched, all manner of vice, immorality and profaneness gains ground and visibly increases, habits of gaming, drinking and swearing are here learnt and contracted, servants defraud their masters, gangs of rogues and thieves are formed and then, after Michaelmas, when these fairs end, they patrol about the streets and make it dangerous to be abroad even early in the evening.... The poor grow even poorer and many families are thrown on their respective parishes".[3]

Holding such views, it is no wonder that the Court sought to

[1] O.C. vol. I, ff. 118-19.
[2] Part of an order against one of the most objectionable of these gatherings which was held at Tottenham Court in the parish of St Pancras in the 1720's, O.C. vol. III, ff. 19-20, 71-2.
[3] O.C. vol. V. ff. 89-90.

repress these assemblies. In 1697, it ordered the various constables of Gore hundred to prevent a concourse of disorderly persons from assembling upon pretence of holding a fair in Whitsun week at Burrows Green, Hendon.[1] Shortly after, upon presentment by the Grand Jury that there was "an unlawful assembly, called the Redoubt, after the Venetian manner, kept at Exeter Change in the Strand, and carried on by persons unknown who, by printed tickets, give notice of games that are not lawful, and tend very much to encourage all manner of vice and debauchery, and that the persons who frequent the same go masqued and disguised", it instructed the constables to repair thither in order to preserve the peace, disperse the assembly and arrest the managers.[2] The May Fair near Hyde Park in St Martin's in the Fields caused much trouble. On one occasion, constables who tried to suppress it were attacked by persons in the habit of soldiers. Several of the peace officers were wounded, one fatally.[3] After a further attempt to keep the peace,[4] which presumably failed, the Court seems to have applied to the Queen for a proclamation against the disorders there[5] and one was accordingly issued.[6] Many other orders were issued against particular fairs,[7] which evidently throve none the less, and the Court in 1746 sent a representation to the Lord Chancellor, Lord Hardwicke, against the various fairs (the majority entirely unwarranted by law), which followed each other in such quick succession that from the beginning of May till the end of September there was generally one within five miles of town. The Justices complained of the danger they ran in attempting suppression, and of connivance at May Fair on the part of gentlemen and others in authority in Westminster. They were at

---

[1] S.B. May 1697, p. 35.
[2] S.B. Feb. 1697–8, p. 35.
[3] S.B. May 1702, p. 35.
[4] S.B. April 1708, p. 76.
[5] S.B. Feb. 1708–9, p. 47, where the address is unfinished.
[6] Crawford, *Tudor and Stuart Proclamations*, vol. I, p. 530.
[7] E.g. against a riotous and unlawful assembly in and about Rosemary Lane in Whitechapel for the buying and selling of old goods, wearing apparel and other things, greatly suspected to be stolen, S.B. Feb. 1699–1700, p. 27. This was commonly called Rag Fair, and attracted attention on several occasions.

a loss how to act unless they received assistance from above.[1] Shortly afterwards, the suppression of fairs was made a standing order.[2] Thus in spite of all rebuffs the Court remained resolute in its determination to put down these gatherings.

As already indicated, the prevention of gaming was one of the objects envisaged in the campaign to suppress fairs.[3] The same object was sought in the due regulation of alehouses. Addressing the Grand Jury in October 1718 on the subject of gaming-houses, Whitlocke Bulstrode spoke of those which undo ordinary men as being "such alehouses that have shovel-board tables, nine-pins and bowling-alleys belonging to them. Here the people I first mentioned come at night, spend and lose that money at one sitting which would keep their families the week following.... Here they get a vicious habit of gaming and sotting, lewdness and swearing and, by degrees, give themselves up to all manner of wickedness; and neglecting their work, leave their wives and children a burthen to the parish".[4] The magistrates of Middlesex and Westminster were, indeed, so anxious to suppress gaming-houses that in 1723 twenty-six of them formed a society with this object and called themselves "The Convention".[5] At the beginning of the period, there is some evidence that offenders were proceeded against by informers[6] and in general there are numerous indictments.[7] We gather, however, that officers were not as ready to prosecute as the Court could have wished, at least at the period of its keen interest in this question.[8] In 1744 the Justices regarded gaming-houses as a main cause of street disorders, as tradesmen, apprentices and

[1] O.C. vol. v, f. 89. Those specially mentioned were: May Fair and Welsh Fair and others at Paddington, Hampstead, Highgate, Mile End, Bow and Tottenham Court.
[2] O.C. vol. v, ff. 125–6, June 1747.
[3] For the way in which these fairs deteriorated from their original purpose as places for sale, *vide* the proclamation against May Fair, Crawford, *op. cit.* vol. I, p. 530.
[4] Charge, p. 24.
[5] Westminster Orders of Court, vol. I, f. 127. The King's satisfaction at what had been done in the previous year was expressed to the Court in a letter from Lord Townshend, Bulstrode, Charge, Oct. 1722, p. 3.
[6] E.g. the information of Thomas Gardiner against Richard Allworth in S.R. Jan. 1662–3.
[7] E.g. S.R. April 1674 and Feb. 1718–19.
[8] *Vide* Sir D. Dolins, Charge in Oct. 1725, pp. 24–5.

others were there ruined and probably made desperate, and they noted that great charges and difficulties attended prosecutions.[1] It is very probable that, to members of the poorer classes, this campaign appeared as an attempt to deprive them of one of their few diversions.[2]

The same may also be said of the attempt to stop the public performance of plays and interludes which, in the minds of those who undertook the moral regimentation of the common people, were very closely connected with unlawful games.[3] When, in July 1709, the Vicar, Churchwardens and other inhabitants of Hampstead complained that a play-house had been lately erected in their town against their consent and that great scandals, annoyances and disorders might be occasioned thereby, the Court suppressed the using and acting of any unlawful games or plays in Hampstead and directed the petty constables and headboroughs to apprehend the players so that they might be punished as rogues, vagabonds and sturdy beggars.[4] This order was apparently ineffective, as another, in terms of similar severity, had to be issued in the following year.[5] In 1735 the Justices petitioned the House of Commons against new playhouses, supporting a bill then depending,[6] while in 1739 the Grand Jury made a presentment against booths for acting and the Court ordered the apprehension of the offenders.[7] Thus it is clear that the Court was very decided in its disapproval of these diversions, but we may well doubt whether it received sufficient outside support to make its policy effective.[8] No doubt these and

[1] O.C. vol. v, f. 46, one gaming-house in Covent Garden kept by a person calling herself the Lady Mordington was particularly mentioned.
[2] Fielding expressly desired to suppress gaming among the lower sort of people "because they are the most useful members of the society", "Charge to the Westminster Grand Jury", *Works*, vol. VIII, p. 349.
[3] E.g. among the vicious practices at fairs.
[4] S.B. July 1709, p. 49.   [5] S.B. July 1710, p. 47.
[6] O.C. vol. IV, ff. 30–31. The Act, 10 George II, c. 28, imposed severe penalties upon those acting without license.
[7] O.C. vol. IV, ff. 134–5. For a presentment against masquerades at the King's Theatre in the Haymarket *vide* Maitland, *History and Survey of London*, p. 545.
[8] Evidence that some action was taken is afforded by six recognisances for acting a stage play for hire, S.R. June 1752. Somewhat similar is the much earlier recognisance of one Scudamore for "being a lewd person and keeping a certain booth for dancing on the ropes and other unlawful exercises in Well

other forms of amusement against which the more respectable magistrates set their faces were too often disreputable and degrading,[1] but unfortunately the campaign for their suppression was waged mainly in the belief that ordinary people should have no public entertainments and a purely negative attitude of this kind was hardly more defensible than successful.

As already shown, the restriction of drinking was one of the leading aims of the eighteenth-century movement for the reformation of manners. It possessed, however, a more permanent interest than other objects of that movement, being more directly connected with the sphere of law and order proper, so that it is still among the important pre-occupations of the magistracy. At first sight, it might be thought that the regulation of common alehouses or victualling houses, which existed "for poor people that are labouring men to refresh themselves after their work that cannot lay in stocks of their own and to entertain travellers in their passage on their lawful occasions",[2] was an essentially economic question but, though the victuallers' license[3] contained provisions against infringing the Assize of Bread and the like, there is little evidence that the magistrates concerned themselves with such aspects of the question. Then as now, they mainly feared, not that licensees would fall short of their proper functions, but that they would exceed them, by allowing excessive tippling, gaming and other amusements and disorders of a more flagrant kind. Licenses to keep common alehouses could, under the Act, 5 and 6 Edward VI, c. 25, be given by any two Justices,[4] and it is doubtful whether General and Quarter Sessions took over any of this work in Middlesex.[5] As in other

Close whereon he is an actor with other lewd persons his servants who use much obscene and profane language, by means whereof many idle persons do assemble, from whence proceed many tumults and disorders, to the great disturbance of "His Majesty's Peace" and that of John Greene, his servant, for "being an actor marvel", etc., S.R. Aug. 1670.
[1] Whitlocke Bulstrode felt strongly that plays and playhouses had degenerated from their original high purpose, Charge, Oct. 1722, p. 18.
[2] Charge of Whitlocke Bulstrode, April 1718.
[3] There are many copies of licenses among the unsorted papers at the Guildhall, as well as in classified sets.
[4] On the whole of this question, *vide* Webb, *History of Liquor Licensing*.
[5] There are usually lists of tipplers in the Sessions Books, but this may simply represent the registration of persons who actually entered into their

matters, the promiscuous—and at times conflicting—action of pairs of magistrates caused trouble, and the Court sought to establish a regular system of licensing sessions half a century before Parliament took the step. It laid down detailed provisions for a single licensing meeting in each hundred and forbade the Clerk of the Peace to issue licenses to persons who did not enter into recognisances there.[1] Naturally, an order of this kind could not hope to enjoy universal permanent respect, and there is continued evidence of conflicting action among licensing justices.[2] Still, an order of 1695 speaks of "the general renewing of licenses in the several divisions of this county",[3] as though that, and not sporadic grants, was the rule. Subsequently, Parliament incorporated the plan in the Act, 2 George II, c. 28, by insisting that licenses must be granted at general meetings of the Justices of each division to be held every September and the Court regarded this as confirming the *status quo*.[4] How thoroughly the fitness of applicants was normally investigated it is impossible to say, but the Court was careful on occasions, such as when it directed churchwardens, overseers and constables to attend licensing sessions with the names of those fit to be renewed or suppressed,[5] thereby anticipating a provision of the Act, 26 George II, c. 31.[6] Those who retailed ale and beer without license might be convicted by Justices out of Sessions, so that the indictments at Sessions, upon which there was a fine of 20*s.* payable to the poor, do not record more than a part of the proceedings actually taken, though they at least indicate that a good deal was done to prevent the breach of the law.[7] The

recognisances before local justices. For evidence of action by the latter, *vide* a petition from four St Pancras victuallers against the discontinuance of their licenses in S.B. April 1673, p. 36.

[1] S.B. Feb. 1674-5, p. 41.
[2] *Vide* S.B. May 1692, pp. 29, 35.
[3] S.B. Feb. 1694-5, p. 33. Similarly, from S.B. Dec. 1682, p. 43, we get the impression that there was a general renewing of licenses in March.
[4] O.C. vol. III, ff. 204-5.
[5] S.B. Feb. 1672-3, p. 42.
[6] In 1717, the Justices announced that licenses would not be granted to persons who had not taken the Oath of Allegiance, Webb, *op. cit.* p. 34 n.
[7] For receipts given by parish officers when the money was paid over, *vide* S.B. October 1664, p. 48; Oct. 1673, p. 49; etc. Doubtless the prosecutors were frequently parish officers, as, for instance, in the case of one Portland to answer the churchwarden of Stepney in S.R. May 1671. This may be

LAW AND ORDER

brewer who sold beer to an unlicensed victualler, over and above that necessary for himself and family, was, by the Act, 4 and 5 James I, c. 4, liable to a penalty of 6s. 8d. a barrel and, though cases under this head are not frequent, there are instances.[1] The Court's interest is shown by orders to constables to return the names of all sellers of ale and beer, so that the unlicensed may be detected,[2] and further by directions for special steps to be taken against particular offenders. In addition, it suppressed the licenses of those who, in its opinion, abused their position by permitting disorders, excessive tippling at unseasonable hours, entertaining the servants of neighbours, and the like.[3] It has been suggested that the early eighteenth century was a period of great laxity in licensing matters,[4] but this is hardly true of Middlesex. At least, the Justices had no idea of consciously pursuing a policy of laissez-faire. They were still ready to lay down careful regulations for the grant of licenses[5] and to punish illicit sellers.[6] It was certainly not for want of orders by the Court if the system was warped and, to a great extent, made valueless by the cupidity of justices' clerks, many of whom saw

attributed, not only to the desire to aid parochial finances by means of the fines, but also to the fear that the multiplication of alehouses would tend to multiply the poor. Hence the churchwardens and overseers of Ratcliff explained that they were so near Mile End that their poor frequented alehouses there, spending time and money, to the impoverishment of their hamlet, and the Court upheld the custom whereby the officers of all the Stepney hamlets searched in each others' territories to "find out all such who keep disorderly houses, or permit people to be tippling and drinking in their houses in time of Divine Service, or such who, thinking to evade punishment, do keep arbours and sheds on the back side of their houses, the better to obscure idle company in the time of Divine Service", S.B. July 1679, p. 55.
[1] E.g. the cases of Page and Gay in S.R. August 1671 and October and December 1743. The indictment for keeping a disorderly house may, on inspection, appear to be really for unlicensed ale selling, e.g. in S.R. Oct. 1719.
[2] S.B. July 1700, p. 42; September 1707, p. 42.
[3] E.g. S.B. Dec. 1671, pp. 35–6; July 1691, p. 56; Oct. 1691, p. 49. One Clerkenwell offender sought to escape detection by means of a drawbridge across the New River, over which he was in the habit of conveying his disorderly company when a search was in progress, but the stratagem did not save his license, S.Reg. vol. VIII, p. 169.
[4] Webb, *op. cit.* p. 15.
[5] E.g. in 1718, O.C. vol. I, ff. 28–9.
[6] S.R. May 1718, Oct. 1719, etc.

nothing in it but a source of revenue and asked nothing of the would-be victualler beyond the payment of a fee.[1]

During the second quarter of the eighteenth century, the Court was engaged in a struggle against the excessive drinking of gin and other spirituous liquors.[2] Parliament was at first disposed to encourage the production and consumption of home-distilled spirits in the interest of agriculture and of the national revenue, but later discovered its mistake and made desperate efforts to repress the habit it had fostered, though, even after the fatal consequences of excessive drinking had been widely canvassed, there were still some vacillations towards the earlier policy.[3] Our Justices were becoming anxious on the question as early as 1721[4] and Sir Daniel Dolins referred to the evil and to the need for legislative action in his charge at the October Sessions in 1725.[5] The Grand Jury made more than one presentment on the subject[6] and the Court held various enquiries into the circumstances and effects of the mania,[7] and petitioned the House of Commons for remedial measures.[8] The committees of justices that went into the matter painted gruesome pictures of the havoc wrought among the populace of the Metropolis—of the prevalence of drunkenness, impairment of health, unfitness for work, increase of poverty, begging and stealing and so on. They showed that Parliament's attempts to meet the evil through a system of licenses with heavy duties proved quite ineffective owing to the impossibility of preventing unlicensed selling, which was carried on by ordinary traders such as weavers and chandlers, and also by hawkers. The en-

---

[1] For this evil, and the elaborate regulations prescribed to combat it, vide especially O.C. vol. I, ff. 28–9. The Court was restricting such fees as early as 1694, S.B. Jan. 1693–4, p. 57.

[2] For fuller accounts of this episode, vide Webb, op. cit. p. 23 et seq.; George, London Life in the Eighteenth Century, p. 27 et seq.

[3] On the baneful effects of "the poison called gin", especially when consumed by the "most useful part of the people", vide especially Fielding, op. cit. section 2, and the Speech of Nathaniel Blackerby at a general meeting of Justices for Westminster on April 1st 1738.

[4] O.C. vol. I, f. 118.

[5] Charge, p. 31.

[6] E.g. in September 1735, O.C. vol. IV, f. 46. The Court ordered this to be printed in two newspapers.

[7] E.g. in 1726 and 1735, O.C. vol. III, ff. 41–3; vol. IV, ff. 54–7.

[8] E.g. in Feb. 1750–1, O.C. vol. V, f. 225.

forcement of the various laws was defeated by the interest which a large proportion of the peace officers had in the illicit traffic, by the cost of securing convictions and by the fact that the lawbreakers had a common fund for their defence and were not at all reluctant to employ force against those who informed.[1] The Court did all that it could by frequent orders for the stringent enforcement of the law. So anxious was it that nothing should stand in the way of this, that it sent a representation to the Duke of Newcastle (to be transmitted to the Council) against a magistrate who demanded fees from informers.[2] However, little improvement seems to have been achieved for some time as, in 1751, the Justices were still petitioning Parliament for further legislation.[3] The Act, 24 George II, c. 40, which may have been due to this application to Parliament, apparently opened an era of amelioration, but this belongs mainly to a period subsequent to that with which we are concerned.

Despite a prima facie appearance to the contrary, the question of recusancy forms a natural branch of the general subject of law and order, inasmuch as those who refused to conform to the Established Church were to a great extent punished for political reasons.[4] It is significant that Protestant Dissenters received a large measure of toleration immediately after the Revolution, when they became a support, rather than a danger, to the Government. During the first part of the period, however, they were looked upon with no favour by those in authority and various punitive acts were passed, more particularly against them. This may be illustrated by a case of the severe punishment of persons attending unlawful conventicles which occurred in 1664, when

---

[1] We even hear that churchwardens and overseers were in the habit of returning the poor's half of the £5 fine for selling without license on the ground that the offenders were poor, and the Court instituted precautions against this, O.C. vol. IV, ff. 106–7.
[2] O.C. vol. IV, ff. 107–8.
[3] O.C. vol. V, f. 225.
[4] On the whole question of the political implications of religious disunion, especially in publishing the divisions and weakness of the kingdom to foreign princes, vigorous presentments were made by the grand juries of the county and of Ossulston hundred in 1682, S.B. Dec. 1682, p. 41 *et seq*. For a recital by the Court that the peace was "daily endangered by the great resort of Papists and reputed Papists" in the county within ten miles of London, *vide* S.B. Sept. 1690, p. 41.

twelve people who had been convicted twice already were found guilty and sentenced to seven years' transportation to Jamaica.[1] Those indicted for recusancy might, of course, be either Catholic or Protestant, and no doubt people of both persuasions are involved in the numerous cases at this time. In 1674, Frances Beddingfield of the parish of Fulham was fined £180 for this offence[2] and at one Sessions about the same time well over 300 people were indicted for the same crime, most being convicted and fined upon their non-appearance.[3] Orders against both Catholic and Protestant recusants were especially vigorous during the disturbed last years of Charles II, when George Jeffreys, as Chairman of Sessions and otherwise, apparently exercised much influence on the Court.[4] Apart from the general stringent instructions to enforce the laws, it is interesting to note an unusual anxiety as to unlicensed schools at this time. The Justices, or some of them, would seem to have thought upon reflection that action had been too severe, or at least that such energy should not continue indefinitely. At all events, at the beginning of 1685, on discovering that there were in the New Prison for not taking the oath tendered to them a second time, seven persons who were poor and of peaceable behaviour (one of them had been in custody since 1681), and also that Mr Baxter and other dissenting preachers had been bound over to their good behaviour at several Sessions by direction of Lord Chief Justice Jeffreys, the Court instructed one of its members to ascertain from the Lord Chief Justice or Attorney-General whether the prisoners might be released and the recognisances discharged.[5] During these years we see that special pressure could be put upon alehouse-keepers by threatening to refuse licenses to those who neglected to receive the Sacrament and attended conventicles, while the religious orthodoxy of the

[1] S.B. Dec. 1664, pp. 29–31. The offenders had to pay the Sheriff his charges in carrying out the sentence.
[2] S.R. Jan. 1673–4. She was at the same time acquitted on a charge of keeping a school without license, but, as will appear shortly, her school attracted further attention.
[3] S.R. April 1674.
[4] S.B. Oct. 1681, pp. 43–5; Dec. 1682, pp. 41–3; Sept. 1684, p. 56; Jan. 1684–5, p. 50.
[5] S.B. Jan. 1684–5, p. 49.

LAW AND ORDER

poor could be encouraged by making relief conditional upon due observance of the law.[1] Thus there is plenty of evidence that the Court did not allow the church laws to lie idle, but a study of Quarter Sessions Records will not enable us to form a quantitative estimate of the amount of action taken, since much could be done by Justices out of Sessions. The summary method was easier and cheaper than that of indictment and was no doubt largely employed. Evidence of such proceedings is occasionally available, as in a series of convictions of one William Oyles for which £24 was levied upon him.[2] Another illustration is afforded by the appeal of Timothy ffly of Uxbridge against a conviction by Ralph Hawtry, J.P., the Justices being "doubtful whether the same ought to be received by them or not by reason of several errors and words of false Latin therein, as also whether they should receive a like appeal of William Kisten because the same is written in English".[3] After the Revolution, there are various signs of the new position of Protestant Dissenters. In particular, we find the names of teachers of Dissenting congregations entered in Sessions Books[4] and also entries of the meeting-places of such congregations.[5] The new toleration was not, of course, extended to Roman Catholics, who continued to suffer under the old laws and some new ones. Owing to the critical political situation, action against them was probably for a time more determined than before. Among new Acts passed, was one for the seizure of their horses[6] and the Justices gathered information under this head in 1690 and 1695, presumably with a view to carrying out the confiscation.[7] In addition, there is good ground for presuming that those who paid fines for refusing to take the appointed oaths or were committed in default were Catholics.[8] There was special fear of the influence of Rome in the neighbourhood of the capital and Papists were legally required to remove from within a radius of ten miles of London and West-

[1] S.B. Oct. 1681, p. 44; Dec. 1682, p. 43.
[2] S.B. April 1683, p. 45.
[3] S.B. Oct. 1670, p. 38. The problem was referred to the judges.
[4] E.g. S.B. Jan. 1690-1, p. 82.
[5] S.B. April 1692, p. 66.
[6] 1 William & Mary, c. 15.
[7] S.B. Sept. 1690, pp. 41-2; July 1695, p. 41.
[8] *Vide*, for such entries, S.B. Feb. 1694-5, p. 35.

minster. Among miscellaneous papers is a certificate of such removal, dated April 1696 and signed by magistrates. In December 1698 the Court was informed that a school for the education of young women in the Popish religion was kept in the house of Mrs Beddingfield at Hammersmith and that divers Popish priests sheltered in and near Hammersmith. It thereupon ordered the High Constable of Kensington to take steps to apprehend such women and suspected priests and bring them before one of His Majesty's Principal Secretaries of State to be proceeded against.[1] At the same time, it was disturbed by the information that many Popish priests were coming from abroad.[2] After the passage of a decade had dimmed the memory of James II and his pro-Catholic policy, the Justices appear to have ceased to initiate positive steps against the members of the hated church. Still, the hostility between England and France and the existence of the Pretenders did not allow them to forget their fears altogether. Whitlocke Bulstrode was keenly aware of the perils of Popery[3] and the preparations for the 1745 Jacobite Rising spurred the Court to send a loyal address to the King in which it laid much stress on the preservation of the Protestant religion.[4] The Lords of the Privy Council wrote to the Duke of Newcastle, *Custos Rotulorum*, requiring him to charge the Justices strictly to execute the laws against Papists and Non-Jurors,[5] and the readiness with which the Court issued instructions for this purpose shows that they did not consider that the penal laws against Roman Catholics should under all circumstances remain in abeyance.[6] Thus although Burn, writing at the end of our period, stated that "these laws in the present age have been permitted to sleep in a great measure",[7] the attitude of the Middlesex Justices shows—what is abundantly clear from the general history of the country—that hostility to, and fear of, Roman Catholics were very slow to die.

After the Revolution there is evidence of considerable interest in Sunday observance, and this continues to some extent

[1] S.B. Dec. 1698, p. 47.
[2] *Ibid.* p. 48.
[3] *Vide* the Preface to his Charge, April 1718.
[4] O.C. vol. v, f. 18, Feb. 1743-4.
[5] *Ibid.* f. 19.
[6] *Ibid.* f. 21.
[7] *Justice of the Peace*, p. 595.

LAW AND ORDER

right down to the end of the period.[1] On July 9th 1691, Queen Mary wrote to the Justices against the "profanation of the Lord's Day, by people travelling, selling or exposing anything to sale by exercise of their ordinary callings thereon or by using any other vain employment or sports, and especially by tippling thereon or on any part thereof, and neglecting the worship and service of God", and the Court ordered the Clerk of the Peace to have her letter printed and affixed to the great gates of Hicks Hall and to the church doors and other public places of each parish.[2] Shortly afterwards, the Court was informed, in this connection, that Sir Richard Bulkeley, Bart., had set up an office in Lincoln's Inn to superintend the action of the county justices, had several orders and warrants printed without lawful authority and, aided by Ralph Hartley, J.P., caused several unlawful convictions to be made.[3] It learned later, for instance, that one Francis Askew, distiller, had been distrained upon under a warrant for exercising his trade on the Lord's Day, although the nature of the offence was not specified and he was given no opportunity to answer the charge.[4] "Since that, by the rash and unadvised action of several persons, pretending great zeal, many illegal and irregular warrants of conviction have been issued out against a multitude of innocent persons for suffering tippling in their houses and exercising their ordinary callings on the Lord's Day, without summoning or hearing their defences, whereby it might appear whether they were works of charity or necessity", and "to the end that so religious an intention may not miscarry", the Justices resolved to encourage all legal informations, to deliver summonses without charge and to go in person upon searches.[5] Further orders on the same subject were issued

[1] For an earlier case, *vide* the recognisance of a schoolmaster named Manby for using the trade of a barber on the Lord's Day in Shoreditch, S.R. Jan. 1671–2. For later references, *vide* the Charge of Whitlocke Bulstrode, Oct. 1718, p. 5, and that of Sir D. Dolins, Oct. 1726, p. 39.
[2] S.B. July 1691, p. 78.   [3] S.B. Oct. 1691, p. 53.
[4] S.B. Dec. 1691, p. 50. The Justices unanimously decided to petition the Commissioners of the Great Seal to put Ralph Hartley out of the Commission of the Peace, *ibid*. p. 58.
[5] S.B. Jan. 1691–2, p. 57. For a fine of 5s. for using the art of a gardener and selling produce on Sunday, *vide* S.R. May 1693. For indictments (without judgment) for uttering beer, and for tippling during Divine Service, *vide* S.R. April 1691 and May 1693.

within the next decade,[1] one being in response to a proclamation by Queen Anne, and Sunday observance was one of the pious and virtuous practices which it was sought to encourage under the Hanoverians.[2] The continued vitality, though ill enforcement, of the Sabbath laws was clearly revealed in 1734. Several butchers[3] informed the Court that, for some years past, they had entered into agreements to prevent the profanation of the Lord's Day by the sale of meat. They had expended money in convicting offenders, but had failed to achieve their object, for there was "every Sunday morning, and oftentimes all the day, a certain market kept and great quantities of meat publicly set forth and exposed to sale and sold by divers butchers in Turnmill Street, in the parish of Clerkenwell, in the time of divine service", to their great prejudice and to the annoyance of the inhabitants going to church. The petitioners complained that officers were negligent and that there was no indictment for this offence, only forfeiture of the goods sold, and they were consequently unable to stop the evil. The Court therefore directed the Justices of Finsbury to execute the laws and report back their action.[4] The offenders appear to have fought hard for their freedom, but, about 1740, the Court decided that they could be indicted,[5] and a Committee of Justices evidently thought that, by 1746, this offence had been checked, though certainly not altogether stopped. This committee was appointed in response to a petition from barbers, on lines very similar to the butchers' complaint just noted, and it reviewed at great length the arguments for and against the laws in question. Its conclusion was definitely favourable to them and, in particular, it dismissed the contention that many people were not paid in time to obtain their provisions

[1] S.B. Aug. 1700, p. 46; April 1702, p. 21.
[2] *Vide* Sir D. Dolins, Charge in Oct. 1725, p. 29 *et seq.*, and Charge in Oct. 1726, p. 39.
[3] For Whitlocke Bulstrode's objection to Sunday trading by butchers, in various markets, *vide* his Charge, Oct. 1718, p. 5.
[4] O.C. vol. IV, f. 4.
[5] O.C. vol. V, f. 100. In Jan. 1739–40, seven persons, including six butchers, were indicted, as common Sabbath breakers, three being fined 13*s.* 4*d.*; one, 6*s.* 8*d.*; and one, 20*s.* At the Sessions in May and August following, six bills against butchers were not found, S.R. Jan. 1739–40, May and August. 1740.

on Saturday night. It pointed out that retailers who had scruples were forced by competition to put them aside, and it thought that the laws were in the interest of all parties.[1] The Court endorsed its findings,[2] and so placed itself definitely on the side of the legal *status quo*.

The foregoing paragraphs fall far short of constituting an exhaustive description of the action of Quarter Sessions in supervising morals, manners and religion. Magistrates were, for instance, anxious to suppress swearing, blasphemy and atheism, as well as the grosser personal vices. What has been said, however, brings out the more prominent features of their policy and, moreover, shows it controlling those parts of private conduct that are most closely connected with the maintenance of external order. We cannot believe that this part of the Justices' work was particularly successful, and much of it clearly failed utterly. From a modern standpoint, not a little of this failure would seem desirable rather than otherwise, but an administrative system must be judged by the objects it sets out to achieve. Although we must attach due weight to the lessened disposition to enforce many laws and though it is not easy to form definite conclusions, our study does suggest a verdict of inefficiency.

[1] O.C. vol. v, f. 100. [2] *Ibid.* f. 102.

CHAPTER III

THE POOR LAW

CONSIDERING the amount of work already done on the subject, alike by modern and older historians, it could hardly be expected that the study of the Middlesex records would throw any very striking new light upon the working of the Old Poor Law. From a very large mass of tedious matter, it is difficult to disentangle much of real interest. Still, no account of the work of Quarter Sessions could be complete without a discussion of a problem which occupied an immense amount of the Justices' time and thought and, though there is little that is new to relate, there is perhaps still value in an account of the extent, manner and duration of the execution of the various branches of the laws relating to the poor in a county such as Middlesex.

The Tudor poor law system was destined to stand or fall largely by its success or failure in solving the problem of employing the able-bodied poor, a problem which was, to a great extent, new in the sixteenth century. The solution attempted was in the event a complete failure, and in this weakness, more than in any other, lay the seeds of the ultimate decay of the whole structure. In this sphere, in particular, the inadequacy of the parochial unit and of amateur management is patent, yet these were of the essence of the system. True, Tudor statesmen could not be expected to foresee the destruction of the central control upon which they placed so much reliance, but no council could have imbued the inexperienced and annually changing officers of a multitude of parishes with enough zeal and insight to cope with a problem which still awaits a real solution.

We cannot be surprised to find that the indications of parochial employment of the able-bodied are scanty. Had the churchwardens and overseers been seriously attending to their duty to set the able-bodied poor on work, we should expect to find evidence of the fact in the parochial accounts which were constantly submitted to Quarter Sessions by officers claiming payment of arrears and by parishioners appealing against over-

THE POOR LAW

rating or malversation. The accounts are not set out in full, but we should expect to hear something of the expense of purchasing the stock of wool, flax, hemp, iron and other stuff, and of the profits arising from the sale of articles manufactured. Such items are, however, not mentioned.[1] Parish out-work on a large scale was so impracticable that workhouses had to be instituted by those who seriously tackled the problem. Most of these were of comparatively late origin and attributable to the influence of eighteenth-century reformers, but at least one Middlesex parish took early steps in this direction, despite the obvious obstacles to such an undertaking in so small a unit.[2]

The Court did not try to stimulate the parochial provision of work, less, it would seem, from lethargy, than from the consciousness of the hopelessness of the system as Elizabeth had left it, since, quite early in the period, the Justices took part in an attempt to organise employment over a wider area and, in so doing, anticipated an expedient which later came much into vogue.[3] The problem of vagrancy was naturally acute in the years immediately following the Restoration, and this drew attention to that of employment. Hence the Act of 1662,[4] whose most famous provisions concerned settlement, attributed existing evils partly to defective provision of employment and, while emphasising the normal duty of the parish to provide work, made provision for a special corporation for the area in which the Government was most directly interested and in which the difficulties were probably at their maximum. On May 9th 1661, a proclamation against rogues and vagabonds was issued, directing, among other things, that penalties for drunk-

---

[1] For a single late exception in connection with the parish of St George's, *vide* S.B. Sept. 1755, p. 69.

[2] The Churchwardens and Overseers of St Clement Danes petitioned the Court that their poor were very numerous and many of them fit to be set on work. They had begun to build a workhouse, but needed £400 more to complete it, and asked for a rate to raise that amount. The Court, well liking the project, complied with their request, but it seems unlikely that the house was completed, S.B. Jan. 1661–2, p. 31. Later we have references to workhouses at St Giles' in the Fields (O.C. vol. 1, ff. 93–4), Shadwell (S.B. June 1731, pp. 55–6), Ealing (S.B. April 1733, pp. 67–9), St Luke's (S.B. Oct. 1737, p. 39), St George's (S.B. Sept. 1755, p. 69), etc.

[3] For these later schemes, *vide* Webb, *The Old Poor Law*, chap. III.

[4] 14 Charles II, c. 12.

enness should go towards buying stock to employ the poor.[1] This came before the Middlesex Justices at their October Sessions, when two Justices were detailed to confer with the Lord Mayor and other Justices of London and Westminster as to its execution.[2] Probably as a result of this conference, there was introduced into the House of Commons, on January 17th following, a "Bill for the Better Relief and Employment of the Poor and the Punishment of Vagrants and other disorderly persons within the Cities of London and Westminster, and the Liberties thereof, and the Bills of Mortality".[3] Perhaps the main object of this measure was to confirm the authority of the Corporation within the City of London, which had been founded in 1647, but the Act, like the recourse to the conference just mentioned, witnesses to a perception that the problem was wider than the City limits. The adoption of the Corporation scheme in Middlesex may be traced partly to the example of London and partly, perhaps, to the influence of Sir Matthew Hale, who possibly inspired another bill, introduced about the same time, for the establishment of similar corporations in all the towns of England and Wales.[4] In the event, the latter more general project was dropped and, in the single Act which emerged as the result of the deliberations of Parliament on these and two other measures submitted to it, the innovation was confined to London and Westminster and the district on both sides of the Thames within the Weekly Bills of Mortality. For this area one or more corporations were to be established and, for the parts within the Counties of Middlesex and Surrey, Quarter Sessions were empowered to nominate the officers—a president, deputy-president, treasurer and assistants—to take their accounts, to raise money from the parishes not exceeding the amount of the poor rate in any one year and to approve their orders and by-laws. The Corporation was to apprehend rogues and vagabonds and set them to work, but, over and above this, Quarter Sessions might signify to the Privy Council the names of those fit to be transported.

[1] *Cal. S.P. Dom.* May 9th 1661.   [2] S.Reg. vol. VIII, p. 208.
[3] Webb, *op. cit.* p. 325; Journals of the House of Commons, Jan. 17th 1662.   [4] Webb, *op. cit.* p. 325.

THE POOR LAW

In July 1662, our Justices appointed a committee to consider how this Act might best be executed,[1] and, doubtless upon its recommendation, ordered "that from henceforth there be one Corporation settled in this County within the parishes mentioned in the Weekly Bills of Mortality consisting of a President, a deputy to the President, Treasurer and Assistants for the said Corporation, that there be likewise three workhouses within the same places for the employing and setting the poor to work". The Earl of Southampton was appointed President, Edwin Rich, Esq., Deputy-President, and Humphrey Weld, Esq., Treasurer, and every Justice of the Peace was to present six or more fitting persons to be assistants.[2] To all appearance, only one workhouse took shape, that at Clerkenwell, but it was on a large scale, for in January 1662-3 the President and Governors of the Corporation certified to the Court that they required the sum of eighteen thousand eight hundred pounds, "for building twelve thousand pounds, for materials of hemp and wool to work upon two thousand pounds, for implements of household and household stuff two thousand five hundred pounds, for tools and implements to work withal eight hundred pounds, and for officers' and servants' wages for a year from Lady Day next fifteen hundred pounds". Thereupon the Court voted £3980. 5s. 3d., setting out specific amounts for the various places within the area concerned.[3] Clearly, the institution had been planned on an ambitious scale as, from the exalted position of its leaders and patrons, we should expect. The building must have been completed within little more than a year as the next assessment desired by the President and Governors was only for "furnishing of the new workhouse at Clerkenwell with materials and provision of clothing and victuals and for a stock to employ the number of six hundred poor at work and maintenance of a hundred aged and blind persons uncapable to labour".[4] This is surprising, seeing that less than four thousand pounds had been assessed and probably still less actually collected. We can only conclude that the plan had been whittled down.[5]

[1] S.B. July 1662, p. 16. [2] *Ibid.*
[3] S.B. Jan. 1662-3, pp. 28-31. [4] S.B. April 1664, p. 31.
[5] The *Account of the General Nursery or College of Infants* published in 1686 put the cost of building at £5000.

The collection of the Corporation's funds under the orders of the Court rested with the officers of the various parishes, and we find evidence of slackness and obstruction in this quarter,[1] especially towards the end, when St Giles' without Cripplegate and St Andrew's, Holborn, proved very refractory, partly, perhaps, because the Corporation was being wound up.[2] The tardiness of collection and payment is emphasised by the fact that the Act 22 and 23 Charles II, c. 18, laid down that all moneys assessed since March 1st 1665 should be paid over by September 29th 1671. This implies an insufficiency of coercive power which must have been a serious embarrassment to the Corporation. And there was slackness also within the Corporation itself, for in January 1664-5 the Court was informed that the work was being carried on by a few only of those entrusted with it, as many of the assistants had seldom or never found leisure to afford their advice.[3]

By contrast, the Corporation, in answer to a petition, received ready royal patronage and encouragement. On January 12th 1664-5, the King wrote to the President and Governors, referring to their petition "in the behalf of the good and public work which hath been intrusted to you by us and our Parliament for the setting of the poor on work, of the preventing the many evils which have arisen in our government for want thereof, we are so well pleased with the endeavour you have already employed, and the good affection and forwardness we find you have for perfecting that useful work, that we have resolved by ourself and our ministry (*sic*) you all manner of encouragement and assistance in the prosecution thereof, and whilst we think fit to approve and commend the industry and the charity of such as have attended and advanced this work to so hopeful a degree and condition, we cannot but take notice of the backwardness and neglect of those who, having been joined with you, do yet

---

[1] *Vide* two prosecutions for not collecting sums in S.B. July 1663, pp. 7-8. In April 1664 it was found necessary to order overseers to collect arrears and to stipulate that none could be discharged from their offices until they had paid them over or shown cause to the contrary, S.B. April 1664, p. 30.

[2] S.B. June 1670, p. 42; June 1671, p. 27. In July 1671, the late churchwardens of St Giles' were indicted for not collecting certain sums and one of them was fined 3*s*. 4*d*. upon confession, S.R. July 1671.

[3] S.B. Jan. 1664-5, p. 29.

withdraw themselves from bearing their part in a duty, whose success cannot but conduce even to their private benefit and advantage".[1] At the same time, he wrote to the Middlesex Justices, requiring them to give the Corporation all possible countenance.[2] Two days later there followed a more tangible token of interest. Under the date, January 14th 1663-4, we read: "His Majesty expresses himself to be perfectly well satisfied with the care and industry of those worthy persons who have taken pains in the good and pious work expressed in this petition, and as much dislikes the remissness of those who have withdrawn their hands from it. And for a better mark of his own royal intention to encourage it, hath appointed the Lord Treasurer to furnish one thousand pounds to it, as a beginning and earnest of what he means to do further hereafter for the advancement, recommending it in the like manner to all honourable and charitable persons to follow his royal example herein, according to their respective abilities".[3]

Upon the internal affairs of the Corporation, it is unfortunately not possible to glean much information. As already seen, it had been originally planned to accommodate six hundred able-bodied and one hundred impotent poor, and the building erected is styled "large" in an order of a later date,[4] though, as already shown, it seems unlikely that the scheme was carried out in its entirety. A representation of the President and Governors speaks of "those of a better and more ingenious condition employed in the several manufactures",[5] and evidently their products included sail-cloth and canvas.[6] The difficulty of making such work remunerative has been too often proved to need elaboration here and, from a retrospective survey, we gather that our corporation was handicapped, as compared with the similar institution in the City of London, by the fact that the

[1] S.P. Dom. Charles II, Entry Book 17, p. 2.
[2] *Ibid.* p. 3. [3] Entry Book 18, p. 3.
[4] S.B. June 1679, p. 35. [5] S.B. Jan. 1664-5, p. 29.
[6] Among the Admiralty papers for 1666, we find Francis Pointz of Holborn tendering Bridewell sail-cloth at 1s. 6d. per yard—Cal. S.P. Dom. 1666-7, p. 390. Earlier, in a letter to the Navy Commissioners, John Harris adjudged Mr Pointz's canvas worth 1s. 6d. and 12d. the yard, not considering the rise in price from the present scarcity of canvas, Cal. S.P. Dom. March 1st 1665-6.

county had no charities to supplement the income derived from the sale of products.[1] Even so, considering that Quarter Sessions was empowered to raise funds for it equal to the annual poor rate of the parishes covered, the Corporation's task in maintaining its solvency does not, on the face of it, appear very formidable.

Its position was, however, seriously shaken by the Great Plague of 1665. This impoverished the district from which its external revenues were derived, and the pestilence removed all or most part of the master workmen and all but fifty-six out of about one hundred and thirty poor belonging to the House.[2] It consequently wholly frustrated an agreement made by the President and Governors with one Francis Pointz of Holborn, the nature of which remains obscure. From a maintenance dispute we learn that he had undertaken to look to the poor in the Clerkenwell Workhouse, whom he was to receive under warrant of two Justices,[3] and he also had the disposal of the produce of the inmates' labour.[4] Seemingly, then, he was in some way farming the establishment, but whether this was a temporary arrangement owing to the Plague crisis it is impossible to say. The precarious position of the institution led the Court to approve proposals made by certain unnamed persons of eminent quality, who offered to raise privately a stock to maintain it without charge to the county.[5] It does not seem that these proposals came to fruition, as the President and Governors themselves continue to submit accounts to Quarter Sessions.[6] It is probable that the Corporation never recovered its balance after the Plague catastrophe, and its doom was sealed by Parliament in the Act, 22 and 23 Charles II, c. 18, which significantly makes no allusion to its productive work. This Act reduced the legal annual assessment upon parishes to one-fourth of their poor rate and provided that no further sums should be raised after September 29th 1675. In view of the previous financial condition of the Corporation, this was clearly tantamount to a

[1] S.B. Feb. 1705–6, p. 38. [2] S.Reg. vol. IX, pp. 317–19.
[3] S.B. April 1669, p. 40. [4] *Vide* p. 49, n, 6.
[5] S.Reg. vol. IX, pp. 317–19.
[6] S.B. July 1671, pp. 33, 49; Oct. 1672, p. 50. Unfortunately the accounts are never set out.

THE POOR LAW

deferred dissolution.[1] At all events, the result was that, in submitting its accounts in October 1672, the Corporation tendered the surrender of its authority and rights[2] which was later accepted.[3]

The failure of this scheme did not permanently discourage our Justices. Within seven years, we find them again active in the matter of employing the poor, and this, so far as we know, on their own initiative. Their attention would be drawn to the matter by the fact that, owing to the burning down of the New Prison, they were obliged to convert part of the Corporation Workhouse into a temporary prison. Very likely some of those who had borne the expense of its erection protested against this appropriation, and the Court felt obliged to do something to further the original object of the institution by ordering that the residue of the buildings should be used for setting to work the poor of the parishes within the Bills of Mortality, "and more especially for the making of shoes and stockings to be sent into His Majesty's plantations and other places in parts beyond seas, by which means this Court conceives the said parishes will be very much eased of their said poor, the native commodity of this kingdom will be consumed, the manufacture promoted and the said plantations will be supplied with useful commodities and His Majesty's Customs thereby very much advanced".[4] The plurality of aim here contemplated betrays a refreshing optimism. The urban parishes were evidently again the main interest, and the problem of the increasing burden of pauperism was seen to be common to them and to the City of London. The Lord Mayor and Aldermen desired to consult the Justices as to how to set the poor on work, in order to ease the parishes and discourage pauperism, and a committee was appointed to confer

[1] The proviso in the Act that auditing Justices should be non-governors suggests a suspicion of irregular practices.
[2] S.B. Oct. 1672, p. 50.
[3] Under the Act of 1662, the City of Westminster established one or more Corporations on similar lines, about which the City Records furnish some information. The Act, 22 and 23 Charles II, c. 18, which deprived the Middlesex Corporation of its revenue from rates, expressly exempted that of St Margaret's, Westminster, from this virtual dissolution, but this undertaking does not appear to have survived longer than 1678.
[4] S.B. June 1679, p. 35.

4-2

with the City authorities.[1] Evidently this conference did not solve the difficulty, as the Court next sent a deputation to the Committee of Council on Trade and Plantations "in order to the maturing of some good method for setting the poor to work upon the native commodities of England and for transporting the same, ready wrought, to some of His Majesty's foreign plantations and other places, that the said poor may in some measure relieve themselves and ease those who now relieve them and yet not injure those of the same trades here in England".[2] As a result, Secretary Jenkins wrote to the Middlesex Justices on April 15th 1681 that, according to their petition, His Majesty had appointed a committee of Privy Council to treat with their committee as to the execution of 43 Elizabeth.[3] The following day the Justices appointed another committee to attend the Committee of Council,[4] but it does not appear that any good came of these negotiations. Certainly the Corporation Workhouse was not, for any length of time, restored to its original use, as it was shortly afterwards suggested for the accommodation of French Protestant refugees,[5] and was later leased by Sir Thomas Rowe for the foundation of a school for poor children.[6]

During the following three-quarters of a century, we find no trace of any attempt by our Quarter Sessions to organise work for the unemployed in order to fill the void left by parochial administration, although the need for some such provision was widely recognised. Thus the old law and the old administrative framework were in this respect a complete failure and left a clear field for the reformers and philanthropists of the time.

Destitute children must always form one of the main concerns of any poor law authority. Their management is of special interest in that here, more than in any other branch of the system, there is scope for a really constructive policy. The transformation of the child pauper into a self-supporting adult worker is an ideal so obvious that it is difficult to see how it could altogether fail to attract even the most perfunctory administrators, while the

---

[1] S.B. Aug. 1679, p. 49.　　　　　[2] S.B. Oct. 1680, p. 49.
[3] Cal. S.P. Dom. April 15th 1681.　　[4] S.B. April 1681, p. 48.
[5] Cal. S.P. Dom. Nov. 12th 1681; S.B. Dec. 1681, pp. 48–9.
[6] *Vide* p. 59.

THE POOR LAW

difficulties are less serious than in the case of adult pauperism. On the other hand, juveniles are more susceptible to oppression and neglect, and consequently fall an easier prey to greedy, tyrannous or negligent officers. Their treatment is therefore a particularly good test of any poor law administration.

The first duty of the parish was, of course, to maintain its destitute children and, as usual, there was the correlative obligation of the Justices of Peace, in and out of Sessions, to enforce that duty. The children themselves were hardly in a position to make their voices heard, so that we do not find the stream of petitions for relief which we have from adults, but rather quarrels between various possible sources of relief—between the parish and the relatives of the child, or between one parish and another.[1] The Court is constantly called upon to decide such disputes, but the decisions fall more conveniently into the categories of maintenance or settlement. What we are here concerned to ascertain is the attitude of the Justices to the kind and manner of relief given by parishes, and the general policy, if any, governing that attitude. In strictness, we should distinguish two classes of child paupers: those with parents who remained responsible for them but lacked the means to maintain them, and those who, through the death or desertion of their parents, had been cast entirely upon the parish. The position of the former is inextricably bound up with that of their parents who, in their petitions for relief, always make much of their family responsibilities. The Court, if it sees fit to comply with their requests, does not make any special provision for the children, but relies upon the parents to make proper use of the assistance given. The Justices did not generally concern themselves as to the way in which these children were maintained, and we may therefore concentrate our attention upon those for whom the parish was immediately responsible.

The younger ones were normally put out to nurse, and we do not find the Court objecting to this method in principle or seeking to compel parish officers to provide a common establishment for their reception. Its most constant concern with the

---

[1] But no doubt local Justices would frequently make orders upon their own observation or common report.

matter arose from the flow of petitions from nurses who had not been paid their allowances.[1] All that was here necessary was, in case of doubt, to refer the matter for enquiry to some local Justices,[2] or, if the case was clearly made out, to order payment.[3] A parish officer who thereafter refused to pay the arrears might be committed to prison.[4] The Court does not stop to ask how the children have been maintained; it merely looks to the contract into which the parish has entered. Its further attention was, however, arrested in 1694 by the conviction of one Mary Compton for starving and murdering several parish children put to nurse with her. The trouble appears to have been due to the fact that parish officers had been putting out their children for lump sums, so that the nurses could make substantial profits by speedily disposing of their charges, while the parishes would have no further interest in them. The Court forbade this practice in April 1694,[5] laying down that payments must be by the week or month. It further ordered churchwardens and overseers to make lists of all their children, stating where they were at nurse, what was paid for their maintenance, how many died, when and where they were buried, etc., and to deliver these lists to the Clerk of the Peace at each Easter Sessions. Such data would have enabled the Justices to maintain a very close supervision of parochial administration in this connection; but there is no evidence that, when the immediate scandal had passed over, they continued their vigilance.

The provision of maintenance was only a temporary expedient, and there remained the task of fitting the child for after life. This was attempted through the system of apprenticeship.[6]

[1] One such petition among the Miscellaneous Papers, c. 1698, states that the child had been put to nurse at 1s. 6d. per week and 2s. 6d. per quarter for clothes.
[2] E.g. S.B. Oct. 1679, p. 68.
[3] E.g. S.B. July 1675, pp. 25–6. In S.B. July 1699 (p. 35) the churchwardens and overseers of St James's, Westminster, were ordered to pay forty-five nurses sums amounting to £35. 9s. 6d.
[4] E.g. S.B. May 1673, p. 53.   [5] S.B. April 1694.
[6] Miss Dunlop and Mr Denman, in their *English Apprenticeship and Child Labour*, chap. XVI, distinguish parish apprenticeship from ordinary apprenticeship on the ground that the former was intended to provide maintenance rather than training. The educational aspect of the system, however, certainly cannot be ignored, cf. Dalton, *Country Justice*, p. 94.

THE POOR LAW

By this means, the child would begin to maintain itself by its own labour (though an initial premium was sometimes paid) and, it was hoped, would learn some useful occupation which would be an equipment for after life. Parish officers did not require any encouragement to adopt this method of relieving themselves of their burdens, but many of them undoubtedly needed direction as to the sort of masters and trades to which the children should be apprenticed if the real object of the system was to be achieved. We do not find the Justices prescribing any general rules to be followed nor, from their decisions on specific cases, do we gather that they paid very much attention to the future prospects of the apprentice. These cases do, however, shed light on the working of the system. Parish children were legally apprenticed until the age of twenty-four,[1] and, to all seeming, this provision was generally observed,[2] so that, character apart, they were more profitable to their masters than ordinary seven-year apprentices. Still, a premium was sometimes paid at the time of binding, the amount, when stated, usually being about five pounds.[3] As will appear later on, the officers could compel masters in their own parishes to take poor children, so that a premium was necessary only when the master belonged to some other parish, but the officers were encouraged to seek out such masters by the principle of settlement by apprenticeship. The method of paying lump sums as premiums would, to some extent, be open to abuses similar to those already noticed in connection with nurse children, so that, whether the master was compelled or bribed to relieve the parish of its juvenile charge, the latter could not expect very considerate treatment at his hands. Apprentices would generally be older and more able to take care of themselves than the children who were merely put out to nurse, while their masters would, in their labour, have an incentive at least to keep them alive. It does not appear that this interest always carried them much further. Indeed, the apprentice was not even sure of continued maintenance, but was liable

---

[1] This was the age for boys. Girls were to be bound until the age of twenty-one or marriage, 43 and 44 Elizabeth, c. 2.
[2] There are instances in S.B. Jan. 1664–5, p. 45; Sept. 1693, p. 57; etc.,
[3] E.g. S.B. Jan. 1708, pp. 45–9.

to be deserted and left destitute, as were James May, apprenticed to a mariner by the churchwardens of Limehouse, William Martin, bound to a tailor by St Botolph's without Aldgate, and Francis Blady, bound to a leather-dresser by Holborn.[1] In such cases, there was nothing to be done but to dissolve the bond in the hope of being able to place out the apprentice afresh.

One suspects that a good many parish apprentices would have been quite pleased to be deserted. We shall see that many ordinary apprentices had no easy or comfortable life, and children put out by parishes were clearly in a much worse condition, since they often lacked friends to complain on their behalf, especially if they were sent to a distance, while the surviving remnant of supervision by guilds and companies afforded them no protection.[2] We hear a good deal of cruelty to such children and find the Court not infrequently obliged to release them from their servitude.[3] The officers of the child's parish sometimes made the application, but they would clearly only be sufficiently interested to do so under special circumstances. Thus in one case of such a petition from the Overseers of Chelsea, the child, after repeated ill-treatment, had run away and again become chargeable to them.[4] In case the child absconded or was likely to do so, they would, if they had paid a premium, be anxious to recover all or part of it. Although it had no explicit legal authority to do so,[5] the Court did, at times, order masters to repay such money.[6] Where the child had been sent to a distance, and usually also where he had not, there was no hope of such intervention, and the only remedies were the hazardous expedient of unauthorised flight and the no less dubious undertaking of a personal application to Sessions. Under these circumstances, it cannot be doubted that a majority of the worst cases of

---

[1] S.B. Sept. 1692, p. 54; Aug. 1733, pp. 84-5; Dec. 1747, p. 37.

[2] Dunlop and Denman, *English Apprenticeship and Child Labour*, p. 253.

[3] Of the apprenticeship discharges by the Middlesex Sessions given by Mrs George in Appendix IV to her *London Life in the Eighteenth Century* (pp. 421-2), Nos. 24 and 26 show parish children bound respectively to a victualler and a pump-maker being discharged for cruelty.

[4] S.B. Jan. 1750-51, p. 35. In S.R. June 1671 we have the recognisance of Ann Tarling to answer the Churchwarden of Limehouse "for giving her apprentice, Diana Jeager, immoderate and unlawful correction".

[5] *Vide* p. 141.   [6] E.g. a fisherman in S.B. July 1707, p. 55.

oppression never reached the ear of the law. The Act, 20 George II, c. 19, met the case to some extent by empowering two Justices to discharge parish apprentices, thus bringing redress nearer home; but the later history of the system shows that this was an entirely inadequate safeguard. The worst abuses of the practice of sending cart-loads of parish children to the northern manufacturing districts do not fall within our period, but it is clear that, from the point of view of the children, there was already much to be said against the system.

In view of the dangers to which parish apprentices were exposed, and the length of time for which they were bound, it is easy to understand the reluctance to enter such service. Hence, if the system was to work at all, compulsory powers were essential. No doubt the mere refusal to maintain children of suitable age would often be sufficient, while poor orphans could offer little resistance; but by 43 and 44 Elizabeth, c. 2, all children chargeable to the parish were apprenticeable and coercion was at times required in the case of those with parents. Accordingly, in May 1715 and July 1718,[1] the Court made pensions to parents conditional on their allowing their children to be apprenticed. In the latter of these cases, the children were to be twelve years old and, generally, we infer that the Justices saw danger in apprenticing very young children.[2] Although parish apprentices were bound for an exceptionally long term, their general character clearly made masters far from eager to receive them. The Act, 43 Elizabeth, c. 2, gave no explicit authority to compel masters to take them, but was interpreted as giving it by implication.[3] Such an interpretation was, however, open to dispute. Hale, in fact, stated in clear terms that the Act provided "for the putting of poor children apprentices; but no compulsory for any to receive them".[4] Hence we cannot be surprised to find that some intended masters questioned the right of parishes to foist their

[1] S.B. May 1715, p. 60; July 1718, pp. 59–61.
[2] In the Westminster Book for July 1718 we find the Justices discharging a boy apprenticed by St Martin's in the Fields to a chimney-sweep at the age of five and a half.
[3] "All persons of ability are compellable to take apprentices according to this Statute", Dalton, *Country Justice*, p. 95.
[4] Quoted by Burn, *History of the Poor Laws*, p. 141.

children upon them, especially as, even if the general principle of compulsion were admitted, it could only operate within certain limits, which parish officers would at times transgress. Hence we find the Court deciding such cases, when parish officers seek to coerce unwilling masters, or masters appeal against being compelled to take undesired children.[1] Although in 1664, under the direction of the Lord Chief Justice, the Court ordered that any master refusing to take a child duly put to him should be bound to appear at the Gaol Delivery,[2] the law continued to be questioned until the Act, 8 and 9 William III, c. 30, explicitly affirmed the obligation to receive parish apprentices under penalty of ten pounds to the poor. The officers of Mile End exercised this authority with excessive zeal and at one Sessions the appeals of ten masters to whom they had bound children were allowed.[3] If the child could be proved to be morally unfit, the Court would excuse the master,[4] and it was always willing to listen to charges of definite misconduct against apprentices who had actually been received into service, and such proceedings throw light on some of the drawbacks of the system from the master's standpoint.[5]

Our records do not, from their nature, warrant a final judgment on the system of parochial responsibility for destitute children, but they certainly illustrate some of the defects of the haphazard arrangements practised during our period. In the light of general considerations and later experience, we cannot but conclude that there was a widespread failure to provide either suitable maintenance during childhood or adequate training for after life. There was therefore ample scope for supplementary action by the Justices of Peace. We find no

[1] *Vide* the recognisance of John Bening of Tottenham to answer the churchwardens for refusing to take a parish child put to him with the assent of two Justices, S.R. Feb. 1663-4. He alleged that the child was diseased and under ten years of age, and the Court accepted the objection in principle, ordering him to take the child if ten years old, otherwise some other boy of that age, or failing that, a girl, S.B. April 1664, p. 27.
[2] S.B. April 1664, p. 27.
[3] S.B. Jan. 1700-1, pp. 43-5. For an unsuccessful attempt by a goldsmith to escape the obligation, *vide* S.B. Jan. 1718-19, p. 57.
[4] E.g. in the case of a girl of notorious character, S.B. Sept. 1699, p. 51.
[5] *Vide*, for instance, the complaints of a fringe-maker named Carrington, and a victualler named Dickenson, S.B. Sept. 1690, p. 55; Jan. 1671-2, p. 31.

THE POOR LAW

evidence that in Middlesex they did much to direct parochial administration in the matter and only one instance of an attempt by them to provide an alternative system. This, however, was an interesting experiment.

In January 1683-4, the Grand Jury presented that "some consideration may be taken for the relief of the poor besides the provision made by the Statute of the 43 Elizabeth, the poor growing very numerous, especially by the water side by the accidents of the sea, (insomuch that the inhabitants are not able to relieve them) either by an hospital for the providing for and educating of seamen's children for sea service, which His Majesty hath been graciously pleased to encourage, or by such other ways as shall be thought meet ".[1] This may have suggested the idea of a county school for poor children which was evolved by Sir Thomas Rowe, one of the Justices. In July 1685, he took a lease from the county of part of the disused Corporation Workhouse[2] and, with some others, fitted it up "at great charge "[3] as a nursery or college for poor children. We read that the Justices "having observed great inconveniences from the loose way of breeding up of parish children, whereby very few of them come to good ", ordered "a great part of the Corporation Workhouse at Clerkenwell for their reception, and the same is fitted up for that purpose, and excellent rules and methods are there taken for their education in true religion and virtue, and the care thereof is committed to Sir Thomas Rowe". The Court therefore ordered the officers of the urban parishes of Middlesex and the City of Westminster to send specified numbers of children[4] and issued other orders commending it to the Justices of the Tower Hamlets[5] and also to the Justices of the rural divisions.[6] The new institution appears to have earned very wide approval, though the officers of St Clement Danes resisted the order to send children, on the ground that they themselves could make provision more cheaply.[7]

[1] S.B. Jan. 1683-4, p. 29.   [2] S.B. July 1685, p. 61.
[3] S.B. April 1686, p. 81.   [4] S.B. Feb. 1685-6, p. 35.
[5] S.B. May 1686, p. 37.   [6] S.B. July 1686, p. 68.
[7] *Ibid.* Five of the parish were indicted for disobedience, S.R. Aug. 1686. The Court evidently suspected that the parish was carrying economy too far and instituted a drastic enquiry into the history of the parish's apprentices, S.B. Dec. 1686, p. 44. For the abuses disclosed, *vide* George, *London Life in the Eighteenth Century*, p. 215.

Fortunately, further information regarding the experiment is supplied by a published account of the institution,[1] from which we learn that its staff included "an excellent writing master to teach all the children to write", "a schoolmaster who teaches all the boys to read, say their prayers and Catechism", "several other persons of several trades to teach the children general sorts of works and bring them up therein", "a school mistress for the girls to teach them to read, say their prayers and Catechism", "a seamstress who teacheth all the girls to work and make all the linen used in the House".[2] It is clear that the founders of the establishment had planned it with some care, intending to provide much more than bare maintenance for the inmates, though the industrial training given was meant to be a preparation, not a substitute, for apprenticeship. The churchwardens and overseers of parishes appointed to send children thought that the poor children were "provided for and educated much beyond the imaginations of any persons that do not go to see them and to the great satisfaction of all that do",[3] while the Grand Jury found that "all the children there are well lodged, well clothed, kept neat and clean, taught to read and write and well instructed in the religion of the Church of England" and that the enterprise was a great advantage to the several parishes.[4] Parishes were not the only sources from which children were to be sent, as one of the main objects was to stimulate charitable persons to provide for children there, "whereby the charge of the maintenance and education of the poor may be at least eased, if not wholly taken off". More striking still is the fact that the House catered for children who were in no way dependent either on their parishes or upon charity, but whom it happened to be inconvenient to rear at home, if, for instance, their fathers were seamen.[5] The Nursery continued in existence for some years, though, as time passed, the parishes became less

[1] "An Account of the General Nursery or College of Infants set up by the Justices of the Peace for the County of Middlesex (1686)", Brit. Mus. 1027. 1. 30. There appear to be two pamphlets bound together, the second covering dates in 1687.
[2] "An Account of the General Nursery", pp. 2–3.
[3] *Ibid.* p. 9.
[4] *Ibid.* p. 11.
[5] *Ibid.* pp. 3–6, where the charges are set out in detail.

regular in sending their children.[1] By 1696, Sir Thomas Rowe was dead and the Court was treating with his executors as to arrears of rent [2] and it was probably owing to inability to pay these that the school was moved to Hornsey.[3] What became of it afterwards, we do not hear, but the absence of further information in our records seems to indicate that its connection with the county was at an end.

This, then, was the one attempt by the Middlesex Quarter Sessions to supplement parochial care of destitute children. Having regard to the deficiencies in that care, deficiencies to which the Court bore ample witness, the Justices might have been expected to do very much more, though in this, as in other cases, they could plead multiplicity of business against any charge of personal negligence. At all events, whether the blame rests upon those who created the administrative machinery or on those who operated it, it is fairly clear that destitute children were not treated in a manner calculated either to give them a good start in life or to reduce the social burden of poverty.

The supervision of ordinary poor relief demanded a degree of detailed knowledge and personal contact which the Justices in Sessions could not easily acquire. The immediate control of this matter was therefore left, for the most part, to local Justices. As in other departments, the Court was constantly employed with cases on appeal. Moreover, since Hicks Hall was very accessible to the suburban parishes, many applicants preferred to approach the Court in the first instance, rather than repair to the house of some Justice of their own parish, interested as he was in keeping down the rates. Such a procedure clearly lent itself to abuse, as the Court could not generally have sufficient data for a correct decision. Direct applications to Hicks Hall were therefore

[1] In 1690 Sir Thomas Rowe petitioned the Court to order parishes to send their children in such numbers and upon such terms as formerly to his College "for the education of poor infants in the Protestant religion". The fact that this request was merely referred to a committee may indicate lessened zeal on the part of the Court, S.B. June 1690, p. 55.
[2] S.B. July 1696, p. 66.
[3] The parish of Hornsey complained that Isaac Adams had come with about sixty poor children, "the inventory" of the late Sir Thomas Rowe, who might become chargeable. Adams was ordered to give security against this contingency, S.B. Jan. 1696–7, p. 36.

strictly forbidden in 1678,[1] but the Court soon forgot its ruling and resumed the hearing of direct applications for relief which, added to the cases on appeal, gave the Justices in Sessions much work.[2] On more general matters, we find the Court in 1694 ordering all parish pensioners to wear badges, to prevent their begging in other parishes,[3] thereby anticipating the statutory requirement contained in the Act, 8 and 9 William III, c. 30.

Naturally the parish, before accepting responsibility for the relief of any poor persons, attempted to lay the burden on other shoulders. It might remove the pauper to some other parish, for which purpose it would have to depend on the law of settlement; or it might seek to fix the obligation on some private person, in which case it would be concerned with the comprehensive body of law defining personal responsibility for relatives and dependents. This latter law was, for the most part, administered by Justices out of Sessions, who were empowered to issue maintenance orders, but, as usual, the Court was called in to deal with many cases on appeal, as well as with a considerable number at first instance. This need not be discussed at length, since it was largely a routine matter, the orders being, either to maintain personally, or to pay a contribution to the parish in respect of some person chargeable to it.[4] Most trouble was naturally caused in connection with those for whom least personal responsibility was felt—illegitimate children. Affiliation and maintenance orders under the Act, 18 Elizabeth, c. 3 were to be made by pairs of Justices, but the parish authorities frequently applied in the first instance to Sessions, so that we constantly find the recognisances of the putative fathers to appear there, and the Court's orders of reference back to local Justices. Less frequently, there are appeals against orders of such Justices,[5] proceedings against women for false accusation,[6] and against men

---

[1] S.B. Aug. 1678, p. 41, *vide* p. 193.
[2] For typical cases, *vide* S.B. Oct. 1673, p. 43; Jan. 1673-4, p. 36; Oct. 1700, p. 51; May 1715, p. 60; Feb. 1726-7, p. 60; etc.
[3] S.B. Oct. 1694, p. 57.
[4] For illustrations, *vide* S.B. July 1662, p. 24; Jan. 1675-6, p. 39; Jan. 1689-90, p. 41; July 1723, pp. 73-4; Jan. 1729-30, p. 68; etc. The Court's anxiety to lighten parochial burdens did not lead it to order maintenance if it was not satisfied that the relative was of sufficient ability, S.B. Oct. 1702, p. 30.
[5] E.g. S.B. Jan. 1690-91, p. 63.   [6] S.B. Oct. 1715, p. 45.

for disobeying affiliation orders.[1] In fact, it is doubtful whether a Sessions ever passed without the Justices being in some way occupied with this matter. The impression is that they handled it with some strictness.[2] We have no means of judging whether, as has been suggested, this system of maintenance actually increased the amount of immorality. For whatever cause, this amount seems to have been large, but the affiliation law apparently saved the public from most of the resulting expense.

The Justices in Sessions normally took no direct part in the appointment of overseers of the poor. These were, by law, to be named by two neighbouring Justices, but there was a tendency for parishioners to make their wishes felt, either by submitting a list from which the Magistrates could choose (as in the case of surveyors of highways), or by actually nominating persons to serve, in the hope that Justices would be content with the right of formal confirmation. There was here ample room for conflict, since, even within the letter of the law, there might be rival appointments by different Magistrates, while, in the domain of custom, friction was much more likely, for Justices were always at liberty to insist on their full right of unfettered choice, insistence which would be resisted by parishioners who tended to regard their customs as their rights. Hence we cannot be surprised at the numerous disputes which were referred to Quarter Sessions.[3] Over the country as a whole, it is thought that retiring overseers practically nominated their successors,[4] but it is not clear how far this custom operated in Middlesex.[5] The office was, of course, unpaid and compulsory, and clearly there was plenty of anxiety to escape it. The overseer's duties were tedious and, unless he indulged in malversation or oppres-

---

[1] S.R. Sept. 1715.
[2] *Vide* S.B. Oct. 1673, p. 43; Dec. 1680, p. 39; Jan. 1722-3, p. 58.
[3] *Vide* S.B. June 1676, p. 41; May 1683, p. 37; April 1719, pp. 60-61; April 1724, p. 67; June 1758, p. 55; etc. It is impossible to infer how much weight the Court generally attached to the claims of the parishioners, but it certainly did not always ignore their views.
[4] Webb, *Parish and County*, p. 31 n.
[5] The right to appoint churchwardens was very indeterminate (*Ibid.* pp. 22-3), and, seeing that the prestige and influence of the office caused it to be coveted, one might have expected to find the quarrels of rival candidates coming before Sessions. Such is, however, not the case, probably because the Court had no legal position in the matter.

sion, there were no compensations.[1] Hence nominees frequently sought to be exempted from the unwelcome office, and the Court allowed a wide variety of pleas.[2]

We are left in no doubt as to the existence of a great need for supervision and stimulation of the parish officers. Their unfitness is, perhaps, the most oft-repeated explanation of the bad working of the Poor Law. Burn quite forgets his accustomed sober judicial air when he comes to expose their deficiencies, and the institution of general superintendents to supervise them is one of his main proposals.[3] He lays great stress on the absence of payment in producing slackness in these, as in more exalted offices. Officers who neglected their duty or refused to obey orders could be indicted and, in that case, the Justices in Sessions would be called upon to act in their judicial capacity. The method of indictment was, however, recognised to be clumsy and ineffective, and was certainly not used much in Middlesex in this connection.[4] In the last resort, substitutes for the delinquent officers might have to be found.[5]

The Court was always much occupied with the financial aspect of poor relief, although the more direct control rested with the local Justices out of Sessions or in their informal Petty Sessions. The intervention of Quarter Sessions was constantly sought by individual parishioners who considered themselves over-rated,[6] by groups who objected to the method of assessment[7] or to the

---

[1] The prestige and influence of the office of churchwarden compensated for its burdens, Webb, *op. cit.* p. 18. This doubtless accounts for the absence of attempts to escape it.

[2] A list of exemptions by Common and Statute Law is given by Mr and Mrs Webb (*op. cit.* p. 16 n), but the Court went beyond these limits.

[3] *History of the Poor Laws*, p. 211 et seq.

[4] For two indictments for neglecting to execute the office of overseer, *vide* S.R. May 1697. A similar offender was fined 3s. 4d. a little later, S.R. Oct. 1697. For an interesting case in which the Court ordered certain overseers to be indicted for misconduct, *vide* S.B. Oct. 1717, pp. 75–7.

[5] E.g. S.B. June 1662, p. 36; May 1703, p. 26. In view of the size of parishes and the amount of work required, the Court at one period appointed additional overseers to assist those named in the ordinary way, S.B. May 1683, p. 39; July 1683, p. 54.

[6] Individuals' Rate Petitions are most commonly grounded on alleged inequality of assessment, on the fact that the property assessed is legally exempt or that the petitioner is poor, *vide* S.B. Dec. 1676, p. 44; April 1685, p. 65; Jan. 1689–90, p. 41; April 1707, p. 59; Oct. 1715, pp. 63–4; etc.

[7] The most interesting cases of group petitions arose from the clash of

THE POOR LAW

manner in which parish funds were being spent or accounts rendered,[1] and by parish officers who could not obtain reimbursement for their expenses or who were at cross purposes among themselves.[2] By 43 and 44 Elizabeth, c. 2, overseers were required to submit their accounts to a Justice of Peace, but the efficacy of such audit, if it had ever been great, was seriously reduced by the ruling that if the overseer swore to the account, he need not produce details.[3] Again, the signatures of two Justices were required before a rate could be collected, but this also was in practice an illusory safeguard, since it was decided that they had no power either to refuse to sign, or to alter the assessment.[4] In any case, single Justices or pairs of Justices were not very satisfactory arbiters, as Magistrates of the parish concerned might be parties to the dispute, perhaps on opposite sides, while those of other parishes would generally know too little of the circumstances to form an equitable decision. In many parishes, custom gave to a more or less formal meeting of inhabitants some control over taxation and expenditure. Such usages were not legally enforcible, and might be broken by officers who did not fear the disapproval of their neighbours. Breaches of this kind do, in fact, partly account for many of the appeals to Sessions. The Court, on its part, seems to have taken for granted that the more substantial and ancient inhabitants would have a voice, but the general terms it employed would not

interest between landholders and others in a parish, it being especially difficult to allocate the rate burden between those two classes while the "discretionary rate" was in vogue. For disputes in this connection, *vide* S.B. July 1663, pp. 33–4; Sept. 1675, p. 44; April 1679, p. 71. There were also charges of general irregularity and fraud, such as that a rate had been made by a minority or that the assessors had favoured themselves: e.g. S.B. July 1675, p. 47; July 1677, p. 41; July 1723, p. 62; Oct. 1747, pp. 40–41. One method of obviating the arbitrariness of the "discretionary rate" was to introduce the "pound rate" and the Court sometimes used this expedient, but even this did not work entirely satisfactorily, owing to the difficulty of valuing properties and the need for an abatement in favour of the poor, *vide* S.B. Aug. 1663, p. 39; April 1673, p. 47; July 1715, pp. 58–9; Oct. 1715, p. 90; Jan. 1715–16, p. 77.

[1] *Vide* S.B. May 1676, p. 35; Oct. 1678, p. 40; April 1679, p. 87; Dec. 1692, p. 40; Jan. 1692–3, p. 54; Feb. 1692–3, p. 36.
[2] *Vide* S.B. Dec. 1670, p. 37; Oct. 1675, p. 42; April 1677, p. 42; April 1680, p. 40; July 1711, pp. 53–4; Oct. 1711, p. 79.
[3] D. Marshall, *The English Poor in the Eighteenth Century*, p. 58.
[4] *Ibid.* pp. 58, 257 n. Burn, *Justice of the Peace*, p. 582.

be a serious check on autocratic officers and, in any case, usually put the emphasis on local custom, to the exclusion of the natural rights of any individuals or groups of individuals. Considering this lack of control alike by local Justices and parishioners, we cannot be surprised that persistent use was made of the right to appeal to the Justices in Sessions.[1]

As at the present day, the size of the rating area caused difficulties in connection with the equitable distribution of financial burdens. Indeed, the trouble was probably more serious then, when the chief burden was that of poor relief, so that the magnitude of the charge and ability to pay would tend to vary inversely. There are a number of applications to the Court for relief in this connection,[2] but the authority of Quarter Sessions to order a rate in aid was very limited[3] and it does not seem that the inequality of the rate burden was redressed to any appreciable extent.[4]

The principle of parochial responsibility, which lay at the foundation of the Elizabethan Poor Law, required extremely precise definition, for, before the obligation to relieve could be enforced, it was necessary to determine to which of the multi-

[1] The right was easily abused, vide S.B. Jan. 1672–3, p. 39; July 1724, p. 101.
[2] Especially from the hamlets into which the parish of Stepney had been divided, S.B. Aug. 1670, p. 43; Dec. 1670, p. 37; Jan. 1670–71, p. 23; Aug. 1676, p. 46. There is one similar petition from Shoreditch, S.B. April 1700, p. 41.
[3] 43 and 44 Elizabeth, c. 2; Burn, *Justice of the Peace*, pp. 584–5.
[4] Justices in and out of Sessions were further concerned with the financing of poor relief because the penalties under many statutes were allocated, in whole or in part, to the poor, though the importance of this source of revenue was much reduced by laxity in prosecuting. Of the matters adjudicated at Sessions, much the most prominent was unlicensed beer-selling, vide p. 34. The Court also interested itself in cases cognisable out of Sessions, when, for instance, it sought to deal with abuses committed by unscrupulous clerks to magistrates, O.C. vol. I, ff. 46–7. It also had to deal with the apportionment of such forfeitures, e.g. for recusancy, S.B. April 1683, p. 45. Allocation disputes also arose under the Act, 30 Charles II, c. 3, to enforce burial in woollen shrouds, as there were two Jewish cemeteries at Mile End and the latter hamlet sought to keep for itself the whole of the fines arising from the Jewish custom of burying in linen, S.B. Jan. 1679–80, p. 29; July 1680, p. 51. The appeal to Sessions against convictions of this type is illustrated in connection with 4 George I, c. 7, prohibiting the use of buttons and buttonholes made of, or bound with, cloth, S.B. Oct. 1718, p. 67; Jan. 1718–19, p. 58; April 1719, p. 84; July 1720, p. 68.

THE POOR LAW

tude of separate entities the pauper or potential pauper belonged. Precise classification of human beings and human relations is never an easy undertaking and, in this instance, it proved far more perplexing than the originators of the scheme foresaw, giving rise to the complex law of settlement. Orders for removal were normally made by pairs of Justices out of Sessions, but appeal lay to Quarter Sessions with which, therefore, rested the further adjudication of the persistent attempts of parishes to shift their burdens on to their neighbours' shoulders. Although the great Act of Settlement was not passed until 1662, the administration of the Poor Law from the first presupposed some conception of what constituted a settlement, and we find the Justices doing their best to make this principle explicit in spite of its vagueness[1] and their slender legal authority in the matter.[2] The Act, 14 Charles II, c. 12, began the process of resolving these doubts and also legalised the removal, irrespective of actual chargeability, of newcomers not occupying tenements worth £10 per annum, unless they gave security against becoming chargeable, and so encouraged the parish authorities to scent danger even where there might be none.[3] Of the qualifications for settlement laid down in precise terms by this and subsequent Acts, that most frequently in question is naturally the forty days' residence.[4] There are also cases of settlement by

[1] *Vide* Burn, *Justice of the Peace*, p. 530, and *History of the Poor Laws*, p. 108. The shortest period of residence allowed by the Middlesex Justices in the years immediately preceding 1662 appears to have been from All Hallows to Shrovetide, S.Reg. vol. VIII, p. 307. In one case they divided the burden between the parish of birth and that of residence, S.Reg. vol. VIII, p. 169. They also regarded the father's settlement as the determining factor for children, S.B. Aug. 1662, p. 29.

[2] At the Summer Assizes at Cambridge in 1629, Sir Francis Harvey delivered it that "the Justices of the Peace (especially out of their Sessions) were not to meddle either with the removing or settling of any poor, but only of rogues", Dalton, *Country Justice*, p. 99.

[3] For cases of removal determined by the occupancy of £10 houses, *vide* S.B. May 1670, p. 29; July 1675, p. 51; etc.

[4] The Court apparently felt itself justified in using some discretion even in regard to this, as it refused to recognise as adequate forty days' residence in a house with a bill "to be let", S.B. Sept. 1672, pp. 41–2. It was to counter such expedients that the Act, 1 James II, c. 17, insisted that the period should only count from the time when written notice was given, and that III William & Mary, c. 11, further stipulated that such notice was to be read in church.

68   THE POOR LAW

apprenticeship[1] and service.[2] There is little evidence that settlements were determined by the payment of parish dues[3] or by serving parish offices, probably because the very poor were usually allowed to escape the burdens of paying rates and serving offices.

Settlement litigation was carried on in no half-hearted manner by the parishes concerned and its amount constitutes a severe commentary on parochialism, at least after the decay of central control, since it entailed a great deal of expenditure of time and money[4] and a good deal of suffering,[5] without in the least helping to relieve pauperism. Indeed, pauperism was probably aggravated, since labour tended to be either immobilised or moved to places where it was not wanted. The amount of the Court's time occupied by settlement cases must always have been considerable and continued to increase as the law was made more meticulous by successive Acts of Parliament. Not infrequently, there were more than twenty cases at a single Sessions.[6] At times the Court's work was increased by the refusal of parties to comply readily with orders.[7] It was also employed, in a judicial capacity, in punishing the practice of dumping poor persons, especially impotent poor and children, in parishes where they had no settlement—a practice to which, one suspects, parish officers were often parties, though the Records do not indicate the fact. The number of cases under this head increases towards the end of the period, as also does the severity with which they were treated.[8]

[1] E.g. S.B. Oct. 1676, p. 51.   [2] E.g. S.B. Feb. 1662–3, p. 30.
[3] For a case of settlement by paying scavenger's rate, *vide* S.B. Jan.1710–11, p. 59.
[4] In a parcel of miscellaneous papers dated 1696–8 is a document recording the expenses of the parish of Stanmore in a suit with Harrow regarding the settlement of Mary James, single woman, and her newly born child. The items show that the officers spared neither pains nor money, and total £11. 19s. 6d.
[5] For a case in which the Court stayed removal, which was legally justified, but which would entail special hardship, *vide* S.B. Feb. 1689–90, p. 40.
[6] E.g. S.B. Jan. 1726–7, April 1729 and Jan. 1741–2. For Cambridgeshire, Miss Hampson estimates that "quite one-half of the time of the Bench must have been occupied in settlement disputes", "Cambridgeshire County and the Poor Laws", *Camb. Hist. Journ.* vol. II, p. 289.
[7] *Vide* S.B. April 1670, p. 32; May 1670, p. 27; Oct. 1674, p. 37.
[8] *Vide* S.R. Sept. 1709, Oct. 1709, June 1746, April 1748 and Feb. 1755. Fines range from 3s. 4d. to £5 and imprisonment is sometimes added.

THE POOR LAW

In dealing with the question of vagrancy, we are naturally concerned in the first place with methods of repression. Though earlier rigours had been softened to some extent, the authority to order whipping or detention in the House of Correction for any of the wide range of activities that could be brought under the vagrancy laws gave the Justices in and out of Sessions a very broad discretionary power. We could not expect them to exercise that authority at all fully at a time when the increasing mobility of trade and population was rendering the old rigidity quite unsuitable, especially in the neighbourhood of the Metropolis, but the power remained and might be vigorously employed as, from time to time, various evils seemed to demand it.

It was only to be expected that, immediately after the Civil War, there should be much vagrancy and, during the first decade of our period, there is evidence of a fairly energetic attempt to eliminate it in Middlesex, partly, it seems, under pressure from the central authorities.[1] There are more indications of the punishment of vagrants than at any other period,[2] and, in accordance with the Act of 1662, the Justices in January 1664-5 certified to the Council the names of several vagabonds and sturdy rogues and beggars, not living by honest labour, as being fit for transportation.[3]

From 1670 onwards, our cases are closely associated with hawking. The indictment is usually for being a vagabond and colouring vagabondage by offering for sale wares of various kinds.[4]

[1] The proclamation of May 9th 1661 displayed special interest in London and Westminster and their neighbourhood, Crawford, *Tudor and Stuart Proclamations*, vol. I, p. 396. In Oct. 1661, the Court appointed two Justices to consult with the Lord Mayor and other Justices of London and Westminster as to the execution of His Majesty's Proclamation to suppress rogues, vagabonds and beggars, S.Reg. vol. VIII, p. 208.

[2] The entries are mostly in the House of Correction calendars (e.g. S.B. June 1665, p. 55; Oct. 1667, p. 50), lists of names which, unfortunately, are not annotated with sufficient regularity to enable us to draw reliable conclusions as to the extent to which, and the regularity with which, vagrants were committed. One, Thomas Robinson, was indicted as an incorrigible rogue who would not reform himself, but no further proceedings are recorded, S.R. July 1667.

[3] S.B. Jan. 1664-5, p. 36. One of them, committed from a conventicle, would not disclose his settlement, saying that his habitation was with God.

[4] The goods hawked include glasses, knives, baskets, linen cloth, Scotch and Holland cloth, silk, turner's wares, brass and pewter, meat, stockings and books, *vide* p. 198.

The wandering habits of these people would naturally be frowned upon by the authorities,[1] but, from the character of the prosecutors who were often traders in the goods being hawked, we may infer that the initiative was taken by established trading interests threatened by these interlopers.[2] To many of the recognisances there are no indictments, some of those indicted are acquitted, and the sentence of whipping, when given, was respited.[3] Probably, then, the Court was already handling the question less stringently. Later we occasionally have fines in place of the statutory whipping, the amounts being no more than 3s. 4d.[4] and 12d.[5] In some instances where the offender confesses, no judgment is entered.[6] Such leniency was not shown where political considerations were involved, for in January 1683-4 the Grand Jury presented "that Scotch pedlars and petty chapmen may not be suffered to pass this county and kingdom without examination and licence"[7] and, in reply, the Court ordered all pedlars travelling with packs or horses or wares without license to be taken up as vagrants.[8] That this was no idle threat appears from an order to whip three people wandering with Scotch and Holland cloth[9] and also from a petition "by several Scotchmen inhabiting in the City and Liberties of Westminster and suburbs of the City of London and parts adjacent, showing that some of them have lately been whipped as vagabonds and passed away to their own country, and that they are natural-born subjects of his now Majesty, capable of the same privileges as Englishmen born, and that they have wives and families in England and pay scot and lot in the parishes where they live, praying the liberty to exercise their occupations to gain their livelihoods without such like punishments".[10] With

---

[1] It is interesting to note how completely such peddling was denied the virtue of labour.
[2] *Vide* p. 167.
[3] E.g. in the cases of Ann Woodward and Alice Hall, indicted in S.R. Jan. 1670–71 for wandering with linen cloth, the ground for postponing punishment being pregnancy.
[4] Two cases in S.R. April 1685.
[5] S.R. Jan. 1684-5 and three in Jan. 1687-8.
[6] E.g. S.R. Aug. and Oct. 1687.
[7] S.B. Jan. 1683-4, p. 29.   [8] *Ibid.*
[9] S.R. April 1684.   [10] S.B. Feb. 1683-4, p. 25.

THE POOR LAW 71

regard to the latter, the Court stated that several such wanderers had had the Oaths of Allegiance and Supremacy tendered to them and had refused to take them, and that some of them had been carriers of intelligence in relation to the recent conspiracy against the King.[1] After the Revolution, there continue to be prosecutions of hawkers, but our evidence of punishment disappears altogether. As often, the fine appears to have gradually shaded off into a license which, under restrictions, permitted a form of trading which was almost indispensable in a rapidly growing urban area and which had the additional advantage of bringing in revenue to the Government.[2] Hence in January 1697-8 we find three indictments from St Martin's in the Fields for wandering without license[3] and then nothing more of the kind for a long period. Much later, there is a case of forging a hawker's license in order to defraud His Majesty of four pounds,[4] and in 1753 a man was prosecuted for assaulting an officer appointed to apprehend unlicensed hawkers and for rescuing his, the offender's, wife who had been apprehended for not showing a license, to the great hindrance of His Majesty's revenues.[5]

The Justices, however, did not lose interest in a question which occupied so much of the time of Parliament and which, on its financial side, came to demand a great deal of their own attention. The licensing system only covered hawking, which was but one of the types of vagrancy. For the rest, the laws remained in full force and even became more stringent and complex. The fact that Quarter Sessions were not enforcing them directly does not prove that they were inoperative, for the bulk of the work had always been done by Justices out of Sessions.[6] The interest of the Court continued to be displayed in the issue

[1] S.B. Feb. 1683-4, p. 25.
[2] James II used this expedient, *vide* the Proclamation in Crawford, *op. cit.* vol. I, p. 464. It was regularised by the Act, 8 and 9 William III, c. 25.
[3] S.R. Jan. 1697-8. They were all removed by Certiorari.
[4] S.R. April 1756.
[5] S.R. April 1753. The Bill was not found.
[6] We gain occasional glimpses of their activity, as, for instance, from an order censuring Mr Troughton, J.P., who had bailed out a man committed to the House of Correction as a vagabond for returning after being passed by two Justices from Sunbury to London, he, Mr Troughton, not having sent to the two committing magistrates, O.C. vol. III, f. 136, 1728.

of general injunctions to Justices and peace officers to enforce the laws,[1] the object of such orders coming more and more to be the reduction of the financial burden of passing vagrants which fell upon the county. The zeal of constables and others was stimulated by rewards as well as punishments from 1662 onwards, but this led to abuses of its own.[2] Twice, at least, in February 1729 and June 1741, the Grand Jury dealt at length with the evil of street begging.[3] On one of these occasions, they took no pains to hide their dissatisfaction with the conduct of the Justices. "Though we are sensible the vast increase of poor may be in some measure owing to the distressed circumstances which we apprehend ourselves to be in," ran part of their presentment, "yet we hope the evil we now complain of will be cured without waiting till the flourishing state of our commerce abroad is restored. For as we have effectual laws in being to prevent begging in the streets, for want of a due execution of which that nuisance is now become an intolerable burden as well as a disgrace to us, we think the utmost care of the magistrate is required to relieve us from it.... Therefore we hope this honourable Court will take so manifest and great a grievance into their serious consideration, and will apply without delay the proper remedies, that we may not be thus troubled with the poor, at the same time we are every day more loaded with taxes to provide for them, and His Majesty's subjects may have the passage of the streets, as in former happy times, free and undisturbed, and be able to transact that little business which the decay of trade has reduced us to, without molestation."[4]

The continuous stream of statutes on the subject of vagrancy bears eloquent testimony to the sense of the uncertainty and

[1] E.g. S.B. July 1709, p. 58; April 1715, pp. 73–6; O.C. vol. I, ff. 126–8; in the last two of these orders, the laws were to be administered by means of frequent petty sessions. In 1721, danger of infection was seen in the begging of loose, idle and disorderly people who were lame, had distorted limbs, etc., so that mendicancy ranks among other nuisances, such as slaughter-houses and hog-keeping.

[2] In particular, there appears to have been extensive collusion between constables and Justices' clerks who shared these rewards, *vide* an exhaustive report on the whole question of the expense of passing vagrants in O.C. vol. VI, ff. 116–18.

[3] Webb, *The Old Poor Law*, p. 357.

[4] Maitland, *History and Survey of London*, vol. I, pp. 543–4.

THE POOR LAW

clumsiness of the growing body of relevant law. This is well illustrated by a petition presented by our Justices to the House of Commons in 1742, complaining of the uncertainty of the laws relating to the poor, settlement and passing, particularly in that, whereas it had been thought that the Justices living in or near any parish were to act for it, there had been a recent decision to the contrary, on the ground that they were interested parties. The Justices considered this inconvenient as, if the loose, idle and disorderly people resorting to London and its neighbourhood "cannot be passed away by those Justices who are likely to be the greatest sufferers by them, it is not to be expected others will exert themselves with the same diligence to remove a nuisance which does not affect themselves nor the parish in which they reside".[1] Following the Act, 17 George II, c. 5, there is a noticeable increase of severity in dealing with vagrants, prompted mainly by the growing cost of the passing system.[2] In 1749, upon representation that it would be of service for vagabonds to be publicly corrected before being passed, the Court directed that a fresh order to that effect should be drafted[3] and, as a result, the next order, setting out the rates to be paid for passing, directed magistrates to have rogues or vagabonds whipped or sent to the House of Correction before being passed.[4] All this failed to check the evil or the expense of passing, and the Court found it necessary to appoint a committee to review the whole system. Its report, presented in April 1757, emphasised the ill execution of the laws, particularly as to punishment before

---

[1] O.C. vol. IV, f. 270. The Act, 16 George II, c. 18, thereupon authorised Justices to act in regard to the poor, vagrants and highways, in parishes where they were rated, but they were not to participate in determining appeals to Quarter Sessions from any order in such parishes.

[2] One man adjudged a rogue is sentenced to three months' detention in the House of Correction and public whipping, S.B. Dec. 1747, p. 49. Another who has returned without a certificate after being passed is committed for a month and to have due correction, S.B. Feb. 1748-9, p. 50. Yet another is committed for two years for leaving his children and refusing to give an account of his settlement, S.B. April 1749, p. 47.

[3] O.C. vol. V, f. 179.

[4] O.C. vol. V, ff. 188-9. One drawback to this was the extra expense involved, as illustrated by a note that one delinquent in the House of Correction was to be publicly whipped if Isleworth would bear the charge, S.B. Dec. 1750, p. 82. For a further stringent order for punishment, *vide* O.C. vol. V, f. 235.

passing and as to the harbouring of vagrants. It pointed out the futility of enforcement in particular parishes or districts and suggested that the Surrey Justices should be approached in order that the entire area comprised within the Weekly Bills of Mortality might be covered. It advocated the publication of the vagrancy laws and of the intention to execute them and, since many of the vagrants came from other parts of the country, suggested that the Court's resolutions should be posted up on the roads leading to London. Peace officers must be charged to do their duty. The committee considered indiscriminate passing too expensive, and thought that severe whipping would drive away the sturdy, so that only objects of real distress need be passed. The penalties upon incorrigible rogues were inoperative owing to the difficulty of detecting those who returned and it was therefore suggested that the Keeper of the House of Correction should keep a book containing the names and descriptions of those passed, so that those who returned might be identified. His memory might be quickened by the offer of a reward for the conviction of every incorrigible rogue. On receiving this report, the Court issued a detailed order for the execution of the law[1] and, in July, embodied in an eight-page order the suggestions of the committee, not only as to the method of passing, but also as to the public whipping of sturdy beggars and counterfeit objects of distress, together with its scheme for the detection of incorrigible rogues.[2] We should not look for the main effects of these proceedings in the Sessions Records, but we find evidence of the action taken by the Court against the more serious offenders, notably forgers of counterfeit passes.[3]

So much for the attempt to repress vagrancy, an attempt which, it must be concluded, was far from successful. We have now to

[1] O.C. vol. VI, f. 116.
[2] O.C. vol. VI, ff. 126–30: 500 copies were to be printed.
[3] Thus Patrick Ryley was indicted twice for forging a counterfeit writing under the hand of an Essex Justice allowing two seamen's wives, one with a child, to pass to Reading within ten days and to be allowed necessary relief on the way, he, Ryley, intending to dispose of the forgeries to idle and disorderly persons who might thereby wander and beg. On one bill he was acquitted, but on the other he was sentenced to be whipped from the upper end of the Haymarket along Piccadilly to St James's Church, S.R. April 1757 and S.B. April 1757, p. 47.

THE POOR LAW

consider the method by which vagrants were passed to their places of settlement and, more particularly, that by which the resulting expenses were met. The duty of passing rested upon the constables and headboroughs of the parishes on the route to a vagrant's settlement. Expense was naturally involved and the Act, 14 Charles II, c. 12, empowered the peace officers, together with the churchwardens and inhabitants, to make a rate to reimburse themselves. As constables did not always receive the willing co-operation of these other officers and inhabitants, they had frequently to appeal to the Court for injunctions. From 1673 there was a fairly considerable stream of such petitions, the Court, in reply, either referring the request to the local Justices or itself ordering a rate to be made.[1] The method must have worked clumsily and the burden fell with disproportionate weight on the parishes lying along the main roads through which a large proportion of the vagrants were passed. Hence the Act, 11 William III, c. 18, in seeking to reorganise the whole system on a more workable basis, transferred the duty of raising the necessary funds to Quarter Sessions.[2] As a result, we find from July 1700 onwards, assessments by Quarter Sessions for money to repay constables,[3] and at less frequent intervals the rates at which allowances were to be made were similarly prescribed.[4] As usual, there was difficulty in obtaining payment of the rates. The county engaged in a long dispute with the City of Westminster and the Liberty of the Tower as to their liability to contribute to the county rate,[5] and had to give way in both

---

[1] E.g. S.B. Oct. 1673, p. 36; June 1676, pp. 42-3.

[2] In ordering the conveyance of vagrants, Justices were to give a certificate to the peace officer, stating the number of vagrants to be conveyed and the method to be employed, with an allowance for his loss of time and expenses. The high constables were to pay these allowances out of the Gaol and Marshalsea Money. If these funds proved insufficient, as they certainly would, Quarter Sessions were to raise additional funds as they did upon the Gaol and Bridge Rates. [3] S.B. July 1700, p. 43.

[4] At first these rates were fixed at 3*d.* per mile for a cart and 1*s.* 6*d.* per day for a horse, but some discretion was still left to the passing Magistrate, S.B. July 1700, p. 43. Later, the mileage along the most frequented routes was sometimes added for the information of Justices, e.g. O.C. vol. v, ff. 188-9. For the allowances authorised by the Hertfordshire Justices in 1719, which were much more liberal, *vide* Hardy, *Hertford County Records*, vol. II, pp. 52-3.

[5] S.B. July 1703, p. 52; O.C. vol. II, ff. 87-93; S.B. May 1736, pp. 102-8.

instances. High constables were very remiss in bringing in their accounts, as also were collectors in paying over their quotas.[1] In 1734, the officers of Saffron Hill moved King's Bench against Mr John Higgs, the General Treasurer, for issuing a precept to raise the money in their liberty.[2] The Justices came to the conclusion that the opposition had been organised by Thomas Robe, J.P., in revenge for their proceedings against him in connection with the office of Clerk of the Market.[3] There followed representations and counter-representations to the Lord Chancellor as to his conduct.[4] Several rates were quashed despite the best endeavours of the Court to meet the requirements of the law and avoid formal defects.[5] It had apparently become impossible to frame an order to which some exception could not be taken and the new legislation which was imperatively demanded took shape in the Act, 12 George II, c. 29. This, besides strengthening the Court's control over collectors, unified all the county rates, which were in future to be paid by the churchwardens out of the poor rate for each parish. It also brought Westminster under the Middlesex rate and, most important of all, directed that rates should not be quashed simply for want of form and restricted the Certiorari.[6] After this, in making an £800 assessment for the purposes of the Act, the Court took the precaution of directing the County Treasurer to attend the Solicitor-General, so that the latter might peruse and settle the order,[7] and though the money was at first slow in coming in,[8] we find that, on the whole, the opposition had died down, so that the accounts which follow each other at short intervals do not show serious arrears. We may therefore leave the

---

[1] The only remedy was the clumsy and expensive method of indictment, O.C. vol. II, ff. 87–93. Orders to constables to account for and pay over their balances follow each other in wearisome succession. In 1732 three high constables were fined five pounds and one ten pounds, S.B. April 1732, p. 59; May 1732, p. 96. These and other penalties were of no avail, yet the committee appointed to consider remedies could suggest nothing but indictment, O.C. vol. IV, f. 24.

[2] S.B. Feb. 1734-5, p. 67.   [3] O.C. vol. IV, f. 26. *Vide* p. 162.
[4] O.C. vol. IV, ff. 29, 36-7, 41, 63-4.   [5] O.C. vol. IV, f. 63, etc.
[6] Our Justices played some part in promoting this Act, *vide* O.C. vol. IV, ff. 83, 124, 139. Perhaps their main interest in the matter arose from Brentford Bridge rather than vagrancy, *vide* p. 127.
[7] O.C. vol. IV, f. 150.   [8] O.C. vol. IV, ff. 191-2.

THE POOR LAW

problem of raising the money and turn to the consideration of its expenditure.

As already shown, the normal method of passing was from constable to constable along the route to the vagrant's settlement. This was a clumsy arrangement, since peace officers might misdirect their charges, while the latter, in the course of their gradual progress, could easily evade their constantly changing conductors and practise upon the inhabitants of the numerous parishes in which they halted. In 1711, following complaints to this effect, the Court ordered that vagrants should be carried by the peace officer who first received them right through the county to the first parish in the adjoining county and not to any other parish or place in Middlesex. This direct passage would, it was stated, be less costly than the system of passing parish by parish[1] and had, as a matter of fact, been envisaged by the Act, 11 William III, c. 18. Payment was by the piece, upon certificates which constables received with the pass warrants,—clearly a clumsy arrangement, giving opportunities for fraud by constables, which were the subject of many orders. In addition, it entailed considerable work on the passing Justices and made an elaborate audit indispensable if any check on expenditure was to be maintained, and constables' demands are constantly being referred to committees of magistrates or petty sessions for inspection of certificates.[2] Apart from the impossibility of sufficiently minute enquiries for this purpose, it was difficult to ensure that only real vagrants should be passed at the charge of the county, for the allowances to constables were liberal enough to make them quite willing to extend their business,[3] while parishes were very willing to save themselves expense by having ordinary poor passed upon the county rate.[4]

---

[1] S.B. Jan. 1711–12, p. 78.

[2] For disallowance by auditors of amounts in excess of the rates prescribed by Sessions, *vide* S.B. May 1720, p. 53.

[3] A report in 1759 estimated that some constables had made above £50 a year, O.C. vol. VII, ff. 129, 135. We can therefore understand why these officers opposed a change of system.

[4] Upon all these difficulties, *vide* the Report of April 1757 in O.C. vol. VI, ff. 116–18. Mr and Mrs Webb also point out that parishes were tempted to pass their poor as vagrants because they thereby precluded appeals, *The Old Poor Law*, p. 380.

The idea of contracting for all vagrants to be passed in consideration of a fixed periodic payment had therefore much to recommend it and was very much in keeping with the practice of the times. It had been introduced quite early in the case of two constables who always had a great deal of work to do—those of South Mimms and Enfield on the northern roads.[1] For the rest, the old arrangements remained in force, with the exception of a brief interval regulated by the Act, 13 George II, c. 24,[2] until almost the end of the period. Despite most elaborate precautions by way of receipts, audits, etc., abuses seem to have increased rather than diminished, entailing an ever-growing burden upon the county. The committee which carefully examined the whole question in 1757 contended that severe whipping would be enough to drive away the sturdy, so that passes need only be used for objects of real distress, who should be passed from Bridewell. For these it considered that stage waggons would be cheaper than the existing method of conveyance and suggested the appointment of some person to carry this out once a week or oftener.[3] Thereupon the Court approved a contract with one Sturges Adams to clear the Bridewells twice a week, conveying the vagrants in covered carts, those to the north on one day, those to the south and west on another. He was to be paid £10 a month and 6*d*. for the sustenance of each vagrant.[4] The new method at once produced great economies,

---

[1] The salary of the constable of Enfield was at first £60 but was subsequently reduced to £40, S.B. Oct. 1712, p. 69; O.C. vol. III, f. 96. In the case of South Mimms the old piece-rate system was reverted to in 1735, O.C. vol. IV, f. 52. The Enfield salary also disappears.

[2] This provided that long-distance passing should be from House of Correction to House of Correction. For payments to the Keeper of the House of Correction at Clerkenwell in respect of this service, *vide* O.C. vol. IV, ff. 194–5, 232, 265, etc. From Dec. 1740 to June 1744 payments were ordered of sums totalling £925. 8*s*. 4*d*. It is not therefore surprising that the Justices, in petitioning the House of Commons, urged the inconvenience and expense of this method of passing and they evidently took part in framing the new Act, 17 George II, c. 5, which restored the old system, O.C. vol. IV, f. 270; vol. V, f. 48.

[3] O.C. vol. VI, ff. 116–18.

[4] O.C. vol. VI, ff. 118–19. At the same time, the 10*s*. reward was pronounced excessive and Justices were to proportion it to the time and trouble involved in each case. The contract system had been introduced in Hertfordshire at least as early as the reign of George I, Hardy, *Hertford County Records*, vol. II, p. 76.

THE POOR LAW

although it was at first marred to some extent by the opposition of constables and the slackness of magistrates.[1] The Court enforced its new policy energetically[2] and the close of the period therefore witnessed the most successful attempt to lighten the burden of vagrancy upon the county finances.[3]

The sub-division of cottages and taking of inmates involved a triple danger to the inhabitants of a locality. Overcrowding aggravated the danger of epidemics, always great in a growing urban area at a time of primitive sanitary arrangements; the fact that the people taken in were normally of the poorest class with little or no property threatened the parish with the burden of maintaining them at some future date; there was also the fear of harbouring lawbreakers, especially, in the eighteenth century, street robbers. On the whole, the danger of pauperisation seems to have carried most weight with those upon whom the execution of the law depended, so that this matter is most conveniently dealt with as a Poor Law question. True, the danger of infection was placed by the jurors in their presentments before that of pauperisation and, in 1721, a report on various nuisances conducing to infection called attention to inmates and especially to the custom of receiving unknown people at a penny or more a night, lodging them without beds, fifteen or twenty in a small room, where some of them were often found dead.[4] On the whole, however, aspersions upon

---

[1] From July 1756 to July 1757, there had been issued 1951 orders to convey, costing £678. 11s. 9d. and 474 orders to reward 498 people, costing £246, making a total of £924. 11s. 9d. From July 1757 to July 1758, 1240 orders to convey cost £325. 19s. 0d. and 131 orders to reward, £67. 17s. 6d., amounting with the £120 for the contract and £40 extra maintenance allowance to a total of £553. 16s. 6d. Of this, £149. 13s. 0d. had been spent contrary to order of Sessions, but there still remained the substantial saving of £370. 15s. 3d., O.C. vol. VII, ff. 129–35.

[2] After ordering remonstrances to be sent to two Middlesex magistrates and to the Clerk of the Peace for the North Riding of Yorkshire regarding irregularities, it received explanations and promises of future compliance, O.C. vol. VII, ff. 45, 47. The sending of vagrants without stating any act of vagrancy was persisted in by Mr Bell, a Justice of the Peace for the North Riding, against whom the Court threatened to move King's Bench, O.C. vol. VII, f. 59.

[3] In one attempt at the more questionable economy of shifting burdens, the Court found the law against it, when it unsuccessfully tried to transfer the expense of relieving sick vagrants to the churchwardens and overseers of the parishes where they fell ill, O.C. vol. V, ff. 156, 168, 171.

[4] O.C. vol. I, ff. 126–8.

the character of the unwelcome guests seem merely intended to give point to the danger of their chargeability. This danger is stressed even in the order of February 1665-6, following immediately upon the Plague,[1] which, so far as our period is concerned, practically inaugurates proceedings in this connection. In this case, stringent instructions were given that divided houses should be restored to their original condition, that inmates or undersitters should be removed and that persistent offenders should be prosecuted. As a result, there were, at the following Sessions, more than twenty indictments for committing the nuisance in question[2] and, though this number is exceptional, there is a fairly continuous stream of them almost until the close of our period. The legal penalty of 10s. a month[3] was not exacted at all regularly and a large proportion of cases have no fines entered, so that it is probable that the indictment was generally at most a method of putting pressure upon offenders, to be allowed to drop if the annoyance was removed.[4] As in other branches, the slackness of unpaid, overworked and more or less unwilling officials ensured that the law should not be enforced with anything approaching completeness[5] and the Court was not very persistent in its attempts to stimulate them in this direction. It is a sign of their fitful activity that cases tend to come in batches from particular parishes and that at some

[1] S.Reg. vol. IX, pp. 294-5.
[2] S.R. April 1666.
[3] 31 Elizabeth, c. 7.
[4] For a case of the legal fine, *vide* S.R. Feb. 1739-40, where an inhabitant of St Luke's is fined 40s. and committed until he paid "for suffering several families as inmates to lodge in a certain cottage in the said parish for the space of four months there". One Richard Collins was fined as much as £13. 6s. 8d. for dividing his house into twelve separate habitations, and Elizabeth Major, £3. 6s. 8d. at the same time, S.R. July 1678. Quite often no more than 12d. is exacted, e.g. S.R. Sept. 1684 and April 1715.
[5] In 1673 the Court attributed the increasing charge of the poor to the negligence of constables, headboroughs, etc., in not searching for inmates and strangers or presenting those taking inmates and dividing tenements. It ordered them to perform their duty, so that newcomers might be removed and necessary proceedings taken, S.B. Sept. 1673, p. 41. The churchwardens and overseers had perhaps the most direct interest in prosecuting offenders and we sometimes see them in action—as, for instance, in the recognisance of Mary Pilkinson to answer the churchwardens of St Giles' "for crowding her house with inmates which are likely to become a great charge to the said parish"— S.R. March 1670-71.

THE POOR LAW

Sessions practically all the cases come from a single parish.[1] During the last sixteen years of the period there is a marked slackening of administration under this head. No doubt the difficulty of enforcing the law and the hardship which would have resulted from its rigorous execution grew as the eighteenth century advanced. Our Justices do not appear to have shared Child's view of the imprudence of the law in relation to cities and great towns of trade,[2] but to have considered it ineffectual, since, in their representation to the Duke of Newcastle on the subject of street robberies, they urged the need for legislation against those harbouring inmates, especially loose, idle and disorderly people, reputed thieves or vagabonds, "there being at present no law for the speedy and effectual punishment of them".[3] Hence it would seem to have been in opposition to the policy of the Court that the latter half of the reign of George II witnessed a definite relaxation of the Tudor restrictions.

Closely akin to the sub-division of existing houses was the practice of erecting large numbers of new cottages upon small areas of land,[4] but it is fairly certain that the objection to this latter practice was even more definitely the fear of pauperisation. The records exhibit a considerable number of indictments for erecting or continuing cottages without the statutory four acres of freehold land,[5] and, for reasons which do not appear, the maximum activity is at the turn of the century.[6] After 1720, cases become extremely infrequent with rather marked suddenness. Throughout, the treatment of offenders is characterised by great leniency. Many cases remain without any entry of proceedings, many were removed by Certiorari and, in the later years, the

---

[1] E.g. S.R. Oct. 1670 and Aug. 1694.
[2] For Child's view, *vide* Burn, *History of the Poor Laws*, p. 166.
[3] O.C. vol. v, ff. 46–7. This was just at the time when prosecutions at Sessions became scanty.
[4] Both were forbidden for the like unspecified inconveniences by the Act, 31 Elizabeth, c. 7. The true bills do not indicate the nature of the danger that they were combating.
[5] E.g. the indictment of a Tottenham butcher named Boone for erecting a cottage and a further indictment against him for continuing one, S.R. Oct. 1671 and April 1672. Naturally, the builders are often carpenters, e.g. in S.R. May and June 1671. For a prosecution for converting a barn to serve as a cottage for habitation, *vide* S.R. April 1684.
[6] *Vide* S.R. April, Oct. and Dec. 1700 and Sept. and Oct. 1701.

proceedings were often stayed.[1] The Justices were authorised to license the continuance of cottages without four acres if satisfied that they were needed and were innocuous, and we find them using this power when they permitted John Peacocke of Acton to continue four cottages which he had lately built without the required four acres, a certificate being presented under the hands of the officers and numerous distinguished inhabitants of the parish "that the said cottages stand in convenient places and that the said John Peacocke hath been a laborious, painful man in his trade aforesaid and been lately sore afflicted with sickness and hath a wife and six small children". Still, the license was only granted for twenty-one years if the owner lived so long and subject to the proviso that the parish must be indemnified from any charge arising from the poverty of the tenants of these cottages.[2] The fact that this Act might be used against squatters is illustrated by the recognisance of Amos Cox of East Barnet, carpenter, "for setting up a cottage in the night time on the waste in Finchley without the consent of the Lord of the Manor and inhabitants of the parish and without four acres of ground laid to it".[3] This apparent strictness does not, however, prevent us from concluding from the Records as a whole that the law against landless dwellings was never vigorously enforced in Middlesex between the Restoration and the death of George II and that, during the reign of the latter, it was virtually a dead letter.[4] If further evidence is needed as to the views of the Justices, it may be found in the fact that, while cottages without four acres were among the matters to be enquired into by the Grand Jury at the Easter Sessions in 1682,[5] they appear to have been entirely passed over by eighteenth-century chairmen in their charges.

Before leaving the subject of the Poor Law, it will be well to

[1] The statutory penalty was £10 for the erection, and 40s. for every month of the continuance, of a cottage without the legal acreage. For a case in which the former penalty was imposed, *vide* S.R. July 1677. For much smaller fines, *vide* S.R. Jan. 1720–21.
[2] S.B. April 1677, p. 43. For another similar license, *vide* S.B. Oct. 1679, p. 76.
[3] S.R. Oct. 1668.
[4] There was apparently a similar trend in Hertfordshire, *vide* Hardy, *Hertford County Records*.
[5] *Vide* the articles of enquiry appended to the printed copy of Sir William Smith's Charge, p. 10.

THE POOR LAW

consider briefly a type of assistance closely akin to that rendered by the ordinary destitution authorities—that which was provided by means of collections upon briefs. The brief is one of the many institutions borrowed by the post-Reformation state from the medieval Church.[1] It had been one of the expedients used by the Papacy for raising money from the well-disposed for particular religious and charitable objects and was adopted by the secular state for kindred purposes. We are not here concerned with its extensive use for ecclesiastical objects, of which the most common was the repair of decayed churches; but, through its employment as a means to make good personal losses due to severe accidents, it impinged upon the Poor Law. It might be regarded as a method by which the relief of exceptional catastrophes bearing upon particular persons and localities was transferred from the parishes where they occurred to the country as a whole. Contributions under briefs remained voluntary and they also retained their medieval character in that they were sought by the reading of the brief in church, though there might be a house to house collection. Authorisation for these collections was obtained *ad hoc* by Letters Patent, under which special undertakers and collectors were appointed, but, before such Letters Patent were granted, it was necessary that a certification of the losses to be made good should be sent by the Justices of the county to the Lord Chancellor or Lord Keeper. Hence sufferers applied in the first instance to Quarter Sessions and we find the resulting certificates entered in the Records of the Court. The most frequent ground of application for a brief was loss by fire,[2] and Wapping was particularly frequent in its

---

[1] A historical account of the system is given in *By-gone Briefs* by the Author of *Local Government in Westminster*. Appendix I gives specimen copies of briefs, while Appendix II comprises a schedule of 1021 briefs laid in the parish of St Margaret's, Westminster, between 1644 and 1793, and is therefore a most valuable index of the extent and variety of uses to which this machinery was put.

[2] Occasionally other types of loss are in question. In one of the parcels of miscellaneous papers, dated 1701–30, is an application, dated Aug. 1702, by one Welburne who had lost one ship, a Levantine called *The Sussex*, coming from Turkey, through its being taken into Toulon. Later, when he had bought another, *The Fleetwood*, and was ready to sail, it was burnt, together with some other shipping, the loss amounting to £3115. 10s. 0d. The Court granted him a certificate, a copy of which is preserved. It also used the brief

applications for help in repairing the damage caused by catastrophes of this kind.[1] Despite elaborate precautions as to procedure,[2] fraud was still possible and not uncommon, mainly, no doubt, owing to the fact that the charitably disposed would not be sufficiently critical of the credentials of collectors. In one instance, however, the dupe was no less a personage than the Lord Keeper.[3] There are a number of cases of the severe punishment of forgers, mainly towards the end of the period. One Matthew Broom, for instance, who appears to have offended more than once, was adjudged an incorrigible rogue and sentenced to hard labour in the House of Correction for two years and to be "twice stripped naked from the middle upwards and publicly whipped within the first year of his said confinement by the Keeper of the said House of Correction or some person acting for him at a cart's tail, each time until his body be bloody, upon a

on behalf of the poor Palatines in 1709 and on one occasion it granted a certificate for the rebuilding of a church, that of Ealing, S.B. Sept. 1709, p. 44; April 1733, pp. 67–9.

[1] *Vide* S.B. May 1703, p. 33; April 1727, pp. 63–4; July 1727, pp. 80–84; Jan. 1735–6, p. 41. In 1727, the Court was informed that 130 dwelling-houses and warehouses had been burnt to the ground there and granted a certificate to make good the loss which was estimated at £5178. 16s. 10d., S.B. April 1727, pp. 63–4. There were other similar catastrophes in the same parish, for in 1682 a proclamation was issued for a brief for a fire there upon petition of the churchwardens and certificate of the Middlesex Justices. The houses of 1500 families were said to have been destroyed, the value being £35,446 of houses and £20,948 of goods, Crawford, *Tudor and Stuart Proclamations*, vol. I, pp. 453–4. Briefs on account of this parish were laid in St Margaret's, Westminster, in 1704, 1722, 1728, 1742 and 1759, *By-gone Briefs*, Appendix II.

[2] For a case in which the Court rejected an application, that of a Holborn broker, *vide* S. Reg. vol. IX, p. 317. The petition of a carpenter, bricklayer and mason as to their loss amounting to £4178. 6s. 0d. through the destruction of new buildings in Bedford Row was certified by surveyors and the Court granted its certificate upon recognisances of five people, amounting to £8000, that the patent should not be converted to the use of the Landlord or any other person, S.B. July 1718, p. 62.

[3] *Vide* the bill against George ffoxcroft, labourer, for forging a certificate under the hands of two Derbyshire Justices as to a loss by fire amounting to £3755, supposed to have been sustained by Richard Burton, lead-merchant, who, it was also alleged, had lost £2000 in trade during the Dutch wars, had been a man of great industry and credit and had brought up nine children. ffoxcroft was further accused of forging an authorisation to himself to elect a treasurer who was to receive what should be collected. Armed with these documents, he had obtained from Lord Keeper Bridgeman Letters Patent to receive charity in several counties and had actually collected several sums from divers people. Judgment is not entered, Gaol Delivery Roll, Dec. 1670.

THE POOR LAW

Friday, being market day, the first time from Smithfield Bars unto and over against Clerkenwell Church in this county and back again to Smithfield Bars, and the second time from the end of Drury Lane in Broad Street to St Giles' Pound in the said county and back again to the end of Drury Lane aforesaid, and the person who whips him is required to do his duty".[1]

The Justices also took some action to prevent the outbreak of fires, the most frequent cause of the distress which briefs were intended to mitigate. It appears that they did not enforce the building restrictions which had been instituted with this in view,[2] but it did provide for some precautions as to dumps of gunpowder, which were apparently common in the eastern suburbs, and caused much uneasiness.[3] Parishes did something on their own initiative,[4] but clearly failed to do enough,[5] while insurance was still in its infancy. The real solution lay partly in the substitution of brick for timber in building, partly along the lines pioneered by the insurance companies through their "fire porters", leading ultimately to the establishment of special fire brigades. These developments are, however, irrelevant to the present purpose, for which the main interest of the question lies in the inability of eighteenth-century administration to cope with a really serious evil. The evil remained throughout our

[1] S.B. Dec. 1748, p. 49. For other sentences, *vide* S.B. Dec. 1682, p. 54; S.R. May 1745 and Dec. 1755. The elaborate precautions instituted by 4 and 5 Anne, c. 25, which among other things prohibited the practice of farming, were evidently inadequate.

[2] For a case in which these were in question, *vide* S.B. Dec. 1729, p. 66. For an order to remove a nuisance, which threatened the danger of fire at a time when that was very much in the public mind, owing to the Great Fire, *vide* S.Reg. vol. IX, pp. 387-8.

[3] S.B. Jan. 1718-9, p. 51. As a result of a fire in Wapping in Jan. 1741-2, the Grand Jury suggested an Act of Parliament against landing gunpowder, with encouragement to informers, O.C. vol. IV, ff. 239-40. Restrictions were imposed by the Acts, 5 George I, c. 26, 15 George II, c. 32 and 21 George II, c. 38.

[4] Watches had, among other duties, the prevention of fire, *vide* S.B. Oct. 1672, p. 44. St Sepulchre's had a water engine and ladders as early as 1677— S.B. Sept. 1677, p. 41—and Parliament made such provision compulsory for all parishes within the Bills of Mortality by 6 Anne, c. 58 and 7 Anne, c. 17, and also inserted provision for pumps for fire-engines in some of the Acts for new waterworks, e.g. 8 George I, c. 26.

[5] Hence prevention of fires is one of the objects of the new commissions to regulate the watch, e.g. for Saffron Hill by 10 George II, c. 25 and for Christ Church by 11 George II, c. 35.

period and, with it, the brief to remedy the distress caused. The remedy no doubt had many defects but, for the time, its existence was amply justified.

In conclusion, it must be admitted that the study of Middlesex administration does nothing to shake the belief that, at any rate after the Civil War, the Tudor Poor Law was fundamentally a failure. True, we have found no reason to suppose that, so far as concerned the permanent section of the poor—the impotent—the attitude of the Justices was either harsh or indifferent. Nor have we found them entirely acquiescing in the failure of the parish as the unit of administration, a failure which really doomed the whole system. They wrestled incessantly with the financial problems of the parish and at times attempted to stimulate its officers to more vigorous action. Nor, again, have we found them disposed blindly to enforce antiquated laws which, under changing circumstances, would involve severe hardship or an undue obstruction to progress. Many enactments had become dead letters long before they were erased from the Statute Book. Still, a destitution authority without a curative policy cannot claim to be really adequate. Curative measures, so far as that authority is concerned, must concentrate upon the able-bodied and children and, with regard to these, it would be idle to claim that the Middlesex Justices were other than negligent. As things then were, failure to remedy meant, not merely stagnation, but deterioration, since, in the absence alike of general principles and of systematic administration, it was impossible to prevent the continuance of a body of able-bodied poor who, if they had had more opportunity or incentive, could to a great extent probably have found work for themselves. Perhaps the position was hopeless so long as the Act of Settlement remained law. At all events, apart from its reiteration of the need for severity towards vagrants, the only measures at all consistently pursued by the Court which could be styled remedial were those designed to repress or restrict certain activities which were thought to conduce to pauperisation as well as to immorality—drinking, especially gin-drinking, gaming and the like.[1]

Most of those who thought seriously on the problem of

[1] *Vide* chap. II.

destitution came to the conclusion that radical innovations were essential if the poor were to be properly treated or the burden of rates kept down.[1] Many of them, like Henry Fielding, based their proposals on experience gained in Middlesex,[2] and it would be strange if other Justices besides Fielding were not convinced of the deficiencies of the law which they were called upon to administer. Some Magistrates would doubtless have pleaded this conviction against any accusation of negligence. In fact, as has already been shown, Quarter Sessions adopted a scheme for a special corporation for the poor in the suburban area at the very commencement of the period.[3] Later, a still more radical project was laid before the Court and received its qualified approval. This envisaged the subscription of three hundred thousand pounds by persons who were to be formed into a corporation to maintain the impotent and employ the able-bodied of the whole kingdom for a period of twenty-one years, while every parish should pay over to the corporation annually a sum equal to its average expenditure on the poor during the preceding seven years.[4] Revolutionary as this scheme was, our Justices evidently gave it their general approval, though they considered twenty-one years too long a term and apparently thought the change over from parochial to national administration too drastic and would have preferred a separate act for each county.[5] This helps us to gauge the Magistrates' lack of faith in the system for which they were responsible,[6] and it was probably

[1] *Vide* Burn, *History of the Poor Laws*, chaps. VI and VII; Webb, *The Old Poor Law*, chap. III.

[2] For Fielding's scheme, *vide* Burn, *op. cit.* p. 196.

[3] The main interest of this enterprise is in its attempt to provide employment, but it was intended to maintain 100 impotent persons, so that it was an attempt to supersede the Elizabethan system except in regard to children.

[4] A copy of these proposals is in the parcel of miscellaneous papers dated 1696–8.

[5] This information is supplied by a paper in the same parcel as the proposals, which is dated Jan. 13th 1697 and headed "Minutes above stairs". These notes do not explicitly mention the scheme but, from the subject-matter and the numbering of the comments, it is clear that they refer to it.

[6] Owing to the dislocation caused by the recoinage, the Government, by a proclamation on July 2nd 1696 had specially impressed on magistrates their duty to provide relief and work for the poor, Crawford, *Tudor and Stuart Proclamations*, vol. I, p. 501. In response, the Court issued an order for monthly petty sessions to consult how the poor might be relieved, S.B. July

owing to conflict of opinion on the details of the scheme that it was never put into practice. If, then, by the end of the seventeenth century, the Justices were already convinced of the need for radical reform, we should perhaps not blame them for their apparent slackness in administration, but we should expect them to take some steps to secure the reform whose necessity they recognised. In fact, however, the only legislation which the Court appears to have played any part in promoting concerned details of the old system and offered no remedy for its larger shortcomings.[1] It would, no doubt, be difficult to secure agreement upon sweeping innovations, but there is no evidence that the Court gave any further consideration to the question of radical reform. Some of the Justices may, as individuals, have taken part in promoting the Acts which, towards the close of our period, began to entrust the care of the poor, along with other public services, to new bodies operating in certain limited areas within the county.[2] The Court itself, however, seems to have been content to shirk the wider issues and administer so much of the existing law as it could, without any very clear object in view beyond the avoidance of too rapid a growth of rates. Many thinkers who took this narrow fiscal point of view doubted the ability of the existing machinery to secure even this negative object and experience was to prove them right. The Old Poor Law in the long run failed both to benefit the poor and to prevent them from becoming a severe burden on the rest of the community.

1696, p. 65. Experience of the futility of such consultations would leave the Justices in a frame of mind ready to give a hearing to any proposal which offered something better.
  [1] E.g. the Act, 17 George II, c. 5, referred to previously.
  [2] E.g. 23 George II, c. 35, for St Martin's in the Fields, 25 George II, c. 23, for St Margaret's and St John's, Westminster, 26 George II, c. 97, for St George's, Hanover Square, 26 George II, c. 98, for Christ Church and 29 George II, c. 53, for Marylebone. The first three of these actually dealt with places within the liberty of Westminster.

CHAPTER IV

HIGHWAYS AND BRIDGES

IN the maintenance of highways, as in other departments of administration, direct action by the county, represented by its Justices of Peace assembled in General or Quarter Sessions, is only in question to a comparatively small extent. The county is seen mainly as a stimulating, supervising and co-ordinating authority. Its closest and most constant relations were naturally with the parish. Upon this unit the Act, 2 and 3 Philip & Mary, c. 8, had finally settled the responsibility for all highways whose maintenance was not a specific charge on some other person or body. By prescription it was responsible for many bridges. We therefore find the Court of Quarter Sessions judicially enforcing these duties, supervising their execution and aiding the parish by compelling its members to play their part and by supplying it with financial resources, partly by imposing and paying over to it fines on various types of offenders, partly by giving it explicit authority to levy rates. To a great extent individuals presented themselves to the Court simply as members of their parish, under obligation to give it their labour or that of their teams, to serve its offices and later to pay it rates, duties which the Court was constantly called upon to enforce. In so doing, it was aiding the parish to do its work. But individuals had other duties more distinctly their own. Their old duties were to keep highways and bridges in repair when bound so to do by reason of tenure of land and to abstain from committing nuisances; the newer ones imposed under the special circumstances of town life, entailed the performance of definite services to the streets adjoining their houses—to sweep, to pave and to light them. Here, too, there was need of the compelling and controlling authority of the Justices. The county itself was directly responsible for the upkeep of certain bridges and this liability occupied a good deal of the attention of the Court, since here it was both judge and minister, with power both to punish defaults and to remedy them. Finally, the Court was, during the latter part of the period, brought into relation with the new bodies established by Parliament to take over the care of certain highways from the older authorities. Hence it is necessary to give some attention to the connection between the Court and the turnpike trusts, and to see how the former partly restrained and partly assisted the latter. From the standpoint of administrative method, there would be advantages in treating this whole subject primarily from the point of view of the responsible persons or bodies and in sub-dividing this chapter accordingly. We should then consider highway service as an affair firstly of the parish, secondly of the individual citizen, thirdly of the county and fourthly of the turnpike trust. Such a treatment would, however, be clumsy and entail much repetition, since most questions would need to be discussed from more than one point of view and therefore in more than one section. It therefore seems best to make the service rendered the main classification and to deal in passing with any significant points arising from the character of the renderer.

First, however, it will be well to say something as to the organisation of the Justices themselves for highway business. Much of the detail work was done by the local Justices out of Sessions, and for this organisation was convenient.[1] The Act, 3 William & Mary, c. 12, directed Justices in their respective divisions to hold special sessions for highways every four months, but this provision had been anticipated by the Middlesex Justices, not by the establishment of special highway sessions at regular intervals, but by the gradual and unsystematic development of local meetings for the transaction of all business which Justices were empowered to perform either singly or in pairs, of which that relating to the highway formed no small part. This is seen very clearly from the proceedings of the Brentford Justices, whose meetings, usually held at the Red Lion Inn, became fairly regular much earlier than those in other districts.[2] But clearly the movement here was only greater in degree, not different in kind from that in other districts. A petition from St Giles' in the

---

[1] The general question of local organisation has already been discussed, p. 7 *et seq.*
[2] *Vide* the Brentford Calendar, *passim.*

HIGHWAYS AND BRIDGES

Fields asking for a highway rate under the Act for cleansing the streets[1] suggests that it be employed as the Justices usually present at the Petty Sessions in the parish shall appoint, and the application is referred by the Court to Petty Sessions.[2] From this we may conclude that the transaction of highway business at the local meeting in this parish was already an established practice.

The Court, when making orders of reference upon petitions relating to the highways, usually mentions the referees by name. It names certain magistrates to supervise the collection and expenditure of rates ordered in the years 1670–72; and it does the same in December 1672 when, after recommending Justices to present decayed highways and supervise their repair, it deputes groups of Justices to take care of the various main roads.[3] It is certain, however, that these were usually the local magistrates, and at times the "Justices in their respective divisions" are explicitly charged with duties, as in the earlier part of the order of December 1672 just mentioned and in an order of May 1686 directing that special attention be given to the Uxbridge Road.[4] It sometimes recognises their local organisation by referring a matter to their next meeting as, for instance, a complaint of inhabitants of Hayes against their Surveyor[5] and a bill in connection with Staines Bridge.[6] When it orders the surveyors of highways generally to arrange their statute work under the direction of Petty Sessions, as it does in April 1682,[7] or of Justices in their Monthly Meetings,[8] it apparently thinks that the whole county will be covered by such meetings; and the Act, 2 William & Mary, c. 8, warrants this conclusion so far as the Metropolitan district is concerned by entrusting to Petty Sessions the provision of laystalls, a necessary part of the scavenging arrangements then provided for. We must not, of course, read too much into the term Petty Sessions or picture stable groups of magistrates holding regular sessions for carefully delimited areas; but it is clear that the Act of 1691 did not

---

[1] 2 William & Mary, c. 8.
[2] Miscellaneous Papers, c. 1690.
[3] S.B. Dec. 1672, pp. 46–9.
[4] S.B. May 1686, p. 34.
[5] S.B. Dec. 1674, p. 41.
[6] S.B. Jan. 1686–7, p. 35.
[7] S.B. April 1682, p. 37.
[8] S.B. Dec. 1684, p. 44.

create the local meetings and it is doubtful whether it materially affected them by causing either greater regularity or differentiation of business. The Brentford Justices continue to intersperse highway with all kinds of other business;[1] so, at a much later date, do those of Marylebone.[2] The Court still refers highway business to Justices by name or to Justices in their divisions or to Petty Sessions. We hear something of "Special Sessions",[3] but the use of this term is the exception rather than the rule and, even when it is employed, it would be dangerous to infer that only highway business was dealt with at the meeting in question. It would seem that the Act of 1691 made little difference in Middlesex; that after, no less than before, this measure, the Justices held local meetings over the county where they were prepared to transact any business legally cognisable out of General or Quarter Sessions, and that the growing regularity of these meetings, which made them better able to deal with all such matters, was a natural development, not appreciably influenced by Parliament.

Parochial road maintenance covered the vast majority of highways at the commencement of our period and may be regarded as the primary and normal type of road service.[4] This

[1] *Vide* the Brentford Calendar.
[2] Minutes of Marylebone Petty Sessions, 1730–56.
[3] For the Tower Division in S.B. July 1694, p. 45; for some area including St Giles' in the Fields in S.B. April 1714, p. 52, and including Islington in 1716—Miscellaneous Papers.
[4] The roads for which particular persons were responsible were not in themselves peculiar and the liability of such persons was legally prior to that of the parishes, but the sphere of this obligation seems to have been very restricted in Middlesex, our evidence on the subject being extremely scanty. A number of bills were found against the Mayor, Commonalty and Citizens of London in their capacity of Lord of the Manor of Finsbury, for not repairing highways on the east and south of the New Artillery Ground in St Giles' without Cripplegate, S.R. Oct. 1671, April 1680 and Oct. 1693. On one occasion, John Green, their common solicitor, confessed two indictments and they were fined 13s. 4d. on each, the money being repaid for the use of the highways, S.R. Oct. 1671. From an order of the Court in 1686, it seems that the Governors of the Hospital of Charterhouse had been prosecuted for not repairing a highway in Clerkenwell, S.B. Oct. 1686, p. 62. In the roll for April 1727 there is an obscure memorandum of a presentment, by two Justices, of the decayed condition of High Holborn in St Giles' in the Fields, which goes on to state that certain persons are to repair various parts of it. Each is fined £10 unless he makes it good before May 10th and two confess, being fined 3s. 4d.

HIGHWAYS AND BRIDGES

has to be considered from several points of view, so that it is necessary to treat separately of the legal obligation of the parish itself, the duty of the inhabitants to do the actual work, the provision of revenue for the purpose and the local officers who directed and organised the whole.

From the fundamentally judicial character of the General and Quarter Sessions it followed that their primary duty in relation to parochial highway obligations was to enforce them judicially. If a parish neglected to keep its public roads in good order, it was indicted at Sessions and further steps rested with the Court. Such indictments are in evidence from the very outset of our period[1] and continue with considerable regularity throughout the greater part of it until, with the gradual supersession of parochial liability for the more important roads, their main *raison d'être* ceased to operate. Of the dilatoriness of the method of indictment we hear much in all connections and its weakness is most marked where the defendant is a community and not an individual, since it would be more difficult to frighten a parish than an ordinary person into confession. In connection with all matters, the number of jury convictions in our records is very small and there are not more than one or two in relation to highways.[2] A parish which put itself on the country and stood its ground firmly rendered itself, therefore, virtually immune from punishment unless some more effective weapon could be devised. Fines, even when imposed, were in the normal case so small—6s. 8d. or 13s. 4d.—as to be a negligible stimulus and they could only be levied by distress upon individual parishioners whose fate might not greatly interest their neighbours. Still, extreme obstinacy was perhaps dangerous and, in a large number of cases, parishes did, sooner or later, take steps to remedy the evil in question, though this may have been partly due to their own recognition of the need. Eventually, Justices who were often deputed to view roads that had been out of repair, were frequently able to report that the defects had been

---

[1] *Vide* those of St Martin's in the Fields and Marylebone in S.R. Oct. 1660.
[2] For instances, *vide* the cases of Kensington in S.R. Jan. 1685–6 and of Hornsey in S.R. May 1677.

made good, in which case a small fine was imposed, but the proceedings might be protracted for years.[1] Sometimes proceedings were stayed altogether upon certificate of repair, without any confession or fine,[2] so that parishes were apparently allowed to neglect their duties for years with complete impunity.

Under the Act, 5 Elizabeth, c. 13, the formal bill of indictment might be dispensed with if one or more Justices of Peace presented a decayed highway. This procedure was no doubt quicker and less expensive and the direct action of some neighbouring magistrate might well carry more weight with surveyors and parishioners than the more remote pronouncement of a Grand Jury. We find such a certificate against Hammersmith in October 1671,[3] and this method was adopted by the Court and recommended to all Justices in the following year when the expedient of conditional fines was introduced. It is doubtful, however, whether such presentments should have ranked merely as indictments which could be traversed or whether they amounted to convictions.[4] Our Justices considered that a fine might be assessed even before the parish concerned had notice of the presentment and, although the levying of it was generally postponed, we do not gather that a subsequent conviction by confession or verdict was considered a necessary preliminary to the estreat when the period of grace had elapsed.[5]

[1] Marylebone which, as already mentioned, was indicted in Oct. 1660, did not confess until May 1664, when it was fined 6s. 8d., S.R. Oct. 1660.
[2] E.g. in the case of Shoreditch in S.R. April 1665, in which the certificate was not presented until July 1669.
[3] S.R. Oct. 1671. For such a presentment in the reign of James I, vide Jeaffreson, *Middlesex County Records*, vol. II, p. 89.
[4] Mr and Mrs Webb think that "originally this presentment by a single Justice may have been made in person at the Quarter Sessions with little formality, the assembled magistrates then and there proceeding to fine the parish in default" in which case, it would appear to constitute a conviction. But they add: "Presently, however, this presentment was dealt with more formally and was treated merely as equivalent to the finding by the Grand Jury of a true bill on an indictment of the parish", *The King's Highway*, p. 51. Burn, also, differing from Dalton, interprets the Act as allowing the delinquent parish the full right to traverse the presentment, *Justice of the Peace*, p. 367.
[5] In Dec. 1674, the Court ordered the fines set upon St Pancras and Islington to be estreated simply upon information from Mr Atkins, the presenting Justice, that the highways were still unrepaired, S.B. Dec. 1674, p. 45.

HIGHWAYS AND BRIDGES

Later, the fines were to be levied immediately, without giving the parish any time to appear or make good the defect.[1] Yet the presentment does not take the place of the ordinary conviction since, in many cases, even after the conditional fine had been estreated, the parishioners confessed the indictment and were thereupon fined the usual trifling amount.[2] It would therefore seem best to equate the Justice's presentment as such to a true bill and to regard the conditional fine as an additional instrument which (with what authority does not appear) was often used in conjunction with it. When the two are employed together, the process comes to resemble conviction upon view of a Justice, which is common in regard to offences cognisable by Justices out of Sessions.

The combined method was introduced by the Middlesex Bench at the time when the temporary rating powers conferred by the Act, 22 Charles II, c. 12, were expiring. Finding "by sad experience that, by neglect of the inhabitants of very many parishes within this county of Middlesex for several years last past in not substantially repairing the highways and roads within their several parishes leading out of many parts of this kingdom to the cities of London and Westminster and places adjacent and by the neglect of the constables, surveyors for the highways and other officers of such parishes from time to time in not presenting the defects of repairs of the said highways in His Majesty's Court of King's Bench at Westminster or at the Quarter or other General Sessions of the Peace of this county, the said highways and roads are rendered in many places of this county very dangerous and almost unpassable to His Majesty and his subjects with horses, coaches and other carriages in and by the same ways riding and travelling", the Court ordered all Justices, at the next and subsequent Sessions, to present the inhabitants of defaulting parishes in order that it might proceed to impose fines unless the inhabitants should, by the time appointed, make good the defects. Upon the recording of such presentments, an officer of the Court was to give written notice to the officers and substantial inhabitants of the parishes, so

[1] E.g. those upon Tottenham, Hackney and Shoreditch in S.R. April 1682.
[2] *Vide* the case of Friern Barnet in S.R. Dec. 1672.

that equal rates and taxes might be rated for raising money to repair the highways that had been presented. The money so raised was ordered to be employed under the close supervision of the magistrates in the various divisions and the care of the principal roads in the county was entrusted to various Justices by name.[1] No time was wasted before beginning to carry out these injunctions. The presentments and conditional fines actually begin at the Sessions at which the order was issued and continue with almost uninterrupted frequency for nearly twenty years. Here, the Court had a very powerful lever, for the fines that were held up in order to give the parishes time to amend their roads were large enough to constitute a real threat and incentive. £100 was the commonest amount imposed, but it was sometimes as much as £300[2] and quite often £200. Moreover a single parish was often liable for two or three such fines at one time. That much good resulted appears from the large number of cases in which, at the end of the period of grace, the Justices certified the highway to be well and sufficiently repaired, whereupon the fine was discharged and the parish was generally fined the usual small amount. If compliance was delayed because of unfavourable circumstances, the Court would further postpone the estreat,[3] but it has to be remembered that the parish, as represented by its surveyors, was powerless if its members refused to play their part, and this seems to be the explanation of most of the continued defaults by parishes. In such a case, the conditional fine could be made absolute and could be used to strengthen the authority of the parish over its members[4]. The Act, 3 William &

[1] S.B. Dec. 1672, pp. 46-9.
[2] The case of St Pancras in S.R. Sept. 1690.
[3] E.g. for Islington, on petition that its roads were nearly nine miles in length, that there had been heavy rains, and that harvest hampered work, S.B. July 1675, p. 56.
[4] Thus, the Court being informed that various surveyors had expended money upon road repair which they could not recover from their parishioners through voluntary rates, ordered the fines which it then made absolute to be levied upon "such of the refractory persons in opposing or negligent persons in making voluntary rates for the reimbursement of the said surveyors and perfecting the work of reparation of the highways in the said respective parishes, townships and places under the direction of Justices of Peace of the respective divisions", S.B. Dec. 1673, pp. 45-7. Here the fiscal aspect of the matter is predominant. On another occasion, estreats were ordered to be issued against all inhabitants of lower Wapping mentioned in a presentment of

Mary, c. 12, restored to General or Quarter Sessions the authority to order rates when necessary and, with the passing of what we must conclude to have been the chief reason for its existence, the expedient of conditional fines fell into desuetude and was only very occasionally used subsequently.[1] In the last twenty-five years of the period, owing to the creation of turnpike trusts, there is a great reduction in the amount of highway business done at Sessions and, though there continue to be occasional presentments of parishes,[2] it seems that, with the taking over of the more important roads by the new authorities, there ceases to be any strong disposition to enforce parochial responsibility for the less important thoroughfares whose dilapidation would be rather a private than a public nuisance.[3]

The basis of parochial highway maintenance was the labour of the parishioners. So far as the ordinary individual was concerned the primary duty in relation to road repair consisted, not in personal responsibility for any particular highway, but in the obligation to work for his parish upon its highways—either to work himself or, if he occupied a ploughland or owned a draught, to send a team with two men. It is unnecessary to dwell long on this matter, since it is the counterpart of parochial obligations already discussed, but something must be said regarding the definition and enforcement of the duty. In the matter of definition, difficulties were caused by the position of non-resident landholders and the indeterminateness of the term "ploughland", whose acreage had not been fixed by Parliament but varied from one part of the country to another according to the nature of the soil. Both these questions were dealt with by

the surveyors, doubtless for not doing their statute work, S.B. Oct. 1679, p. 81. Mr and Mrs Webb consider that the conditional fine tended to undermine the old system, since those who personally worked would still be liable for such fines on their parish, *The King's Highway*, p. 56. Discretion in levying the fines would, however, counteract this tendency and transform them into new weapons for the enforcement of old obligations.

[1] For later instances, *vide* S.B. June 1697, p. 43; S.R. Dec. 1711, July 1720 and Jan. 1720–21.

[2] E.g. three in S.R. Aug. 1752. Fines are either absent or negligible. Hayes, for instance, was fined 12*d.* for the road from Cranford to Uxbridge, S.R. Oct. 1749.

[3] Even in regard to these, the paving of closely inhabited areas was continually reducing the sphere of parochial obligation, *vide* p. 107 *et seq.*

the Court in 1680, when it decided against the claim for exemption put forward by non-resident landholders who, it was informed, occupied very great quantities of land in some parishes. Where they occupied ploughlands, which it defined for Middlesex as fifty acres, it affirmed their duty to send carts as if they were parishioners.[1] This definition, however, did not fit the circumstances of urban parishes, where there might be no owners of fifty acres. Parliament partly met this difficulty in the Act, 7 and 8 William III, c. 29, under which land worth £50 per annum was to be deemed a ploughland, so including comparatively small sites of high value. Another difficulty arose in interpreting the term "draught" in the Act, 2 and 3 Philip & Mary, c. 8. In October 1722, the Court took the view that a coach was not a team,[2] reducing its owner's assessment to that of an ordinary householder. If this meant that all coaches were exempt, it would seriously restrict the supply of carts and horses for work in the thickly populated districts, but the report on the liability of the parishes covered by the Islington Turnpike Trust shows quite considerable numbers of persons as liable to send teams.[3] At the other end of the social scale, among those who worked personally, the very poor must have felt the loss of six days' labour every year a very considerable hardship and the Court was prepared to give them special consideration.[4] If the idea of exempting the poor was interpreted at all liberally, it would lead to the exclusion of a very large proportion of the inhabitants of suburban parishes. These parishes could ill afford to lose this labour and it is very doubtful if they in fact did so. At all events, the committee of Justices appointed to confer with the Islington Turnpike Trust as to the liability of the

[1] S.B. Sept. 1680, p. 53.
[2] S.B. Oct. 1722, p. 79.
[3] 624 in Islington, 396 in Clerkenwell, 234 in Cripplegate, 204 in Hampstead, 396 in Hornsey and 486 in St Pancras, O.C. vol. IV, ff. 60–62.
[4] It recommended some abatement for the poor in 1676. In 1682 it directed that none who did not pay poor rate should be summoned to work and, a little later, recommended the exemption of the poor to the Justices in their monthly meetings, as parish officers were accused of burdening the poor more severely from prejudice or favour, S.B. May 1676, p. 33; April 1682, p. 37; Dec. 1684, p. 44.

HIGHWAYS AND BRIDGES

parishes covered by that Trust returned large numbers as, without qualification, liable for six days' labour.[1]

In the matter of enforcement, it was the duty of the surveyors to present defaulters—those who would neither do their work nor pay the fine for their neglect.[2] These fines were an important source of revenue and were fixed by the Act, 22 Charles II, c. 12, at 1s. 6d. per day for a labourer and 10s. per day for a team. In case of refusal they could be levied by warrant of two Justices of Peace and no doubt a large proportion of such presentments by surveyors were dealt with at the local meetings of Justices which grew up all over the county.[3] In Middlesex, however, the regular indictment at Sessions was extensively used to enforce the obligation. Such indictments for not working or sending teams are not very numerous during the early part of the period,[4] but later we find very large numbers[5] and the frequency of fines shows that the procedure was no empty threat.[6] The method was, however, illegal, as Parliament had not provided for it and was so pronounced by King's Bench in 1729.[7] This judgment put a stop to the practice in Middlesex and the indictment for not working or sending teams disappears from the Records.[8] By this time, owing to the growth of turnpike trusts, the public importance of parochial work was growing less. Still, the turnpike acts laid down that those already liable for highway maintenance should continue to carry out their duties, but now, so far as the roads specially provided for were concerned, this would be done under the direction of the trustees,

---

[1] 2598 in Islington, 8934 in Clerkenwell, 16,272 in Cripplegate, 14,352 in St Giles', 1992 in Hampstead, 1056 in Hornsey and 1212 in St Pancras, O.C. vol. IV, ff. 60–62.

[2] In S.R. Oct. 1666 there is the recognisance of a surveyor for not returning such defaulters.

[3] *Vide* the Brentford Calendar, *passim*.

[4] For a batch of 14, *vide* S.R. Oct. 1667.

[5] Some 60 from Whitechapel in S.R. June 1687 and batches of from 30 to 40 from other parishes at a single Sessions, as in S.R. April 1710, July 1711 and April 1719.

[6] About three-quarters of the Whitechapel offenders just mentioned were fined 6s., i.e. four days' composition.

[7] Burn, *Justice of the Peace*, p. 369. Bond, in his *Complete Guide for Justices of Peace* (1685), gives the form of an indictment for not working.

[8] It was no doubt largely owing to its legal weakness that, in most counties, the method of indictment was not much used.

not of the parish surveyor. It remained for the trustees to secure the performance of this statutory work and, as will appear later, from 1735 they were constantly applying to the Court to allot them a proportion of the statute work of the parishes through which their roads ran. The quotas allocated were not large if, as we may well suppose, the bulk of parish work had previously been done on these main roads. From this, and from the infrequency of proceedings against parishes in respect of their remaining highways, we may conclude that the latter part of the period witnessed a great reduction of the burden of highway maintenance falling upon the ordinary inhabitants.[1] In any case, the obligation ceases to have any place in our Records.

The labour of parishioners and their teams provided the surveyors of highways with a strong force of men and transport for work on the roads, but there remained a need for funds with which to meet pecuniary liabilities. Probably it had never been possible altogether to avoid such expenses and, with the growth of traffic, especially of wheeled traffic, they grew apace. This was particularly so in parishes lacking adequate supplies of gravel and stones.[2] Originally, however, parishes had no legal authority to raise money directly by rates and had to rely mainly on a variety of fines allocated by Parliament to the use of the highways. The fines for not working or sending teams, which tended to develop into money compositions in lieu of service, have already been noticed. Inasmuch as the method of indictment was used in this connection, the Court was a means of

[1] In 1735 we read of Islington that "The method the parish usually takes for raising the composition to pay the Trustees and answer the demands for the repairs of the roads of the rest of the parish is by the parishioners being defaulters for three days' statute work", while in Clerkenwell the inhabitants defaulted for only two days and in St Pancras for four days, O.C. vol. IV, ff. 60–62. It may be that, in the rural areas, the surveyors, with the help of the local Justices, continued to some extent to oblige their parishioners to turn out for highway work. There also, however, turnpike trusts were being given charge of the main roads. The Colnbrook Trustees abandoned the policy of applying to Sessions to allot statute work and so, presumably, took the burden of their road entirely off the adjacent parishes, *vide* p. 132.
[2] In one case, a Limehouse surveyor was detained in prison by a gravel factor, S.B. Feb. 1674–5, p. 40.

HIGHWAYS AND BRIDGES

providing the revenue for the parochial authorities.[1] The same is true in regard to the ordinary indictment of the parish for unrepaired highways, though the revenue was less important, as negligent parishes were naturally less numerous than defaulting individuals and the fines were very small in the ordinary case. Fines upon negligent surveyors also went to the use of their office.[2] There were offences, rather less directly connected with road maintenance, whose penalties were appointed for the same purpose,[3] and others not in themselves having any connection with the roads, forfeitures upon which went to swell the funds at the disposal of the surveyors.[4] Such funds were, however, altogether insufficient to cope with the increased use of the roads from the seventeenth century onwards.

This being so, parishes naturally wished to raise further revenue by rating their inhabitants, as they were empowered to do in connection with poor relief. An Ordinance of 1654 legalised a 1s. rate, to be made by a meeting of parishioners, and apparently a good deal was done with its help, but it lapsed at the Restoration.[5] An Act of 1662[6] for three years allowed a 6d. rate, but it does not appear to have been much employed.[7] Something was done through "voluntary rates", and the fact that these were at all feasible argues a lively sense of responsibility or of the advantage of good roads on the part of the inhabitants of at least some parishes. In 1666 the inhabitants of Kentish Town in St Pancras complained "that having made and collected an

---

[1] Receipts were sometimes entered in the Sessions Books when the money was paid over, e.g. S.B. Dec. 1692, p. 57.
[2] For a fine of 40s. upon a Heston surveyor, vide S.R. Jan. 1679–80.
[3] In S.B. Feb. 1672–3 (p. 55) there are receipts for £3. 6s. 8d. and 3s. 4d. levied upon two inhabitants of Bromley for not scouring their ditches, the money being received from the Clerk of the Peace for the use of the surveyor there. For other nuisance fines similarly earmarked, vide S.R. April 1699.
[4] For five Hanwell cases of unlawful measure, in which half the 5s. fines are for the use of the surveyors, vide S.R. Oct. and Dec. 1706.
[5] Webb, *The King's Highway*, p. 20.
[6] 14 Charles II, c. 6.
[7] Mr and Mrs Webb have found only one instance, op. cit. p. 22. Our Records supply none, but, as the rate was to be made by the surveyors with two or more householders and to be confirmed by a neighbouring Justice, action by Sessions was not directly involved. In Hertfordshire, a 6d. rate was made by the surveyors of Furneux Pelham in 1663, Hardy, *Hertford County Records*, vol. I, p. 159.

assessment on the said inhabitants for repairing the highways in the said parish and having by their surveyors of the highways carefully employed the same in repairing and mending the same, yet by reason of the very frequent and unusual passing of waggons, carts and carriages upon and through the said highways they are become so much broken and decayed that the moneys so collected for the repair thereof are not sufficient to defray the charges which the said inhabitants have been put unto for the repairing of the highways and the discharging the indictments preferred against them for not repairing the same", and desired an order for an assessment, to amount to £21, upon non-resident landholders as upon resident inhabitants. This the Court granted. If any refused to pay, his name was to be returned at the next Sessions "to answer such his refusal and further to be dealt withal according to justice", but it is doubtful if he could have been dealt with very effectively.[1] When the inhabitants of Marylebone asked for an assessment to be ordered because "the highways within that parish are become exceeding ruinous, broken and torn and in great decay for want of repairing and amendment thereof, for the which they have been often indicted and several issues have been levied upon them, to the great impoverishment of them and that the said inhabitants of themselves are not able to repair and amend the same according to the ordinary means", the Court, "being ready and willing to further so good a work", directed two Justices to be desired to cause an assessment to be made for such money as they thought needful "if by law they may justly do the same".[2] Here we have a striking testimony to the impotence of the parish and the weakness of any attempt to help on the part of the Court.

The Act, 22 Charles II, c. 12, gave temporary authority to the Justices in Sessions, if satisfied that the highways of a parish could not be sufficiently repaired by the existing laws, to assess a rate not exceeding 6*d.* in the pound upon such parish. A good deal was done in Middlesex under this Act during its three

---

[1] S.Reg. vol. IX, pp. 392–3. For a reference to sums collected at St Pancras, *vide* S.B. Feb. 1670–71, p. 24.
[2] S.B. April 1670, p. 35.

years' continuance,[1] but the order of 1672 already referred to[2] suggests that the roads were not much benefited.[3] This Act expired in 1673, but the Court was not content to allow matters to slip back into the old state of inaction. At the very next Sessions after the last rating order it inaugurated the system of conditional fines which has already been discussed in its punitive aspect. This not only provided funds to defray expenses which could not otherwise be met, but supplied a direct means of strengthening the voluntary rate, inasmuch as it could be deliberately levied on those who refused to contribute. Thus when the surveyor of Limehouse, after alluding to various defaults, informed the Court that he was engaged to workmen for £58. 14s. 6d. more than he could receive, the Court ordered a high constable to levy this amount, under an estreat in his hands, upon the most refractory inhabitants and to repay the officer.[4] Again, ten Fulham inhabitants refused to pay money assessed upon them by the "chiefest of the inhabitants" and the Justices directed that a £100 fine outstanding against the parish should be levied upon them according to their assessment.[5] As a result of similar action at Lower Wapping, John Batty complained that, for his refusal to pay a 4s. assessment, the high constable had levied £5 upon an estreat against the parish. The Court directed the surveyors out of the next rate to repay £4. 12s. 0d., retaining double his assessment as a punishment for his refusal and ill example.[6] But the best illustration of the close connection between the fine and the rate comes from Hampstead, where the high constable had distrained goods for a £100 fine upon presentment. Being informed that the parish had made an adequate rate, the Court ordered him to go round with the

---

[1] Some 24 rates were made in the years 1670 and 1671.
[2] *Vide* p. 95.
[3] Not only lands but any personal estate usually rateable to the poor were rated, and Justices were deputed to supervise the collection and expenditure of the money, *vide* for instance, the rate for St Pancras in S.B. June 1670, pp. 29–34. Sometimes the Court itself appoints assessors and collectors of the rates, as, for instance, in a number of cases in S.B. July 1671. The Tottenham vestry elected two rival collectors for one of these rates, but the Court brushed their claim aside and confirmed those originally appointed by its own order, S.B. December 1672, p. 41.
[4] S.B. Sept. 1674, p. 40.   [5] S.B. Oct. 1674, p. 44.
[6] S.B. Feb. 1675–6, p. 40.

collectors and return the goods to those who paid their quota, otherwise to retain them.[1] Such an arrangement involved great trouble, and it is clear that in most cases the estreat was only an imperfect substitute for a compulsory rate. Usually the high constable would distrain upon only a few parishioners for comparatively large amounts, so that a rate was still needed to make good their losses and distribute the burden equitably.[2] It was therefore in response to a real need that the Act, 3 William & Mary, c. 12, empowered General or Quarter Sessions to order a rate, not exceeding 6*d.* in the pound, if satisfied that the highways of any parish could not otherwise be sufficiently amended.[3] Thereafter, circuitous expedients for raising money were superfluous. The rating powers were naturally used very unequally by different parishes. St Giles' in the Fields, Islington and Hornsey secured orders for rates in most years.[4] Heston, St Pancras, Ealing and Harmondsworth also occur. Shoreditch, on the other hand, never had a rate, the statute work and penalties being sufficient.[5] After the new rating provisions had been in operation for about twenty years, there is an apparent falling off in the use of them.[6] This is surprising in view of the fact that the turnpike trusts had not yet made much headway and the Act, 1 George I, stat. 2, c. 52, so far from impairing the rating power of Quarter Sessions or countenancing the idea that it was superfluous, expressly confirmed it, adding that it was not necessary to wait until all statute work was performed, as had

[1] S.B. July 1688, p. 41.
[2] £90 was levied by the sheriff upon one inhabitant of Shoreditch. The parish took up £100 at interest to reimburse him and satisfy other charges and prayed an order of Court for a rate to meet this debt. The Justices complied, S.B. Aug. 1671, p. 31. For a similar case, *vide* S.B. Feb. 1680-81, p. 29.
[3] This is shown by a petition of the churchwardens and other officers and inhabitants of St Giles' in the Fields, preserved in the Miscellaneous Papers, which set forth that they had usually made an annual rate for highways, but many had refused to pay, and prayed an order according to the late Act that those usually present at the making of other parish rates should have authority to raise money for highways, to be employed as the Justices usually present at the Petty Sessions in the parish should appoint.
[4] St Giles' in the Fields received authority for a 1*d.* rate as early as April 1691, S.B. April 1691, p. 77.
[5] S.B. Oct. 1724, pp. 110-12.
[6] After 1715 St Giles' in the Fields seems to be the only parish for which the Court ordered assessments.

HIGHWAYS AND BRIDGES

been supposed. This points to the development of the rating principle as a substitute for, not merely a supplement to, the older method. Moreover, there are one or two incidental references to rates,[1] and a report on the Islington turnpike implies that Islington, St Giles' without Cripplegate and St Pancras had rates up to the turnpike era.[2] We must conclude that rates were becoming familiar enough to pass without the formality of approval by Sessions, perhaps being allowed by Justices at their local meetings.[3] With the development of turnpike trusts, it is easier to believe that rating powers fell into disuse. The report of February 1735-6 shows that the nominal compositions payable by the parishes covered by the Islington Turnpike amounted to only £241 out of about £1900 annually expended by the Trust on their roads, and even these modest contributions were much in arrear. A 6d. rate in Islington and a rate of unspecified amount in St Pancras had become unnecessary.[4] Still, we do not find a complete cessation of this line of action.[5] Though turnpike action continued to increase, statute labour diminished, and the net result was to leave the rate an indispensable adjunct to parochial road maintenance.

It is necessary to say something regarding the surveyors of the parish highways, since one method by which the Justices could exercise control of road administration was through the medium of the responsible officials. Under the Act, 2 and 3 Philip & Mary, c. 8, these were to be chosen by the constables, churchwardens and inhabitants of their parish, but by 3 William & Mary, c. 12, the inhabitants were merely to submit a panel from which the actual appointments were to be made by two Justices

---

[1] S.B. Jan. 1719-20, p. 54; April 1720, p. 64.
[2] O.C. vol. IV, ff. 60-62.
[3] The Brentford Calendar does not suggest that the latter course, which would in any case appear to have been irregular, was widely adopted, but we do read there of a rate for Willesden being seen and allowed in June 1709, p. 145. The Minutes of the Petty Sessions at Marylebone show that rates continued there for some time, though there is no record of their being allowed by the Justices. One of the annual surveyors' accounts, for instance, includes the item: "received per the book, £160. 3s. 6d.", Minutes, July 5th 1731. There are frequent proceedings for non-payment of highway rates, but mention of them seems to cease after 1746.
[4] O.C. vol. IV, ff. 60-62.
[5] *Vide* S.B. Oct. 1739, p. 41; Oct. 1758, p. 39.

of the division at a special sessions. It is doubtful whether this legal change made much difference in practice, for the Court had apparently, even before this, claimed for the local Justices some voice in the selection of surveyors.[1] We have evidence that the bilateral control was in force later,[2] though, in our instances, it was the discretion of the magistrates, not that of the inhabitants, which the Court restrained.[3] In the case of an unpaid post, entailing such extensive duties, duties, moreover, which brought its occupant into very unpleasant relations with his neighbours, compulsion to accept nomination was indispensable. There seem to be no explicit prosecutions for refusing to accept office,[4] but indictments for neglecting to execute the office usually allege total neglect and would, therefore, cover passive resistance to appointment. As in other cases, refusal to serve might be compounded for, and we meet references to such fines, which went to the service of the highways.[5] The Court also allowed many appeals against nomination on a variety of grounds.[6] When parishioners had been compelled to take upon themselves the undesired office, it still remained to induce them to carry out its onerous duties with a reasonable measure of energy and intelligence.[7] The "spiritless, ignorant, lazy, sauntering people called surveyors of the highways"[8] needed constant supervision by Justices in and out of Sessions, and it is clear that a certain amount was done in this direction in Middlesex. Proceedings are naturally most noticeable at times of vigorous highway administration[9] and prosecutions of surveyors go hand in hand

[1] S.B. Dec. 1672, p. 49. The true bills for neglecting the office continue to mention only nomination and election by the inhabitants, cf. the bills against the surveyors of Islington in S.R. Oct. 1680 and against those of Hammersmith in S.R. Aug. 1694.
[2] *Vide* the Marylebone Minutes, Jan. 3rd 1738.
[3] S.B. Jan. 1720–21, p. 35; April 1730, pp. 66–7.
[4] In connection with the removal of two inhabitants of Shoreditch, it was suggested that they had gone in order to escape the office, and the Court directed that, if this were so, they were to be bound over, S.B. Jan. 1672–3, p. 37.
[5] E.g. S.B. Oct. 1674, p. 41.
[6] S.B. May 1676, p. 36; Jan. 1691–2, p. 47; Jan. 1698–9, p. 35.
[7] Between 1680 and 1683 Hornsey farmed out the office of surveyor to one Richard Hall for £10 yearly, S.B. Dec. 1686, p. 44.
[8] Burn, *History of the Poor Laws*, p. 239.
[9] There are nine recognisances for neglecting the office in S.R. June 1673.

HIGHWAYS AND BRIDGES

with indictments of their parishes, serving the same purpose.[1] Fines range from 40s.[2] downwards and were for the use of the roads. One or two prosecutions relate to specific negligences, such as allowing overloaded vehicles on the highway[3] and not presenting unscoured ditches.[4] As the money raised for the highways increased, its disposal grew in importance and the Court had to deal with surveyors who refused to submit accounts,[5] with those who converted highway money to their own use[6] and with the extravagance of others.[7] Another type of difficulty arose from the temptation which the surveyors were under to arrange the road work to suit their own or their friends' interests.[8] From many points of view, therefore, since the parishioners themselves had very slender means of controlling their officers, a tight hand from above was essential. Naturally such control could most easily be exercised by the local Justices, and we see the Court constantly referring one matter after another to their attention, with or without general injunctions how to proceed. In fact, it is possible that a large proportion of the complaints to Court as to the conduct of surveyors represent, not so much specific grievances, as attempts by parishioners to assert control over their officers by inducing the Justices to allow or disallow items in their accounts or to issue desired regulations as to the management of the work. The Court evidently saw the need for public accounts at least.[9]

Up to the present we have been dealing with normal highway administration, and so far our evidence may be regarded as typical of what went on throughout the country. It has to be remembered, however, that Middlesex was not a typical county.

[1] In April 1680 Islington was conditionally fined £50 on each of two presentments and in the following October its four surveyors were indicted for totally neglecting to execute their office, S.R. April and Oct. 1680.
[2] S.R. Jan. 1679-80. [3] S.R. Oct. 1673.
[4] S.R. July 1669. [5] E.g. S.B. May 1676, p. 33.
[6] *Vide* the indictments of the four Shoreditch surveyors in S.R. April 1680.
[7] Those of Shoreditch for 1673 "in giving where they list and spending near £20 in breakfasts", and those of Acton who were accused of charging nearly £5 for labourers and gravel which was spent in alehouses and charging 30s. for gathering the money, S.B. Dec. 1674, p. 44; April 1708, p. 65.
[8] *Vide* S.B. Dec. 1674, p. 41; Jan. 1729-30, pp. 24-5.
[9] *Vide* an order to surveyors to account annually to the vestry in S.B. April 1687, p. 61.

Its proximity to London alone would cause the traffic upon its roads to be much greater than the average and, in the light of this consideration, it is probable that the demands made upon those who were charged with their maintenance were abnormally heavy. A further complication, however, was introduced by the fact that a considerable and growing portion of the county was actually covered by the Metropolis, and here the density of the population gave rise to a great deal of local traffic. The more or less regular gravel surface which was the most that parochial administration achieved was not at all suited to stand such continuous wear and tear, while it does not seem that the parish could usually be made responsible for the new streets which were constantly being opened out.[1] The encloser (including, no doubt, the encloser for building purposes) of land adjoining the highway was legally bound to maintain the half of the road adjacent to his holding, and this was, we may suppose, the foundation for the arrangement adopted to meet the case of all streets as they came to be fully built on. The customary obligation to keep in repair such streets as by some means had become paved appears vague, but of more importance were the definite provisions of several acts passed in the sixteenth century as to certain streets in the metropolitan area.[2] Thus, from the very beginning of the period, the Court was concerned in enforcing the duty of paving and keeping in repair certain specified streets, but for several years we meet hardly any indictments.[3] The Act, 14 Charles II, c. 2, provided special commissioners, to be nominated under the Great Seal and accountable to the Exchequer, to pave certain streets as well as to perform other services. Owners or inhabitants were to pay them at the rate of 16*d.* per square yard—an interesting early example of the idea of substituting compulsory payment to a public body for the

---

[1] Burn, *Justice of the Peace*, p. 353.
[2] For a list of such Acts, *vide* Webb, *Statutory Authorities*, p. 277. The Act, 34 and 35 Henry VIII, c. 12, after reciting the noisome condition of certain streets, required all persons with lands and tenements fronting them to pave them with stone as the streets in the city of London were paved upon penalty of 12*d.* per square yard.
[3] In 1660 the Court ordered constables to return defaulters in St Giles' and Holborn, S.B. Oct. 1660, p. 35. There is a fine of 3*s.* 4*d.* in S.R. April 1666.

HIGHWAYS AND BRIDGES

obligation to perform a service in person—but little is known of the Commissioners of Scotland Yard, as the new authority came to be called.[1] For the rest, the Act reaffirmed personal liability for pavement where it existed and the Great Plague brought the question of public health into prominence. As a result, an order was issued under the direction of the Lord Chief Justice enjoining the repair of pavements as well as the strict execution of the cleansing regulations.[2] More vigorous prosecutions followed and a number of fines were imposed during the following year.[3] There follows a relaxation and indictments are not numerous enough to indicate vigorous administration. As, however, Justices out of Sessions could convict under the Act of 1662, this evidence is not conclusive.[4] The parish as a whole was interested in the enforcement of individual responsibility for pavement, as this reduced the extent of parochial highways,[5] while individual default might involve the parish in prosecution.[6]

---

[1] Webb, *Statutory Authorities*, p. 240 n.

[2] S.Reg. vol. IX, p. 393.

[3] These included a fine of 20s. upon one of two Stepney scavengers indicted for not repairing pavement, S.R. April 1667.

[4] That something continued to be done is shown by an order for the inhabitants of White Horse Street to remove a pump, posts and rails, in order that the inhabitants of Ratcliff might pave it, S.B. July 1683, p. 57. Perhaps the parish authorities at times introduced paving, thinking it cheaper in the long run for much-frequented thoroughfares. In S.R. June 1687 St Clement Danes is fined 6s. 8d. for pavement in the Strand, but the position there must have been anomalous, as John Mayrock, common pavior, was fined 3s. 4d. for deceitfully and insufficiently repairing pavement there before the house of one Peter Smith. Evidently he was employed by the several inhabitants, since the bill alleges intent to deceive and defraud Peter Smith, S.R. Jan. 1687-8.

[5] We find the churchwardens and others of St Giles' in the Fields petitioning that the high street had formerly been repaired at the general charge but, conceiving that it ought to be paved by the several inhabitants, they desired that it might be viewed, S.B. April 1672, p. 44.

[6] The ancient inhabitants of Shoreditch complained that many indictments had been laid against them and great issues returned into the Exchequer, mainly owing to the fault of certain inhabitants in not paving the street and highway before their respective lands and tenements, as had been heretofore accustomed and ought to be done. The Court ordered all streets usually paved to be made good, everyone paving the portion before his lands or tenements as far as the middle of the street, S.B. July 1671, p. 44. Doubtless as a result, three Shoreditch people were indicted and fined at the following Sessions, S.R. August 1671.

The Act, 2 William & Mary, sess. 2, c. 8, reaffirmed the duty of inhabiting householders and owners of unoccupied houses to keep paved streets in repair and, what was of more importance, greatly extended the operation of the law and increased the duties of Justices in the matter by empowering a Justice to certify new streets as fit to be paved, whereupon Quarter Sessions was to order the owners and inhabitants, according to their several interests, to pave them upon pain of 40s. per perch for every week's default. As a result, there was an immediate stiffening of the existing liability[1] and we find frequent orders, grounded upon certificates of Justices, for the inhabitants of new streets to pave the way before their walls as far as the "denter stone" or middle of the street.[2] The Records do not warrant the making of any definite inference as to the vigour of enforcement, since Magistrates out of Sessions could convict. There are fairly numerous indictments for a time, then noticeably fewer.[3] Slackness in enforcement is very probable, considering that there was no official specially charged with the duty of prosecuting defaulters. This work fell mainly upon the constable, and we know that that officer was far from energetic even in spheres where he was spurred on by frequent exhortations and threats from his superiors and by the offer of rewards. The absence of Sessions orders to stimulate him, when contrasted with their frequency in other connections, argues a lack of interest on the part of the Justices.[4] A further stage is marked by the temporary Act, 2 George II, c. 11, which directed the vestrymen of parishes within the Bills of Mortality to return a list of inhabitants to two or more Justices at a special Sessions. The Justices were, from such lists, to appoint surveyors to make returns of unrepaired

[1] There are 16 indictments in S.R. April 1691 and about 30 in the following October.
[2] E.g. S.B. April 1691, pp. 80–82. For the difficulty of sharing out the burden between those with various interests in tenements, vide S.B. July 1691, p. 64; April 1692, p. 54. For the paving and amending, as well as the cleansing, of Kensington Square, 3 William & Mary, c. 12, empowered Sessions to make a rate upon the inhabitants of old and new streets alike. It is not clear why the burden on the residents was thus lightened.
[3] Against some 50 bills between April 1700 and April 1706, there are not 10 in the corresponding period from 1710 onwards.
[4] But the Court was roused to action regarding paving, as well as cleansing, by the plague of 1720, vide p. 116.

HIGHWAYS AND BRIDGES

pavements to them, the Justices, by whom they were to be presented at Quarter Sessions. Notice of default was to be given in church and, if they were not amended within twenty days, the surveyors were to repair it and to be reimbursed. They were also empowered to pave before empty houses and levy the expense on the next tenants. The surveyors might be allowed £8 per annum. As a result of this Act, there is, at the Guildhall, a volume of "Presentments of Surveyors of Streets", covering the years 1729-31. Its ninety-one pages comprise lists of presentments by the surveyors of various parishes and divisions. Most are signed by surveyors, but the names at the foot of some of the lists would appear to be those of the Justices who returned them to Sessions.[1] Following each list is a Latin note, under a different date, presumably added after the presentment had been returned to the General Sessions, that all the persons mentioned are fined £3. 6s. 8d., to be levied unless the pavements are repaired either before a certain date or within a certain time. There is no evidence of orders to surveyors to carry out the repairs themselves, but perhaps the conditional fine was used instead.[2] Nor do we hear of any payment to the surveyors.[3] The new system apparently did not work well, though we do not gather why,[4] and Parliament allowed it to expire after three years. So far as the Quarter Sessions was concerned, the position then became what it had been before the new Act. There continue to be orders to pave and sporadic prosecutions,[5] but the general impression is one of slackness and lack of interest. It is doubtful if this can be attributed to a perception of the inequitability of laying upon the residents the burden of maintaining roads which might be thoroughfares in extensive general use.[6] The enthusiasm of administrators may

---

[1] E.g. at the foot of Nos. 1 and 9 for St Giles'.
[2] For the estreat of a fine of £3. 6s. 8d. for three yards of pavement, vide S.B. April 1733, p. 70.
[3] There are a few presentments for laying and allowing rubbish before houses, also with conditional fines of £3. 6s. 8d., e.g. on p. 36 of the volume.
[4] The Court appointed a committee to consider defects, O.C. vol. III, f. 265.
[5] S.B. April 1734, p. 77; Jan. 1738-9, pp. 27-8. There were nearly 30 prosecutions in Swan Alley, Clerkenwell, in S.R. Oct. 1756.
[6] Under 2 William & Mary, c. 8, ancient streets repaired and paved in any other manner were to continue so and it is doubtful how far the new system

well have been damped by the obvious difficulties in the system. So long as each inhabitant was responsible for his own piece of pavement, it was almost hopeless to expect uniformity. An irregular pavement might be dangerous enough to be worse than no pavement at all.[1] Empty houses were also a difficulty, while water companies caused much annoyance by taking up pavements in order to lay pipes and not replacing them satisfactorily.[2] Hence we cannot be surprised at the constant complaints as to the condition of the streets[3] nor that these complaints finally led to the institution of new authorities to carry out paving as well as other street functions.[4] Before the close of our period, such bodies had begun to operate in some parts of the urban area.[5] Parliament thereby accepted the view that the old system was no longer adequate.[6]

The growth of a large urban area adjacent to the city of London much aggravated the difficulty of keeping the highways in a reasonably sanitary condition. Throughout our period, interest was concentrated on the state of the public roads, as distinct from the private homes, but clearly the two could not really be kept separate. The presence of filth in the highways was, for the most part, the direct result of its production in large numbers of closely packed houses, coupled with the absence of adequate provision for its removal. Theoretically, of course, the

was applied to really important roads. A special grievance was caused by the use of paved streets for market purposes, particularly when, as in the case of hay and straw, an extensive use of waggons was involved. Following a precedent set by 14 Charles II, c. 2, the Act, 8 and 9 William III, c. 17, established a system of partial maintenance by the users in the case of the Haymarket at Westminster by imposing tolls which were to be paid to persons appointed by the Justices of Middlesex and Westminster. The affairs of this market consequently came before the Court very frequently.

[1] For two indictments for erecting pavement above the ancient level, damaging the highway by obstructing a watercourse, *vide* S.R. Sept. 1759.

[2] For this evil in Westminster, *vide* Sir John Gonson's Charge at Quarter Sessions, April 24th 1728, p. 25. For Middlesex, *vide* S.B. Dec. 1714, p. 84.

[3] *Vide* Webb, *Statutory Authorities*, p. 280 et seq.

[4] At least one of the turnpike acts had included provision for paving, Oxford Street being so covered by 7 George I, c. 26.

[5] In Red Lion Square under 10 George II, c. 15. and in Wapping, Shadwell and Ratcliff under 29 George II, c. 87.

[6] Outside the metropolitan area, some paving was carried out at Brentford, *vide* the Brentford Calendar, pp. 54, 66, but there seem to have been no proceedings at Quarter Sessions in this connection.

HIGHWAYS AND BRIDGES

evil might have been met by strict execution of the law against nuisances, but, unless some positive solution were offered, this would be hardly practicable, especially as there were no officials exclusively charged with its administration. Hence the institution of public scavengers, like the provision of common sewers, is really a constructive attempt to abate a large class of nuisances to the highway. As such, it is an excellent illustration of the manner in which the inadequacy of private action gradually, by force of circumstances, leads to a general perception of the need for public provision.[1] Apart from the prohibition of positive nuisances to the highway, there was an old duty of householders to keep clean the pavement in front of their tenements, failure to fulfil which constituted a passive nuisance,[2] but it is doubtful whether the enforcement of this was ever seriously attempted. Clearly, the provision would be illusory unless some means of removing the dirt were provided by municipal or other local enterprise, as was done in the cities of London and Westminster and many other towns. Something had already been done along these lines in the county of Middlesex,[3] but such extra-legal developments were obstructed by the difficulty of raising the necessary funds.[4] Remedial measures were soon undertaken, as the Act, 14 Charles II, c. 2, which made special provision for the cleansing as well as the paving of certain streets, went on to deal with the problem in the rest of the district adjacent to London and Westminster. It ordered all householders to sweep the street before their doors twice a week and directed that all dirt was to be regularly removed by scavengers or other officers coming round with carts. Scavengers were to be annually elected for each parish and compelled to take office, and a yearly rate was to be made to pay the wages of the raker or other person employed for the

[1] Webb, *Statutory Authorities*, p. 316 *et seq.*
[2] *Ibid.* p. 317.
[3] *Vide* an order regulating nuisances in St John Street, which refers to scavengers and rakers, S.B. Jan. 1662–3, p. 33. For similar arrangements under the Protectorate in the parishes of St Giles' in the Fields, Shoreditch, Clerkenwell, St Sepulchre's, St Giles' without Cripplegate and Whitechapel, *vide* Jeaffreson, *Middlesex County Records*, vol. III, pp. 226–8.
[4] For an illustration of this in Hertfordshire, *vide* Hardy, *Hertford County Records*, vol. II, p. 93.

purpose, which rate was to be confirmed by two Justices. The Act was only to be in force until the first session of the following Parliament, but this, as it happened, meant a fairly long life. The new provisions were not allowed to remain idle long,[1] and the Court came to stand, in relation to the duty of cleansing, in a position analogous to that which it occupied in relation to repairing the highway. It had to deal with scavengers who neglected their duties[2] or who refused to submit accounts,[3] or to pay over their balances,[4] and with inhabitants who refused to pay their rates[5] or considered themselves over-rated.[6] It also entertained appeals against election to the office of scavenger and, when it thought fit, discharged nominees.[7] A difference is introduced by the absence of proceedings against parishes in their corporate capacity[8] and by the greater degree of professionalism in the department of cleansing. While the office of scavenger was unpaid and compulsory, provision had, as we have seen, been made for payment for the work of actually removing the refuse, which the ordinary inhabitant would not usually care to undertake. The expedient of hiring substitutes or rakers removed the need for an annual change of staff[9] and made it easier to secure that the work should be undertaken by people with capital and initiative.[10]

[1] In February 1662–3, the Court ordered the scavengers of Ratcliff to pay £20. 10s. wages for cleansing the streets for half a year to a man hired by the inhabitants for that purpose, an assessment having been made according to the late Act, S.B. Feb. 1662–3, pp. 31–2. In the roll for the same month, one Stanford of Limehouse is charged with altering the book of assessment for scavenger's rate after it had been signed by the inhabitants and allowed by Justices. *Vide* also S.B. Oct. 1663, p. 40; Dec. 1664, p. 37.

[2] Three scavengers of St Giles' in the Fields were indicted in S.R. Feb. 1666–7, two fined 20s. and one 10s.

[3] Two scavengers of Whitechapel were fined 12d. for not accounting, S.R. Oct. 1749.

[4] A Bethnal Green scavenger was fined 12d. for not paying over his money, S.R. Oct. 1733.

[5] One was fined 3s. 4d. in S.R. April 1684.   [6] S.B. July 1691, p. 71.

[7] S.B. April 1665, p. 41; April 1672, p. 33; April 1676, p. 38; May 1692, p. 29; April 1707, p. 36; April 1737, p. 75; April 1738, pp. 70–71.

[8] Moreover, proceedings never seem to have been taken at Sessions against householders for not sweeping the streets.

[9] One Silver Crispin was raker of Holborn for at least eight years, S.B. April 1758, pp. 32–3.

[10] In St Giles' in the Fields, Thomas Rowe stated that he had laid out above £1000 in purchasing the business from the widow of Windsor Sandys and

HIGHWAYS AND BRIDGES

The expiration of the Act of 1662 left the legal position doubtful[1] and the Court therefore took part in promoting fresh legislation after the Revolution.[2] The Act, 2 William & Mary, sess. 2, c. 8, after reciting the impossibility of enforcing the execution of the office of scavenger or the payment of scavenger's rate and the resultant throwing of dirt into the streets, re-enacted, with little alteration, the provisions of the expired Act on these matters, which were to apply to the parishes within the Weekly Bills of Mortality and Kensington. Following this, the Court issued a general order for the execution of the new law, directing scavengers to go round every day except Sundays and holidays.[3] The organisation had been developed in conjunction with the provisions for paving,[4] being most needed in those densely populated areas which were intended to be paved, but it would have been unfortunate if delay in paving had barred the introduction of these other necessary improvements, and the Court expressed its opinion that those distant from the pavement should take part in the scavenging arrangements.[5] The disposal of the refuse was not without difficulty. It was needed as manure, and country carts returning empty after delivering their loads of hay, straw, etc., afforded a convenient means of transport. But it was necessary to provide facilities for the transfer from rakers to farmers and, to this end, the Act allowed scavengers and rakers to lodge their dirt in convenient vacant places in the neighbourhood, by order of Petty Sessions, giving satisfaction to the owners, whose demands might be moderated by the Justices. Appeal lay to Quarter Sessions, so that the Court was occasionally occupied with this compulsory use of private property for public purposes.[6] Needless to say, it was necessary for the Court to be on the alert against general slackness. Single magistrates could convict offenders, and doubtless the local resident Justice would usually be interested in the

---

buying horses and other goods, and a further £1000 in carrying on the work. The Court found that he had carried away nearly 2000 loads of dirt and ashes between Christmas and Lady Day, S.B. April 1681, p. 27.

[1] S.B. May 1682, p. 34. *Vide* also the preamble to 2 William & Mary.
[2] S.B. Jan. 1690–91, p. 54.   [3] S.B. Jan. 1690–91, p. 50.
[4] *Vide* the Acts and Webb, *Statutory Authorities*, p. 316.
[5] S.B. April 1691, p. 86.   [6] E.g. S.B. July 1751, pp. 35–9.

enforcement of the law. The ordinary inhabitants, too, would be sufficiently alive to the necessity of the system to make general neglect less likely than, for instance, in the case of highway repair, where the users were, for the most part, not the providers of the service.[1] The Court itself was most active in the matter in the years 1720–21, when plague was raging on the Continent. Upon complaint that "by the great negligence of the scavengers, rakers and other officers, as well as an almost entire neglect of the inhabitants in sweeping their doors, etc., as directed by the statutes, the streets, lanes, alleys and public places are in a most ruinous and dirty condition, not only in respect to the pavements being broke and wore down in most of the high streets, but also by the poorer sort of people laying at their doors dust, dirt, coal-ashes, dung and other filth and rubbish", and finding that, though extracts of the laws had been printed and the Justices had pressed the inhabitants to obey and had "made examples by convicting and levying the penalties on some of the most remarkable offenders", more vigorous execution was still necessary, the Court unanimously resolved to enforce the laws in the most effectual manner possible, ordered extracts of the statutes to be widely distributed and recommended Justices to hold Petty Sessions one day a week at least in order to deal with this matter.[2] The measures were not as effective as could have been wished, and a long report on the various practices and negligences conducing to infection was submitted to the Court in October 1721, when Justices were again urged to give the whole question their most careful attention.[3] At this crisis, public health for its own sake, not merely the sanitary condition of the King's highway, was kept clearly in view, and it is likely that the energetic action of the Justices in and out of Sessions

---

[1] Evidence that the need was keenly felt, at least in some cases, is afforded by an order allowing the inhabitants of Blue Anchor Alley in the Liberty of Grub Street, St Giles' without Cripplegate, to employ and pay a labourer to cleanse it, such payment to be over and above their contribution to the scavenger's rate, S.B. April 1703, p. 29. *Vide* also S.B. Jan. 1684–5, p. 53.
[2] O.C. vol. I, ff. 109–10, *vide* p. 194. Among the Miscellaneous Papers for 1711–20 is a copy of the printed abstract, giving a very full summary of the law and penalties, covering paving, cleansing and nuisances. Several thousand copies were printed, O.C. vol. II, f. 2.
[3] O.C. vol. I, ff. 126–8.

HIGHWAYS AND BRIDGES 117

did help to ward off the infection. It must be remembered, however, that their efforts were severely restricted by the narrowness of the area covered by the cleansing legislation.[1] As the eighteenth century progressed, many parishes outside the Bills of Mortality were built over and became an integral part of the metropolis. For these, the Justices were not empowered to make any provision, though the need was acute enough to call forth at least some voluntary action.[2] When, in addition, we remember that parochial organisation was necessarily clumsy, and that the negligence of those responsible prevented its possibilities from being fully exploited, it is clear that the system under consideration went but a little way to meet the growing needs of the time. Parliament therefore followed its usual course by superseding parochial administration under the supervision of Justices of Peace and establishing, in its place, new bodies charged with this, along with other lines of improvement.[3] Thus, as in connection with most of the other questions considered in this chapter, we leave the administrative system, of which Quarter Sessions was the head, already condemned and in the process of being supplanted by new bodies.

Street lighting provides an interesting illustration of the transition from the imposition of an obligation upon individual inhabitants to the public provision of the service at their expense. Illumination became a necessity with the growth of the metropolitan area, partly in order to lessen the danger of accidents, partly in order to make robberies somewhat less easy than they must have been in a city of dark streets and ineffective police.[4]

[1] The Act, 1 George I, stat. 2, c. 52, empowered Justices in Sessions to appoint scavengers and order an assessment not exceeding 6*d*. in the pound for any city or market town not covered by any former law. Under this, upon complaint by a local Magistrate, the Court appointed two scavengers and ordered a rate for Brentford, S.B. Oct. 1716, p. 46; Dec. 1716, pp. 61–2.

[2] Marylebone, for instance, had no scavengers in 1756, but a person was employed to carry away the ashes and received £50 a year by voluntary contribution, Maitland, *History and Survey of London*, vol. II, p. 1373.

[3] For Shoreditch by 22 George II, c. 50, for St Martin's in the Fields by 23 George II, c. 35, for Bethnal Green by 24 George II, c. 26, for St Margaret's and St John's, Westminster, by 25 George II, c. 23, for St George's, Hanover Square, by 26 George II, c. 97, St Luke's by 27 George II, c. 25, Marylebone by 29 George II, c. 53, and Wapping, Shadwell and Ratcliff by 29 George II, c. 87.

[4] For the consideration of robberies in this connection, *vide* the representation to the Duke of Newcastle in 1744, O.C. vol. V, ff. 46–7.

Provision for this need therefore takes its place with other attempts to improve the highway, or at least to prevent its deterioration. Parliament followed its usual course by ordering all householders to hang out candles or lights every night from Michaelmas to Lady Day.[1] The Middlesex Justices appear to have taken no action under this Act, which expired with the Cavalier Parliament. Shortly afterwards, however, we find them ordering householders to put candles in or near their windows from six to nine o'clock, as was done in London.[2] Two years later, they ordered lamps to be hung out when there was no moon.[3] The Court appears to have had no definite authority for these proceedings, but its hands were strengthened by the Act, 2 William & Mary, sess. 2, c. 8, which re-enacted the duty to hang out lights, from Michaelmas to Lady Day, as it grew dark until midnight, the penalty for default being 2s. A proviso was included for those agreeing to contribute to common lamps approved by Justices of Peace, an arrangement which marks an interesting step towards public provision. The obvious waste involved if every householder hung out a good lamp, and the inferiority of a crowd of miserable lights to a few good ones, led private speculators to undertake the provision of adequate lamps at intervals along the streets, most of the inhabitants being only too pleased to pay them the small necessary contribution and so escape all personal trouble. The order enjoining the execution of the new Act which, as already shown, also dealt with paving and cleansing, put the question of lighting first, and this suggests that the Justices were more interested in this than in any of the other clauses.[4] A little later, they again dealt with the matter, stating that patentees for lamps put them at too great distances, while many people neither hung out lamps themselves nor contributed to these. Magistrates were to regulate the distances and certify their approval to Sessions, and constables were to enforce the duty.[5] The negligence of householders was not the

---

[1] 14 Charles II, c. 2.   [2] S.B. Oct. 1680, p. 49.
[3] S.B. Dec. 1682, p. 45. For a fine of 12d. for not hanging out a light at night, vide S.R. April 1684.
[4] S.B. Jan. 1690–91, p. 54.
[5] S.B. July 1691, p. 82. For another similar order, vide S.B. April 1694, pp. 53–5.

HIGHWAYS AND BRIDGES

only defect in the system, for great confusion was caused and evasion facilitated by the approval of various kinds of lamps.[1] It would seem that individual responsibility, even with an optional arrangement for common provision, could never supply a really satisfactory service. In 1744 the Court advocated legislation "for obliging all housekeepers who pay to the poor's rate to pay also to the public lamps, it being found by experience that the inhabitants hanging out lights of their own does not ensure the end in regard of the number of empty houses and of persons out of town in the dark quarters between Michaelmas and Christmas, when there is the greatest occasion for them, and of those who do hang out lights of their own, few light them so soon or let them burn so long as they ought".[2] Parliament in fact handed over this, along with other public services, to the new bodies which it created for various localities in the urban section of the county.[3] A considerable fraction of that area was covered so that, by the close of the period, the service of lighting had become of much less importance in the administrative work of the Justices of Peace.

The law as to nuisances covered a very wide field, but, of the cases explicitly prosecuted as nuisances in Middlesex in our period, a vast majority related to the highway, and it seems probable that their predominance fairly reflects the general public attitude on the subject.[4] This is partly explained by the fact that many things which would now be regarded as essentially questions of public health were then viewed mainly from the standpoint of the highway and the travellers thereon.[5] The

[1] S.B. Jan. 1704-5, p. 48.   [2] O.C. vol. v, ff. 46-7.
[3] For Christ Church in 11 George II, c. 35, Shoreditch in 22 George II, c. 50, Bethnal Green in 24 George II, c. 26, St Luke's in 27 George II, c. 25, and Wapping, Shadwell, Ratcliff, St Ann's and Well Close in 29 George II, c. 87.
[4] Burn, who treats nuisances in general somewhat cursorily, *Justice of the Peace*, p. 504 *et seq.*, gives a very careful exposition of the law of nuisances to the highway, *ibid.* p. 357 *et seq.*
[5] Health is usually mentioned, as in a conviction of several persons "for a very great and common nuisance by laying of great quantities of dirt and dung near the highway, in the parish of Whitechapel, to the great annoyance of all the King's liege people passing thereby and to the endangering the health of all the inhabitants there", S. Reg. vol. VIII, pp. 206-7. But the highway is the first consideration and is brought in even where the gravamen of a charge of pouring out filth is that it pollutes a spring and endangers health, S.R. April 1753.

abstention from committing nuisances is primarily a passive duty, but it might involve action as, for instance, in removing annoyance caused by unscoured ditches. When this was so, public provision for the regular performance of the duty was very desirable and was sometimes eventually developed.[1] It is clear that such action might with advantage have gone further, since parochial care bestowed upon roads was liable to be nullified by the negligence of adjacent landholders.[2] The only remedy for the great majority of nuisances was the prosecution of offenders. This was, in a special sense, the duty of constables, and we know that they had many other things to do and, as they were not stimulated by the offer of rewards, it was not to be expected that they would come near to exhausting the very wide scope for action offered by the existing law and existing abuses. From time to time, the Court tried to rouse them to a more vigorous performance of their duties, either upon outside complaints[3] or with some particular public object in view.[4] Such orders do not, as might have been expected, produce a noticeable increase of judicial proceedings. The most energetic period in this connection was the decade immediately preceding

---

[1] E.g. in the case of scavenging.

[2] The Act, 3 William & Mary, c. 12, provided that, when nuisances were not removed within thirty days after notice, the surveyors should remove and amend them at the expense of those who should have done so, but there is no trace of the use of this power in our Records.

[3] In 1716, in response to complaints as to annoyances within the Bills of Mortality through cellar doors left open into the footways, stalls, stands, wheel-barrows, baskets of herbs, fruit and other goods, decayed pavements, assemblies of disorderly persons singing and dispersing seditious songs, ballads and pamphlets, gaming-houses, disorderly victualling-houses and beggars, it ordered the petty constables and headboroughs to perform their duty. As a further precaution, high constables were to take a view one week before every Sessions and present the neglects of the inferior officers, O.C. vol. I, f. 8. The result was not satisfactory, and a further order eighteen months later required high constables, under threat of severe penalties, to submit a written account of proceedings in their divisions, O.C. vol. I, f. 25. Some of the resulting reports have survived among the Miscellaneous Papers.

[4] E.g. the prevention of plague in 1720–1, *vide* p. 116. The presence in the streets of wheel-barrows with oysters, oranges, decayed cheese, apples, nuts and ginger bread and other wares was objected to, not merely because they caused obstruction, but also because the sellers often used false weights and carried dice with which to tempt the unwary, S.B. Jan. 1709–10, p. 53; Dec. 1710, p. 50; Jan. 1714–15, p. 65; etc. For a case in which the convenience of the Court itself was involved, *vide* S.B. Jan. 1662–3, p. 33.

HIGHWAYS AND BRIDGES

the Revolution, and there is no obvious explanation of this, other than the general vigour displayed by the Justices at that time. Presumably their zeal affected the number of prosecutions more through their extra-sessional activities than through the promulgation of general orders, a conclusion which is supported by the occurrence of very large numbers of cases from a single parish at a time when most other parishes are quite unrepresented.[1]

It remains to give some account of the treatment of a few specific nuisances and for this purpose it will be convenient to give one illustration of each of the three main classes—those which caused direct damage or obstruction to the highway, those which involved danger of accident to passengers, and those which menaced their health by polluting the air. The first category may be illustrated by the regulation of the method of drawing vehicles and the number of draught animals to be used. Among the expedients for preserving the roads, none was more persistently exploited by the Parliament of our period,[2] but this enthusiasm is not reflected in our Records. True, one magistrate could convict, so that indictment was unnecessary, but the Court does not betray interest by orders to enforce the laws, as in so many other branches. The absence of licenses to exceed the legal limit when travelling up specially steep hills[3] supports the conclusion, which we naturally draw from the need for frequent alteration and re-enactment of the law, that the regulations were not enforced to any great extent. The interest of the matter lies in the light thrown upon the abuses that were apt to arise from the attempt to secure the enforcement of laws by bribing informers. The Act, 22 Charles II, c. 12, forbidding waggons (with exceptions) to go with more than five horses at length, divided the 40s. penalty between the highways, the poor and the informer. In August 1689 we find one Edwards petitioning that he and

---

[1] Following the order of 1716, Holborn is the only parish that is at all prominent in the subsequent rolls.
[2] E.g. by 14 Charles II, c. 6, 22 Charles II, c. 12, 7 and 8 William III, c. 29, 6 Anne, c. 56, 9 Anne, c. 23, 1 George I, stat. 2, c. 11, 5 George I, c. 12, 14 George II, c. 42, and 27 George II, c. 20.
[3] For a Hertfordshire illustration of this license, *vide* Hardy, *Hertford County Records*, vol. II, p. 100.

other waggoners had been convicted by John Littlehailes and Pointer for drawing with more than five horses at length. The prosecutors had secured this conviction from a Justice who was not of the division and had seized the waggoners' horses without giving them any opportunity to defend themselves.[1] We do not hear what came of this complaint, but Littlehailes was convicted of flagrant offences in this connection.[2] At the Old Bailey in January 1700 he was charged upon three indictments for extorting money from Robert Cook, Thomas Southgate and Richard Hurst, upon pretence of a warrant for drawing with six horses at length. Cook deposed that, for some years past, he and his father had paid the prisoner a guinea a quarter, he pretending to license them to go with six horses. From August 1698 he had paid him nearly £50 in addition, the prisoner pretending to be a Deputy-Surveyor for the Highways and to have a license from Esquire Lawrence. Littlehailes said that he had only borrowed the money, but was found guilty.[3] Parliament had been conscious of the evil some years before. The Act, 7 and 8 William III, c. 29, allotted the fines exclusively to the surveyors of the highways owing to the abuses just mentioned, but this measure was too heroic and was modified by 6 Anne, c. 56, and 9 Anne, c. 23.

Danger to travellers may be illustrated by that which confronted pedestrians in the narrow streets of greater London, thronged, as they were, by waggons and carriages of all kinds, each drawn by anything up to five horses at length and more if in pairs. The Justices tried to mitigate the evil by forbidding carters to ride in their carts and ordering them to lead their horses. An order in this sense was issued in 1663[4] and was repeated a year later, under the direction of the Lord Chief Justice of King's Bench and Mr Justice Windham, then present.[5]

---

[1] S.B. Aug. 1689, p. 7.
[2] Among the Miscellaneous Papers is a warrant, dated 1705, signed by Sir Edward Northey, Attorney-General, acknowledging satisfaction for fines upon Littlehailes for extorting money for drawing with six horses.
[3] *Proceedings of the King's Commission of the Peace and Oyer and Terminer and Gaol Delivery of Newgate*, p. 4.
[4] S.B. June 1663, p. 29.
[5] S.B. July 1664, pp. 33–4.

HIGHWAYS AND BRIDGES

For a few years after this there are a number of prosecutions[1] and they reappear later following a fresh order in 1683.[2] The evil was, however, not stopped and, in January 1691–2, the Grand Jury made it the subject of a presentment which the Court answered by a fresh prohibiting order.[3] No prosecutions seem to have resulted and later, when Parliament legislated on the matter, one Justice might convict,[4] so that action at Sessions was unnecessary. What had already been done, however, affords an interesting illustration of the way in which the Justices were ready to act in advance of Parliament in dealing with evils which they considered serious.

Probably the most frequently prosecuted of all nuisances was the keeping of pigs. It requires no effort of the imagination to conceive how intolerable an annoyance this was in thickly populated districts. Neighbouring residents would, of course, be the chief sufferers but, as usual, much attention was given to the highway and the travellers thereon. The Court did not single out this annoyance in special orders, so it is probable that prosecutions were instigated by the immediate sufferers; but from the outset of the period it was ready to deal with cases brought before it, not, apparently, under any definite statute, but under the general Common Law as to annoyances. From the time of the Great Plague onwards, they are never long absent, though, as usual, action is spasmodic and both the number of prosecutions and the size of fines vary greatly. In October 1682 there are no less than eighteen indictments, and one offender is fined £3. 6s. 8d.[5] So far, hog-keeping could be punished only where definite annoyance was proved. A more radical and undoubtedly necessary measure was taken by Parliament when, in the Act, 2 William & Mary, sess. 2, c. 8, it altogether prohibited the practice so far as the inhabitants of paved streets were concerned. To

---

[1] For fines of 3s. 4d. vide S.R. Aug. 1667 and June 1668. One offender made matters worse by assaulting those appointed to stop the practice, S.R. Oct. 1669.
[2] S.B. August 1683, p. 50.
[3] S.B. Jan. 1691–2, p. 56; Oct. 1692, p. 58.
[4] 1 George I, stat. 2, c. 57, and 24 George II, c. 43.
[5] S.R. Oct. 1682. The fine is as high as £5 in one instance, S.R. July 1689, but is often no more than 12d.

the extent that the paving provisions were carried out, this offered a means of removing the evil in the crowded areas where it was most acute, but the trouble continued to a great extent and the keeping of hogs, especially by brewers and starch-makers, was among the practices condemned in October 1721 by the committee on nuisances conducive to infection.[1]

In connection with the highway services so far discussed, the county as a whole was not directly responsible. The work of Quarter Sessions in this connection consisted in enforcing, regulating and assisting the performance of the obligations of others. In regard to bridges, however, the county had direct responsibilities which occupied a great deal of the time and attention of the Justices in Sessions. The Act, 22 Henry VIII, c. 5, had made precise the liability of counties for all bridges whose maintenance did not fall by a definite obligation from tenure or prescription upon other bodies or persons, and the county, in defending itself upon an indictment for non-repair, could only excuse itself if it could show whose duty such repair was. Hence, before dealing with the county, the residuary legatee, it will be well to notice briefly such prior obligations as appear to have been a reality. In regard to these, Quarter Sessions plays its usual part as judge and enforcer of the duties of others.[2] In this connection, proceedings are surprisingly rare, considering the unsatisfactory state of bridge building at the time.[3] Moreover, outlays on bridges are seldom mentioned in petitions from parish officers for reimbursement or rates.[4] Slackness is hardly likely to have been the whole explanation, and it must be remembered that bridges were still not considered necessary where rivers were fordable. Such indictments as were preferred against parishes and individuals nearly all fell between 1670 and 1710, fines being very rare and,

---

[1] O.C. vol. I, ff. 126–8.
[2] A report on bridges compiled for the Court in 1825, a copy of which is preserved at the Guildhall, gives a valuable review of the whole of this subject.
[3] Proceedings were much more frequent in Hertfordshire, Hardy, *Hertford County Records, passim.* In Middlesex, hundred bridges are not in evidence at this period.
[4] Rates for bridge repair were granted for Holborn in 1673 and for Clerkenwell in 1726, S.B. June 1673, p. 49; April 1726, p. 85.

HIGHWAYS AND BRIDGES

when they did occur, small.[1] It is surprising to find the King being indicted for not repairing a bridge at Hampton, called King's Bridge, which, it was alleged, he should have maintained by reason of his tenure of lands adjoining, but, as might have been expected, the charge was not pressed.[2] In cases at Harrow we find both the parish and the Lord of the Manor, Sir J. Rushout, involved.[3] In the case of Colnbrook Bridge, there were involved, not only the parishes of Langley Marsh and Horton in Buckinghamshire, and Stanwell in Middlesex, but also the Corporation of Colnbrook, to which had been granted certain tolls and profits of fairs for the maintenance of the bridge.[4] When the care of the main roads was handed over to the turnpike trusts, the obligation to repair bridges was not shifted, but the trustees were empowered, in default of repair, to carry it out themselves, charging the cost to those who had neglected the duty. This may in some measure account for the disuse, in the eighteenth century, of the indictment of parishes and persons for not repairing.

Of the more important county bridges, there were at this time in Middlesex only three—that over the Brent at New Brentford, that over the Thames at Chertsey (which was maintained jointly by Middlesex and Surrey) and that over the Brent at Hanwell.[5] The last-named gave little trouble—so that the Court was at one time actually not certain of its responsibility for it[6]—but the other one and a half made up for this by being a constant

---

[1] 6s. 8d. upon Chelsea in S.R. June 1676 and upon Sir J. Rushout in S.R. Oct. 1685 and April 1686; 3s. 4d. upon Saffron Hill in S.R. August 1685. One Chittle of St Giles' without Cripplegate was fined as much as 40s. in S.R. April 1668 and the conditional fine was used at least once, in the case of Chelsea in S.R. June 1676.

[2] S.R. Oct. 1670.   [3] S.R. Oct. 1685.

[4] S.B. Jan. 1690–91, p. 55.

[5] This is rather surprising since, as the Act, 1 Anne, c. 12, recites, any county was hampered in litigation on this question, because its inhabitants, being interested parties, were not accepted as witnesses. The Act redressed this grievance, and it was not until the end of the century that counties began to find themselves charged with a rapidly increasing number of bridges formerly maintained or recently built by other bodies and persons, Webb, *The King's Highway*, p. 99. By 1825 the number of county bridges in Middlesex had increased tenfold, partly owing to the shifting of old burdens, partly owing to the growing need for more and better bridges.

[6] O.C. vol. II, f. 133.

source of anxiety.[1] Bridge proceedings might be initiated by indictment or information in King's Bench[2] or by ordinary indictment at General or Quarter Sessions.[3] In the latter case, the Court itself was in a position to set a fine upon the county after some inhabitants had confessed the charge.[4] In Middlesex, moreover, rates for bridge repair were, from the Restoration onwards, imposed by Sessions, although, until the passing of the Act, 1 Anne, c. 12, four Justices were entitled to levy money for the purpose.[5] Thus the Court first sat in judgment upon the county and then itself proceeded to take steps to remedy the defect on the county's behalf. There was an obvious temptation to dispense with judicial forms and, without waiting for an indictment, to order repair as soon as any magistrate or other person made its necessity known.[6] This would make bridge maintenance a purely administrative function and would often save much delay and expense,[7] but, by a strict interpretation of the law, a presentment was required prior to a rate, and, though the records show that this formality was usually observed, the obstruction which the Court encountered over several years was based partly on the neglect of this procedure. The Act, 12 George II, c. 29, still insisted on presentment, and thereafter the Court carefully observed the provision.[8] It does not follow, however, that the Court actually lost the initiative that it had previously exercised, for it could take steps to provide the Grand Jury with the information upon which to base a presentment. Middlesex at this time had no regular bridge surveyors, provision for whom was included in the Act of 1531. The Court's practice was to entrust the general care of the bridges to committees of Justices. The latter would employ some local artificer

---

[1] At one time it seemed that the county would be saddled with half the responsibility for the bridge over the Thames at Staines, but this was happily avoided, S.B. Sept. 1684, p. 59; April 1685, p. 61; Dec. 1686, p. 43.
[2] *Vide* S.B. June 1662, p. 33; Dec. 1669, p. 35.
[3] E.g. in S.R. April 1677.
[4] *Vide* S.B. Feb. 1686-7, p. 33. In this case, it was intended to use the estreat against influential inhabitants of certain parishes which had refused to pay a rate.
[5] 22 Henry VIII, c. 5.
[6] *Vide* S.B. Oct. 1723, pp. 77, 83.
[7] Webb, *The King's Highway*, p. 90.
[8] E.g. in September 1739, O.C. vol. IV, f. 151.

HIGHWAYS AND BRIDGES

to survey defects and estimate for repair, whereupon they would submit reports, often in great detail, to the Court. This obviously entailed much work upon those Justices and the bridge treasurers, for which, of course, they received no payment.[1]

The expense of bridge maintenance can be gauged to some extent from the fact that, from 1662 to 1735, rates imposed by Sessions for the purpose amounted to some £6500. It must not be concluded that these sums were collected in their entirety, for constables on whom fell the duty of collection were apt to be very negligent and reluctant to pay over the money,[2] while the Liberty of Westminster claimed, and in practice to a great extent secured, exemption from the county rate.[3] Obstruction reached its height in the years following 1730.[4] In January 1735–6, following a presentment of Brentford Bridge by the Grand Jury, a rate of £200 was ordered.[5] By the following May only £70 had been collected[6], and in June the Court found itself in the humiliating position that no one would contract for the repair owing to the obstruction to the raising of the necessary funds.[7] After further strenuous efforts to ensure payment,[8] the rate order was removed by Certiorari, and in December the Court could do no more than order payment for the bridge out of the first rate allowed by King's Bench.[9] The opposition, which was apparently led by a member of the Commission,[10] was successfully supporting its resistance by insisting on legal niceties, and the only hope was to invoke the intervention of Parliament. The Court therefore sent a petition to the House of Commons, explaining that two rates had been quashed and officers prosecuted for collecting them. Others had been removed and were

---

[1] Apart from two dinners at Chertsey, which were ordered to be paid for in September 1743, the only compensation that is recorded is a payment of £20 to Mr Mainwaring, J.P., for trouble and expense in connection with Chertsey Bridge, and Mainwaring occupied a quite exceptional position at the end of the period, O.C. vol. v, f. 10; vol. vii, f. 35.
[2] The threat of indictment was used, e.g. against the high constable of Kensington in 1727 (O.C. vol. iii, f. 97), but it was a clumsy weapon.
[3] S.B. July 1713, pp. 46–8.
[4] For similar difficulties and obstructions in connection with vagrant rates, vide p. 76.
[5] S.B. Jan. 1735–6, pp. 61, 67.
[6] O.C. vol. iv, f. 65.
[7] Ibid. ff. 68–9.
[8] Ibid. f. 72.
[9] Ibid. f. 79.
[10] Vide p. 76.

liable to be quashed, "considering the great niceties and forms requisite in such cases, although your petitioners have, by themselves and counsel, used their utmost care and caution therein, whereby it is become extremely difficult, if not impossible, for your petitioners to execute the trust reposed in them, or to make any contracts either for repairing county bridges or gaols or to support the continual charge of passing vagrants ".[1] In response to this, and another petition,[2] Parliament, in the Act, 12 George II, c. 29, unified all the county rates, which were in future to be paid by the churchwardens and overseers out of the poor rate to the high constables and so to the county treasurers. A rate was not to be levied until three-fourths of the previous one had been spent, and bridges were not to be repaired until after Grand Jury presentment. The Westminster rate was definitely amalgamated with that for Middlesex, while the county Justices were to have the same authority at General as at Quarter Sessions. At the same time, the power to enforce collecting and accounting was strengthened and the use of Certiorari was restricted. Under the circumstances, perhaps the most vital provision was that orders were not to be quashed for want of form only. After some further delay,[3] the opposition broke down and thereafter the accounts show that the bulk of the new general rates was collected.

As the period advanced, the increase of wheeled traffic made the existing wooden bridges more and more inadequate, and repairs became ever more frequent and more expensive. This was particularly the case with regard to Brentford Bridge, situated, as it was, on the much-frequented Bath Road. One characteristic expedient was that of restricting the passage of vehicles over the bridge and trying to force them to go below when the state of the river made that practicable.[4] This apparently failed, and eventually the Court adopted the more heroic remedy of rebuilding this bridge of brick and stone, employing Charles Labelye, Engineer to the Westminster Bridge Commissioners, to supervise the work.[5] The cost appears to have been in

[1] O.C. vol. IV, f. 88.   [2] *Ibid.* f. 124.   [3] *Ibid.* ff. 188–90.
[4] S.B. July 1707, p. 51; Oct. 1712, pp. 27, 32; April 1715, p. 112.
[5] O.C. vol. IV, ff. 141–3, 151, 171, 175, 217.

HIGHWAYS AND BRIDGES

the neighbourhood of £3350,[1] but, even so, a twelve years' respite was all the Court gained, for by 1755 the bridge was again out of repair, and in December 1759 the Clerk to the Brentford Turnpike wrote to the Court as to its condition.[2] Chertsey Bridge was less affected by traffic, but had its own engineering problem, caused by the tumultuous habits of the Thames. Divided responsibility also caused difficulty, though at times there was close co-operation with the Surrey Justices. It was not rebuilt of stone until 1780,[3] so that there was no single outlay upon it comparable with that just noted in connection with Brentford Bridge, but frequent smaller bills amounted, in the aggregate, to a heavy charge, while half measures certainly involved the Justices in more personal trouble.[4] By December 1748, the middle was again out of repair and, within two years, it was severely damaged by barges.[5] Throughout, it is clear that the system of leaving bridge maintenance to be supervised by amateurs was very unsatisfactory. A group of magistrates could hardly be expected to give a sound judgment upon the very considerable engineering problems involved, and they must have been thoroughly perplexed by discussions as to the merits of campshotts, starlings and rampires. The idea of contracting for the continued maintenance of the bridges, instead of for specific pieces of work, had much to recommend it and was very much in keeping with current practice. It was not, however, adopted by the Court as a general principle, though a contract for maintenance for a term of years was sometimes coupled with that for carrying out some special repair,[6] while, at the time of the reconstruction of Brentford Bridge, the pavior undertook to keep the pavement in repair for three years, and thereafter for a further eighteen years at £1 per annum for every hundred yards.[7] In general, the system of immediate supervision by Justices remained in force, and it is something of a tribute to

[1] O.C. vol. IV, ff. 257, 267, and S.B. Jan. 1742-3, p. 57.
[2] O.C. vol. VI, f. 63; vol. VII, f. 45.
[3] *Report on Bridges*, p. 264.
[4] When the repair of Chertsey Bridge was carried out by the two counties in 1744, the cost to Middlesex was at least £1200, O.C. vol. V, ff. 65-8.
[5] O.C. vol. V, ff. 165, 215, 217.
[6] E.g. at Chertsey in 1724, O.C. vol. II, ff. 120-22; vol. III, f. 23.
[7] O.C. vol. IV, f. 251.

their partial success in spite of difficulties that no Parliamentary measures were taken to supplant their authority. It must be remembered that in this matter they were not faced with the problem of enforcing and organising universal unpaid and unskilled service. Except under special circumstances, they were able to raise as much money as they deemed necessary and to employ the most skilled workmen they could find. This no doubt is the main reason why bridge maintenance contrasts favourably with other highway services, but we cannot in fairness deny the Justices some of the credit of their achievement.

During the last half of the period, there was, as has already been indicated, a growing perception that the old highway administration, even when supplemented by certain new powers, was inadequate. Small alterations were insufficient, so that the only hope was to develop an entirely new form of organisation. This was done, and new bodies rapidly took over the maintenance of the more important roads, thus, as has been shown, greatly reducing the amount of highway business done by the older authorities, including Quarter Sessions. The main reason for the innovation—the growth of wheeled traffic—is clearly brought out by a petition to the House of Commons, dated December 1711, praying for a special act to repair the road from Stanmore to Kilburn Bridge.[1] The Court refused to subscribe to this petition, but this can hardly have been due to satisfaction with things as they were, since some magistrates participated from the first in the trusts established by Parliament. Although, therefore, it seems that the Court played no direct part in the establishment of the new bodies, it was brought into relations with them—relations which consisted, partly in control and restraint, partly in co-operation and protection. As regards control, the various turnpike acts gave authority to Quarter Sessions to appoint persons to survey the roads and enquire into the application of tolls and, upon their report, to determine questions as to the misapplication of funds or the abuse of power. For the Islington Trust,[2] which controlled various roads leading to Highgate Gatehouse and Hampstead, the Court appointed a Committee of

---

[1] This is preserved among Miscellaneous Papers at the Guildhall.
[2] Under the Act, 3 George I, c. 4 (private).

HIGHWAYS AND BRIDGES

Enquiry in 1718, and ordered the Clerk to the Trustees to attend with journals, books of orders, accounts, etc.[1] The Trustees, however, proved truculent and sought to thwart the enquiry.[2] The Committee strongly criticised the manner in which the Trust had been carried on, and suggested rules to prevent abuses in the future.[3] Faced with continued opposition, the Court finally ordered the Trustees to be indicted in King's Bench for contempt.[4] It is not clear how the dispute ended, but this much is sufficient to indicate that there was need for some such control as Parliament had put in the hands of Sessions. The Middlesex Justices do not, however, seem to have exercised this supervision in a general way,[5] and, as time passed, their responsibility was lessened in proportion as Parliament conceded more and more independence to the new bodies.[6] On one or two occasions, the Court intervened upon complaint as to specific grievances due to the activities of trusts. At Hammersmith, for instance, a gate was erected on a road other than that intended by Parliament[7] and obstructing access to the chapel there, whereupon the Justices ordered the Sheriff to remove the gate.[8] Again, they sought to prevent the Trust for the road from Shoreditch to Enfield from committing encroachments and nuisances upon the lands of the alms-houses built by the Ironmongers' Company.[9]

Turning to the sphere of collaboration, we find that the most important matter in which the trusts needed the co-operation of the Justices was the enforcement of statute labour, since the establishment of new machinery, with permission to levy tolls on road users, was not intended wholly to disburden those previously responsible for highways. The surveyor of a trust, no less than the surveyor of a parish, depended on the Court to enforce

---

[1] S.B. Oct. 1718, p. 69.   [2] O.C. vol. I, ff. 51–9.
[3] *Ibid.*   [4] O.C. vol. I, ff. 86–7.
[5] In regard to the road from Tyburn to Uxbridge, which was provided for by 1 George I, c. 25 (private), a committee of enquiry was appointed in response to complaints by the inhabitants of neighbouring parishes, but these complaints were pronounced groundless and the order quashed, S.B. June 1721, p. 39.
[6] Webb, *The King's Highway*, p. 119.   [7] 4 George II, c. 34.
[8] S.B. Oct. 1732, pp. 84–8; Jan. 1732–3, pp. 38–40.
[9] S.B. Oct. 1736, p. 73; April 1737, p. 79.

the performance of this duty. Parishes might prefer to pay an annual sum as a composition for the labour of their inhabitants[1], and many apparently did so.[2] Where, as seems often to have been the case, the agreed sums were not paid, or where no composition was made, the Trustees retained the right to call on the inhabitants for their labour and that of their teams. In the Minutes of the Colnbrook Trust,[3] we find the Trustees deciding to apply regularly to Quarter Sessions to enforce statute labour[4], but they later abandoned this policy owing to the expense of the Sessions orders.[5] To a great extent, the allocation of statute work came to be performed by Justices out of Sessions,[6] but our Records exhibit no trace of this procedure in Middlesex at this time. It is therefore probable that neighbouring parishes escaped all or most of their liability for an important section of the Bath Road, but the Islington Trust, perhaps owing to its proximity to Westminster and Hicks Hall, thought statute work worth fighting for.[7] In response to applications, the Court instituted a careful enquiry into the whole position in that area,[8] and thereafter issued frequent orders for various persons from the lists submitted by the parish surveyors either to do a certain number of days' work for the Trustees or pay them their statutory composition.[9] The amounts of work allotted are, however, extremely small in relation to the numbers shown to be liable in the various parishes[10] and, though the parishes remained responsible for roads not specially provided for, it seems certain that the trusts greatly reduced the weight of parochial

[1] This arrangement was introduced at Hackney by the original Act for the Road from Shoreditch to Enfield, 12 Anne, c. 19.
[2] As early as 1719, the surveyors of Clerkenwell had compounded for their grand road for £25, S.B. Jan. 1719–20, p. 54. For other similar cases, *vide* the report on the Islington Turnpike in O.C. vol. IV, ff. 60–62.
[3] This was established by 13 George I, c. 31. Volumes of its minutes and accounts are preserved at the Guildhall.
[4] Minutes, pp. 40, 44, 56; S.B. April 1729, p. 34.
[5] Minutes, p. 60.
[6] Webb, *The King's Highway*, p. 117.
[7] The statute work on these roads was specially dealt with by 8 George II, c. 12.
[8] S.B. June 1735, pp. 77–9; August 1735, p. 92; Dec. 1735, p. 73. O.C. vol. IV, ff. 60–62.
[9] S.B. June 1736, p. 63; Sept. 1737, p. 73; etc.
[10] Full particulars are given in O.C. vol. IV, ff. 60–62.

HIGHWAYS AND BRIDGES

burdens. In its more purely judicial capacity, the Court was of course concerned with offences committed against trusts. To deal with the opposition—often violent—which these bodies aroused, Parliament passed numerous Acts imposing severe penalties on offenders. Many of these offences could be dealt with by magistrates out of Sessions but, even allowing for this, the number of cases that can be traced in the Sessions Records is surprisingly small and the sentences remarkably lenient. There are some cases of assault upon turnpike collectors, especially those of the Islington Trust,[1] an instance of breaking open a gate[2] and a forgery of turnpike tickets.[3] The Records may therefore be held to suggest the tentative conclusion that Parliamentary severities went too far and that the laws were not enforced.

It is hardly possible to summarise conclusions on the numerous and largely distinct questions that have necessarily been discussed in this chapter. Still, merely from the amount of material provided by our Records, it is clear that the Justices devoted a large amount of time to the fulfilment of their various responsibilities in connection with the highways. Much of this attention was bestowed involuntarily, at the instance of others who suffered from bad roads, or who needed help in performing their own duties. To this extent, the Justices were but passive instruments and could claim no credit. But it would be doing them less than justice to suggest that they confined their activities to this necessary minimum. At times, as we have seen, they took a very decided initiative of their own, and spared no pains in their endeavour to bring about some improvement. Still, we cannot suggest that the provision of good communications was one of their major interests. Highways and bridges figured among the articles which the constables were ordered to present at the Sessions of April 1682,[4] and they were given in charge by Whitlocke Bulstrode in April 1718;[5] but in the latter case, the cursory reference to them contrasts strongly with the long discussions on several other matters. This subject certainly engaged much less

---

[1] S.R. July and August 1734.
[2] S.R. July 1753.   [3] S.R. August 1721.
[4] Charge of Sir William Smith, April 1682, p. 10.
[5] Charge, p. 31.

of the thought of the great majority of Justices than did questions relating to the constitution, to social morality and pauperism.

In fact, after 1700 the Court ceased to display initiative in relation to ordinary road maintenance. If vigorous presentment of decayed highways was necessary in 1672, it was certainly not less so thirty or forty years later, but we look in vain for any general resolution to use this weapon. True, the conditional fine was no longer the only method of providing funds for parishes with obstinate inhabitants, but there was still need for pressure upon the parishes corporately in order to oblige them to utilise their new rating powers. Sixpence was, in any case, a modest maximum for parishes responsible for the main roads to London, and there was room for the fine as a method of supplementing this revenue.[1] Some of the instances of conditional fine in the eighteenth century may be thus explained, but the Court took no steps to press this policy. Whether the Revolution or the Act of 1691 was responsible for the change is not clear. Probably both events helped to make the Court more willing than formerly to act merely as the agent of others, lending its authority when rates were asked for or indictments lodged, but not troubling to take action on its own account. In relation to the special problems of the metropolitan district, more energy is visible. The Justices of the neighbourhood would be too conscious of the evils there prevalent to allow either themselves or their colleagues to remain idle, but the measures taken were, as we have seen, inspired more by the needs of public health and order than by the desire to provide good facilities for transport.

Here, perhaps, more than in any other of the branches of administration that concern us, we can see the fatal consequences of heaping such an enormous variety of responsibilities on a single body of men who were, after all, only amateurs devoting a part of their time to the business. In proportion as they were roused to activity by one problem or group of problems, their interest in matters which had no special call upon their attention was bound to flag. More specialisation was essential if this tendency towards compensation was to be obviated.

[1] Webb, *The King's Highway*, p. 56.

HIGHWAYS AND BRIDGES

A committee system would have met the need, at least to some extent, by assuring those Justices specially appointed to deal with highway repair or scavenging that, if they devoted themselves wholeheartedly to these duties, other matters which they might consider more urgent would not be neglected, since they were the particular care of other Justices. Specialisation, too, would have given greater knowledge and experience, which became increasingly necessary for the adequate maintenance of roads and bridges in proportion as the increase of traffic made the engineering problems involved more serious. In fact, the Justices charged with the care of the two main county bridges do seem to have tended to form something in the nature of a standing committee, and here, perhaps, is a partial explanation of the considerable enterprise shown in this connection. The more obvious explanation is also significant—the Justices in the neighbourhood of Brentford and Chertsey were not absorbed in the peculiar difficulties of maintaining order and morality in a town which had far outgrown its administrative machinery. Hence, while the Brentford Petty Sessions might be able to give a fairly adequate amount of attention to highways and bridges, it did not follow that a similar unspecialised meeting for the Tower Division or Finsbury would be equally satisfactory. Parliament may have been conscious of this need when it sought to regularise the special highway Sessions, but it did not suggest that certain Justices should be permanently deputed for this purpose and freed from some of their other responsibilities. Moreover, it is doubtful whether these special Sessions were of much importance in Middlesex. In any case, they would only cover a portion of the field, there being no provision for *ad hoc* organisation for Justices to supervise paving, cleansing and lighting, and no attempt to differentiate the functions of the General Sessions. When finally driven to take more drastic steps, Parliament did not attempt to introduce specialisation among the Justices themselves, but set up entirely new bodies to take over the maintenance of the highways. It is true that, in the urban district, some of the new bodies were charged with several highway services and also with other functions such as poor relief; but their responsibilities were still only a fraction of those of the

Justices and, of course, ordinary turnpike trusts were highway authorities pure and simple.

It is not suggested that the very understandable negligence of the Justices and the need for specialisation were the primary causes of the failure of the old highway régime. The new users of the roads were producing a problem which the amateur surveyors with their armies of amateur assistants had not originally been intended to solve, and the slight additional help afforded by Parliament was not in the least commensurate with the new difficulties. Still, it is of interest to observe that, on the eve of the turnpike era, our Justices were apparently giving a decreasing, instead of an increasing, amount of attention to the admittedly deplorable highways, and this fact must partly account for the early introduction and rapid spread of the new machinery in Middlesex.[1] Towards the end of the reign of George II, a beginning was made, as already shown, with the process of transferring the other services considered in this chapter, with the exception of bridge repair, to new authorities, so that by the year 1760 the administration we have been studying stood condemned in almost all its branches and was in course of being superseded. The verdict of Parliament was unequivocal and must be accepted as final.[2]

[1] Within the short space of five years, the following roads were covered by successive acts: Kilburn Bridge to Sparrows Herne by 10 Anne, c. 7; Highgate Gatehouse to Barnet Blockhouse, by 10 Anne, c. 33; Shoreditch to Enfield, by 12 Anne, c. 19; Shenley Ridge to South Mimms, by 1 George I, c. 11; Tyburn to Uxbridge, by 1 George I, c. 25 (private); from several places towards Highgate Gatehouse and Hampstead, by 3 George I, c. 4 (private), and from Counters Bridge in Kensington to the Powder Mills in the road to Staines and to Cranford Bridge in the road to Colnbrook, by 3 George I, c. 14 (private).

[2] We might also cite the criticism of Sir John Hawkins, himself a Middlesex Justice, in his *Observations on the State of the Highways*, 1763, quoted in Webb, *The King's Highway*, pp. 30, 35.

CHAPTER V

THE LABOUR CODE

THE Statute of Artificers may well be regarded as the most ambitious of all the measures taken by Tudor statesmen with the object of controlling and directing economic forces. It was concerned, not with particular groups of people or with exceptional crises, but with the ordinary business life of the great bulk of the community, and the regulations contemplated were nothing if not minute. Consequently, as material circumstances and political ideas passed out of the stage in which Elizabethan legislators found them, or thought they found them, these provisions inevitably became inapplicable to the former and antagonistic to the latter. In addition, there was the unexpected destruction of that central control and direction by which the Tudors had laid so much store. We cannot therefore be surprised that, after the lapse of a century, little more than the shadow of the structure remained, though Cecil himself would doubtless have been painfully astonished at the meagre contents of this chapter. It will, however, treat only of so much of the Elizabethan code as concerned the conditions of employment in the more modern sense, to the exclusion of the regulations governing the position of the master craftsman.[1] Although, however, the system in which one set of persons continuously employed another set had, to a great extent, already taken possession of the economic field, it had of course not yet assumed the precise form in which we know it. In particular, the status of apprenticeship, which falls first for discussion, was still of great importance and gave rise to problems which we do not meet to-day.

During the first half of the period, a considerable number of indentures of apprenticeship, almost always in Latin, were

[1] At the period with which we are concerned, facts appear to warrant this treatment, though it involves certain disadvantages, such as the discussion of apprenticeship in two different chapters. Here we are concerned with it as a status, with the interest and behaviour of the parties to the bond while still in force. As a qualification for the exercise of crafts it will be considered in chap. VI.

138 THE LABOUR CODE

entered in the Sessions Books.[1] Hardly any years before 1700 are without such entries, which, however, become infrequent at the beginning of the eighteenth century and cease from 1719 onwards.[2] The statutory term for apprenticeship was seven years, but we do not find a rigorous adherence to this. Longer periods were admissible and the Court generally treated indentures entailing them as valid.[3] Shorter terms were sometimes, though not invariably, considered to invalidate indentures.[4] Other grounds for pronouncing an indenture invalid are that it had not been enrolled[5] or indented,[6] that the apprentice had been bound without his father's consent,[7] and that the master was an alien, therefore not capable of taking an apprentice.[8] The approved legal opinion seems to have been that the obligation of an indenture ceased with the death of the master or mistress,[9] but the Middlesex Justices often held that the executor or executrix, usually the master's widow, was entitled to the rest of the apprentice's service, if she continued to exercise the trade or provided instruction and maintenance in some other way.[10] The

[1] The Court does not seem to have enforced the restrictions regarding those who might take or become apprentices, except that in one case it discharged the apprentice of an alien on the ground that the latter was incapable of taking an apprentice, S.B. Aug. 1670, p. 44.

[2] This cessation is perplexing, but may be connected with the system of stamping indentures under several Acts passed during the reigns of William III and Anne. It certainly cannot be supposed to indicate any sudden break in the practice of apprenticeship, though it is of interest to note that prosecutions of unapprenticed workmen slackened about the same time, *vide* p. 176.

[3] Terms of eight years and thirteen years were tolerated in the cases of Humphrey Turner and Arabella Yarwell, S.B. Dec. 1692, p. 45; May 1705, p. 44. Yet John Rooksbee, who complained of ill-treatment by his master in "not only compelling him to drink water, but also giving him abundance of violent blows", breaking his head, disabling his left hand, etc., was apparently discharged simply because his indenture was for ten years, S.B. Oct. 1728, p. 90.

[4] In the case of Katherine Lambert, apprenticed for two years, and Margaret Berry, bound for six years, S.B. July 1694, p. 39; April 1708, p. 78. At least one master was indicted for taking an apprentice for a short term, S.R. Feb. 1679–80. The Court did, however, occasionally pass indentures for less than the statutory term, e.g. S.B. Dec. 1692, p. 42.

[5] S.B. Jan. 1691–2, p. 50.   [6] S.B. Sept. 1714, p. 71.
[7] S.B. Oct. 1706, p. 62.   [8] S.B. Aug. 1670, p. 44.
[9] Burn, *Justice of the Peace*, p. 37.
[10] S.B. July 1691, p. 63; May 1705, p. 44. When the Court discharged the apprentice of a deceased carver, its reason was, not the death of the master, but the fact that the widow no longer followed the trade, S.B. Sept. 1736, p. 67.

THE LABOUR CODE

pressure was most frequently put upon the apprentice at the instance of the widow since, as the term of service drew to its close, the connection came to be more and more in the interests of the master or mistress, but proceedings were sometimes taken by parish officers, fearful that children turned adrift might become chargeable.[1] Unless and until an indenture was pronounced invalid or was cancelled by order of four Justices of Peace, both parties were bound to carry out its provisions, and we find constant proceedings to compel them to do so. Those against masters are frequently begun at the instance of the parish for reasons just mentioned,[2] while, where the apprentice or his friends initiated the suit, the object was frequently to recover all or part of the premium paid at the time of binding.[3] Prosecutions of apprentices for deserting are much more numerous than those of masters for turning out their apprentices. It is seldom, however, that the apprentice himself is punished, probably because some other person was considered to have seduced him and therefore to be primarily responsible, while the master's main object would be to recover, not to punish, his apprentice. There are frequent prosecutions for enticing, deluding, lodging and entertaining apprentices, and the like, the offenders being either new masters or friends of the apprentices.[4] After 1720, proceedings of this kind become much less frequent.[5]

The records of Quarter Sessions are hardly an adequate basis for a general judgment on apprenticeship, concerned, as they

[1] *Vide* an order that James Dormer, who had married the widow of George Fox, vintner, should provide for the latter's apprentice, who had become destitute and chargeable, S.B. Dec. 1698, p. 42.

[2] Grace Dukeson was committed to prison for want of surety for turning her apprentice out of doors, who had since fallen sick of the small-pox in St Sepulchre's parish, and one Maryott was bound to answer the churchwardens of Shoreditch for neglecting his apprentice and allowing him to be taken as a vagrant, having received £6. 10s. with him, S.B. Dec. 1670, p. 44, S.R. Jan. 1675-6; S.B. Jan. 1675-6, p. 39. *Vide* also S.B. Sept. 1714, p. 77.

[3] E.g. S.B. April 1670, p. 36.

[4] In one case where both the apprentice and the seducer were punished, the former was fined 12d., the latter 3s. 4d., S.R. Jan. 1709-10. Apprentices never seem to be fined more than 3s. 4d., while the penalty exacted from the seducer might be 20s. or 40s., S.R. May 1677 and Feb. 1677-8.

[5] This reinforces other evidence that the bond of apprenticeship was weakening at the time, but there continues to be evidence that an undissolved indenture constituted a serious barrier to the apprentice's freedom, e.g. S.B. Feb. 1731-2, p. 60.

are, mainly with its failures. Still, in discounting the evidence afforded by prosecutions of misdoers and applications for annulment, we must remember that many of the worst cases of ill-treatment of friendless apprentices certainly never came into Court. With this consideration in mind, it is impossible to avoid the conclusion that the defects and abuses of the system vitiated it over a large field and appear so natural as to cast great doubt upon any eulogistic estimate. At all events, the system seems to have worked far from well in the period with which we are concerned, when guild control was waning, and the Justices did not—perhaps could not—do much to correct its deficiencies.[1] It should be judged mainly by its success or failure in its main object, that of affording the apprentice a satisfactory training for life and work. The Records are particularly unsuitable material for a broad judgment of this kind, yet our suspicions cannot but be aroused by the occurrence of housewifery as the mystery to be learnt, particularly when the supposed instruction is to be given, not by a housewife, but by a writing-man.[2] Indentures to persons of unspecified occupation do not sound very promising openings to efficient vocational training.[3] Indeed, some indentures state only that the apprentice is to serve, without mention of his learning the trade.[4] We also find instances of apprentices lent by their masters to persons in other trades.[5] Still, the Justices at times gave consideration to the educational aspect of the bond, and were willing to discharge apprentices whose masters neglected their duty in this respect.[6] In 1695 they discharged Edward Green, apprentice to Roger Gately, surgeon, as the latter did not practise the art of a surgeon, and

---

[1] *Vide* George, *London Life in the Eighteenth Century*, chaps. v and vi. Mrs George's unfavourable impression is, of course, largely based on Middlesex Records.

[2] S.B. Dec. 1747, p. 35.   [3] S.B. July 1671, p. 56.

[4] E.g. S.B. Dec. 1699, p. 69; July 1700, p. 61.

[5] A shoemaker's apprentice let out to a brickmaker, a hemp-dresser's apprentice assigned to a chirurgeon, and a cordwainer's apprentice lent to a chimney-sweep, S.B. May 1673, p. 35; July 1707, p. 62; July 1726, pp. 52-3.

[6] E.g. in the case of a silk-stocking-weaver who was so poor that he had no frames or materials and was incapable of instructing his apprentice who, therefore, would never be able to learn the trade, S. Reg. vol. viii, p. 95.

compelled Green to be "a rope-dancer, tumbler and jack-pudding ".[1] They were especially critical of masters who took to beer-selling, and discharged apprentices in such cases.[2]

A serious defect in the whole nexus was the divergence of interest between master and apprentice. The latter was clearly an encumbrance during his early years of service, when receiving the bulk of his instruction, and a fee was therefore usually paid at the time of binding. This involved danger since, the premium once paid, an unscrupulous master was tempted to resort to unjustifiable measures such as ill-treatment or false accusation, in order to get his apprentice discharged; he might even make away with the apprentice or abscond himself. If, however, he retained and taught the apprentice, the latter was subject to similar temptations as his term drew to its close since, by that time, he was profitable to his master and could probably do better if free to dispose of his own labour. This was especially so when the term was long and became more serious as the seven-year qualification for exercising trades was less rigorously enforced. When either party absconded, there was, of course, no remedy.[3] At other times the Court apparently tried to reach a fair balance of interests, though we cannot tell how successful it was in the attempt. It sometimes explicitly,[4] often tacitly, allowed the master to retain the premium, even when the apprentice was discharged for ill-treatment, but this may be due to the consideration that, after providing training and maintenance for the earlier part of the term, he was losing the apprentice's services during the profitable later years. Legally, the reason for discharge would be irrelevant until the Court obtained the right to impose penalties upon masters who abused their authority, a right which it does not seem to have had during our period. Indeed, it had no real authority to order repayment of any part of the premium,[5] but it frequently assumed this right, when there seemed good ground, particularly if the discharged

---

[1] S.B. Oct. 1695, p. 41.
[2] S.B. Oct. 1660, p. 32; May 1707, p. 26.
[3] *Vide* S.B. Sept. 1692, p. 59. In this instance, a milliner absconded after receiving £20 premium.
[4] E.g. S.B. Sept. 1690, p. 51.
[5] Burn, *Justice of the Peace*, p. 36.

apprentice was to be placed out afresh with a further premium.[1] A similar difficulty arose when there was question of paying compensation to the master for the loss of his apprentice's labour. The master might seek to turn his hold of the apprentice into a source of unjustifiable profit.[2] Such exactions were apparently not considered inequitable even where the master was personally to blame for his loss.[3] In case of misconduct of either master or apprentice, the aggrieved party would naturally apply for remedy to some local Justice who, if he failed to settle the dispute, was required to pass it on to Sessions. As already mentioned, there seems to have been no authority to punish the master, so that the numerous recognisances for ill-treating or neglecting apprentices were presumably merely preliminary to discharge proceedings. There are, however, one or two cases of fine for maltreating apprentices.[4] On the other hand, one or more Justices might commit an apprentice to the House of Correction for misbehaviour, and there was danger that masters would not be sufficiently reluctant to resort to this drastic and undesirable step.[5]

The final remedy against disorderly apprentices and the usual one against unsatisfactory masters was the dissolution of the

[1] For orders to repay the whole premium in view of a fresh binding, *vide* S.B. April 1670, p. 36; Oct. 1680, p. 51. One man was committed to prison for refusing to repay half a £20 premium received with an apprentice to his wife, a seamstress, the apprentice having been discharged because she had not been instructed but set to do household work which she could not perform, S.B. Aug. 1688, pp. 46–7. A mistress was committed to New Prison for similar obstinacy and for detaining the apprentice's indenture and clothes, S. Reg. vol. VIII, p. 171. In 1693, the Court ordered a master to repay £6. 13s. 4d. although the apprentice was discharged for theft, S.B. Sept. 1693, p. 51.

[2] A watch-maker's apprentice, in complaining of beating, alleged that his master meant to make him purchase the remainder of his term as he, the apprentice, had recently come into a small estate, S.B. July 1737, p. 41.

[3] A watch-maker was allowed compensation for an apprentice who was discharged for ill-treatment, S.B. June 1728, p. 70; Aug. 1728, p. 64. For a case of compensation to the son of an absconded master, *vide* S.B. Jan. 1736–7, p. 64.

[4] Eleanor Holland fined 13s. 4d. for assaulting and inhumanly, cruelly and excessively correcting her apprentice, Rebecca Cooley, and Mary Rest fined 3s. 4d. for a like offence, S.R. Aug. 1671 and Aug. 1694. For an indictment for neglecting to provide for an apprentice (removed by Certiorari), *vide* S.R. Dec. 1697.

[5] For cases of apprentices so committed, *vide* S.B. Jan. 1689–90, p. 51; April 1711, p. 26.

THE LABOUR CODE

bond. If the law was strictly interpreted, the Court could only take this final step after application had been made to a neighbouring magistrate and he had failed to compose the quarrel. In practice, however, the Sessions exercised an original jurisdiction in the matter,[1] and, among the multitude of discharges ordered by the Middlesex Sessions during our period, it is seldom that there is any definite evidence of a previous application to a single Justice. From the comparative weakness of the apprentice and his lack of real remedy so long as he remained in tutelage, we should naturally expect most applications for cancellation to come from his side, and we certainly find this to have been so in the great majority of instances in which the Court found sufficient grounds for discharge. The bulk of such orders show the apprentice as petitioner and the master as offender, in ill-treating or neglecting his apprentice, sometimes absconding completely.[2] Occasionally apprentices secure release because they find the trade prejudicial to their health.[3] Where complaint comes from the side of the master or mistress, apprentices are discharged for pilfering,[4] for selling goods below cost price,[5] for deserting service,[6] and the like offences. The Act, 20 George II, c. 19, empowered two Justices to discharge a parish apprentice or any other apprentice at whose binding not more than £5 was paid, but this did not produce any perceptible reduction in the number of applications to Sessions. Probably its main result was to open a door of escape to the poorest and most oppressed apprentices who would have difficulty in gaining access to the Court, particularly those living at a distance.[7] At all events, cases continued to come to Court in large numbers and, in 1752, the Justices found it necessary to order that no apprenticeship petitions should be received after the second day of Sessions, as they hindered other business in

---

[1] Burn, *op. cit.* p. 35.
[2] As Mrs George has already published a summary of 34 cases taken from the Middlesex Records (*London Life in the Eighteenth Century*, Appendix IV) it is unnecessary to deal at length with this aspect of the question here.
[3] S.B. Feb. 1724-5, pp. 55-7; April 1739, p. 35.
[4] S. Reg. vol. VIII, p. 188.   [5] S.B. Jan. 1689-90, p. 43.
[6] S.B. Jan. 1685-6, p. 44.
[7] For the discharge of an apprentice by Petty Sessions upon complaint by his master, *vide* the Marylebone Minutes, April 1760.

the latter part of the week.[1] Thus it is clear that, during the century under review, the Middlesex Justices by no means neglected the subject of apprenticeship. It does seem, however, that the attention they gave it was mainly involuntary and that, for the most part, they merely took the necessary minimum of action when parties to the bond invoked their aid. We cannot suppose that *ad hoc* intervention of this kind was an adequate substitute for continuous and expert regulation by trade guilds, or that it did much to retain the virtues of the system once those directly concerned in its working had lost interest in the more valuable side of the status of apprenticeship.

There was no very clear line of demarcation between apprenticeship and ordinary work for hire. Our Records afford no evidence that the payment of wages was at this time ever included as one of the stipulations embodied in indentures, but, within limits which do not seem to have been very clearly defined, a master was permitted to let out his apprentice to some other master, in which case wages would often be paid and the legal master, not the apprentice, was entitled to receive them. The same was true if the apprentice earned money for any other reason, if, for instance, he was impressed. Disputes in this connection came before the Court on several occasions.[2] Apart from this consideration, there was, between the apprentice and the ordinary paid employee, a class of indentured or covenant servants. They were bound for longer than the statutory year, for periods varying, in our cases, up to five years. An indenture is sometimes mentioned,[3] and apparently instruction might or might not be given.[4] Instruction was included in articles between a servant and a coach-maker and was alleged to have been

---

[1] O.C. vol. v, f. 252.
[2] E.g. S.B. April 1672, p. 25. For an order to an apprentice to pay his master's widow four years' wages earned since the death of his master, *vide* S.B. March 1662–3, p. 21.
[3] E.g. on the recognisance of one Watson in S.R. July 1671.
[4] In June 1662, in a dispute between a tailor and his covenant servant, the Court ordered the latter to remain until 1664 and the master to find her sufficient meat, drink, lodging and apparel, but there is no mention of instruction, S.B. June 1662, p. 37. On the other hand, we hear of a man becoming a servant for three years to a gardener, who was to instruct him and pay him £3. 10s. a year, S.B. Feb. 1680–81, p. 31.

THE LABOUR CODE

neglected, but the Court decided that, as there was no indenture, it could not intervene.[1] The tutelary position of the servant, at least in some cases, is indicated by the fact that, in a dispute as to the discharge of Anne Ward, covenant servant of Michael Wright and his wife, it is not the girl but her mother who is a party, and the former is left at the disposal of the latter.[2] These long contracts were, however, of doubtful validity. When, for instance, a girl, bound by indenture to serve a silk-thrower for five years, left without warning, she was ordered to return, not necessarily for the whole period, but was to give three months' notice if she intended to leave at the end of the year.[3] Akin to these long hirings was the indenture for service in the plantations. It was by no means uncommon at this time for persons to be "spirited away" beyond sea, usually to the plantations, and sold into what was often actual slavery and at other times was probably not much better.[4] To meet this evil, an arrangement was introduced in 1682 whereby servants intending to emigrate were to execute an indenture in duplicate before a magistrate. A register was to be kept by the Clerk of the Peace[5] and this doubtless explains the presence of a considerable number of such indentures among the Guildhall papers.[6] These indentures cover the years 1682–4, and are signed by Abraham Bayly, Esq., one of the county Justices. Those bound vary in age from children to middle-aged men, and the indenture frequently bears a note indicating that the servant was "friendless", "wandering", "from the House of Correction", "from Whitechapel Gaol where he had lain for pilfering", "no apprentice" and the like. Sometimes there is a stipulation that he is to have an opportunity to seek his redemption. Very many of the bindings are to masters of

---

[1] S.B. May 1687, p. 33. [2] S.B. Oct. 1670, p. 36.
[3] S.B. July 1679, p. 58.
[4] For a discussion of the activities of "spirits" in Middlesex, vide the Preface to vol. IV of Jeaffreson's *Middlesex County Records* (p. 41 et seq.), where the lightness of the penalties inflicted is emphasised. We may well believe that apprentices were most subject to such treatment and, in this connection, we read that John Marsingall of Poplar, mariner, was bound by recognisance to produce John Bennett, his apprentice, whom it was believed he had transported and sold beyond seas, S.B. June 1673, p. 65.
[5] Crawford, *Tudor and Stuart Proclamations*, vol. I, p. 453.
[6] They are in a parcel dated 1682–95.

ships[1] and, this being so, the trade at which the servant is to work is naturally not specified. The masters doubtless disposed of their interests to colonists, but they were bound to provide passage, lodging and necessaries. Four years seems to have been the usual term, but some indentures are for six or seven years. Barbadoes was apparently the most popular destination, but there were also emigrants to Jamaica, Pennsylvania and Maryland. It is of course impossible to throw any light on the working of the system after the binding had been duly performed, but interest attaches to this evidence that the machinery was employed to a considerable extent.

That the status of apprenticeship should be carefully regulated by national legislators and administrators seems natural even to modern eyes, seeing that it concerned persons who supposedly were unable to look after their own interests. Such inability was not, however, supposed by Tudor statesmen to be by any means confined to those of tender years and, for this reason and also to provide for national interests where they did not coincide with those of individuals, they made provision for an equally careful supervision of wage contracts between adults. That a man should be free to engage an employee or enter employment for as long or short a period as he pleased was not considered beneficial either for the parties concerned or for the country as a whole, and the Act, 5 Elizabeth, c. 4, therefore sought to enforce annual hiring. Though this law remained on the Statute Book, there is little evidence that it was anything more than a dead letter after the Restoration. The Middlesex Records show that annual bonds were in use to some extent during the early part of our period, and the Court was prepared to enforce such contracts as were made. There is, however, no indication that the Justices presumed contracts to be for a year when no term was stated[2] or that they urged the observance of the annual bond. In fact, so far as there is any trace of a general object prompting the enforcement of annual contracts, it is the prevention of chargeability.[3] Usually there is no sign of any interest beyond that of

[1] E.g. to Joseph Bull, Captain of the *Hopewell*.
[2] This was the legal construction, Burn, *Justice of the Peace*, p. 646.
[3] *Vide* a complaint by the churchwardens and overseers of the Rolls Liberty regarding a servant retained for a year who had been turned out

THE LABOUR CODE

the parties directly concerned,[1] and the statutory penalty of 40s. seems never to have been imposed upon masters who broke the law. The breach might, of course, be on the other side and, as late as January 1709–10, a labourer retained for a year was indicted for departing without leave.[2] The absconding servant was to be committed to ward until he should become bound to continue his service, so that it is probable that some of the persons in the House of Correction who are ordered to be sent to master or mistress are runaway servants. In addition, there is at least one case of undoubted punishment, a fine of 6s. 8d. upon Thomas Hide, who had been retained for a year by John ffeild for £6, together with meat, drink, washing and lodging, and left within two months without any reasonable cause first allowed by a Justice of Peace or the leave of his master.[3] Third parties might be prosecuted for enticing or entertaining hired servants, no less than apprentices, and, for this offence, there is at least one fine of 6s. 8d. and one of 12d., both at the period when an attempt was being made to enforce other labour regulations.[4]

The requirement of testimonials from those seeking fresh employment had, to all appearance, completely lapsed by the commencement of our period. Burn, writing at its close, lamented this fact and found in it the explanation of the dearness of labour, since the fixing of wages in one county would simply induce servants to move elsewhere.[5] This is perfectly true if, as in his and most of his contemporaries' view, fixing meant

"without any leave or approbation" of Justices of Peace, S.B. Oct. 1663, p. 37. Cf. an order for Antony Gray to keep and maintain a servant who had become sick and subject to strange fits of lunacy until "the full end and expiration of the term of his said service", and also the recognisance of Gray for contempt of an order made for the relief of the parish of Sandon, Hardy, *Hertford County Records*, vol. I, pp. 146, 142.

[1] E.g. in the recognisance of one Payne, victualler, for putting away his hired servant within her term without lawful warning or testimonial or cause allowed before a Justice of the Peace, S.R. Oct. 1663.

[2] S.R. Jan. 1709–10.

[3] S.R. Aug. 1686.

[4] S.R. May 1682 and Oct. 1687. The Brentford Justices were also interesting themselves in the method of dismissal at this period, as we see from the prosecution in 1683 of Richard Pluckington, who was to show cause why he turned away Robert Ashwell, his servant, without lawful warning, Brentford Calendar, p. 83. There was a similar case in 1693, *ibid.* p. 112.

[5] *Justice of the Peace*, p. 649.

reduction. Some attempt was made to revive the system in Middlesex during the latter part of the reign of Charles II, but we should attribute this to a general feeling on the part of the paternally-minded governing class that the common people were too much out of control, rather than to a deliberate policy of lowering wages, although, as will appear shortly, the question of wages was under consideration at the same time. In October 1683, the Court ordered the strict enforcement of the law, on the ground that it was "generally experienced throughout this whole county, as well by the nobility and gentry as other good householders inhabiting the same, that servants having no such certificates and testimonials when they depart out of one service and come to be retained into another service, and the neglect of putting the said law in execution giveth great occasion to very many servants to become idle, loose and of evil behaviour and often times to cheat and purloin from their masters and mistresses, and when they come to be retained in a service upon liking without a testimonial, take their first opportunity to run away with their masters' or mistresses' goods".[1] In the following January, the Grand Jury presented "that the testimonials for servants may be made universal in all the kingdom, otherwise this county will have little benefit of the order made by this Court".[2] They prayed that this presentment might be laid before the King, a request which the Court granted, and their action may be partly responsible for the issue, on October 21st 1684, of a proclamation against servants being taken without testimonials.[3] The requirement can hardly have been enforced with vigour, for there is no sign of the prosecution of offenders who, one imagines, would be in the majority. The only indictment for retaining a servant without testimonial appears to be that of Style of Sunbury in 1694.[4] For the rest, it is significant that indictments for retaining servants already bound to other

[1] S.B. Oct. 1683, p. 59. It is interesting to note that, more than a century earlier, similar evils were attributed to the slack execution of this regulation, *vide* the proposals on the matter printed in Bland, Brown and Tawney, *Documents*, pp. 333–5.
[2] S.B. Jan. 1683–4, p. 29.
[3] Crawford, *Hand-List of Proclamations*.
[4] S.R. Oct. 1694. It was quashed for insufficiency.

THE LABOUR CODE

masters do not allege the absence of a testimonial, which would have afforded a very easy ground for action. We may therefore conclude that the testimonial as an instrument of general economic policy was extinct throughout our period.

The fixation of the amount of wages is generally regarded as one of the most advanced forms of paternalism, and it is certainly one of the most difficult to administer intelligently. Burn went so far as to assert that the Elizabethan laws on this subject "always have been and always will be impracticable",[1] so that, in view of the decay of central government and the absence of compulsion, we cannot be surprised to find that our Justices did little under this head. In place of the elaborate scale of wages which they were expected to issue every Easter, we only find, incorporated in the annual order as to the Assizes of Bread and Ale which was inserted in each April Sessions Book, the formal provision "that rates of servants' wages, labourers and artificers, upon the Statute of quinto Elizabeth, do stand as they were at the last General Quarter Sessions of the Peace held for this county after the close of Easter" with the appropriate date. Action had sunk to this merely formal level as early as 1610,[2] and the order was inserted in practically every April Sessions Book down to 1725. The reissuing of wage schedules was, of course, quite common,[3] but clearly it here passed the bounds of practical policy. Variation according to the plenty or scarcity of the time and other circumstances was of the essence of the Elizabethan

---

[1] *History of the Poor Laws*, p. 243.
[2] Cal. of Sessions Rolls, etc. vol. II, p. 50. Miss McArthur does not adduce specific evidence for her view that "in the county of Middlesex... the Justices certainly acted in accordance with the Statute during the Stuart period" but seems to base it on these annual entries in the Sessions Register, *Eng. Hist. Rev.* vol. XV, p. 445. Such perfunctory action cannot be regarded as real execution of the careful provisions of 5 Elizabeth, c. 4. If this is the only ground, her inference as to the probability of contemporaneous action in the City of London loses its force. Rather the provision in 18 and 19 Charles II, c. 8, for the rebuilding of London that "in case of combination or exaction of unreasonable wages" the Justices of King's Bench, upon complaint of the Lord Mayor and Aldermen, might assess wages, especially in the building trades—a provision which Miss McArthur mentions—gives strong ground for supposing that here also the ordinary machinery for wage assessment by Justices of Peace had ceased to be effective.
[3] The Wiltshire scale of 1605 was continued almost unaltered until 1654, and that for 1655 until 1684, *Hist. MSS. Comm.* vol. I, p. 161 *et seq.*

enactment, and it would be idle to expect any attempt to enforce a completely rigid scale over a period of more than a century. In April 1682, the Court ordered that "no wages shall be allowed by the Justices but according to the rates settled by this Court and that whosoever retains servants or pays wages not according to the Statute shall be punished according to it".[1] This might conceivably refer to the usual order, which is included in the Sessions Book for that month, but one would think that the rates of at least three-quarters of a century earlier would appear so obviously inapplicable[2] that, on deciding to enforce regulation, the Justices would take the trouble to compile a new scale. In their then vigorous frame of mind, they may well have undertaken this task, though no resulting assessment has yet been found.[3] At all events, there is no sign of the prosecution of offenders and, whatever the Court's intentions and actions were, we cannot suppose that they produced much effect on wages. The same is true of one or two other symptoms of activity which, if they do nothing more, show that there continued for a time longer to be some interest in wage regulation. In April 1694, when there is the usual order regarding wages, the Court, "taking notice that the rates of wages for labourers and artificers published in this county are little regarded and that there are no rates set for coachmen and other servants", deputed a number of Justices "to examine and consider of the said rates set for the year last past and what rates ought to be set for this present year".[4] Thus the evidence forthcoming for the period 1660 to 1760 amounts to very little. It does not show that compulsion was ever actually brought to bear upon any one master or employee or affected the daily life of

[1] S.B. April 1682, p. 37.
[2] The original assessment for Middlesex has not yet been found, so that the antiquity of these rates cannot be precisely stated.
[3] It is interesting to note that the period 1682–8 is one for which wage assessments for some counties survive, Hewins, "Regulation of Wages", *Economic Journal*, 1898, p. 27.
[4] S.B. April 1694, p. 6. Among the minutes for Thursday, April 8th 1703, is the entry: "wages of labourers and servants on Saturday", Miscellaneous Papers. This may indicate that the question was being seriously considered, but may only refer to the promulgation of the usual order, which appears in its customary place.

THE LABOUR CODE

any person. When adjudicating upon suits for the recovery of wages, we never find the Court determining its award, as the Kent Sessions did as late as 1734, "according to the rates of wages for servants in husbandry, as the same stood limited, rated and appointed for this County, according to the statute in that case made and provided".[1] The Justices may at times have thought the old law worth reviving, but this is the most that can be said. From 1725 onwards, we look in vain for the faintest sign of the most perfunctory action, and Fielding who, as a magistrate for the county, was intimately acquainted with its administration, may be adduced as witness to the neglect of the labour laws in general " particularly as to that which relates to the rating the wages of labourers; a law which at first, it seems, was too carelessly executed, and which hath since grown into utter neglect and disuse".[2]

More interesting is the special case of the tailors within the Weekly Bills of Mortality. The Act, 7 George I, c. 13, passed against combinations of journeymen to raise wages and shorten hours, fixed the hours in this trade at from 6 o'clock in the morning till 8 o'clock at night (with $1\frac{1}{2}d.$ for breakfast and an hour for dinner), and the maximum wages at 2s. from March to June, and 1s. 8d. for the remainder of the year. Quarter Sessions was empowered to alter them when necessary, according to plenty or scarcity and other circumstances. In 1751 the Court received a complaint from several master tailors of Westminster and the Middlesex suburbs "that a great many journeymen tailors have, since the commencement of the present year 1751, exacted and insisted to have much greater wages for their work in making up men's or women's clothes than are settled and ascertained by an Act of Parliament...". The masters "in order to prevent such exactions for the future were willing that the journeymen tailors should be allowed greater wages than were settled by the said Act of Parliament" and applied for an alteration to be made by the Court which, after

---

[1] Waterman, "Some New Evidence on Wage Assessments in the Eighteenth Century", *Eng. Hist. Rev.* vol. XLIII, p. 401.
[2] "Enquiry into the Causes of the Late Increase of Robbers", *Works*, vol. VIII, p. 577.

hearing counsel for both parties, ordered "that every master tailor inhabiting or residing in the said City and Liberty or in any other part of the said county of Middlesex within the Weekly Bills of Mortality shall pay unto every journeyman tailor or other person employed or to be employed or retained as a journeyman tailor for his work from six of the clock in the morning until eight o'clock at night, excepting only that there shall be allowed by the master three-half-pence a day for breakfast and one hour for dinner in the time aforesaid, the wages and sums following (that is to say) from the 25th day of March to the 29th day of September 2s. 6d. a day, and from the 29th day of September to the 25th day of March 2s. a day, instead of the sums mentioned in the aforesaid Act, and in case of non-payment, to be levied in such manner as by the said Act is directed".[1] This action did not have the desired result, and in 1756 the masters again sought the aid of the Court, stating "that the petitioners did with all thankfulness acknowledge the favour and protection which this Court was pleased to show them upon their application made at the General Quarter Sessions of the Peace for this County held after Midsummer 1751 in relation to the differences then depending between the petitioners and their several journeymen", but that their men had entered into "unlawful combinations for refusing, and now actually refused to work the several and respective hours by the said order prescribed and directed, and likewise that they do frequently and many times go off and leave their work unfinished, to the petitioners' great loss and disappointment, as well as the displeasure of their customers, in direct contravention and defiance of the said order of Sessions". The Court then strictly enjoined obedience to its previous order, and recommended licensing Justices "to take due notice of the conduct and behaviour of such persons in their several divisions who are keepers of such victualling houses which are commonly called Houses of Call", as the masters had complained of their conduct, no doubt in facilitating concerted action by the men.[2] It does not appear

[1] S.B. July 1751, p. 29. This order was to be published in newspapers and otherwise, and payments for printing and posting up were subsequently ordered, O.C. vol. v, ff. 242, 254-5.
[2] S.B. Sept. 1756, pp. 44-5.

THE LABOUR CODE

whether this second order proved efficacious. The only prosecutions of offenders were at an earlier date, when there were two cases of fine for paying excessive wages and one acquittal.[1] There is no indication that journeymen were committed to the House of Correction for refusing to work or for taking higher wages. It is therefore unlikely that even in this instance much practical result was produced by the Justices' intervention.

The Justices had no clear authority to order and enforce the payment of wages, but in practice they were allowed this power in connection with wages fixed by them under 5 Elizabeth, c. 4, and, more generally, in connection with wages in husbandry.[2] Although the fixing of wages was moribund, the Justices in and out of Sessions were active in enforcing payment of wages, not according to authoritative assessment but according to contract. In so doing, they undoubtedly met a crying need. There are many petitions from employees among the miscellaneous papers at the Guildhall, warrants against the masters being allowed. In the rolls, we find recognisances of the masters and mistresses for refusing to pay.[3] The Court itself was prepared to order payment[4] and at times committed masters for default.[5] When, however, oaths were made as to wages due to several servants of Sir John Benett, the Court merely instructed the Clerk of the Peace to forward the particulars to Sir John.[6] The need for some such remedy as the Court provided may be gauged from the fact that in one instance the wages were due for no less than three years five months.[7] However, even the cost of application to Sessions would put servants at a disadvantage, particularly if non-payment of their wages had left them penurious. In 1674

---

[1] S.R. Oct. and Dec. 1744. In one of these, the prosecutor was the journeyman, who received both the extra pay and half the forfeiture, *vide* p. 199.
[2] Burn, *Justice of the Peace*, pp. 647–8.
[3] E.g. three in S.R. Dec. 1670.
[4] E.g. two orders in S.B. Feb. 1695–6, p. 30.
[5] In 1705 it committed one for not paying £7. 17s. 6d., S.B. Oct. 1705, p. 42. We sometimes find masters and mistresses on the prison calendars, e.g. three in S.R. May 1671. One master was allowed to pay by instalments, S.B. April 1690, p. 54.
[6] S.B. Jan. 1674–5, p. 53. The money was, at least sometimes, paid into Court by the master and so to his employee, *vide* a receipt in S.B. Oct. 1678, p. 112.
[7] S.B. Feb. 1710–11, p. 39.

we find the Court ordering William Draper of Willesden to pay Jane Cox 30s. wages and 5s. costs in getting the order.[1] Probably therefore the extra-sessional assistance of the magistrates was more valuable because more accessible. The Brentford Justices were very active in this connection.[2] Towards the close of the period, however, one master successfully took his stand by the strict interpretation of the law. Solomon Jonas appealed against a warrant of Thomas Lediard, J.P., ordering him to pay Gerritt Mennes "therein mentioned to be his yearly hired servant in husbandry the sum of nine pounds nine shillings and two pence for wages pursuant to the direction of the Statute in such case made and provided and the said appellant by his said petition alleged that there was no wages due from him, the said appellant, to the said Gerritt Mennes, neither the said appellant ever employed the said Gerritt Mennes as a servant in husbandry but only as a labourer and workman in a peel mill". The warrant was pronounced "defective and insufficient in law",[3] and Mennes may well have been obliged to go without his pay. By that time, however, all might have been well had the mention of husbandry been omitted, as the Act, 20 George II, c. 19, gave a single Justice authority to order payment and issue distress warrants for small sums. As a matter of fact, the Justices in Sessions do not seem to have played any part in the enforcement of wage payment during the last forty years of the period. Probably their outside activities were accomplishing as much as could be attempted in the existing state of the law and, when these received explicit recognition, action by the Court became unnecessary.

Considering the state of the law of conspiracy, and the frequent special acts of Parliament against combinations of workmen in particular trades, we hear surprisingly little on these kindred subjects. In 1720, we find the recognisances of seven men for conspiracy and combination to enhance the rate of journeymen artificers' wages and work in the art and mystery of

[1] S.B. Jan. 1673–4, p. 37. The servant's plight was much worse if the master removed the case to King's Bench by Certiorari.
[2] *Vide* the Brentford Calendar.
[3] S.B. Oct. 1753, pp. 39–40.

sail-maker.[1] In July 1729, one Newton of Spitalfields, weaver, was prosecuted for mutiny and unlawful assembly of weavers,[2] while, some years later, nine men were indicted for conspiracy not to work as journeymen wheelwrights save at certain prices and hours.[3] Much earlier, trouble had been caused in the Spitalfields silk district by the introduction from Holland of ribbon looms or "loom engines", and there were serious riots in the summer of 1675. One of our rolls contains the recognisances of the prosecutors,[4] but the offenders were dealt with at the Gaol Delivery in September, not by our Justices. Particulars of the charges and the punishments inflicted have already been published elsewhere,[5] so that it is unnecessary to do more than mention the incident here. It constitutes an interesting anticipation of the Luddite riots. In the tailoring dispute, the workmen, as has already been shown, were acting in combination, but there is no sign that they were proceeded against on this ground. Thus our evidence gives little help in estimating the importance of the conspiracy and combination laws at this time, though, so far as it goes, it suggests that they were not enforced to any considerable extent.

Our Records do not shed much light on the general sociopolitical conceptions which lay at the foundation of the labour code. This absence of evidence is, of course, partly attributable to the nature of our materials, but it is of some significance. Compulsion to work, which was so important an element in the Elizabethan system, was intended as a cure for poverty, vagrancy and vice generally, as well as to promote industrial expansion, and such compulsion implied regulation of working conditions. Hence we find that writers on the poor laws were naturally led on to a discussion of wages and conditions of work, a discussion which, in the eighteenth century, usually led to the conclusion that wages were too high and must be reduced if the

---

[1] S.R. Sept. 1720.
[2] S.R. July 1729.
[3] S.R. Oct. 1734. Six of these bills were not found, one removed by Certiorari, and there is no note as to the other two.
[4] S.R. Aug. 1675.
[5] Jeaffreson, *Middlesex County Records*, vol. IV, pp. 61–5. For action taken by the Council in this matter, *vide* Cal. S.P. Dom. Aug. 11–13th 1675.

rise in poor rates was to be stemmed.[1] Similarly Fielding, in probing into the causes of street robberies and other vices, was drawn on to the same discussion and the same conclusions.[2] Concern for the balance of trade, the one purely economic motive which remained powerful, pointed in the same direction, since lower wages were expected to increase exports and reduce imports.[3] Thus the thinkers of the time might well regard the labour code as a primary factor in industrial prosperity and as a cure for poverty, vice and crime, yet those responsible for its administration allowed it to fall into almost complete desuetude. This fact becomes all the more significant when we remember that these administrators were far from being without interest in the wider issues and were constantly occupied with the problem of vagrancy which focused all those issues. The inference then is that the great majority of those responsible for the country's administration had come to the conclusion that it was impracticable to enforce the old labour code. It is very noticeable that the eighteenth-century chairmen, though they show a marked penchant for philosophising and though they were always obsessed with the idea of the idleness and debauchery of the lower orders, left this code entirely out of the range of possible remedies, and this remark applies to Fielding himself when occupying the chair of the Westminster Sessions.[4] To some extent, the notion of the duty to work survived for police reasons, an aspect which has already been illustrated by the momentary attempt to enforce the use of testimonials in order to secure better order among servants by strict supervision of their movements. Such measures were not solely in defence of masters, as the latter were expected to a great extent to stand surety for the good behaviour of their servants. This standpoint is illustrated by recognisances for living out of service where actual vagrancy is not alleged.[5] It was felt that people out of service would

---

[1] D. Marshall, *The English Poor in the Eighteenth Century*, p. 26.
[2] "Enquiry into the Causes of the Late Increase of Robbers", *Works*, vol. VIII, p. 577 *et seq.*
[3] *Ibid.* p. 581. Furniss, *Position of the Labourer in a System of Nationalism*.
[4] Charge to the Westminster Grand Jury, June 29th 1749.
[5] E.g. that of Mary Marshall of Whitechapel to answer the Churchwardens for her evil life, living idly at her own hand out of service, and that of a

THE LABOUR CODE

naturally fall into evil courses and would probably resort to bad practices in order to maintain themselves, while, if in employment, they would not be under the same temptation and would be well supervised. A corollary to this was the master's right to punish his servants himself[1] and, in the last resort, to bring them to the Justices for correction. We hear something, though not much, of this disciplinary side,[2] but nothing of the other corollary, the duty to provide work. There is no sign of any pressure upon masters to keep their employees in work, as in the old days of vigorous administration by the Council. Thus the old conception of service had survived in a one-sided and therefore a corrupt form—a form, moreover, which could not possibly recommend it to the employee, since it meant restraint without compensating advantages. The notion of decadence must not be pressed too far, for it has to be remembered that, even in the heyday of Tudor and Stuart paternalism, many scales of wages prescribed maxima and not minima. Still, without unduly idealising the Tudor system, we must admit that its conceptions had deteriorated greatly by the eighteenth century and had ceased to be a possible basis for a just or practical economic policy.

Harrow husbandman for being a lewd and idle person and refusing to go to service, S.R. July 1661 and April 1673. We find the Brentford Justices ordering three women to go to service or, in default, to be sent to the House of Correction as vagrant persons, Brentford Calendar, p. 77. Under the designation "idle and disorderly persons", 17 George II, c. 5, classed persons who, not having wherewith to maintain themselves, live idle and refuse to work for the usual wages, with those threatening to run away and leave their families to the parish, those unlawfully returning after being passed and with ordinary beggars. They were liable to be arrested and, in 1759, we hear of the issue of comprehensive warrants to apprehend all loose, idle and disorderly people who can give no good account of their way of living—a prosecution of peace officers for neglecting to execute in S.R. Oct. 1759.

[1] Burn, *Justice of the Peace*, p. 650.
[2] E.g. when punishment developed into ill-treatment, as in the recognisance of Richard Robes for giving his servant immoderate and unlawful correction, S.R. August 1670. There are also recognisances of disorderly servants, e.g. in S.R. Sept. 1754.

CHAPTER VI

THE REGULATION OF PRODUCTION AND DISTRIBUTION

THE most cursory glance at any contemporary manual on the office of Justices of Peace or at a model charge for chairmen of Sessions[1] at once shows us that the Justices were charged with the execution of a mass of law governing the production and distribution of goods, law which is quite astonishing in its extent, variety and minuteness. General legislation upon weights and measures is to be expected, and was among the earliest symptoms of the interest of the growing nation state in economic matters. But an embryonic central government and Parliament did not attempt, and certainly would not have achieved, immediate uniformity. Even what may be called the common denominators could not at once be made identical throughout all trades—troy and avoirdupois weight, water and Winchester measure subsisted side by side for different purposes. But this, and some continued local variation, accounted for but a small part of the complexity. More important was the impossibility of compelling people to buy and sell in terms of these common denominators. The continuance of the practice of selling by various specialised measures, lots and pieces, necessitated an elaborate definition of the standards to be used for various commodities—sacks, barrels, loads, trusses, billets and the like. As a consequence, the mere supervision of weights and measures was no small task. A further group of regulations concerned the manner and place of sale and frequently developed into the fixation of prices. These owed their origin to the ease with which small localised markets could be dislocated or manipulated and were in essence measures of self-protection devised by those dependent on such markets. Political unification could only slowly break down this economic separatism and the central

[1] E.g. that of Lambard, quoted by Holdsworth, *History of English Law*, vol. VI, p. 543 *et seq.*

government therefore long found it necessary to preserve these medieval restrictions, but the need for them passed away with the growth of trade mobility and enterprise, so that they have little counterpart to-day. The quality of goods sold is another matter which no government can ignore. At the period with which we are concerned control went far beyond the simple protection of the consumer from common fraud and, over a wide field, went on to impose rigid standardisation and precise definition of the classes of persons who might make and sell various goods and of the manner in which they were to do so. This clearly indicates much more than a general interest in the health of consumers and the veracity of sellers. Faith in the sufficiency of free competition was very weak and, since good quality of products was seen to be a primary factor in the prosperity first of the town and later of the nation, a minute circumscription of the freedom of the individual producer was deemed essential to his own, and still more to his society's, welfare. Naturally this belief waned with the growth of individualist philosophy, but it would be dangerous to read a definite creed into the evidence on this subject supplied by Quarter Sessions records. Justices of Peace and those upon whom fell the duty of prosecuting offenders had very much else to do, a great deal of which they personally would consider of more importance and could understand far better because it was less intricate. From the very beginning of the period we look in vain for evidence of the enforcement of the bulk of the law governing production; and at this date it would certainly be rash to infer any definite belief in the virtues of laissez-faire, the more so since Parliament was not for a long time to show any perception that minute regulation was becoming less necessary or beneficial. Here more than in any other sphere we must take into account the remoteness and complexity of the subject from the point of view of the amateur magistrates and officials and, to the extent that we give weight to this consideration, we shall attribute the non-enforcement of the relevant law less to actual disbelief in its value than to the unsuitability of the machinery provided for its execution. Before going further, some consideration must be given to certain officials who were specially concerned with the subject of this chapter and who interest us in so far as they came in contact with the Justices of Peace.

In connection with the supervision of quality, weights and measures, it is interesting to discover traces of the survival of the old manorial office of aleconner or aletaster. In August 1664 we find the recognisance of a Shoreditch chandler to answer one Vanse, aleconner, for using false scales and weights to the oppression of the poor,[1] and this same officer was active in enforcing the Assize of Bread, as also was Nash, aleconner of Shadwell, ten years later.[2] Some attempt was made to enforce the execution of the office, since in March 1667–8 William Edwards and Geoffrey Bowles were indicted on the ground that, though elected aleconners for Staines on October 6th 1667, they had totally neglected their office, and both were fined 3s. 4d.[3] In August 1670 Francis Ford complained to the Court that, having been duly chosen aleconner of Spitalfields, he was disabled from executing the office for want of scales, weights and measures. He had applied to the officers and inhabitants, but they had not provided any. The Court ordered the churchwardens and overseers to do so, in order that he might perform the office "and the great oppression, frauds and abuses of victuallers, bakers, chandlers, butchers and other retailing traders may be from time to time discovered and punished".[4] Aleconners must, however, have been quite exceptional. Parliament usually relies entirely on the constables and headboroughs to enforce its regulations,[5] as also does the Court itself.[6] Though we hear of aleconners for Twickenham as late as October 1709[7] and for Spitalfields in 1766,[8] it is certain that they were not general enough to constitute a real executive force. In the lack of such a body of officials specially charged with their enforcement may be found no small part of the explanation of the feebleness of the

[1] S.R. Aug. 1664.
[2] *Vide* p. 180.
[3] S.R. March 1667–8.
[4] S.B. Aug. 1670, p. 45. For a similar order to Ealing made by the Brentford Justices in April 1669, cf. the Brentford Calendar, p. 50.
[5] E.g. in the Act, 22 Charles II, c. 8.
[6] For this in connection with the Assize of Bread, *vide* p. 179.
[7] Brentford Calendar, p. 146.
[8] Entick, *History and Survey of London*, vol. IV, p. 436.

PRODUCTION AND DISTRIBUTION

execution of the laws governing the standards of quality and quantity in the sale of goods.

The office of Clerk of the Market was on a different plane. It provided much more than specialised machinery for the prosecution of trade offences, exercising a jurisdiction of its own which enabled it to punish, as well as to detect, offenders. Its authority was thus, in a limited sphere, on a par with that of the Justices of Peace, and it must have been at once a rival and relief to magistrates charged with such comprehensive powers and duties as were the Justices. The Tudors and early Stuarts had found in this specialised machinery a more adaptable and more incisive instrument for the execution of their elaborately detailed supervision of trade and industry and had taken considerable pains to develop and perfect it. The position is somewhat difficult to gauge accurately owing to the fact that there were two sets of officials bearing very similar titles, namely the Clerk of the Market pure and simple, and the Clerk of the Market of the King's Household. As the title of the latter is not always given in full, confusion is easy.[1] Sheppard, in his book on the Office, makes it clear that, at least after the Restoration, the distinction was quite definite, and that the Clerk of the Household was restricted to the Verge of the Court, so that it was the ordinary Clerk of the Market who was the administrative instrument for the general enforcement of justice and uniformity in weights and measures, and his office was mainly exercised by Justices, mayors and similar officers, along with other jurisdictions.[2] There is hardly any evidence of action by these

---

[1] Even in the Act, 16 Charles I, c. 19, which limited the sphere of the Clerk of the Market of the King's Household to the Verge of the Court where it then was, implying that he had been usurping a wider jurisdiction, the reference to "the undue execution of the Office of Clerk of the Market" appears ambiguous.

[2] "There is a Clerk of the Market for the King's Household only...and there is a Clerk of the Market for all other places. And there are laws for both of them. For the first, he is to execute his office duly and to burn false weights and measures. He is to execute his office within the Vierge only and not elsewhere.... For the other Clerk of the Market, we are to know this, that albeit his power be much lessened by the distribution of it to, and exercise of it by, Justices of Assize, of Oyer and Terminer, and Justices of Peace; yet his office doth still remain, and he hath a jurisdiction still. This officer hath a court which he may still keep, and hold plea therein of that which belongs to

officials during the period[1] and it is very unlikely that we should have heard nothing of them if they were of real importance.[2]

Similar oblivion does not shroud the Clerk of the Market of the King's Household, for we hear not a little of opposition to his activities,[3] and this, at one period, developed into a keen controversy between our Justices and the occupants of the office. In January 1726–7, the Court was informed that the deputies and agents of Thomas Robe and John Matthews, who held the office, "have and do exact and receive great sums of money of tradesmen and alehouse keepers in this county, under pretence of weighing of their weights and measuring of their quarts, pints and other measures, and that such proceeding is illegal and oppressive and cannot be justified".[4] Mr Robe, himself a Justice of the Peace, produced his patent and, after a consultation at which all Justices were asked to be present, the Court reached the opinion "that the said patent or grant doth not extend any further than to the King's Palace and the precincts thereof commonly called the Little Verge" and ordered copies of this opinion to be delivered to all Justices and high constables. It also pronounced illegal a warrant to the High Constable of the Tower Division for the appearance of jurors and traders at the King's Arms, Shoreditch, and expressed the intention to support all officers who acted according to its resolution.[5] In the roll for October 1728, we find the recognisances of Edward Evans and Thomas Fielding, each "to answer such misde-

his Office, and for that purpose send out his process and warrants to the Sheriffs and Bailiffs to bring a jury before him, and give charge, and take a presentment...", Sheppard, *Of the Office of Clerk of the Market*, p. 117.

[1] For the Westminster Clerk, *vide* p. 187 n.

[2] In April 1718, Whitlocke Bulstrode charged the Grand Jury to enquire "Whether the Clerk of the Market does his duty; he ought twice a year to summon in all weights and measures, and break them that are less than they ought to be, according to the Standard", Charge, p. 32. It must, however, be remembered that many of the topics briefly touched on in these charges were of little more than antiquarian interest.

[3] Two recognisances for abusing the Deputies of the Clerk of the Market of His Majesty's Household within the Verge, because they found weights and measures false at Hammersmith, S.R. Feb. 1663-4. Recognisances of Turvill and Shute for extortion, "sitting at the sign of the Exchequer, Uxbridge, as Deputy for William Hempson, Clerk of the Market for the King's Household", S.R. May 1675.

[4] O.C. vol. III, f. 83.   [5] O.C. vol. III, ff. 87–8.

PRODUCTION AND DISTRIBUTION 163

meanours as shall be objected against him for his extorting several sums of money from Anne Hale, widow, Richard Collins and divers other inhabitants within the township of Uxbridge...under pretence of being deputies of the Clerk of the Market and without any legal authority".[1] At the same time, bills were found against them for extortionately receiving the sum of 6*d*. for fee to the Clerk of the Market of the Household of the Lord the King, but were removed by Certiorari.[2] By way of retaliation, Mr Robe lodged a complaint against John Weedon, J.P., who had taken the recognisances, touching matters contained in an affidavit of Fielding and Evans sworn before Lord Chief Justice Raymond, the affidavit stating that, when Fielding and Evans were carried before Mr Weedon and other Justices at Uxbridge, Mr Weedon had returned several recognisances against them, whereas they maintained that they had only entered into one.[3] The Court upheld Mr Weedon's action and, being informed that the Deputies of the Clerk continued to exact money as before, appointed a committee to enquire into their proceedings "and to consider of the most proper and effectual methods to prevent and put an end to the oppressions of His Majesty's subjects dwelling within this county under colour of the said patent".[4] Those acting under the patent persisted and indicted Richard Norwood of Uxbridge, High Constable, for neglecting to appear before them at the Chequer Inn, to return a warrant for the appearance of jurors.[5] John Matthews menaced the Grand Jury to have this bill found, for which he was presented by them, and the Court resolved to apply to King's Bench for an information against him.[6] Norwood's prosecutors, doubtless fearing the hostility of the Justices, removed their action by Certiorari and the Court resolved that his defence should be paid for by the county.[7] The Justices learned that, in Michaelmas Term 1730, King's Bench ruled in this action that the Clerk had a jurisdiction "beyond the

---

[1] There is a second recognisance against each of them for similar extortion from other persons, S.R. Oct. 1728.
[2] *Ibid.*
[3] O.C. vol. III, ff. 156, 159.
[4] O.C. vol. III, f. 159.
[5] S.R. Jan. 1728–9.
[6] O.C. vol. III, ff. 184–6.
[7] O.C. vol. III, f. 192. For payments, *vide* O.C. vol. III, ff. 279, 286, 303.

Little Verge, through the circuit of twelve miles from the Palace where His Majesty shall be resident for the time being ", but that he was not entitled to the fee of 4*d*. twice a year for examining weights and measures. They therefore recommended all magistrates to see that no more than the legal fees were taken and declared their opinion that "the Clerk of the Market for the time being is entitled to a certain fee, (which he claims to be 4*d*.) for and on his marking or sealing any weights or measures used for gain in trade or dealing, but that no fee is due to him for viewing or examining them without sealing or marking or for reviewing or resealing or marking again any weights or measures before marked or sealed by him or any preceding clerk of the said market, and...no person or persons are obliged or compellable to have any of their weights or measures marked or sealed by the Clerk of the Market unless they shall think fit and desire to have the same sealed or marked accordingly for their own security or satisfaction", and that the Clerk or his Deputy should "carry his standard weights and measures to the dwellinghouses, shops or stalls of such persons as buy or sell by weight or measure in their respective trade or callings in order to view and examine the same". Where he found false weights or measures, he might seize, break or otherwise destroy them and might summon juries and set fines,[1] but it would seem that this interpretation, if accepted, must have robbed the office of any value that it may have had for securing justice between buyers and sellers generally, as distinct from the immediate object of protecting the Court from deceits and exactions. Seeing that the twelve-mile radius would normally include most of Middlesex, there was a real clash of authority and it is clear that the Justices, in opposing the Clerk's proceedings, were in fact espousing the cause of laissez-faire, for they could never hope to give the matter the careful attention that would be possible for a specialised official. They would doubtless contend that the office was a cloak for exactions, without serving any real public interest, and it is highly probable that, in the eighteenth century at least, this was a valid objection and an adequate ground for condemning the whole system.

[1] O.C. vol. III, f. 279, April 1731.

One of the most prominent aspects of medieval economic control was the attempt to restrict the practice of purchase and sale to the minimum compatible with the current division of labour in production, and to concentrate what was indispensable in recognised public markets. This was long justified by the fact that the middleman function was not generally differentiated, so that those who, in ordinary domestic trade, bought goods to sell again in the same form, might usually be presumed to be serving no useful purpose, while the sources of supply of most commodities were so small and localised as to be easily dammed up or diverted, with very serious consequences to those to whom they normally flowed. The establishment of national control did not immediately produce a national economic unit, the only difference being that the interests of each market district were now governed by general legislation which codified earlier regulations and was administered by Justices of Peace.[1] The general prohibition of forestalling, engrossing and regrating sought to prevent mere buying to sell again and to concentrate legitimate transactions in the public markets, while a licensing system was introduced in order to permit the performance of the middleman function where it was seen to be necessary, more particularly where it included the provision of transport. In connection with the general prohibitory law, our period opens with an amount of activity which is never afterwards equalled and which is clearly due to the action of a small group of informers, of whom one Abraham Cornish was the chief.[2] From July 1660 to October 1662, practically every roll contains a batch of informations for forestalling, engrossing, or regrating, there being nearly seventy in one.[3] After a break, they reappear in less profusion from July 1666 to October 1670, when they finally disappear, except for a single very late specimen.[4] Some of the informations, those for forestalling cattle, are against butchers who bought them on their way to London, at Islington, Finchley, Clerkenwell, Knightsbridge, or some such neighbouring place, before they were exposed to sale in any public

---

[1] The most important single Act was 5 and 6 Edward VI, c. 14.
[2] Joseph Rudyard and, in 1670, Thomas Bond, also lodged informations.
[3] S.R. July 1662.   [4] S.R. July 1756, *vide* p. 200.

market. Some allege that the buyer resold them alive without pasturing them for five weeks, a special offence for which the forfeiture was double the normal.[1] Another group allege purchase, with intent to resell, of dead victuals—either meat, poultry, butter and eggs, or wheat, wheatmeal, rye, oats and peas. The fact that all the informations in a group frequently specify the same quantities and prices[2] seems to prove that the allegations were purely formal. In concluding his information, the informer prays the advice of the Court and that the offender shall forfeit the value of the goods, half to himself and half to the King, and be imprisoned for two months. The Court then orders the defendant to appear. The latter appears and prays license to compound, which license is usually granted to the informer upon condition that he shall report the nature of such composition before the end of the following Sessions. This is the last we hear of the matter, there being no visible record of any composition or proceedings for failure to report. The objects of the informers are by no means clear, for, if the prospective forfeiture was the lure, it is difficult to see why more did not enter the field,[3] while, if some trade interest was involved, it is strange that single informers dealt with various types of offence.[4] After the information had been superseded by the method of indictment, there are still the endorsements on the bills to help us to discover the identity of prosecutors, and these at times give more definite evidence of the motives for proceedings. In the middle period of the reign of Charles II, forestalling was closely connected with vagrancy which, it will be remembered, partook largely of the nature of hawking at that time.[5] The recognisance of a pedlar sometimes adds forestalling to his or her other

---

[1] E.g. S.R. Aug. 1660.
[2] Nine informations of Joseph Rudyard as to wheat, flour, rye, wheatmeal, peas and oats, S.R. Oct. 1662. Seven of Thomas Bond regarding veal, hens, pigeons, rabbits, butter and eggs, S.R. Oct. 1670. More than 50 by Cornish are identical with those of Rudyard, S.R. April 1661.
[3] In one instance the fine totalled £1606. 13s. 4d., S.R. July 1660.
[4] Joseph Rudyard informed against keepers of gaming-houses as well as corn engrossers, while Cornish concerned himself with cattle, cereals and the retail price of wine. It is interesting to find Rudyard prosecuted for giving a false kidder's license to a baker named Raylton, S.R. Jan. 1664-5.
[5] *Vide* p. 69.

crimes,[1] and we find that prosecutors are persons trading in the goods being sold.[2] The regular and established trading interests wished, it seems, to repress a form of distribution which, though it might be objectionable in some respects and was certainly difficult to control, was undoubtedly useful in a growing urban district during the time of transition from the market to the shop. The new traders were recognised by Parliament after the Revolution and were subjected to a licensing system, from which, however, sellers of fish, fruit and victuals were exempted.[3] In the meat trade, the position was complex, there being several groups of middlemen, whose rivalry and monopolistic practices caused much misgiving and called forth Parliamentary intervention on several occasions.[4] One of these Acts is responsible for a number of documents in our Records,[5] but it is certain that such legislation accomplished little, if anything.[6]

[1] Recognisance of Mary Manering for "being a hawker and forestalling of the market by selling linen cloth from door to door about the streets" and of Joan Pitts for being a disturber of her neighbours and forestaller of the market by selling meat from door to door, S.R. Dec. 1671.

[2] A poulterer was indicted for engrossing and for exercising the faculty of a kidder and was, by his recognisance, to answer the Poulterers' Company for hawking and selling poulterers' wares about the streets, S.R. May and June 1673. That the London companies were ready to use the forestalling laws is also shown by the fact that forestalling is alleged on the recognisance of Alice Hall, who was sentenced to be whipped for wandering and selling linen, her prosecutors being the Company of Linen Drapers, S.R. Jan. 1671–2. *Vide* also the Recognisance of William Juott "for commonly going about from door to door...offering and putting to sale mutton, veal, pork and lamb, contrary to law and to the great hindrance and damage of several of His Majesty's subjects who have served apprenticeships, pay great rents, parochial duties and other taxes to His Majesty", S.R. Jan. 1675–6.

[3] 8 and 9 William III, c. 25. It is instructive to find in the Act, 10 William III, c. 13, for making Billingsgate a free market, the complaint that the fishmongers, in the attempt to monopolise the market, would not permit fishwomen and others to buy from the fishermen to sell again in London and elsewhere, so that the fishermen had to sell to the fishmongers at the latter's own prices.

[4] For an account of the position, *vide* Westerfield, *Middlemen in English Business*, p. 190 et seq.

[5] 22 and 23 Charles II, c. 19, forbidding butchers to sell to other butchers. In S.R. Oct. 1671 are four indictments for infringing this provision. The same Act sought to stop jobbing by forbidding jobbers or factors to be employed for buying or selling fat cattle (other than swine or calves) for others within 80 miles of London and, as a result, there is an indictment of Richard Palmer of Northampton, factor for selling fat cattle for others, for selling six cows in St Sepulchre's, S.R. Oct. 1671.

[6] Westerfield, *loc. cit.*

In all this, there is little sign of definite policy on the part of the Justices. As will appear later, they did from time to time issue orders against unlicensed badgers, kidders and drovers, but the numbers of recorded cases do not indicate that there followed any appreciable increase of vigour in the matter. It is significant that, except in 1709 and 1710, we hear little of Brentford and Uxbridge, whose markets were of prime importance to the county at large. This is in keeping with the normal preponderance of the metropolitan district, but it is difficult to see that the welfare of the suburbs was in any way furthered by the type of prosecution usually exhibited by our records. Regrating, when it took the form of petty hawking, was a great convenience to those districts which, moreover, would be able to save trouble by intercepting their meat supply on its way to London before it was exposed in the public markets of the capital.[1] In addition, wheat and other cereals, which are of most general public interest, are not in evidence except at the very beginning of the period and in the crisis of 1709–10.[2] The ready grant of license to informers to compound in the first decade of the period argues that the Court did not regard the offences in question as of serious consequence to the public, and its treatment of indictments supports a like deduction. The number of confessions is exceptionally small, and this is not compensated by any increase on the usual small number of jury convictions. Fines, when inflicted, were not always on the statutory scale.[3]

[1] *Vide* the complaint that hay and straw were not being brought into the Haymarket, but were being sold on the way, O.C. vol. III, ff. 225–8.
[2] Though the Act, 15 Charles II, c. 7, allowed wheat to be engrossed and stored when the price was below 48s.—as it was over most of the period—it was still to be bought in the open market and not sold again within the same market within three months, so that forestalling and regrating remained illegal. That the wheat supply still needed attention is shown in the high-price year 1698–9, when the Justices and Grand Jury petitioned Parliament against the distilling of spirits from corn, as the poor were suffering from scarcity, S.B. Jan. 1698–9, p. 31. Parliament prohibited excessive distilling by 10 William III, c. 4, as well as on other occasions.
[3] In S.R. April 1676 is the conviction of Mary Myas, for buying 150 whiting in Billingsgate and reselling them within four miles, she being fined the value and committed for two months. Elizabeth Wrench, however, was fined only 12d. for regrating large quantities of eggs and butter, S.R. Dec. 1687.

PRODUCTION AND DISTRIBUTION 169

From all this it is clear that the Court was normally far from anxious to press home prosecutions, but, during the high prices of the years 1709–10, it made a determined effort to deal with practices in the corn trade which were then regarded as antisocial. This was, at least partly, due to government pressure.[1] After a general meeting of Justices for Middlesex and Westminster on October 1st, 1709, had ordered strict enquiry into forestalling and engrossing and the practice of farmers who brought only samples of their corn to market, selling the gross quantity at their farms and barns,[2] the Michaelmas Sessions promulgated an order laying down that the current market prices should be adhered to, the victuals specified, together with their prices, being "very good English middling wheat", "barley, the better sort", "very good peas for boiling", "the best sort of grey peas for horses and hogs", "good clean beans" and "English sort of good middling oats".[3] At the same time, there were a considerable number of indictments for forestalling, engrossing or keeping private market[4] and, in this instance, it is clear from the endorsements on the bills that the prosecutors were high and petty constables and headboroughs carrying out the Court's instructions. Some of these bills were not found, while there were no confessions or adverse verdicts, so that the Grand and Petty Juries would appear not to have supported the Justices' action. It may be that the Bench did not wish to go to extremes, but merely to create a little healthy respect for the law. Possibly

[1] Parliament forbade the export of corn, low wine and spirits and revived the Assize of Bread, 8 Anne, c. 2 and c. 19. A proclamation for the execution of the forestalling laws was issued on Oct. 24th, Crawford, *Tudor and Stuart Proclamations*, vol. I, p. 530. The government's instructions were communicated directly to certain Justices of Middlesex and Westminster by Secretary Sunderland and a meeting of magistrates of the county and city was held at St Martin's Court Room on Sept. 29th.

[2] S.B. Sept. 1709, p. 45. For the representation by the Justices of the city and county to the Council, reporting what had been done, stressing the evil effects of market manipulation and suggesting the fixation of the price of bread under the Act 25 Henry VIII, c. 2, *vide* S.B. Sept. 1709, p. 47.

[3] S.B. Oct. 1709, p. 45. For contemporaneous action in connection with the Assize of Bread, *vide* p. 180.

[4] Those prosecuted for keeping private market—that is, allowing purchase and sale in a private place—who appear to have been generally inn-keepers, were virtually forestalling the public markets. There are some indictments for selling out of market at other times, e.g. in S.R. Oct. 1676, Jan. 1677–8, Dec. 1680, May 1700, July 1700, March 1700–1 and Oct. 1702.

its orders, coupled with the Royal Proclamation, may have sufficed to put a check upon some of the most irregular practices, though apparently there was no increase in the demand for licenses and the general impression is one of futility. It is possible that the ineffectiveness of this outburst hastened the decay of the system which was already moribund. In fact, there appear to be no cases of punishment after 1690 and, following the incident just mentioned, there are only a very few prosecutions down to the year 1723, when they cease altogether.[1] Thereafter, the only sign of activity is in connection with the special question of engrossing corn for export.[2] Consequently there is strong ground for believing that, for all practical purposes, the laws against forestalling, engrossing and regrating were a dead letter in Middlesex during the reign of George II.

It remains to describe the administration of the licensing system, whereby necessary infringements of the law against engrossing were permitted. For this purpose, the Act of 1552 provided that badgers, laders, kidders, or carriers of corn, fish, butter or cheese and drovers of cattle should be annually licensed by three Justices in Sessions. As a result, over the first half of our period, the Records of many Sessions include lists of names marked B., K. or D. Drovers are of least frequent occurrence, doubtless because they were only licensed to resell cattle at a distance of forty miles or more, and Middlesex stock would naturally go to London, so that middlemen could not legally intervene in transporting them[3] and there are only a small number of licenses, granted at various Sessions between 1660 and 1693. Badgers and kidders are much more numerous. Legally there was no distinction between these two classes, but in Middlesex the expression "Emptor et venditor granorum" is regularly translated "Badger, buyer and seller of corn and grain", while "Emptor et venditor butyri, casei, ovorum, pullitarum et

---

[1] S.R. Oct. 1711, Jan. 1713–14, April 1714, April 1715, Feb. 1720–1 and Jan. 1722–3.

[2] This was due to an Order in Council and the Court merely referred the matter to Petty Sessions, O.C. vol. IV, f. 180 (1740). There is also the single late occurrence of the information already mentioned, S.R. July 1756.

[3] The Act, 22 and 23 Charles II, c. 19, temporarily prohibited the licensing of drovers within eighty miles of London.

PRODUCTION AND DISTRIBUTION 171

aliorum mortuorum victualum" is rendered "Kidder, lader, carrier, buyer and seller of butter, cheese, eggs, poultry and other dead victuals". Kidders are often women, seemingly hawkers in a humble way, not transporters from market to market, and the Court did not impose a fine of more than 3s. 4d. for exercising the faculty without license.[1] It could hardly be contended that the activities of such people constituted any menace to the food supply. Rather, what has already been said regarding the usefulness of the petty regrator in the growing urban area applies more particularly to them. There was the difficulty of ensuring good quality and measure in such an unorganized system of trading, while licenses were a source of revenue to the Clerk of the Peace, but there is no evidence that either of these possible motives played any part. Something may be allowed for the general dislike of any kind of vagrancy, but it is probable that the prosecution of these people was due mainly to the jealousy of old-established trading interests. The activities of badgers may well have been taken more seriously by the Court, for the multiplication of such traders was still considered a menace.[2] It is therefore probable that these were more particularly in the mind of the Justices when, from time to time, they issued orders against unlicensed badgers, kidders and drovers, instructing constables to make diligent enquiry and to make careful returns of such traders.[3] Had the constables carried out these instructions, one would expect a flood of prosecutions to follow, but such evidence is lacking, except in the

[1] One Ann Stocken, who was indicted for regrating meat at Stepney, told the Bench that she had long had license to buy butter and eggs in the country markets and sell them in places adjacent to London, S.R. Feb. 1672-3 and S.B. Feb. 1672-3, p. 37. She seems to have been a typical kidder and is among those licensed, S.B. Jan. 1672-3, p. 55. A Ratcliff poulterer named Goodman, who was proceeded against by the Poulterers' Company for hawking poulterers' wares, was immediately afterwards indicted for engrossing butter and using the faculty of a kidder, S.R. May and June 1673.

[2] The Act of 1663 disturbed the licensing system by allowing engrossing when prices were below a certain level, so that a genuine badger only needed a license intermittently.

[3] Against this view, it is perhaps an objection that two of the orders, those of 1667 and 1716, were issued in time of low corn prices. For the orders, vide S.B. Aug. 1667, p. 37; May 1696, p. 38; Dec. 1709, p. 46; Sept. 1716, p. 67.

crisis of 1709–10.[1] Even then, no penalties were inflicted, so that there was apparently no intention to press matters to extremes, while, at other times, cases are very few indeed and fines are almost completely absent.[2] Had the Court's orders been effective, one might also have looked for an increase in the number of licenses, since the usual number was so small that energetic repression of irregularities must have led more traders to seek and obtain licenses. The evidence here is again negative if, as seems quite justifiable, we assume that licenses were regularly entered in the Sessions Books or Register. Licenses are most numerous at the very beginning of the period, when informers were active.[3] They fall off considerably after 1662, are few in the eighties and very scarce in the nineties, when they never reach six in a year except in 1699. The close of the century virtually witnessed the cessation of the entry of licenses.[4] This is curious, seeing that orders against, and prosecutions of, those acting without license continue down to 1720 and are particularly energetic in the years 1709–10. It almost lends support to a hypothesis that licenses were being entered elsewhere, but this possibility would seem to be ruled out by the consideration that they did not disappear suddenly and those for badgers, kidders and drovers disappear at different times. To all seeming, we must believe that licensing ceased at the very outset of the eighteenth century, even though this stultifies later proceedings against those acting without license.

Our general conclusion, then, is that, after the Restoration, the Middlesex Justices were never disposed to execute the full rigour of the laws regulating the time and place of sale and that,

[1] Following the general orders against forestalling, 15 unlicensed badgers were indicted in Oct. 1709 and the names endorsed on the bills are mostly those of peace officers. A batch of kidders and drovers were also indicted at the following April Sessions, S.R. Oct. 1709 and April 1710.

[2] For a fine of £5 upon an unlicensed badger and of 3s. 4d. upon an unlicensed kidder, *vide* respectively S.R. April 1680 and Oct. 1672. Unlicensed drovers only seem to occur in S.R. Oct. 1693 and April 1710.

[3] For instance, they were granted to 43 badgers, 22 kidders and 2 drovers in October 1661 and to 37 badgers and 8 kidders in April 1662 and to 54 badgers and 41 kidders in October 1662, S. Reg. vol. VIII, pp. 211–13, 275–6, 366–8.

[4] The last badger appears to be in Jan. 1701–2 and the last kidder in July 1706, S.B. Jan. 1701–2, p. 67; July 1706, p. 34.

PRODUCTION AND DISTRIBUTION

in the Hanoverian period, they allowed them to fall into complete desuetude. It is true that Whitlocke Bulstrode included forestalling in two of his charges, directing the Grand Jury in October 1718 to "Present all forestallers, regrators and engrossers, for these enhance the price of victuals and render the poor less able to support their families".[1] Here was strong enough ground for action had there been a real belief in the value of the old laws and their applicability to existing conditions, but we must conclude that such a belief was lacking, and rightly so. The old conception of the unified market serving its own little town and rural environs no longer corresponded with facts, particularly in London and its neighbourhood. On the one hand, the growth of capitalist enterprise made possible much larger dealings and, for these, sale by sample or on the producer's own premises saved much trouble and expense in transport. On the other hand, increasing specialisation and the growth of London necessitated a great extension of retail trading, which could be provided far better by scattered shops than by centralised markets. Hence, from the Restoration onwards, shops steadily multiplied at the expense of the market system.[2] During the period of transition, useful work could be done by hawkers who brought the goods even closer to the consumer. They involved a still more violent break with the old ideas of well-ordered commerce and were naturally suspect on account of their wandering habits. This being so, it is surprising that the Middlesex Records have not afforded more evidence of repressive measures against them and it suggests that the Justices were in reality reaching a fairly definite recognition of the value of laissez-faire in this sphere.

The attempt to restrict the exercise of crafts to those who had served seven years' apprenticeship in them forms a link in one of the more technical branches of economic regulation. It hoped to ensure good quality in products by preventing the untrained from producing except under the supervision of others. A more direct means of doing this was afforded by the right of search which, being an extremely technical matter, was largely entrusted to bodies specially concerned with each

---
[1] Charge, p. 28. [2] Westerfield, *op. cit.* p. 346.

particular trade, namely to the guilds or companies which the Tudor state had, as it were, adopted and made part of its own administrative machinery. The main duty of Sessions was to prevent those who had not acquired the statutory qualification from entering these crafts—a negative aim which, viewed by itself, might well appear meaningless and in many cases would be entirely so if the person in question were obviously competent. In so far as the regular craftsmen failed to maintain their standard, objection to the restraint imposed by the law would become more positive. Thus we cannot be surprised that the Justices showed no zeal for their rôle in this connection, the more so as, unlike the forestalling laws and the Assize of Bread, this branch was not combating the danger of food scarcity, which always had a special significance for those responsible for the relief of the poor. The Court had many more pressing issues to engage its time and energy and this doubtless goes far to explain why it entirely neglected to issue general orders on the subject of apprenticeship. For the bringing of cases before it, a possible motive is indicated by the fact that the Act, 5 Elizabeth, c. 4, allocated to the prosecutor half the forfeiture of 40s. for every month that an unqualified person exercised any of the crafts which it covered. This hope of pecuniary gain may, in particular, be attributed to a small group of informers who were very active at the beginning of our period, though the fact that they tended to specialise on particular occupations suggests that even they had some trade interests in mind.[1] The latter motive can be seen much more clearly when the prosecutors are the companies concerned with the trade in question. During the first part of the period, this is very frequently the case, so that, among prosecutors under the apprenticeship laws, we find the companies of Paviors, Glovers, Basket-makers, Carpenters, Wax-chandlers, Turners, Weavers, Plasterers, Tinplate-workers,

[1] Thus Jenkin Lloid proceeded mainly against leather-dressers, and Symonds against brewers, S.R. Aug. 1660, Jan. 1660–61 and April 1663. Similarly, where the method of indictment was used, we find the names Watkins and Barton endorsed upon five bills against apothecaries, S.R. April 1663. For the closely connected and similar proceedings of informers regarding forestalling, *vide* p. 165. Two informers, Cornish and Piddock, proceeded against butchers under both heads, S.R. July 1661 and Jan. 1663–4.

Wheelwrights, Barber-surgeons and Fruiterers.[1] The London companies thus called in the aid of the Justices in order to bar out from their trades those who had not legally qualified themselves, and this, we may assume, was part of their attempt to make their membership coincident with that of their trades.[2] The Plasterers were particularly active in the year 1671,[3] this doubtless being part of the attempt of the craftsmen in the building trades to keep for themselves the benefit of the exceptional demand for their labour caused by the rebuilding of London. The activities of companies practically ceased after 1675, but there was a slight revival after the Revolution. Restored by the Act, 2 William & Mary, c. 8, the companies doubtless felt that they must do something to assert their rights, and recognisances show the Glovers, Glass-sellers and Plasterers in action during the subsequent four years.[4] This was but a faint flicker and, after 1692, it died out.[5] Throughout, it is clear that the Court had no disposition to press the enforcement of the law. As has already been mentioned, it issued no general orders to that end. Fines are very uncommon, especially upon jury verdict. Indeed, the juries, when unable to acquit, sometimes show their anxiety to treat the offender as leniently as possible by finding him guilty of exercising the trade for only a part of the time alleged in the bill.[6] Many bills of indictment were not found and many others removed by Certiorari. After 1675, the Attorney-General's writ to stay proceedings comes to the

---

[1] S.R. July 1661, Dec. 1662, Dec. 1669, June 1663, April 1669, Dec. 1670, Oct. 1671, Feb. 1671–2, Oct. 1672, Sept. 1675, April 1677 and Dec. 1731, respectively.

[2] For this attempt, *vide* Unwin, *Guilds and Companies of London*, p. 343. The manner in which interlopers would tend to obstruct the companies' performance of their real function is illustrated by the recognisance of one Brady to answer "two of the yeomanry of the Company of Weavers, London, who accuse him of opposing and obstructing them upon their search and also of exercising and working upon their trade of a weaver, he not having served seven years for the same as an apprentice", S.R. Oct. 1671.

[3] The following year, one Cooper, headborough of Whitechapel, was indicted for refusing to execute a warrant issued at their instance, but was acquitted, S.R. May 1672.

[4] S.R. April 1691, Dec. 1692 and Feb. 1692–3.

[5] As in the case of forestalling, there was a close connection with vagrancy in the middle period of the reign of Charles II, the companies using the severe laws against wandering as a means of repressing irregular traders *vide* p. 69.   [6] E.g. the case of ffalcon in S.R. Oct. 1671.

rescue of some of the offenders.[1] In the eighteenth century, there is a very marked decline in proceedings.[2] Thus the aim of trade exclusiveness and the financial inducement both failed to sustain the energy of prosecutors. The decadence of the companies would also count for something, while it must be remembered that conditions were constantly changing and the Statute of Artificers did not suit new circumstances or new trades. This last cannot be of great importance in our case, since the building trades, which had been the most prominent in litigation, cannot have undergone much change in distribution or technique. Rather it seems that the attitude of the Courts was a chief discouragement to prosecutions. The infrequency of punishments was in itself a deterrent[3] and King's Bench ruled that following the trade for seven years without any actual binding was sufficient qualification.[4] This presumably meant that action could only be taken against persons within seven years after they had begun to defy the Act. In such a decision, the judges must have been strongly influenced by a presumption in favour of freedom of trade which could go far to defeat the original intention of any restraining statute. Such definite evidence of the leanings of our Justices is not available, but it seems certain that they also favoured laissez-faire and that their action hastened the decay of the old restrictions.

In a discussion of the regulation of price, quality and quantity, bread, the staple food of man, naturally takes first place. The Assize of Bread dates far back into the Middle Ages and took definite shape in the Assisa Panis et Cervicie.[5] Like so many

[1] E.g. S.R. Jan. 1675-6. Warrants to enter this are preserved among the Miscellaneous Papers.

[2] As against more than 100 indictments and informations in the decade 1660-70 and some 67 in that from 1700 to 1710, there are only some 24 from 1740 to 1750 and 10 in the last decade of the period. Of these last, seven bills were not found and the remaining three defendants were acquitted. Miss Dunlop considers that "the year 1720 perhaps best dates the time at which the definite collapse (of apprenticeship) began", *English Apprenticeship and Child Labour*, p. 224.

[3] An aggravated case was that of John Smithson who, though found guilty of using the art of a patten-maker for twelve months, was only fined 3s. 4d., instead of the statutory £24, S.R. Jan. 1748-9.

[4] Burn, *Justice of the Peace*, pp. 38-9.

[5] Probably 1266. For a general account of this subject, *vide* Webb, "The Assize of Bread", *Economic Journal*, 1904, p. 196 *et seq.*

other medieval institutions, it was taken over, adapted and regularised by the Tudor monarchy. "The Book of the Assise of Bread", embodying the results of this process of development, was issued by the Council from time to time in the late sixteenth and early seventeenth centuries. The transformation appears to have been carried out without any modification of the old law and an Act of 1709 refers, with good reason, to the obscurity and inapplicability of the legislation of four and a half centuries earlier. Whatever may have been the letter of the law, the duty of setting the Assize out of towns devolved upon Justices of Peace, so that this matter naturally comes up for discussion here. The method of setting the Assize was to vary, not the price, but the weight of standard loaves, according to variations in the price of corn. The books of Assize accordingly contain tables showing these concomitant variations, making an allowance for the baker, so that it only remained for the executive officer to ascertain the current price of corn and publish the corresponding weights of the loaves. The simplicity of this task was, however, more apparent than real. The methods of gathering price statistics were of the most primitive and, in addition, the quality of corn was difficult to standardise. Then, too, when the weight of the loaves had been settled, it was essential to ensure that bakers maintained the correct quality. The expedient here applied was a completely rigid standardisation, with a categorical prohibition of all variation or innovation. The permitted types were the so-called white, wheaten and household bread, which were supposed to be made in certain proportions from each lot of corn.[1] Much confusion was caused by the growth of a taste for whiter flour, which upset the old division of the quarter of wheat and made the old regulations inapplicable. Any real attempt to enforce the Assize entailed the repression of these innovations and therefore severely limited the public's demand. In addition, the growth of milling enterprise—the emergence of millers who, instead of working

[1] An order of 1604 against making not only " bread of odd assizes, made by their own inventions, but also sundry sorts of bread, which are both repugnant to the laws of the realm, and hurtful to the common wealth " is inserted in the various books of Assise.

to the order of bakers, bought corn and sold flour at their own prices—caused the relation between the cost of bread and that of unground corn to be dislocated. Yet it was not until 1709 that it became lawful to set the price of bread according to that of grain, meal or flour, and even then no machinery was provided for carrying the modification into effect.

All this considered, it is not surprising to find that the Assize system was not effectively administered in Middlesex during the period. With but two or three exceptions, the Justices altogether neglected to issue a precise Assize according to the ascertained price of corn, but simply, at each Easter Sessions, passed a general order enjoining the observance of the regulations. From 1661 to 1692 we find, in each April Sessions Book, the order "That the Assize of Bread shall be observed according to the printed book of Assize of Bread in this behalf set forth by Mr Pinkethman".[1] It therefore remained for the Justice or Justices to decide, in each individual case, what the existing price of wheat was, before they could pronounce on any alleged infringement of the Assize. This would clearly be troublesome and it does not appear exactly how they proceeded.[2] The authorities in the City of London were more painstaking, issuing a weekly notice of the weights in the Weekly Bills of Mortality. This was perhaps a strange association of ideas, but it undoubtedly secured the Assize a large measure of publicity and made it so much the easier to enforce. Our Justices saw this and adopted it for their own purposes, seeing that, while it was inapplicable to the rural parts of the county, it would well suit the needs of the suburban district, which was always most in the minds of magistrates and where home baking was no doubt less common

[1] The authority here invoked is apparently "Artachthos" by William Penkethman, one of the commonalty of London, which was checked by a committee of London aldermen and licensed by the Privy Council specially for Middlesex in 1638. The Assize table is arranged in five columns, showing the price of wheat per quarter from 6d. to £5, together with the corresponding weights of the ½d. white, 1d. white, 1d. wheaten and 1d. household loaves, all the weights being given both troy and avoirdupois and worked out to minute fractions. This work was long regarded as authoritative.

[2] The bills of indictment do not state what was the correct weight at the time of an alleged offence, but merely accuse the vendor of baking and selling a loaf or loaves of specified price lacking a certain amount of their just weight appointed by statute.

PRODUCTION AND DISTRIBUTION 179

than in the country. The Court had made use of the London Assize as early as 1610[1] and brought it into play in the high-price year 1662, while Penkethman's book was still the acknowledged authority. It then ordered that "the Assize of all sorts of bread be held and observed throughout the whole county the same with the Assize thereof as is and shall be published by the Lord Mayor and Court of Aldermen in the City of London in the Weekly Bills of Mortality" and directed magistrates to view the bread of bakers in their respective districts twice at least between Sessions.[2] In 1693, also a year of high prices, the usual order is absent in the April Sessions Book but, in October, the London Assize was again brought into operation, the actual weights being given, and Justices were directed to send for constables once a week to attend them to view and weigh bread.[3] Thereafter, until 1709, the London Assize is in the April orders. For this half century, the Records do not point to any strict administration of the Assize, which, having regard to the state of the law, is only what we should expect.[4] A majority of years exhibit no prosecutions whatever, the most barren periods being from 1679 to 1692 and from 1699 to 1709, both periods of low prices. For reasons which do not appear, the most active year was 1669,[5] while very occasionally really heavy penalties were inflicted.[6] It is probable that the occasional outbursts of activity originated in the proceedings of informers,[7] but at least some

---

[1] Calendar of Sessions Rolls etc., vol. II, p. 50.
[2] S.B. August 1662, p. 26.
[3] S.B. Oct. 1693, p. 55.
[4] The Bakers' Company was authorised to view, search, prove and weigh bread for ten miles round the City, but it is not evident whether their control was at all effective at this time. In addition, it is possible, though unlikely, that Justices out of Sessions themselves dealt with offenders. These considerations must be borne in mind when estimating the efficacy of the law.
[5] There were then 32 indictments from Whitechapel and Norton Folgate, more than half with fines of from 3s. 4d. to 26s. 8d. Six bills are against a single baker who was fined altogether £5. 3s. 4d., S.R. Oct. 1669.
[6] In 1683 Gervase Wilkinson was found guilty upon two counts, first for selling 200 1d. household loaves each one ounce light, and secondly of selling one peck household loaf (at this time an illegal proceeding in any case) which was 20 ounces light, and was fined £20 and £13. 6s. 8d. respectively, S.R. Feb. 1683–4.
[7] The name Thomas Jones is endorsed upon nine bills in July and six in Oct. 1669, S.R. July and Oct. 1669.

prosecutors in the earlier part of the period occupied the official position of aleconner.[1]

At this time, the Justices acted, so far as they acted at all, without any pressure from above, since supervision by the Council, which was so characteristic of the Tudor system, had decayed owing to the Civil War. The dearth of 1709–10, however, which temporarily revived the laws against forestalling,[2] directed general attention to the Assize of Bread as a means of mitigating distress (which interested the Government more particularly as it was carrying on war) by controlling the baker's margin of profit. The Act, 19 Anne, c. 11, alluded to the desuetude of the system owing to the obscurity and inapplicability of the Assisa Panis et Cervicie[3] and, outside the limits of corporate towns, explicitly conferred upon two Justices the authority to set the Assize according to the price of grain, meal or flour. The alteration in the basis of calculation had been necessitated by the change in milling practice, but this change made it no easier to determine the standard price. Indeed, the calculation would be more difficult, in that meal was sold in shops, out of market, to a greater extent than corn.[4] The table in the Act was based upon corn.[5] So also was the order issued by six Justices in accordance with its provisions, prescribing the weights of the various loaves

[1] On the recognisance of a Shoreditch chandler named Edwards, the prosecutor, Vanse, is styled aleconner and his name appears at the same time on the recognisance of a Shoreditch baker named Edwards for selling light bread, S.R. Aug. 1664. Again, we find the recognisance of Atkinson of Lower Wapping to answer Nash, aleconner of Shadwell, for making a 12d. loaf 12 ounces too light, and Nash's name is on the back of the bill against Rowe of Shadwell who was fined 6s. 8d. at the same time, S.R. Feb. 1673–4. The aleconners of Twickenham appeared against bakers before the Brentford Justices in May 1675, Brentford Calendar, p. 77.

[2] *Vide* p. 169.

[3] This preamble receives curiously literal confirmation from the fact that, during the preceding decade, there seem to have been no prosecutions whatever in Middlesex.

[4] Gras shows that the chandler selling meal in his shop had become thoroughly established in London before the close of the seventeenth century, *Evolution of the English Corn Market*, chap. VII. From the Act, 3 George II, c. 29, it appears that the City of London at that time had meal-weighers to deliver in prices, but it is very unlikely that the Justices had any such machinery at their command.

[5] Even corn was, as already shown, being increasingly sold out of market, yet the price to be used was still the market price and Parliament would not pass a clause to compel all corn brought to London to be sold in markets.

and ordering bakers to mark all bread with their own initials and with signs to indicate quality and price.[1] Convictions were now to be before single Justices, so that we only have side lights on the matter through proceedings for non-enforcement or against enforcement.[2] The impression is that a good deal was done, that at least some of the Justices displayed vigour and that informers took advantage of the 40s. reward offered them for securing convictions.[3] When prices fell, however, popular alarm would subside and tend to be replaced by irritation at the restrictions of the system. From the Act, 1 George I, c. 26, it appears that the 40s. penalty was considered excessive, so that it is doubtful whether the Act of 1709 enjoyed general approval for any length of time.[4] This was probably due in part to the difficulty of working the law satisfactorily, as, on one occasion, the Court found that four Justices had set the Assize on the assumption of a lower wheat price than that actually ruling.[5] Bakers had petitioned against the order as the recent act had expired and some of them brought actions against Justices before whom they had been convicted and the Court directed that Mr Hardisty, the Clerk of the Peace, should appear in defence of any such Justices at the expense of the county.[6] Later, Mr Fuller, J.P., reported that a verdict had gone against him in the King's Bench and that he had been ordered to pay a baker £23 damages and costs. He requested that, in accordance with the order just cited, this should be paid out of the public money and the Court complied.[7] By this action, the bakers in Middlesex seem to have succeeded in freeing themselves for a long time from the restraint of the Assize. Although the law was revived by succes-

[1] S.B. April 1710, p. 59. The order allowed ½d. loaves and French bread.
[2] There is one indictment in S.R. Oct. 1710 for selling a quartern loaf four ounces short, but this was an exceptional case, since these "Prized loaves" of fixed content and varying price were not legalised until 1 George I, c. 26.
[3] For the memorandum of the conviction before Mr Fuller on the information of one Gilbert, vide the parcel of Miscellaneous Papers dated 1711-20. For appeals to Court, vide S.B. July 1710, p. 60; Oct. 1711, p. 76; Oct. 1713, p. 70.
[4] For recognisances of peace officers for refusing to levy the 40s. distress, vide S.R. Dec. 1712 and July 1713.
[5] S.B. Jan. 1713-14, p. 59.
[6] Ibid. The order is partly decayed.
[7] S.B. Dec. 1714, p. 53.

sive statutes,[1] there is hardly any sign of its enforcement[2] until war and scarcity combined to arouse fresh interest, in the year 1757. In April of that year there was an order on the old plan applying the London Assize to Middlesex[3] and this was repeated a month later with a proviso in case Justices in their divisions should settle it otherwise and Justices were recommended to fix it in their divisions.[4] Later, the Court deputed a committee to attend a committee of the House of Commons as to a bill then pending, and Parliament met the crisis by passing two acts, which sought to remove the complexities arising from varying quality by reducing the legal kinds of bread from three to two.[5] There is evidence that, as a result, Justices out of Sessions took some action under these special circumstances.[6] Normally, however, it seems that the Justices, in so far as they considered the matter at all, thought the Assize superfluous in the eighteenth century.[7] It is very unlikely that any direct benefit accrued from the steps taken in emergencies, for the machinery of the Assize was never sufficiently adapted to changing circumstances, the data upon which it was to be based were inadequate and there was always the danger of simply disturbing private enterprise without properly controlling it. On the other hand, it must be remembered that popular recognition of the necessity and value of a freely determined price was far less complete then than now and public control tended to allay suspicion and apprehension at times of severe scarcity. In a broad view, this indirect benefit may perhaps outweigh the economic unsoundness of the system.

Of other action in connection with price-fixing, there is very

[1] 1 George I, c. 26, 5 George I, c. 25, and 10 George I, c. 17.
[2] There are two indictments in 1728 and two in 1730, S.R. July 1728 and May 1730.
[3] O.C. vol. IV, f. 119.   [4] *Ibid.* f. 121.
[5] 31 George II, c. 29, and 32 George II, c. 18.
[6] Some four recognisances of bakers to prosecute appeals against convictions in S.R. Feb. 1759 and Jan. 1760.
[7] The absence of the April orders may be partly explained by the fact that 1 George I, c. 26, gave legislative sanction to the London Assize for the Middlesex parishes within the Bills of Mortality. As the urban area was usually the primary interest of the Justices, this would largely remove the need for actually setting the Assize, but it does not explain the absence of evidence of enforcement, and the hypothesis that little was in fact done is strengthened by the consideration that the Court considered action necessary during the Seven Years' War.

little evidence, but something must be said as to what was done in a few of the many matters regarding which Parliament had legislated. The Assize of Ale rivals in antiquity that of bread, with which it was associated in the Statute of 1266. Indeed, the ale question seems to have been considered more important—perhaps because home brewing was less common than home baking—for the Statute set out, in its case, a schedule of prices varying with the price of barley and, in response to later changes, the duty of Justices of Peace to set this Assize was explicitly recognised by the Act, 23 Henry VIII, c. 4. In addition, at the beginning of the seventeenth century, Parliament itself fixed prices.[1] However, it is generally considered that this Assize fell into desuetude long before that of bread,[2] and this view is supported by the Middlesex Records. After the Restoration, there is no trace of any fixation of price according to that of grain upon the true Assize principle. From 1661 to 1692, the first clause of the April order which, as already shown, dealt with bread and wages, directed "that the prices and rates of strong beer and ale shall be at 10s. the barrel and not above and the prices and rates of small beer and ale at 6s. and not above and that all greater or lesser measures shall be according to the proportion of the rates respectively". Uniform rates of this kind could hardly be enforcible[3] and there is no sign of any attempt to make them effective, the only prosecution being in connection with the special statutory fixation of price.[4] After 1692, even the formal order is absent. For a short time at the beginning of the period, the price of wine was in question, as the

[1] 1 James I, c. 9.
[2] Webb, "The Assize of Bread", *Economic Journal*, 1904, p. 197 n. Blackerby, writing in 1723 and Burn in 1758, seem not to mention it.
[3] In 1610 the prices were 8s. for strong and 4s. for small beer and ale, *Calendar of Sessions Rolls*, etc., vol. II, p. 50.
[4] The Act, 1 James I, c. 9, fixed the prices at 1 quart of best and 2 quarts of small beer or ale for 1d., and under this we find John Bingham of St Sepulchre's being fined 6s. 8d. for selling to William Atkinson 60 cans of best beer at 1d. each, none of which cans contained a full quart, S.R. June 1665. Later, Thomas Simmonds was fined 20s. for selling to Thomas Jones a pot of the best ale containing less than a full quart for 2d., S.R. Dec. 1668. This last indictment mentions no order of Sessions, merely that his action was contrary to the Statute in that behalf, so that it would seem that the legal maximum had been raised. For other similar prosecutions, *vide* S.R. Feb. and March 1670-71.

Act, 12 Charles II, c. 25, after providing a licensing system, went on to fix prices of various kinds of wine and vested the authority to vary them in the Lord Chancellor, Lord Treasurer, Lord President, Lord Privy Seal and the two Chief Justices, or any three of them. Several of the early rolls contain informations for selling at excessive rates lodged by Thomas Gardiner, Edward Perry and Abraham and Nathaniel Cornish.[1] As in the contemporaneous informations under the forestalling laws, the actual amounts alleged would seem to have been purely a matter of form,[2] and the fact that Gardiner also informed with regard to unlawful games makes it unlikely that trade interests were at stake.[3] The Court, for its part, displayed no particular interest and, at least in some cases, granted the informer license to compound with the offender,[4] and the informations themselves appear to cease after February 1662–3. The only other cases in this connection are a few indictments.[5] The price of horse fodder attracted a good deal of attention during the early part of the reign of Charles II, giving rise to five Sessions orders between 1661 and 1673.[6] In these, the Court laid down the prices to be charged by inn-keepers and stable-keepers for stabling and feeding horses and also the rates at which they were to sell fodder. They are of special interest in that they do not appear to have been prompted either by pressure from above or by the exceptional pinch of high prices. Their provisions are modified to suit the conditions of dearth or plenty and really constitute the most enlightened attempt at price-fixing made by our Justices during the period.[7] The last order was not confined to horse

[1] Proceedings began very promptly, *vide* S. Reg. vol. VIII, p. 172.
[2] They are identical in six informations by Gardiner and four by Perry and one by N. Cornish, S.R. Jan. and Feb. 1662–3. There is, however, some variation in the species of wine mentioned. The price also varies, but the total forfeiture is almost always £225.
[3] S.R. Jan. 1662–3.   [4] E.g. S. Reg. vol. VIII, p. 172.
[5] S.R. Aug. 1671, Jan. 1674–5, April 1686 and Oct. 1686. In the last case there is a fine of 3s. 4d.
[6] S. Reg. vol. VIII, pp. 207–8; vol. IX, pp. 408–9. S.B. Oct. 1668, p. 40; Oct. 1671, p. 43; June 1673, p. 56.
[7] Thus in Oct. 1668, in view of the great plenty and low value of oats, the price of that cereal was reduced to 8d. a peck. John Powel, in his Assize of Bread (F.), gives a scale of charges for delivery for a day and night varying according to the price of the load of hay, but his correlation cannot be traced in the Middlesex orders, as the latter do not specify wholesale prices.

PRODUCTION AND DISTRIBUTION

fodder, but hay takes first place in its expressive preamble which complains of "the excessive rates and prices lately put upon hay, corn, victuals and other commodities for the lucre and gainsake of some that deal therein by indirect ways and means which they use contrary to law and to the great grievance of the poor and abuse of others of this county". Doubtless the growing traffic to London and the need for accommodation in its immediate neighbourhood gave ample opportunity for extortionate charges. Pressure may well have been put upon the Justices by influential victims of such practices, to which, indeed, magistrates themselves would be exposed. It is therefore not difficult to understand their action, but rather surprising that it should have been confined to so short a period. Evidently, however, the orders were rather in the nature of severe warnings than literal statements of administrative policy, as they do not seem to have been followed by punitive measures.[1] Considering how many and varied were the statutes in force which gave Justices of Peace authority over prices, the evidence of the Middlesex Records, which has here been summarised, must be regarded as extremely meagre, and we must conclude that commodities were in fact being sold at rates determined by the ordinary play of supply and demand long before legislators were prepared to acquiesce in such a state of affairs.

Turning to the question of weights and measures, we quite naturally find that more was done and the complaint here, from the modern point of view, would be that action did not go far enough. The Court only showed its active interest by issuing orders in connection with one of the many trades for which elaborate special legislation had been passed. This was in connection with the distribution of ale and beer, the prices of which, as already mentioned, were virtually left to settle themselves. In October 1661, the Court ordered that no licensed

---

[1] It may also be mentioned that, while there appear to be no orders prescribing rates for land carriage in accordance with 3 William & Mary, c. 12, the matter was considered by the Court in 1703, 1716 and 1730, S.B. April 1703, p. 54; April 1716, p. 49, O.C. vol. III, ff. 245-6, 278. While it was widely felt that transport to London needed some regulation of this kind, action by single counties could hardly be effective, as was, in fact, realised by the Middlesex Justices.

victualler or other person should sell beer or ale "by the jug, can or blackpot, wine quart or by any other measure whatsoever other than by the Thurndell quart mentioned and expressed in the statute in that behalf made".[1] Ten years later, another order recited the law as to the contents of the various kinds of barrel,[2] referring to complaints "that the beerbrewers and alebrewers inhabiting as well within the City of London as County of Middlesex have not only caused their barrels, kilderkins and firkins in which they expose their beer and ale to sale, but also their gallon measures by which some of the said brewers do sell and retail their beer and ale to poor people, to be cut, pared, diminished and made less than formerly they were and ought to be, whereby His Majesty's subjects have not their full and just measure and quantities of drink as they should have by law, to the great abuse, fraud and deceit and oppression of His Majesty's subjects and more specially of the poorer sort of people who, by reason of their poverty, are not able to buy their drink otherwise than by the gallon" and ordering a stringent search by constables.[3] Both these orders belong to the beginning of the period, when inn-keepers were also attracting attention in connection with their charges for horse fodder. The absence of later orders suggests that the Court did not maintain its interest in the question,[4] and even in connection with these two orders there is no sign of vigorous prosecution of offenders. It is therefore likely that such cases as the Records do exhibit were, like those as to general weights and measures, due to the action of individuals upon whom fraud had been practised.[5] Turning to

---

[1] S. Reg. vol. VIII, pp. 207–8. [2] 23 Henry VIII, c. 4.
[3] S.B. Aug. 1671, p. 34.
[4] In 1699 it detailed certain Justices to inspect the laws as to buying and selling in liquid measure (S.B. Sept. 1699, p. 58), but nothing seems to have come of their investigations and the need for such an enquiry betrays an ignorance hardly compatible with lively interest or regular enforcement.
[5] These cases led in a few instances to fines, 13s. 4d. upon one Napp for selling ale by unlawful measure, 26s. 8d. upon an inn-keeper named Walter for selling drink by unlawful measure, S.R. Jan. 1663–4 and Oct. 1664. With regard to sale by the barrel, the Company of Coopers had special responsibilities touching the selling of soap, as well as beer, within two miles of London, under the Act, 23 Henry VIII, c. 4. That this Company did something at one moment is evident from prosecutions for impersonating its Wardens, for not permitting the Wardens to inspect vessels and for assaulting the Wardens,

PRODUCTION AND DISTRIBUTION 187

cases for which Parliament had legislated specifically, but on which the Court did not itself issue special orders, we find one or two prosecutions for bad measure in selling horse fodder[1] and a number in connection with fuel. The supply of the latter to London and its neighbourhood attracted a great deal of attention from Parliament during the period, and the fact that exceptionally heavy penalties were levied upon offenders would seem to indicate that the Justices themselves felt keenly on the subject.[2] Penalties as high as £10 and £6. 13s. 4d. were inflicted,[3] but action is not very frequent or persistent.[4] The cases so far discussed relate to products which were the subject of price-fixing regulation and should be viewed, at least to some extent, as subsidiary measures to that end. The more general supervision of weights and measures is represented by a considerable number of prosecutions spread over the whole period, but not by Sessions orders.[5] It is therefore probable that prosecutions originated with individual sufferers from fraud or with those anxious to obtain the money penalties.[6] As always, however, the infliction of fines, particularly of heavy fines, may be construed as indicating that the Court was alive to the serious implications of specific offences when they were brought to its notice. The most active period is between 1678 and 1684, when the Assize

S.R. Jan. 1675-6, April 1676 and July 1675. From the absence of other evidence, it is unlikely that much was achieved by this authority.

[1] Recognisance for selling hay 12 pounds too light in every truss and an indictment for short weight with straw, S.R. June 1679 and Feb. 1701-2.

[2] In the Westminster Sessions Book for April 1666 (pp. 35-6) there are two orders regarding the deceits of wood-mongers and others in selling coals, billets, faggots and tallwood by short measure and instructing Mr Robert White, Clerk of the Market of the City and Liberty, to examine measures, billets, etc., the constables and other officers to assist him.

[3] S.R. Oct. 1662 and Feb. 1667-8.

[4] For other cases, vide S.R. April 1668, June 1668, April 1672, Oct. 1695 and Dec. 1699. For an appeal against a conviction for not observing the special procedure for unloading and carrying coal, laid down by 19 George II, c. 35, vide S.B. July 1749, p. 63.

[5] Whitlocke Bulstrode referred to this question quite strongly, but he did so in connection with the duties of clerks of markets, Charge, April 1718, p. 32. It is unlikely, however, that these clerks were achieving much at the time. An estimate of the amount of action which is based solely on Sessions Records is more likely to be vitiated by the fact that Justices out of Sessions could convict.

[6] For the explicit allocation of fines upon six Hanwell offenders, half to the prosecutor and half to the highways, vide S.R. Oct. and Dec. 1706.

of Bread was also attracting attention[1] and, taking the period as a whole, we find prosecutions in connection with corn,[2] meal,[3] malt,[4] meat,[5] spirits,[6] amber,[7] apples,[8] oysters[9] and iron.[10]

With regard to the attempt to maintain good quality in products it must, in the first place, be borne in mind that the measures adopted by Parliament went far beyond mere protection of consumers from glaring fraud and frequently prescribed methods of production with great minuteness, so that, had they been carried out, they would have constituted a serious obstacle to necessary change and adaptation. The very minuteness of such regulations, however, made them far too technical and remote from general interest to arouse the attention of magistrates who had so many more immediate calls upon their energies. There is no indication that the Court took any steps to secure the enforcement of the bulk of the law on this subject, and the legislators' hope that trade interests and the lure of money forfeitures would ensure the prosecution of offenders proved quite unfounded. Of the very large number of statutes passed by Parliament before and during the period it appears that only those connected with the supervision of the brick and tile industry were ever seriously considered by the Court, and even here it seems to have achieved no real success.[11] More surprising

---

[1] Besides smaller amounts, there are fines of £6. 13s. 4d., £3 and 20s., S.R. July and Dec. 1678 and Aug. 1683.

[2] S.R. June 1731 and Feb. 1756.

[3] A batch of more than 20 recognisances in S.R. June 1673, following the Act, 22 Charles II, c. 8, on the subject.

[4] S.R. June 1730.   [5] S.R. Dec. 1751.

[6] S.R. June 1758.   [7] S.R. July 1760.

[8] S.R. Dec. 1731, recognisance to answer the Master and Wardens of the Fruiterers' Company. Under 1 Anne, c. 9, measures sealed by the Company were valid within three miles of London.

[9] S.R. Oct. 1687.

[10] S.R. Oct. 1687. In S.R. April 1705, four millers were prosecuted for keeping unlawful weights, but no penalties are recorded.

[11] The evils resulting from the use of bad bricks in the building of London are referred to by Mrs George, *London Life in the Eighteenth Century*, p. 74. The Company of Bricklayers and Tilers abused the additional authority given it by 12 George I, c. 35, which prescribed minute regulations as to the times for digging clay, the method of making and the size of bricks and pantiles. 2 George II, c. 15, therefore directed Quarter Sessions to appoint searchers, again adding stringent regulations. For the resulting action of the Justices, their difficulty in finding suitable searchers and stopping illegal methods of production, *vide* S.B. May 1729, pp. 56–7; O.C. vol. III, ff. 202, 207, 228.

PRODUCTION AND DISTRIBUTION 189

is the almost complete absence of prosecutions initiated from outside under the numerous statutes relating to other manufactures.[1] There is not the same silence in connection with the quality of goods handled in the more definitely distributive trades. Prosecutions for selling bad meat are, in fact, fairly well maintained throughout the period, and fines range from 12d. to 20s., £10 and even £20.[2] We also find prosecutions for selling fetid and corrupt lard[3] and corrupt cheese,[4] for watering milk,[5] for exposing to sale pewter not of the true standard,[6] for exposing to sale bad pattens,[7] and a bed filled with fetid feathers,[8] for selling at Uxbridge divers locks of hair with two ounces of powder in them,[9] for selling gold and plate below standard[10] and for selling hay mixed with dung as pure hay.[11] These cases are enough to show that sellers, who now included a rapidly growing class of shop-keepers, were not entirely free to defraud the public, but they fall far short of proving that the public was not extensively defrauded. The loudest complaints of the malpractices of tradesmen come from a later period and it may be that, at the time we are considering, the inordinate growth of the evil was rather potential than real. Still, it is clear that the Middlesex Justices found little time to keep watch on this matter and their omissions became progressively more serious as other means of control decayed. Trade was left mainly to look after itself, subject to such scrutiny as consumers could exercise, and experience was to show that this freedom was fraught with pernicious consequences.

3 George II, c. 22, introduced amendments, but the Justices seem to have done nothing further in the matter.
[1] For an indictment for making and selling defective glass, the offender being fined 20 marks, vide S.R. Sept. 1672.
[2] S.R. Oct. 1694, April 1720, Aug. 1728. There is no sign that the Butchers' Company was active at this time, as it certainly was earlier, vide Calendar of Sessions Rolls, etc. vol. I, pp. 94-5. These volumes show many prosecutions for killing and selling bad meat under James I.
[3] S.R. Aug. 1728, John Stevenson fined £20.
[4] Fined 26s. 8d., S.R. Aug. 1726.
[5] S.R. Aug. 1663, Jan. 1693-4 and July 1729.
[6] S.R. Aug. 1700. At the same time there were indictments for hawking pewter without license, S.R. Aug. and Oct. 1700.
[7] S.R. April 1700-1.   [8] S.R. Aug. 1706.   [9] S.R. Sept. 1738.
[10] Gold in S.R. April 1721 and four cases in S.R. May 1721, two of them fined 6s. 8d.; plate in S.R. July 1742.
[11] S.R. Aug. 1733, two cases, one fined 12d.

CONCLUSION

In bringing to an end this survey of Middlesex government from the Restoration to the death of George II, it is not proposed to summarise results at all fully, as this could hardly be done except by a catalogue of largely independent items. The topics covered are too varied to allow any close synthesis, except in regard to one or two general tendencies. These tendencies, moreover, are already fairly familiar, and chief interest attaches to the way in which and the time at which they worked themselves out in each branch of administration. However, it will be well to recall briefly two main conclusions that have been constantly forced upon us.

In the first place, we have been continually reminded that the Justices of Peace were working with decidedly clumsy and blunt tools. Many of the shortcomings in the administrative machinery were already in evidence when Charles II returned from his travels and the landed gentry, perhaps even more than the King, came into their own. Magistrates were certainly hampered by the lack of an adequate staff under their immediate control, while the inferior organs of local government were not of such a nature as made the task of supervising them an easy one. Then, too, though amateur rule had many advantages, it could hardly be expected that gentlemen with many other interests would devote to their public duties the time and thought necessary for the satisfactory performance of such an extraordinary variety of functions. Again, the triumph recently gained over royal pretensions had its destructive as well as its constructive side, for, though local autonomy made for flexibility and growth, it also permitted slackness to pass unpunished and, in many spheres, entailed the danger that vigorous action, if undertaken, would create chaos and defeat its own end owing to the lack of co-ordination. Such shortcomings naturally increased as time passed and conditions changed, and were at their maximum in Middlesex which, by the eighteenth century, was becoming largely urban in character.

CONCLUSION

For all this sufficient remedies were not forthcoming. Parliament lacked the guidance of a central authority with broad and bold vision. On the other hand, it was composed of those who were wrestling with the immediate problems and who could suggest workable expedients for tackling present difficulties. The result was a flood of statutes carrying out minor amendments in the old law and, in the second half of our period, establishing new *ad hoc* bodies to deal with special problems in particular areas. These policies of piecemeal amendment and sectional reconstruction went some way towards meeting the more pressing needs of the moment by adapting the law to changing circumstances and grafting modern devices on to the main stock of medieval institutions. In the process, however, confusion became more confounded and no permanent solution was provided for troubles which were more general and more deep-rooted than appeared at the time. The task of thoroughly recasting the organisation of local government was thus left over for the nineteenth century and was not seriously attempted until after the reform of the House of Commons.

The second trend that has been fairly constantly in evidence concerns the aims of administration and shows them becoming ever narrower. We have seen that a large proportion of the law which the Justices were expected to carry out was in fact a dead letter long before it was erased from the Statute Book. Tudor paternalism was so broad in scope and detailed in content that we may well doubt whether, even in its heyday, administrative practice came near to fulfilling legislative ideals. At all events, to carry out the whole body of regulations was a gigantic task, and after the Civil War, when conciliar supervision was greatly enfeebled, the Middlesex Justices only attempted, as a regular policy, to cover a part of the field, though they still thought their operations should be extended somewhat in times of special difficulty. Thereafter, we have watched them losing even spasmodic interest in many of these matters and abandoning their hold upon many branches of life which in 1660 were well under control. This attitude is particularly noticeable in connection with a large proportion of the more purely economic matters. So far there is little sign of any general belief in the virtues of laissez-faire, for quite vigorous intervention in some fields was attempted when special circumstances appeared to demand it. On the other hand, it is probable that the Justices had already come to a fairly definite decision that many things were best left alone. Quite apart from conscious policy, inaction was fostered by the clumsiness of the administrative machine and by the tendency of a few pressing matters to attract the exclusive attention of magistrates. The last-named tendency must have been much exaggerated by the absence of specialised standing committees.

It is, therefore, clear that many of Adam Smith's strictures bore upon obsolete theory rather than current practice. It does not follow, however, that they were irrelevant, for, so long as a law remained on the Statute Book, it was liable to be resuscitated under the influence of temporary panic or personal motives. Moreover, it was difficult to think clearly as to what new regulations were needed, so long as the ground was encumbered with a mass of derelict restrictions. The individualists were thus justified both because they cut away dead wood and because they helped to prepare the ground for the growth of new controls. At the accession of George III the needs of the new age were not yet very conspicuous, but we have noticed cases in which the law said too little as well as those in which it said too much. Demolition was certainly required, but events were soon to show beyond a doubt that that was not enough. The edifice of social regulation needed to be reconstructed if the forces of individualism were to be prevented from marring their valuable work by inflicting grievous harm upon the community.

APPENDIX

SPECIMEN DOCUMENTS[1]

[Order regarding applications for poor relief]

Whereas many great inconveniences have arisen and more are like to arise (if not prevented) by orders obteyned from this Court for the Releife of severall clamorous and idle Poore people, who waving the Justices of the Peace living in or neare the places where such Poore doe commonly reside, Doe make their first Applicacions and Complaynts to this Court ffor prevention whereof for the future, It is ordered by this Court That all such peticions Exhibited to this Court in manner aforesaid bee laid aside, unles the truth thereof bee Certified by one or more Justices of the peace living neer the place or parish of such peticioners Residence who are most like to know best the truth of their Condicions (unles where the visible wants of such Poore people cannot admitt of delay, and that in such case the order bee only made pro Tempore and nisi causa, and that the Clarke of the Peace then officiating doe on all such occasions from time to time put the bench in mind of this order.
(S.B. Aug. 1678, p. 41)

Order touching the putting the Laws in execucion which relate to the paveing and cleanseing the streets &c.

Whereas complaint hath been made at this Generall Session of the Peace held for this County That notwithstanding the many necessary and wholsome Provisions made for cleansing and paveing the Streets Lanes and other Publique places comprized within the Bills of Mortality by the Laws and Statutes now in force, Yet by the great negligence of the Scavengers Rakers and other officers as well as an almost intire neglect of the Inhabitants in Sweeping their doors &c as directed by the Statutes, the streets Lanes Alleys and publique places are in a most ruinous and dirty condicion, not only in respect to the pavements being broke and wore down in most of the High Streets, but also by the poorer sort of people laying at their doors dust, dirt, coal-ashes, dung and other filth and rubbish to the great annoyance of his Majestys good Subjects in passing the Streets above [*sic*] their lawfull occasions,

[1] These documents are exactly transcribed, except that the numerous abbreviations have been expanded.

APPENDIX

And Whereas Extracts of all the Laws now in force for paveing and cleansing the Streets have been printed, and the Justices have frequently in the most earnest terms pressd the Inhabitants to pay a due obedience thereto, and have made examples by convicting and levying the penalties on some of the most remarkable offenders, Yet experience sufficiently demonstrates that a more vigorous Execucion of these Laws are [sic] required from the Magistrates to render them usefull to the publique and to answer the good ends intended by our Legislators,

And whereas this Court hath taken into Serious consideracion the great destruction made among mankind in the Southern parts of France by the Plague And considering the wise and necessary precautions taken in all parts of Europe to prevent the contagion Spreading, and being fully satisfied that the cleansing and paveing the Streets and keeping them clean and Sweet will in some measure prevent any contagion wee may fear in this County as well as preserve his Majestys good Subjects in passing the streets.

This Court have therefore unanimously Resolved That they will in the most effectuall manner they are able put all the Lawes in Execution that relate to the paveing and cleansing the Streets, And in order thereto and to prevent any Persons pretending ignorance of the Laws, they have Ordered Extracts of all the Statutes relating thereto to be reprinted and delivered to the Clerks of the respective petty Sessions in every parish and Division, and to be distributed and affixed in such manner as the Justices there assembled shall direct,

And this Court doth likewise give further notice to all Persons concerned that it is recomended to all Justices in their respective parishes and Divisions that they hold a petty Sessions one day at least in every week except in such Week in which the Quarter or General Session shall be held to receive any Informations that may be brought against Parish Officers or Inhabitants offending in all or any of the Premisses,

And this Court doth hereby strictly command that all Scavengers, Rakers, Surveyors of the Highways, Constables, Headboroughs, and Beadles or such and so many of them as the Justices in their Petty Sessions assembled may think proper for this Service do attend them from time to time, and may be sent by the said Justices into every Ward, Division, or district in each respective parish or Division to take Views and report the true State and condition of the Streets and pavements and to obey all such further Orders as they may from time to time receive from the said Justices so assembled, as they will answer the contrary to this Court at their peril,

(O.C. vol. 1, f. 109—Dec. 1720)

APPENDIX

ffeb. Sess. 1720.

To the Right Honourable Thomas Lord Parker Baron of Macclefield Lord High Chancellour of Great Britain, The Humble Representation of his Majesties Justices of the peace for the County of Middlesex in their General Sessions Assembled at Hicks Hall in St John Street the seven and twentieth day of ffebruary 1720.

Sheweth

That Complaint was made to this Court at This present General Sessions of the peace of Several misdemeanours committed and done by Sir William Moore Bart. one of his Majesties Justices of the peace for this County of Middlesex in the Execution of his Office. The particulars of which are as follow (vizt) That the said Sir William Moore did on the Second of January last issue a summons directed To Mrs Ann Charles at her house near Sir John parsons's Stairs Wapping requiring her personal appearance before him at his Lodgings in Buckingham Court near Whitehall on the day after To shew cause why She unlawfully detained from Mr William Milton several goods without any legall warrant and on the fourth day of the said January he did issue his Warrant To apprehend the said Mrs Ann Charles, (which without any just cause appearing he made special) to bring her before him, for illegally and unlawfully detaining the goods of William Milton and Mary his Wife, and keeping them out of their Lodgings no rent being then due, keeping the said William Milton prisoner and Assaulting him and his wife, and Swearing at her so that She went in danger of her Life and for a Contempt in disobeying his former summons; and the said Ann Charles was thereupon compelled to come and did accordingly come to Whitehall before the said Sir William Moore, and was by him admitted to Bayl.

That the said Sir William Moore did on the twentieth of ffebruary 1720 direct a summons To M^r ffortiscue in High Holborn ffishmonger and Constable and to Mr Richard Standford at the Golden Lyon in Little Queen Street directing them personally to appear before him at his Lodgings in Buckingham Court in Whitehall the day after To answer what he had to object against them (whereby he seemed to take upon him to Judge in his own cause) And for the said ffortiscue to bring with him a warrant which he had against Elizabeth Moss Alexander Hall Jarvis Shelton and Elizabeth Langley. and that on the five and twentieth of the same Month the said Sir William Moore issued another Summons directed to the said Mr Stanford and his wife to appear before him on the Seven and twentieth of the said Month to answer the said Elizabeth Moss Elizabeth Langley and others and for a Contempt in disobeying his former Summons (in which former Summons the said Stanfords wife was not included) in neither of which Summons's any particular cause was Assigned, nor any oath made as appears to ground them upon.

That the said Sir William Moore did improperly and illegally on the three and twentieth of ffebruary 1720 Discharge out of the House of Correction at Clerkenwell, by takeing bail for their appearance at the then next Sessions of the peace for this County, Elizabeth Childe and Mary Kecke Comitted the same day by Joseph Haynes Esq[r] for being loose Idle and Disorderly Women, taken the night before wandering the Streets and endeavouring to pick up Men and otherwise misbehaving themselves, and to be put to hard Labour, untill discharged by due Course of Law.

That the said Sir William Moore did Grant several Summons's and Warrants against one John Bonfeild for having two Wives and afterwards being himself in Custody upon an Arrest for debt Sent for the said Bonfield and desired him to become his bayl, and Offered to make the matter Easy to him with respect to the said prosecution, or to that effect as appears by the said Bonfields Affidavit. That several other complaints were made to this Court That the said Sir William Moore had in many instances bailed and discharged many persons Comitted by other Justices without consulting the said Justices, or endeavouring so to do, the Contrary of which has been often and earnestly Recomended by this Court to all Justices in the Comission, and is generally practised to avoyd the Inconveniences that may in any wise arise in bailing or discharging such persons from a want of due Informacion of the nature of the Complaint and Evidence thereupon, unless in particular and special cases, or where the said Justices comitting; cannot as sometimes happens be applyed to.

That the said Sir William Moore did on the Seven and twentieth of ffebruary last discharge out of the House of Correction at Clerkenwell one Richard Herbert Comitted thither by Joseph Hayne Esq[r] the Sixth and twentieth of ffebruary 1720 without acquainting the said M[r] Hayne therewith, and though the Court of General Sessions of the peace for this County was that day sitting.

That by Order of this Court the said Sir William Moore was by a Letter from the Clerk of the peace dated the Seven and twentieth of ffebruary 1720 desired to attend on Wednesday the first of March instant To give an answer to the said Complaints; but did not; but sent a Letter Signed by himself, but wrote in another hand alledging he was very much indisposed with a ffeavor so that he could not attend and desiring the Complaints might be reduced into writing and sent him that he might give his answer thereunto. Whereupon by direction of the Court another Letter was that day wrote and sent to

APPENDIX

him by the Clerk of the peace with a coppy of the said Complaints, To which he was desired to give an answer on the ffriday following (vizt) the third of March or To make it appear to the Court that he was not able to come to Hicks Hall by reason of his Indisposition, otherwise that the Court had resolved to draw up a Representation against him to the Lord High Chancellour for his irregular proceedings, but on the said ffriday the said Sir William Moore did not appear, but sent another Letter signed by himself but wrote in another hand by a porter dated Buckingham Court Whitehall March the third, alledging he was then so much indisposed with a ffeavor and other distempers that he could not go out without putting his life in the greatest danger, though the porter who brought the Letter acquainted the Court that he had the said Letter a very little while before from the said Sir William Moore who was then at the Sun Tavern in the Strand.

Wee think our selves obliged to lay the premises before your Lordship although the said Sir William Moore hath not been heard before us concerning the same in as much as it is manifest (as wee humbly apprehend) that the said Sir William Moore, doth by false suggestions and plain misrepresentations of the State of his Health Endeavour to impose upon the Court, in Order to Evade giveing any answer to all or any the premises, (otherwise than he has thought fit to do in his last Letter to the Court relating to the case of Bonfield,) which with the other Letters and papers relating to the matters above Stated wee have hereunto anexed for your Lordships Consideration.

And Wee humbly Submit To your Lordship whither the said Sir William Moore hath not been Guilty of very great abuses of the power granted by the Commission of the peace, and whither he hath not by colour thereof very much oppressed the said Ann Charles ffortiscue Richard Stanford and his Wife in amesning them before him from very remote places by special Warrants without just reason to their great and unnecessary trouble and expence; and for causes of which he the said Sir William Moore had no Conusance [sic] as a Justice of the peace, or else without any cause at all assigned so as they might know to what they were to answer and whither he hath not greatly prostituted the honour of the Comission in Offering to Ease the said Bonfield in a prosecution of ffelony then depending before himself, to induce the said Bonfield to become Bayl for himself in a private action, And whither the said Sir William Moore, the premises considered is a person fit to be continued in the Comission of the peace.

(O.C. vol. I, ff. 114–115—Feb. 1720–21)

A Presentment made by the Grand jury of this County sitting att Hickshall in Quarter Sessions for the Said County Upon Monday the XIIII*th of January* 1683 *Anno* XXXV *Caroli II*^{di} *Regis*

Wee Present as our opinion (if his Majesty in his wisdom shall think fitt) that for the honor and safetie of this County A High Sheriffe be Appointed of, and to reside in this, as in other Counties

That for the peace and ease of this County some Consideration may bee taken for the Relief of the Poore, besides the Provision made by the Statute of ye 43 Elizabeth the Poore growing very numerous especially by the waterside, by the Accidents of the sea (Insoemuch that the Inhabitants are not able to releive them) either by an Hospitall for the Providing for and educating of seamens children, for sea service which his Majesty hath been gratiously pleased to Incourage or by such other wayes as shall bee thought meete

That Scotch Pedlars and Petty Chapmen may not be Suffered to passe this County and Kingdome without examinacion & Lycense

That noe peace officers may bee permitted to keepe Alehouses during the time they are in such an office.

That the Testimonialls for servants may bee made universall in all the Kingdome, otherwayes this County will have Little Benefitt of the order made by this Court

That great care may bee taken to Suppresse all Conventicles and Seditious Riotous meetings by which the peace of this Kingdome will allwayes bee in danger for itt is visible their hopes and Spiritts are raised uppon their Apprehension of any Advantage and there is a necessity of keeping them downe by the due Execution of ye Lawes especially of the Statute of the 35 Elizabeth by which those who will not Conforme may abjure the Kingdome, Itt being much Better that A member should bee cutt off, then the body endangered by Itt

Wee humbly pray that this our Presentment may by this Honourable Court be humbly layd before his Majesty that such care may bee taken therein as in his Princely wisdome shall be thought meete.
(S.B. Jan. 1683-84, p. 29)

[*Indictment of a Hawker for Vagrancy*]

Juratores pro Domino Rege super sacramentum suum presentant quod Martha Candler uxor Jacobi Candler nuper de parochia Sancti Botholphi extra Algate in Comitatu Middlesex Laborer alias dicta Martha Candler nuper de parochia predicta in Comitatu predicto Spinster existens etatis septem Annorum & amplius Leges & Statuta huius Regni Anglie parvi pendens nec penas in eisdem contentas

APPENDIX

aliqualiter verens Vicesimo Secundo die Augusti Anno Regni Domini nostri Caroli secundi Dei gratia Anglie Scotie ffrancie & Hibernie Regis fidei Defensor &c. Tricesimo et semper postea hucusque & adhuc inhabitans in parochia predicta in Comitatu predicto dicto Vicesimo Secundo die Augusti Anno supradicto & diversis aliis diebus & vicibus tam antea quam postea fuit & adhuc est otiosa persona vagrans & circumforaneus circumvagans cum Carnis vitulini [*sic*] & carnis bovini in parvis peciis & membris Anglice wandring abroad with divers joynts of fflesh meat infra Comitatum predictum Ac adtunc & dictis aliis diebus & vicibus ibidem in parochia predicta in Comitatu predicto & aliis locis in Comitatu predicto portans secum et vendicioni exponens Anglice offering to sale diversis ligeis & subditis dicti Domini Regis diversas pecias & membra Anglice Joynts Carnis vitulini & carnis bovini predicti Ac dicto Vicesimo Secundo die Augusti Anno supradicto apud St Katherines in Comitatu predicto et diversos alios locos infra Comitatum predictum contra Leges & Statuta huius Regni Anglie circumvagavit anglice hath wandred abroad circumferens anglice carrying about secum Martha Candler et vendicioni exponens Carnem predictum Ac in huiusmodi sua circumvagacione apud St Katherines predictam in Comitatu predicto et diversos alios locos infra Comitatum predictum adtunc & dictis aliis diebus & vicibus illicite callide & subtiliter vendidit & utteravit quamplures pecias & membra anglice Joynts Carnis vitulini & carnis bovini predicti diversis ligeis & subditis dicti Domini Regis (Juratoribus predictis adhuc ignotis) in privatis domibus suis & non in apertis feriis sive mercato Ea intencione ad colorandam dictam circumvagacionem Suam & ad escapiendum a punicione pro eius circumvagacione Et sic Juratores predicti super sacramentum suum predictum dicunt quod predicta Martha Candler dicto Vicesimo Secundo die Augusti Anno supradicto ac dictis aliis diebus & vicibus apud St Katherines predictam in Comitatu predicto & dictos alios locos infra Comitatum predictum fuit vagabunda In contemptum dicti Domini Regis nunc legumque suarum In malum exemplum omnium aliorum in huiusmodi casu delinquentium Et contra pacem dicti Domini Regis nunc Coronam & Dignitatem suas &c.
(S.R. August 1678)

[*Indictment of a Tailor for giving excessive Wages*]

The Jurors for our Lord the King upon their Oath present that William Neal late of London Taylor after the first day of May One thousand seven hundred and twenty one that is to say on the twenty ninth day of September in the eighteenth year of the reign of our Sovereign Lord George the second now King of Great Britain &c.

then being a person professing using and exercising the Art or Mystery of a Taylor in making up Mens Work within the Weekly Bills of Mortality did at the parish of Saint Dunstan in the West in the County of Middx and within the Limits aforesaid unlawfully give allow and pay unto Anthony Barfoot (then and there being a person imployed and retained by the said William Neal as a Journey man Taylor in making up Mens Work) the Sum of two shillings and Six Pence for the Wages of him the said Anthony Barfoot for work done at the same Parish and County and within the Limits aforesaid by him the said Anthony Barfoot as a Journey man Taylor for the aforesaid William Neal on the said twenty ninth day of September in the eighteenth year aforesaid from six of the clock in the Morning untill eight of the clock at night (one hour in the time aforesaid being allowed to the said Anthony Barfoot for Dinner) which said Sum of two shillings and Six pence is more than the Wages for the hours of work aforesaid limited appointed and declared (by the Statute in such case made and provided) to be paid to any Journey man Taylor imployed in making up Mens or Womens Work within the Limits aforesaid from the four and twentieth day of June to the five and twentieth day of March (the Wages for the Work aforesaid during the time of year aforesaid being one shilling and eight pence and no more besides one peny half peny for that day's Breakfast) against the form of the Statute in such case made and provided and against the peace of our said Lord the King his Crown and Dignity
(S.R. Oct. 1744)

[*Information for Regrating*]

BE IT REMEMBRED That James Prior of the Parish of St. Sepulchre in the County of Middlesex Yeoman who as well for our Lord the King as for himself in this Behalf sueth in his proper Person cometh here into the Court of our said Lord the King of the General Quarter Session of the peace holden for the County of Middx at Hicks Hall in Saint John Street in the County aforesaid on Monday the Twelfth Day of July in the Thirtieth year of the Reign of our Sovereign Lord George the Second King of Great Britain &c. before George Errington Bartholomew Hammond William Withers George Garrett Esquires and others their fellows Justices of our said Lord the King assigned to keep the peace in the County aforesaid and also to hear and Determine Divers ffelonys Trespasses and other Misdeeds committed in the same County and as well for our said Lord the King as for himself Giveth the Court here to understand and be Informed That JOHN BENNETT of Chalfont St. Peters in the County of Buckingham yeoman on the Eighth Day of May in the Twenty ninth Year of the

APPENDIX

reign of our said Lord the King at Agmondesham in the County aforesaid did buy Eleven Sheep and Eleven Lambs of the value together of Seven Pounds alive And that he the said John Bennet afterwards and within the Space of five weeks then next following to wit on the Thirteenth Day of May in the year aforesaid at the Town of Uxbridge in the County of Middx unlawfully did Sell the Same Sheep and Lambs again alive (he the said John Bennet not having kept and fed the Same Sheep and Lambs by the Space of five Weeks in his own house or Houses Ground ffenn Ground or in any Ground or Grounds Where he the said John Bennet had the Herbage or Common of Pasture by Grant or Prescription) against the fform of the Statute in Such Case made and provided Whereby the said John Bennet hath forfeited and lost the Sum of Fourteen pounds of lawfull Money of Great Britain being the Double Value of the said Sheep and Lambs so by him sold as aforesaid WHEREFORE the said James Prior who as well for our said Lord the King as for himself in this Behalf sueth prayeth the advice of the Court in the Premisses And that he the said James Prior who as well &c. may have one Moiety of the said fforfeiture according to the fform of the Statute in such Case made and provided and that the said John Bennet may come here in Court to answer of and concerning the premisses &c.

PLEDGES TO PROSECUTE { John Doe & Richard Roe.

THE above named James Prior maketh Oath that the Offence in the Information above Specifyed was committed in the County of Middlesex—and not elsewhere and within one year last past as this Deponent verily believes.

Sworn in Court at Hicks Hall this twelfth day of July 1756. } 5th & 6th Edwd. 6th

Waller.

James Prior
D

(S.R. July 1756)

BIBLIOGRAPHY

(a) RECORDS AT THE MIDDLESEX GUILDHALL, WESTMINSTER.

Sessions Books nos. 188 to 1165 (excluding those for the City of Westminster). Each of these contains the transactions of a Sessions, comprising the writ and jury panel, lists of recognisances, memoranda as to cases, verbatim orders of the Court, prison calendars, lists of persons licensed and other miscellaneous entries. The books for each year (new style) along with those for Westminster are bound together in a large volume. The abbreviation "S.B." is used for these records. They have been calendared by W. J. Hardy down to 1751, one volume, covering the period 1689–1709, having been published.

Sessions Rolls nos. 1214 to 3105 (excluding Gaol Delivery and Westminster City rolls). These contain bills of indictment, recognisances, prison calendars, writs and sometimes informations. Abbreviation: "S.R." A selection of documents from these rolls is given in J. C. Jeaffreson's printed extracts from the County Records. The early rolls are being systematically calendared by Mr W. le Hardy, six typewritten volumes covering the years 1609–11.

Process Register Books of Indictment, vols. V to XVI. These act as a calendar to the indictments and usually have notes as to subsequent proceedings upon each case. Each stage is separately dated, but the whole history of a case has, to avoid complexity, normally been quoted under the date of the indictment. The abbreviation "S.R." is taken to cover entries in these books as well as in the rolls.

Registers of Records of Proceedings at Sessions of Peace (ending Oct. 1667), vols. VIII and X. These contain rough memoranda as to cases, lists of licenses and orders in full. Abbreviation: "S. Reg."

Orders of Court (commencing May 1716), vols. I to VII. Abbreviation: "O.C." This material is included in W. J. Hardy's Calendar.

Miscellaneous papers, comprising roughly classified parcels and entirely unsorted documents. These are mainly papers relating to matters before the Court and have only been used to a small extent.

Report of the Committee of Magistrates appointed to make Enquiry respecting the Public Bridges in the County of Middlesex. 1825. (Printed.)

Presentments of Surveyors of Streets, 1729–31.

Calendar to a Volume entitled "The Brentford Journal", being a Record of Proceedings of Petty Sessions held at Brentford, 1651–1714.

Colnbrook Turnpike Trust, Minutes and Accounts.

(b) OTHER AUTHORITIES.

An Account of the General Nursery or Colledg of Infants set up by the Justices of the Peace for the County of Middlesex, 1686. (Brit. Mus.)

Ashby, A. W. One hundred Years of Poor Law Administration in a Warwickshire Village. Oxford Studies in Social and Legal History, ed. P. Vinogradoff, vol. III. 1912.

Ashley, Sir W. Bread of our Forefathers. 1928.

BIBLIOGRAPHY

Blackerby, N. Speech at General Meeting of Justices of Peace for Westminster, April 1st 1738.
Blackerby, S. and N. The Justice of the Peace, His Companion. 1723.
Bland, A. E., Brown, P. A. and Tawney, R. H. English Economic History, Select Documents. 1921.
Bond, J. A Complete Guide for Justices of Peace. 1685.
Bulstrode, W. Charge to the Grand Jury and Other Juries of the County of Middlesex, April 21st 1718.
—— Second Charge, October 9th 1718.
—— Third Charge, October 4th 1722.
Burn, R. Justice of the Peace. 5th ed. 1757.
—— History of the Poor Laws. 1764.
By-Gone Briefs, by the Author of "Local Government in Westminster" (J. E. Smith). 1896.
Cannan, E. History of Local Rates. 1912.
Crawford and Balcarres, Earl of. Bibliography of Royal Proclamations of the Tudor and Stuart Sovereigns. 1910.
—— Hand-List of Proclamations. Aberdeen, 1893–7.
Cunningham, W. Growth of English Industry and Commerce. 1925.
Dalton, M. The Country Justice. 1635.
Deveil, Sir T., Memoirs of the Life and Times of. 1748.
Dowell, S. History of Taxation. 1884.
Dunlop, O. J. and Denman, R. D. English Apprenticeship and Child Labour. 1912.
Entick, J. History and Survey of London. 1766.
Fielding, H. Enquiry into the Causes of the Late Increase of Robbers. Works, 2nd ed. 1762, vol. VIII, p. 509.
—— Charge to the Grand Jury of Westminster, June 29th 1749. *Ibid.* p. 325.
Furniss, E. S. Position of the Labourer in a System of Nationalism. Boston, 1920.
George, M. D. London Life in the Eighteenth Century. 1925.
Gras, N. S. P. Evolution of the English Corn Market. Harvard Economic Studies, vol. XIII. Cambridge, U.S.A., 1915.
Hampson, E. M. Cambridgeshire County and the Poor Laws. Camb. Hist. Journ. vol. II, p. 273.
Hardy, W. J. Hertford County Records. Notes and Extracts from the Sessions Rolls. Hertford, 1905.
—— Middlesex County Records. Calendar of Sessions Books, 1689–1709. 1905.
—— Report on Records of Worcestershire Quarter Sessions. Hist. MSS. Comm. vol. I, p. 320.
Hewins, W. A. S. Regulation of Wages by the Justices of the Peace. Economic Journal, 1898, p. 340.
Holdsworth, W. S. History of English Law. 3rd edition.
Jeaffreson, J. C. Middlesex County Records. 1887–92.
Lambard, W. Eirenarcha. 1619.
Lee, W. L. M. History of Police in England. 1901.
Macray, W. D. Records of Quarter Sessions in the County of Wiltshire. Hist. MSS. Comm. vol. I, p. 65.
Maitland, W. History and Survey of London. 1756.
Marshall, D. The English Poor in the Eighteenth Century. 1926.
Marylebone, Vestry of, Justice Minutes, 1730–57.
—— Petty Sessions Proceedings, 1757–66.

BIBLIOGRAPHY

Marylebone (Marylebone Town Hall. MS.).
McArthur, E. A. Regulation of Wages in the Sixteenth Century. E.H.R. vol. xv, p. 445.
Middlesex, Victoria County History. 1906–11.
Penkethman, W. Artachthos. 1638.
Perry, O. Report to the Standing Joint Committee on the County Records (Middlesex). 1912.
Powel, J. The Assize of Bread, etc. 1684.
Proceedings of the King's Commission of the Peace and Oyer and Terminer and Gaol Delivery of Newgate. Old Bailey, Jan. to Aug. 1700.
Proceedings at the Sessions of the Peace and Oyer and Terminer for the City of London and County of Middlesex. Old Bailey, 1731–2.
Sheppard, W. Of the Office of Clerk of the Market. 1665.
Smith, Sir W. Charge at the Quarter Sessions for Middlesex, April 24th 1682.
State Papers, Domestic, Calendar of.
State Papers, Domestic, Charles II.
Statutes at Large.
Statutes of the Realm.
Unwin, G. Gilds and Companies of London. 1908.
Waterman, E. Some New Evidence on Wage Assessments in the Eighteenth Century. E.H.R. vol. XLIII, p. 398.
Webb, S. and B. History of Liquor Licensing. 1903.
—— The Assize of Bread. Economic Journal, 1904, p. 196.
—— Parish and County. 1906.
—— The King's Highway. 1913.
—— Statutory Authorities for Special Purposes. 1922.
—— The Old Poor Law. 1927.
Westerfield, R. B. Middlemen in English Business. Yale University Press, 1915.

INDEX

Acton, 82, 107 n.
Acts, local, liii–liv; for cleansing, 117; for highways, 136; for lighting, 119; for paving, 112; for the poor, 88; for turnpike trusts, 136
Adams, Isaac, 61 n.
Adams, Sturges, 78
Agmondesham (? Amersham), 201
Aldgate, 56
Ale and beer; measures for, 185–6; price of, 183
Aleconner, the, 160–1
Alehouses, 20, 66 n., 198; gaming in, 31; regulation of, 33–6, 152
Alien, apprentice to, discharged, 138
Allegiance, oath of, 34 n., 71
Allworth, Richard, 31 n.
Anne, Queen, 24, 30, 42
Apprentices, discharge of, 141–43; poor, 54–8
Apprenticeship, 54–8, 137–44, 173–6; settlement by, 67–8
Artillery Ground, New, St Giles' without, Cripplegate, 92 n.
Ashwell, Robert, 147 n.
Askew, Francis, 41
Atkins, Sir Robert, Justice of Common Pleas and of the Peace, 94 n.
Atkinson, —, 180 n.
Atkinson, William, 183 n.
Attorney-General, the, 38, 122 n., 175–6
Australia, introduction of Justices of Peace, xl

Bacon, Francis, lxi.
Badgers, kidders and drovers, 170–3
Badges, for parish pensioners, 62
Bagehot, Walter, lxvii
Bailey, Old, 122
Barbadoes, 146
Bard, Captain Robert, 24
Barfoot, Anthony, 200
Barnes, Thomas, 22 n.
Barnet Blockhouse, 136 n.
Barnet, East, 82
Barton, —, 174 n.
Bath Road, 128, 132
Batty, John, 103

Baxter, Richard, 38
Bayly, Abraham, Justice of the Peace, 145
Beadles, 19 n.
Beddingfield, Frances, 38, 38 n., 40
Bedford Row, 84 n.
Beer, *vide* Ale and beer
Begging, 72
Bell, Mr, Justice of the Peace, 79 n.
Bell Yard, 26 n.
Benett, Sir John, 153
Bengal, xli
Bening, John, 58
Bennett, John, 145 n.
Bennett, John, 200–1
Berkshire, Justices of, lvi
Berry, Margaret, 138 n.
Bethnal Green, 27 n., 117 n., 119 n.; scavenger of, 114 n.
Billingsgate, 167 n., 168 n.
Bingham, John, 183 n.
Blackerby, Nathaniel, Justice of the Peace, 36 n.
Blady, Francis, 56
Blue Anchor Alley, 116 n.
Bombay, xli
Bond, Thomas, 165 n., 166 n.
Bonfield (or Bonfeild), John, 196, 197
Boone, —, 81 n.
Bouch, John, 24
Bow, fair at, 31 n.
Bow Street Police Office, 27 n.
Bowles, Geoffrey, 160
Brady, —, 175 n.
Bread, Assize of, 176–82; in victualler's license, 33
Brent, River, bridges over, 125
Brentford, 112 n., 117 n., 135, 147 n., 154, 168; Bridge, 76 n., 127, 128, 129; Justices of, 90, 92, 157 n., 160 n., 180 n.; New, 9, 9 n., 125; Red Lion Inn, 9 n., 90; Turnpike, 129
Brewers, selling to unlicensed victuallers, 35
Bricks and tiles, 188
Bridewell, 49 n., 78; *vide* House of Correction
Bridgeman, Lord Keeper, 84, 84 n.

INDEX

Bridges, county liability and bridge rates, 125–30; liability of parishes and individuals, 124–5
Briefs for collections, 82–5
Brind, William, 20
Broad Street, 85
Bromley, Middlesex, 101 n.
Broom, Matthew, 84
Bulkeley, Sir Richard, 41
Bull, Joseph, 146 n.
Bulstrode, Whitlocke, Justice of the Peace, 2 n., 3 n., 28, 31, 33 n., 40, 41 n., 42 n., 133, 162 n., 173, 187 n.
Burke, Edmund, xlix n.
Burn, Richard, x, 40, 64, 147, 149
Burrows Green, Hendon, fair at, 30
Burton, Richard, 84 n.
Butchers, 42, 189
Buttons and button-holes, 66 n.

Calcutta, xli
Cambridge, 66 n.
Cambridgeshire, 68 n.
Candler, James, 198
Candler, Martha, 198–9
Carmarthen, xxx n.
Carrington, —, 58 n.
Carters, prohibition of riding in carts, 122–3
Cecil, William, Lord Burghley, 137
Certiorari, writ of, 15 n., 71, 76, 81, 127, 128, 142 n., 154 n., 163, 175
Chairmen of Sessions, charges of, 2, 82, 156, 158; as to Clerk of the Market, 162 n.; as to forestalling, 173; as to gaming, 31; as to highways, 133; as to Popery, 40; as to Sunday observance, 41 n., 42 n.; as to vice and immorality, 28; as to weights and measures, 187 n.
Chalfont St Peters, 200
Chancellor, The Lord, *vide* Lord Chancellor
Charles I, xiii, 18 n.
Charles II, xx, xxxviii, 10 n., 23 n., 38, 52, 59, 70, 71, 95, 125, 148, 166, 175 n., 184, 190, 198; encouragement of the Corporation for the Poor, 48–9
Charles, Mrs Ann, 195, 197
Charterhouse, Hospital of, 92 n.
Chelsea, 56, 125 n.
Chequer Inn, Uxbridge, 163

Chertsey, 125, 127 n., 129 n., 135; Bridge, 127 n., 129
Chester, City of, xx
Chester, Palatinate of, xvii–xxii
Chester, Randle, Earl of, xvii
Chesterfield, Lord, 28 n.
Child, Sir Josiah, 81
Childe, Elizabeth, 196
Chittle, —, 125 n.
Christ Church, Middlesex, parish of, 27, 85 n., 88 n., 119 n.
Church End, Shoreditch, 19 n.
Churchwardens, appointment of, 63 n.
Civil War, the, 69, 191
Clerk of the Market, 161
Clerk of the Market of the King's Household, 162–4
Clerk of the Peace, 11, 41, 54, 101 n., 145, 171, 181, 193, 196, 197
Clerkenwell, 1 n., 8, 9, 35 n., 42, 47, 59, 78 n., 92 n., 98 n., 99 n., 100 n., 113 n., 124 n., 132 n., 165, 196; Church, 85; Workhouse, 50, 51, 52, 59
Coke, Lord, xvi, xvii n., xxi, xxii n., xliii
Cole, Sir Mark, 24
Collins, Richard, 80 n.
Collins, Richard, 163
Colnbrook, 136 n.; Bridge, 125; Corporation, 125; Turnpike Trust, 100 n., 132
Combinations of workmen, 154–5
Commission of the Peace, xii
Commissioners of the Peace *ad hoc*, xviii–xx
Companies, London: Bakers, 179 n.; Barber-surgeons, 174–5; Basket-makers, 174–5; Bricklayers and Tilers, 188 n.; Butchers, 189 n.; Carpenters, 174–5; Chandlers, 174–5; Coopers, 186 n.; Fruiterers, 174–5, 188 n.; Glass-sellers, 175; Glovers, 174–5; Ironmongers, 131; Linen Drapers, 167 n.; Paviors, 174–5; Plasterers, 174–5; Poulterers, 171 n.; Tin-plate Workers, 174–5; Turners, 174–5; Weavers, 174–5; Wheelwrights, 174–5
Compounding, for forestalling, 166; for highway service, 132; as to price of wine, 184
Compton, Mary, 54

INDEX

Conservator Pacis, xi et seq.
Conspiracy, 154-5
Constables, high, 17-18; and the Clerk of the Market of the King's Household, 162-3; and county rates, 6, 76; and highway fines, 103-4
Constables, petty, 18-20
Constables and Headboroughs, and Assize of Bread, 181 n.; and badgers etc., 171-2; and forestalling etc., 169; and highways, 95; and inmates, 80 n.; and lighting, 118; and nuisances, 120; and paving, 108 n., 110; and vagrants, 75-9; and weights and measures, 160, 186
Contracting, for bridge maintenance, 129; for passing vagrants, 78-9
Conventicles, 69 n., 198; negligence of officers in suppressing, 21
Convention, the, 31
Cook, Robert, 122
Cooley, Rebecca, 142 n.
Cooper, —, 175 n.
Cornish, Abraham, 165, 166 n., 174 n., 184
Cornish, Nathaniel, 184
Coroners, 11
Corporations for the Poor: of the whole kingdom, 87; of London, 46; of parishes within the Bills of Mortality, 45-51; of Westminster, 51 n.
Correction, house of, vide House of Correction
Cottages without four acres, 81-2
Council, the, xlvi, 69, 155 n., 169 n., 177, 178 n., 180; Committee of, on Trade and Plantations, 52; Order in, as to engrossing for export, 170; vide also Privy Council
Council Board, orders of, relating to the Plague, 9 n.
Counters Bridge, Kensington, 136 n.
County rates, 5, 6, 12-13; for bridges, 127-8; for vagrants, 75-9
County Treasurers, 12-13, 76
Court Leet, 18, 19
Covent Garden, gaming house at, 32 n.
Cow Cross, whipping post at, 22
Cox, Amos, 82
Cox, Jane, 154

Cranford, 97 n.; Bridge, 136 n.
Cripplegate, 98 n., 99 n.; vide St Giles' without
Crispin, Silver, 114 n.
Cromwell, Thomas, xxxii
Custos Pacis, xi et seq.
Custos Rotulorum, xxxiii, 2 n., 11, 25, 40

Dalton, Michael, x
Derbyshire, lx, 84 n.
Deveil, Sir Thomas, Justice of the Peace, 13 n.
Dickenson, —, 58 n.
Dissenters, Protestant, 37-9
Ditches, fines for not scouring, 101 n.
Doe, John, 201
Dolins, Sir Daniel, Justice of the Peace, 2 n., 3 n., 17 n., 20 n., 28, 31 n., 36, 41 n., 42 n.
Dormer, James, 139 n.
Draper, William, 154
Drovers, badgers and kidders, 170-3
Drunkenness, 46
Drury Lane, 85
Dublin, county of, xxvii n.
Duchy Liberty, steward of, 18
Dukeson, Grace, 139 n.
Durham, Palatinate of, xvi-xvii

Ealing, 45 n., 84 n., 104, 160 n.
East Barnet, vide Barnet, East
East Indies, United Company of Merchants of England trading to, xli
Edgware, 9
Edmonton, hundred of, 6, 9, 12
Edward I, xxx, xlvi
Edward II, xxvi
Edward III, xii, xv n., xxvi
Edward IV, xxxii
Edwards, William, 160
Edwards, —, 121
Edwards, —, 180 n.
Elizabeth, Queen, 45
Elthorne, hundred of, 6, 12
Ely Rents, 27 n.
Enfield, 78, 131, 132 n., 136 n.
Englefield, Sir Thomas, xxxii n.
English, appeal written in, 39
Engrossing, regrating and forestalling, 165-70, 200-1
Enticing, apprentices, 139; servants, 147

INDEX

Errington, George, Justice of the Peace, 200
Essex, Justice of, 74 n.
Essex Street, St Clement Danes, 24
Evans, Edward, 162, 163
Exchequer, 108, 109 n.
Exchequer Inn, Uxbridge, 162 n.
Exeter Change, Strand, 30

Fairs, attempted suppression of, 29–31; at Bow, 31 n.; at Burrows Green, Hendon, 30; at Hampstead, 31 n.; at Highgate, 31 n.; May, 31 n.; at Mile End, 31 n.; at Paddington, 31 n.; Rag, 30 n.; at Tottenham Court, 31 n.; Welsh, 17 n., 31 n.
ffalcon, —, 175 n.
ffanshaw, Thomas, 24
ffeild, John, 147
Fielding, Henry, Justice of the Peace, lxiii n., 25 n., 32 n., 36 n., 87, 151, 156
Fielding, Sir John, Justice of the Peace, 27 n.
Fielding, Thomas, 162, 163
Finchley, 82, 165
Fine, conditional, for a bridge, 125 n.; for highways, 94–7, 103–4; for nuisances, 111 n.; for pavement, 111
Finsbury, 6, 9, 135; Justices of, 42; Lord of the Manor of, 92 n.
Fires, prevention of, 85–6
ffly, Timothy, 39
Ford, Francis, 160
Forestalling, engrossing and regrating, 165–70, 200–1
ffortiscue, Mr, 195, 197
Fox, George, 139 n.
ffoxcroft, George, 84 n.
Friern Barnet, 95 n.
Fuel, measures for, 187
Fulham, 38, 103
Fuller, John, Justice of the Peace, 181
Furneux Pelham, Herts., 101 n.

Gaming, attempted suppression of, 31–2
Gardiner, Thomas, 31 n., 184
Garrett, George, Justice of the Peace, 200
Gately, Roger, 140

Gay, —, 35 n.
Geneva and Geneva shops, 28, 36–7
George I, 9, 12, 26 n., 28, 29, 31 n., 78 n.
George II, 25, 28, 29, 40, 72, 81, 82, 136, 170, 190
George III, 192
Gilbert, —, 181 n.
Gin, excessive drinking of, 28, 36–7
Glendower, Owen, xviii
Gonson, Sir John, Justice of the Peace, 112 n.
Goodman, —, 171 n.
Gore, hundred of, 6, 9, 12, 30
Gray, Anthony, 147 n.
Great Seal, Commissioners of, 41 n.
Great Square, St Giles' in the Fields, 26
Green, Edward, 140, 141
Green, John, 92 n.
Greene, John, 33 n.
Grub Street, Liberty of, 116 n.

Hackney, 95 n., 132 n.
Hale, Anne, 163
Hale, the Right Hon. Sir Matthew, 46, 57
Hall, Alexander, 195
Hall, Alice, 70 n., 167 n.
Hall, Richard, 106 n.
Hammersmith, 94, 106 n., 131, 162 n.; school at, 40
Hammond, Bartholomew, Justice of the Peace, 200
Hampstead, 98 n., 99 n., 103, 130, 136 n.; fair at, 31 n.; playhouse at, 32
Hampton, 125
Hanoverians, the, 27, 42
Hanwell, 101 n., 187 n.; bridge at, 125
Hardisty, Robert, Clerk of the Peace, 181
Hardwicke, Philip, the Right Hon. Lord, 30
Harmondsworth, 104
Harris, John, 49 n.
Harrow, 68 n., 125, 157 n.
Hartley, Ralph, Justice of the Peace, 41
Harvey, Sir Francis, 67 n.
Hatton Garden, 27 n.
Hawkers, 69–71, 173, 198–9; licenses for, 167

INDEX

Hawkins, Sir John, Justice of the Peace, 136 n.
Hawtrey, Ralph, Justice of the Peace, 39
Hayes, Middlesex, 91, 97 n.
Haymarket, Westminster, 12 n., 74 n., 112 n., 168 n.; King's Theatre in, 32 n.
Haynes (or Hayne), Joseph, Justice of the Peace, 196
Headboroughs, 18–21; *vide* Constables and Headboroughs
Health, public, 36, 79, 119, 193–4
Hempson, William, 162 n.
Hendon, 30
Henry II, xxiv, xxxv
Henry III, xii, xxiv, xxv
Henry IV, xxvii
Henry V, xxxi
Henry VII, xx
Henry VIII, xx, xxii n., xxxii, xxxiii
Herbert, Richard, 196
Hertfordshire, 75 n., 78 n., 82 n., 101 n., 113 n., 121 n., 124 n.
Heston, 101 n., 104
Hicks Hall, Clerkenwell, 1 n., 41, 61, 132, 197, 198, 200; Housekeeper of, 11
Hide, Thomas, 147
Higgs, John, 12 n., 76
Highgate, fair at, 31 n.
Highgate Gatehouse, 130, 136 n.
Highways, 89–136; carters riding in carts, 122–3; cleansing, 112–17, 193–4; conditional fines for, 95–6, 103–4; hog-keeping, 123–4; indictment for not working, 99; indictment of the parish for, 92–4; lighting, 117–19; maintained by particular persons, 92 n.; nuisances in, 119–24; presentment of by Justices of Peace, 94–5; rates for, 101–5; regulation of drawing, 121–2; revenue from fines, 100–1, 103–4; sessions for, 90–2; statute labour, 97–100; surveyors of, 105–7; *vide also* Bridges, Paving, Turnpike trusts
Hinchinbrook, Lord, 24
Hog-keeping, 123–4
Holborn, 6, 9, 49 n., 50, 56, 84 n., 108 n., 114 n., 121 n., 124 n.
Holborn, High, 92 n., 195
Holland, Eleanor, 142 n.
DQS

Hornsey, 61, 93 n., 98 n., 99 n., 104, 106 n.
Horse fodder, measures for, 187; price of, 184–5
Horses, *vide* Waggons
Horton, Bucks., 125
House of Commons, lii, lxi, lxxiii, 46, 191; application to committee regarding Assize of Bread, 182; petition to regarding county rates, 127–8; regarding gin-drinking, 36; regarding highways, 130; regarding new playhouses, 32; regarding Poor Law, 73
House of Correction, 12, 69, 71 n., 73, 78 n., 84, 142, 145, 147, 153, 157 n., 196; Keeper of, 11, 74, 78 n.
House of Lords, lx
Hoxton, 19 n.
Hubert Walter, xi
Hundred, the, 6; hundred bridges, 124 n.; hundred courts, xx, 6; licensing meetings in, 34; suit against for robbery, 24 n.; *vide also* Edmonton, Elthorne, Gore, Isleworth, Ossulston, Spelthorn
Hurst, Richard, 122
Hyde Park, 30

Illegitimate children, 62–3
Impotent poor, accommodation of in the Corporation Workhouse, 49
Indentures, of apprenticeship, 137–8, 140; for service in the Plantations, 145–6
India, Justices of the Peace in, xli–xlii
Informations, as to apprenticeship, 174; as to forestalling, etc., 165–6, 200–1; as to gaming, 31; as to wine prices, 184
Informers, and the Assize of Bread, 179; and drawing waggons, 122; and gin-selling, 37; *vide also* Informations
Inmates, 79–81
Inns: Chequer (Exchequer) Inn, Uxbridge, 162 n., 163; King's Arms, Shoreditch, 162; Red Lion, New Brentford, 9 n., 90; Sun Tavern, Strand, 197
Ireland, introduction of Justice Peace into, xxiii–xxviii

14

INDEX

Isleworth, hundred of, 6, 12; parish of, 73 n.
Islington, 92 n., 94 n., 96 n., 98, 99 n., 100 n., 104, 105, 106 n., 107 n., 165
Islington Turnpike Trust, 130, 132, 133

Jamaica, emigration of servants to, 146; transportation to, 38
James I, xx, 94 n., 189 n.
James II, 40, 71 n.
James VI of Scotland, xxxv–xxxviii; *vide also* James I
James, Mary, 68 n.
Jeagar, Diana, 56 n.
Jeffreys, Sir George, Justice of the Peace, Lord Chief Justice, 11 n., 38, 58, 109, 122
Jenkins, Sir Leoline, 52
John, King, xxiv, xxv
Jonas, Solomon, 154
Jones, Hugh, 24
Jones, Thomas, 179 n., 183 n.
Journeymen, *vide* Servants
Juott, William, 167 n.
Juries, of constables, 3 n.; grand and petty, 169
Jury, the Grand, 2, 82; articles to be presented by constables to, 3 n.; conflict with the Under-Sheriff regarding, 10 n.; menacing of, 163; petition to Parliament against distilling, 168 n.; presentment of, 198; presentments, as to begging, 72; as to booths for acting, 32; as to bridges, 127–8; as to carters riding in carts, 123; as to the General Nursery for Infants, 61; as to gin-drinking, 36; as to gunpowder, 85 n.; as to peace officers, 20; as to pedlars, 70; as to the poor, 59; as to recusancy, 37 n.; as to the Redoubt, 30; as to testimonials for servants, 148
Justices of labourers, lvii
Justices of the Peace, autonomy of, xlix, 14; certificates of as to paving new streets, 110; decay of the office, xliii–xliv; early history of, xi *et seq.*; extra-Sessional work of, 6 *et seq.*; introduction outside England, xiii *et seq.*; into the Palatinates, xv–xxii; into Ireland, xxiii–xxviii; into Wales, xxviii–xxxiv; into Scotland, xxxiv–xxxix; into the Empire overseas, xl–xlii; literature regarding, ix–xi, xlvi–xlvii; organisation into local sessions, 7–10, 34, 90–2; presentment of highways by, 94–7; relation to central government, lix–lxii, 14–15; to other courts, lxii–lxiv, 15; reliance of Tudors on, xii; representations to the Lord Chancellor against, 7, 76, 195–7; wages of, 7 n.; *vide also* Commissioners of the Peace *and* Sessions
Justices' Clerks, 66 n., 72 n.; abuses in licensing, 35–6

Kecke, Mary, 196
Keeper, the Lord, 84
Keepers of the Peace, transformation of into Justices of the Peace, xv n.; *vide also Custos Pacis*
Kensington, 6, 9, 93 n., 115, 136; High Constable of, 40, 127 n.
Kensington Square, 110 n.
Kent, 151
Kentish Town, 101
Kidders, 166 n., 167 n.; and badgers and drovers, 170–3
Kilburn Bridge, 130, 136 n.
Kildare, county of, xxvii n.
Kilkenny, Parliament of, xxvi
King's Arms, Shoreditch, 162
King's Bench, lxii, 69 n., 76, 95, 99, 126, 127, 131, 149 n., 154 n., 163, 176, 181
King's Bench, Marshalsea and Hospitals, rate for, 12
King's Bridge, Hampton, 125
King's Household, Clerk of the Market of, 76, 161–4
King's Theatre, Haymarket, 32 n.
Kisten, William, 39
Knightsbridge, 165

Labelye, Charles, 128
Labourers, *vide* Servants
Lambard, William, ix, 2, 158
Lambert, Katherine, 138 n.
Lamps, patentees for, 118
Lancaster, Palatinate of, xvii
Land carriage, rates for, 185 n.
Langley, Elizabeth, 195
Langley Marsh, Bucks., 125

INDEX

Latin, false, 39
Lawrence, Esquire, 122
Laystalls, 115
Lediard, Thomas, Justice of the Peace, 154
Lee, Rowland, xxxii
Licenses: for additional draft animals, 121; for badgers, kidders and drovers, 170–2; to compound for forestalling, 166; to compound for excessive wine prices, 184; to continue cottages, 82; for ginsellers, 36; for hawkers and pedlars, 70–1, 167; *vide also* Alehouses
Lighting of streets, 117–19
Limehouse, 56, 100 n., 103, 114 n.
Lincoln's Inn, 41
Linen, burial in, 66 n.
Liquor, excessive retailing of, 28–9; *vide* Alehouses *and* Gin
Little Lincoln's Inn Fields, 26 n.
Little Verge, 162
Littlehailes, John, 122
Liverpool, lxix
Lloid, Jenkin, 174 n.
Local acts, *vide* Acts, local
Local government of the eighteenth century, *ad hoc* authorities, lvi–lviii; new developments, li–lvi; problem of reform, lxxi–lxxiii; relation to central government, lix–lxiv; separation of powers, lxiv–lxvi; strong and weak points, lxvi–lxxi; survival of medieval institutions in, l–li
London, Bishop of, 18
London, City of, lix, lxix, 9, 10, 20, 26, 27, 37 n., 39, 46, 49, 51, 69 n., 70, 71 n., 73, 74, 92 n., 95, 108, 112, 113, 118, 122, 134, 149 n., 165, 167 n., 168, 170, 171 n., 173, 175, 178, 179, 180 n., 185, 186, 187, 188 n., 199–200; *vide also* Companies
London, Lord Mayor of, 46, 51, 69 n.
Loom engines, 155
Lord Chancellor, xliii; certificate to regarding briefs, 86; instructions from regarding vice, 28; representation to against fairs, 30; representations to against Justices of Peace, 7, 76, 195–7
Lord Chief Justice, 38, 58, 109, 122, 163

Lord-Keeper, the, 84
Lord-Lieutenant, lx, lxi, 11; *vide also* Custos Rotulorum
Lord President of the Council, 23 n.
Lord Treasurer, 49
Lord's Day, *vide* Sunday
Ludlow, xxxii n.

Macquarie, Governor, xli
Madras, xli
Maimed soldiers and mariners, rate for, 12
Mainwaring, Boulton, Justice of the Peace, 127 n.
Maitland, F. W., x, xxii, xxv, xlv, xlvi
Major, Elizabeth, 80 n.
Manby, —, 41 n.
Manering, Mary, 167 n.
Mansfield, Lord, li
Marches, the, and Lords Marchers, xxviii–xxxii
Mariners, maimed, rate for, 12
Market, Clerk of, 76, 161–4
Market prices, promulgation of, 169
Market, selling out of, 169
Marshall, Mary, 156 n.
Marshalsea, Prison, fund for, 12, 75 n.
Marsingall, John, 145 n.
Martin, William, 56
Mary II, interest of in Sunday observance, 41
Maryland, 146
Marylebone, 27 n., 88 n., 93 n., 94 n., 102, 117 n.; petty sessions at, 9, 92, 105 n., 106 n.
Maryott, —, 139 n.
Matthews, John, 162, 163
May Fair, 30, 31 n.
May, James, 56
Mayrock, John, 109 n.
Measures, weights and, 185–8
Meath, county of, xxvii n.
Mennes, Gerritt, 154
Mile End, 31 n., 35 n., 58; Jewish Cemetery at, 66 n.
Milton, Mary, 195
Milton, William, 195
Mohocks, 24 n.
Montesquieu, Charles, Baron de, lxiv, lxv
Moore, Sir William, Justice of the Peace, 195–7
Mordington, Lady, 32 n.

INDEX

Mortality, Weekly Bills of, 10 n., 24, 46, 47, 51, 74, 85 n., 110, 115, 117, 120 n., 151, 152, 178, 179, 182 n., 193–4, 200
Moss, Elizabeth, 195
Myas, Mary, 168 n.

Napp, —, 186 n.
Nash, —, 160, 180 n.
Navy Commissioners, 49 n.
Neal, William, 199–200
New Brentford, *vide* Brentford, New
New Prison, Clerkenwell, 12 n., 38, 51, 142 n.; Keeper of, 11
New River, 35 n.
New Zealand, introduction of Justices of Peace into, xli
Newcastle, Duke of, 25, 40, 81, 117 n.
Newton, —, 155
Northampton, 167 n.
Northey, Sir Edward, 122 n.
Norton Folgate, 179 n.
Norwood, Richard, 163
Nuisances, conducing to infection, 79; *vide also* Highways
Nursery or College for Poor Children, 59–61
Nurses of parish children, 53–4

Old Bailey, 122
Order in Council against profaneness, etc., 28
Ossulston, hundred of, 6, 12, 17, 19, 24 n., 37 n.
Overseers of the poor, 63–4
Oxford, 23 n.
Oxford Street, 112 n.
Oyles, William, 39

Paddington, fair at, 31 n.
Page, —, 35 n.
Palatinates, the, xv–xxii
Palatines, poor, 84 n,
Palmer, Richard, 167 n.
Parish bridges, 124–5
Parish Clerks, Company of, 18 n.
Parker, Thomas, Baron Macclesfield, 195–7
Parliament, petition to against distilling, 168 n.; against gin-drinking, 37; *vide also* House of Commons *and* House of Lords
Paving, 107–12, 193–4
Payne, —, 147 n.

Peacocke, John, 82
Penkethman, William, 178, 179
Pennsylvania, 146
Perry, Edward, 184
Petty Session, *vide* Sessions, Petty
Piccadilly, 74 n.
Piddock, —, 174 n.
Pilkinson, Mary, 80 n.
Pinkethman, *vide* Penkethman
Pitt, William, lxxii
Pitts, Joan, 167 n.
Plague, the Great, 50, 80, 109, 123; of 1721, 116, 120, 124, 193–4
Plantations, 51–2; indentures for service in, 145–6
Plays and interludes, attempted suppression of, 32–3
Pluckington, Richard, 147 n.
Pointer, —, 122
Pointz, Francis, 49 n., 50
Pollexfen, the Right Hon. Sir Henry, 26
Poor, the, 44–88; Briefs 82–5; children: with nurses, 53–4, apprenticed, 54–8, nursery or college for, 59–61; Corporation for the better relief of, 45–51; Employment by the parish, 44–5; Inadequacy of the Poor Law, 86–8; Inmates, 79–81, cottages without four acres, 81–2; Overseers of, 63–4; Rates, 64–6; Relief, 61–2, 193, maintenance, 62–3; Settlement, 66–9; Vagrancy: repression, 69–74, passing, 75–9
Poplar, 145 n.
Portland, —, 34 n.
Powder Mills in the road to Staines, 136 n.
Powel, John, 184 n.
Pretenders, the, 40
Priests, Popish, 40
Prior, James, 200–1
Prisons, 12; *vide also* House of Correction, New Prison, Whitechapel Gaol
Privy Council, 40, 46
Proclamation, regarding briefs, 84 n.; forestalling, 169 n.; May Fair, 30; particular offenders, 26; poor, 87 n.; Rag Fair, 30 n.; rogues and vagabonds, 45–6; Sunday observance, 41; testimonials for servants, 148; vagrants, 69 n.; vice, 28
Protestant refugees, French, 52

INDEX

Quality of goods, attempt to maintain, 187–8
Quarter Sessions, *vide* Sessions, Quarter

Rag Fair, 30 n.
Rakers, 113–15, 194
Ratcliffe, 27 n., 109 n., 112 n., 117 n., 119 n., 171 n.; churchwardens of, 35 n.; scavenger of, 114 n.
Rates, *vide* Highways, Poor *and* Scavengers
Raylton, —, 166 n.
Raymond, Lord Chief Justice, 163
Reading, Berks., 74 n.
Reading, Captain John, 24
Recusancy, 37–40, 66 n.
Red Lion Inn, New Brentford, 9 n., 90
Red Lion Square, 27, 112 n.
Redoubt, the, at Exeter Change, Strand, 30
Regrating, forestalling and engrossing, 165–70, 200–1
Relief of Poor, 61–2, 193
Removal, 67–8
Rest, Mary, 142 n.
Restoration, the, xxxviii, lvii, 45, 101, 172, 190
Revolution, the, xlix, lx, 134, 175
Ribbon looms, 155
Rich, Edwin, 47
Richard I, xi
Richard II, xix
Road Maintenance, *vide* Highways
Robe, Thomas, Justice of the Peace, 76, 162, 163
Robes, Richard, 157 n.
Robinson, Thomas, 69 n.
Roe, Richard, 201
Rolls Liberty, 146 n.
Roman Catholics, special action against, 39–40; *vide also* Recusancy
Rooksbee, John, 138 n.
Rosemary Lane, Whitechapel, 30 n.
Rothes, Earl of, xxxix
Rowe, Sir Thomas, Justice of the Peace, 52, 59, 61
Rowe, Thomas, 114 n.
Rowe, —, 180 n.
Roxburgh, Earl of, xxxix
Rudyard, Joseph, 165 n., 166 n.
Rushout, Sir J., 125
Ryley, Patrick, 74 n.

Sabbath, *vide* Sunday
Saffron Hill, 27, 76, 85 n., 125 n.
St Andrew's, Holborn, 48
St Ann's, 27 n., 119 n.
St Botolph's without, Aldgate, 56, 198
St Clement Danes, 24, 45 n., 59, 109 n.
St Dunstan's in the West, 200
St George's, workhouse at, 45 n.
St George's, Hanover Square, lxix, 88 n., 117 n.
St Giles' in the Fields, 20, 26, 45 n., 90, 92 n., 99 n., 104, 108 n., 109, 111 n., 113 n., 114 n.
St Giles' Pound, 85
St Giles' without, Cripplegate, 22 n., 48, 80 n., 92 n., 105, 111 n., 113 n., 116 n., 125 n.
St James', Westminster, church of, 74 n.; parish of, 54 n.
St John Street, Clerkenwell, 1 n., 113 n.
St John's, Westminster, 88 n., 117 n.
St Katherine's, 199
St Luke's, Finsbury, 27 n., 45 n., 80 n., 117 n., 119 n.
St Margaret's, Westminster, 51 n., 83 n., 84 n., 88 n., 117 n.
St Martin's Court Room, 169 n.
St Martin's in the Fields, 27 n., 30, 57 n., 71, 88 n., 93 n., 117 n.
St Pancras, 29 n., 34 n., 94 n., 96 n., 98 n., 99 n., 100 n., 101, 102 n., 103 n., 104, 105
St Sepulchre's, 22, 85 n., 113 n., 139 n., 167 n., 183 n., 200
Sandon, Herts., 147 n.
Sandys, Windsor, 115; widow of, 114 n.
Scavengers, 113–15, 194; and pavement, 109 n.; rate for, 68 n., 114–15
Scotch pedlars, 70, 198
Scotland, introduction of Justices of Peace into, xxxiv–xxxix
Scotland Yard, Commissioners of, 108–9
Scudamore, —, 32 n.
Secretary of State, letter from as immoralities and robberies, 28 n.
Separation of powers, lxiv–lxvi
Serjeants of the Peace, xvii–xviii, xxx

INDEX

Servants and journeymen, 144–57; annual hiring, 146–7; combinations, 154–5; emigration under indenture, 145–6; indentured or covenant servants, 144–5; testimonials, 147–9; wage fixation, 149–53, 199–200; wage payment, 153–4
Sessions, General and General Quarter, 1; committees of, 13–14, 135; foundation of, xii; Judicial and administrative aspects of, xii, 2–4, 126; relation to central government, 14–15; to high constables, 6; to Justices out of Sessions, 6–8; to parishes, 4–5
Sessions, local or special, for highways, 90–2
Sessions, petty, 64, 72 n., 87 n., 116, 143, 194; early development of, 6–10; *vide also* Brentford *and* Marylebone
Settlement of the poor, 66–9
Sewers, Commissioners of, lvii
Shadwell, 27 n., 45 n., 112 n., 117 n., 119 n., 160, 180 n.
Sheir Lane, 26 n.
Shelton, Jarvis, 195
Shenley Ridge, Herts., 136 n.
Sheppard, W., 161
Sheriffs, the, 10, 104 n., 131, 198
Shoreditch, 19 n., 27 n., 41 n., 66 n., 94 n., 95 n., 104, 106 n., 107 n., 109 n., 113 n., 117 n., 119 n., 131, 132 n., 136 n., 139 n., 160, 162, 180 n.
Shute, —, 162 n.
Simmonds, Thomas, 183 n.
Smith, Adam, lviii, 192
Smith, Peter, 109 n.
Smith, Sir William, Justice of the Peace, 2 n., 3 n., 82 n., 133 n.
Smithfield Bars, 85
Smithson, John, 176 n.
Soldiers, maimed, rate for, 12
Solicitor-General, the, 76
South Mimms, 78, 136 n.
Southampton, Earl of, 47
Southgate, Thomas, 122
Sparrows Herne, Herts., 136 n.
Speenhamland order, lvi
Spelthorn, hundred of, 6, 12
Spencer, F. H., liv
Spiriting beyond seas, 145

Spitalfields, 24 n., 155, 160
Squibb, Robert, 24
Staines, 160; bridge at, 91, 126 n.
Standford, Mrs, 195, 197
Standford, Richard, 195, 197
Stanford, —, 114 n.
Stanmore, 68 n., 130
Stanwell, 125
Star Chamber, the, xlvi
Stepney, 34 n., 35 n., 66 n., 109 n., 171 n.
Stevenson, John, 189 n.
Stocken, Ann, 171 n.
Strand, the, 30, 109 n., 197
Street robbery, 24–6, 117; connection with fairs, 29; with gaming, 31; with vicious habits, 27 n.
Streets, surveyors of, 111
Stuarts, the, 27, 161
Sturgion, Robert, 19
Style, —, 148
Sun Tavern, Strand, 197
Sunbury, 71 n., 148
Sunday, observance of, 40–2
Sunderland, Earl of, 169 n.
Supremacy, oath of, 71
Surrey, 46, 125, 129; Justices of, 74
Surveyors of highways, *vide* Highways
Swan Alley, Clerkenwell, 111 n.
Sydenham, Thomas, 24
Symonds, —, 174 n.

Tarling, Ann, 56 n.
Testimonials for Servants, 147–9
Thames, River, 46, 125, 126 n., 129; bridge at Chertsey, 125, 127 n., 129; bridge at Staines, 126 n.
The Fleetwood, 83 n.
The Hopewell, 146 n.
The Sussex, 83 n.
Tippling, *vide* Alehouses; during Divine Service, 35 n.; on the Lord's Day, 41
Tocqueville, A. C. de, lxviii
Tottenham, 58, 81 n., 95 n.; vestry of, 103 n.
Tottenham Court, St Pancras, 29 n., 31 n.
Tower Division, 6, 9, 23 n., 92 n., 135, 162
Tower Hamlets, 23, 59
Tower Liberty, 75; Quarter Sessions of, 1 n.

INDEX

Townsend, the Right Hon. Charles, Lord, 31 n.
Transportation, 38, 69
Treasurer, the Lord, 49
Treasurer, General, of Middlesex, 12 n., 76
Troughton, John, Justice of the Peace, 71 n.
Tudors, the, 14, 137, 161
Turner, Humphrey, 138 n.
Turnmill Street, Clerkenwell, 42
Turnpike Trusts, 100, 130–3; and bridge repair, 125
Turvill, —, 162 n.
Tweeddale, Marquis of, xxxix
Twickenham, 160, 180 n.
Tyburn, 21, 131 n., 136 n.

Uriel, county of, xxvii n.
Uxbridge, 39, 97 n., 131 n., 136 n., 163, 168, 189, 201; Chequer Inn, 163; Exchequer Inn, 162 n.
Uxbridge Road, 91

Vagrancy, *vide* Poor
Vanse, —, 160, 180 n.
Vernon, Sir Ralph de, xix n.

Wages, assessment of, 149–51; in tailoring trade, 151–3, 199–200; enforcing payment of, 153–4
Waggons, regulation of drawing, 121–2
Wales, introduction of Justices of Peace into, xxviii–xxxiv
Walter, —, 186 n.
Wapping, 27 n., 83, 85 n., 112 n., 117 n., 119 n., 195
Wapping, Lower, 19, 96 n., 103, 180 n.
Ward, Anne, 145
Watch and Ward, 21–6, 85 n.; local acts for, 26–7; paid watchmen, 24; special watch, 26
Watch houses, 22
Water companies, 85 n., 112
Watkins, —, 174 n.

Watson, —, 144 n.
Webb, Mr and Mrs, x, xlvi
Weedon, John, Justice of the Peace, 163
Weights and measures, 185–8
Welburne, —, 83 n.
Weld, Humphrey, 47
Well Close, 27 n., 32 n., 119 n.
Welsh Fair, 17 n., 31 n.
Western, Squire, lxii
Westminster, City and Liberty of, lix, 1 n., 9, 12 n., 26, 27 n., 28, 30, 31, 32 n., 36 n., 39, 46, 51 n., 54 n., 59, 69 n., 70, 75, 76, 88 n., 95, 112 n., 113, 127, 132, 151, 152, 156, 169, 187 n.; *vide also* St James', St John's, St Margaret's *and* St Martin's in the Fields
Whetstones Park, St Giles' in the Fields, 20
White, Robert, 187 n.
White Horse Street, 109 n.
Whitechapel, 30 n., 99 n., 113 n., 114 n., 119 n., 156 n., 175 n., 179 n.
Whitechapel Gaol, 145
Whitehall, 195, 197
Wilkinson, Gervase, 179 n.
Willesden, 105 n., 154
William I of Scotland, xxxv
Wiltshire, 149 n.
Windham, Mr Justice, 122
Wine, price of, 183–4
Wirral, xvii, xviii
Withers, William, Justice of the Peace, 200
Woodward, Ann, 70 n.
Woollen shrouds, burial in, 66 n.
Workhouses, 45–52
Wray, Sir Christopher, xii
Wrench, Elizabeth, 168 n.
Wright, Michael, 145
Writs, Prerogative, lxii, 15; *vide also* Certiorari

Yarwell, Arabella, 138 n.
Yorkshire, North Riding of, 79 n.

For EU product safety concerns, contact us at Calle de José Abascal, 56–1°,
28003 Madrid, Spain or eugpsr@cambridge.org.

www.ingramcontent.com/pod-product-compliance
Ingram Content Group UK Ltd.
Pitfield, Milton Keynes, MK11 3LW, UK
UKHW010851060825
461487UK00012B/1042